THE FOUNDATIONS OF JUDAISM AND CHRISTIANITY

THE FOUNDATIONS OF JUDAISM AND CHRISTIANITY

JAMES PARKES

QUADRANGLE BOOKS
CHICAGO
1960

First published 1960
Quadrangle Books, Inc., Chicago 1

Library of Congress Catalog Card No. 60-13608

Printed in Great Britain

To MAURICE and ROSA
with happy memories of a friendship
now stretching back
for thirty years

A*

By the same author

The Jew and His Neighbour, *1930*
2nd and revised ed., 1938

The Conflict of the Church and the Synagogue, *1934*

Jesus, Paul, and the Jews, *1936*

The Jew in the Medieval Community, *1938*

The Jewish Problem in the Modern World, *1939*
2nd (American) ed., 1946
3rd (German) ed., 1948
4th (Italian) ed., 1953

Oxford Pamphlets on World Affairs:
Palestine, *1940*
The Jewish Question, *1941*

An Enemy of the People: Antisemitism, *1945*
2nd (German) ed., 1948

The Emergence of the Jewish Problem, 1878-1939, *1946*

Judaism and Christianity, *1948*

A History of Palestine from 135 A.D. to Modern Times, *1949*

The Story of Jerusalem, *1949*

End of an Exile: Israel, the Jews and the Gentile World, *1954*

TABLE OF CONTENTS

Acknowledgements and Abbreviations

The Scripture quotations in this publication are from the *Revised Standard Version* of the Bible, copyrighted 1946 and 1952 by the Division of Christian Education, National Council of Churches, and used by permission. For the English edition my thanks are due to the permission granted by Thomas Nelson & Son, Edinburgh, who are the English publishers of the Revised Standard Version, to Messrs. Routledge and Kegan Paul for the quotation from Ch. Guignebert on pp. 135f, and to the Oxford University Press for the quotations from Dr. Oesterley on pages 75f.

Mainly through the work of the Soncino Press and the Jewish Publication Society of America, there is now, fortunately, a collection of the texts of rabbinic Judaism translated into English, adequate to the purposes of a volume such as this. I have deliberately confined my quotations to such texts. All quotations from the Talmud are from the Babylonian version, and the second page number in each refers to the Soncino edition. *The Rabbinic Anthology* referred to is that of C. G. Montefiore and H. Loewe, Macmillan 1938.

Abbreviations of the Tractates in the Soncino Talmud quoted in the Text.

NOTE: When several tractates are bound in one volume, the pagination usually starts afresh for each tractate.

Ab.	Aboth	Meg.	Megillah
A.Z.	'Aboda Zarah	Men.	Menahoth
B.B.	Baba Bathra	Ned.	Nedarim
Bek.	Bekoroth	Pes.	Pesahim
Ber.	Berakoth	R.H.	Rosh Hashanah
B.K.	Baba Kamma	San.	Sanhedrin
B.M.	Baba Mezi'a	Shab.	Shabbath
Dem.	Demai	Shebu.	Shebu'oth
Ed.	'Eduyyoth	Shek.	Shekalim
Er.	'Erubin	Sot.	Sotah
Git.	Gittin	Suk.	Sukkah
Hag.	Hagigah	Ta'an.	Ta'anith
Hor.	Horayoth	Tem.	Temurah
Hull.	Hullin	Yad.	Yadayim
Kid.	Kiddushin	Yeb.	Yebamoth
Mak.	Makkoth	Yom.	Yoma

Introduction

It is unfortunate that Christian scholars of the Old Testament have chosen to call all or part of the period of Jewish history which begins with the return from exile by the title of 'Spät-Judenthum', 'Bas-Judaisme' or 'Late Judaism'. They inevitably imply thereby that Judaism was about to pass away, whereas in fact it had just come into existence; and that its passing was preceded by a decline in stature, whereas the key-note of the period is the attempt to weave the teaching of the prophets into the life of the people. It would be just as accurate to describe the Elizabethan Age as 'Bas Moyen-age', or the early north-Italian renascence as 'spät-Lombardisch'. Bad history cannot be the foundation for good theology.

This attitude to the period arises from their natural desire to show that Christianity is firmly rooted in the Old Testament, and in God's covenant with the Children of Israel. And it has been traditionally regarded as a necessary corollary to this belief to present the Church as the *only* legitimate successor to the grandeur of the prophets and the responsibilities of the covenant. Since, in this view, all that was of permanent value in Jewish history was soon to pass to the credit of the Christian Church, this period following the return is automatically, if unconsciously, looked at through spectacles which focus the sight only on evidence for the decline and passing of the spiritual authority of Judaism.

To such scholars loyalty to prophetic religion has to be equated with exclusiveness, and concern for Torah with superficiality and legalism. The Judaism of Palestine has to be sharply distinguished from that of the Diaspora, and the universalism inherent in the religion of Jewry has to be confined to the dispersed element in the people. One strange result of these presuppositions is that the literature of the period cannot be seen as a whole, and as the natural product of the diversity of interests and opinions which mark any dynamic society. All that is good in it has to be treated as an almost individual and isolated reaction against what is assumed to be the obscurantism of the overwhelming majority. The main item of interest during these centuries has to be found in the growth of belief in a personal and supernatural messiah, and other aspects have to be reduced in stature or relegated to the background. Just at the first moment in Jewish history when Jews set as their goal the teaching of prophetic ideals and conduct to the whole people, it is proclaimed as clear that the covenant relationship with a nation has been transferred to a remnant, so that it might subsequently be transferred to an individual.

There is no more important aspect of the divergence between the attitude of Christian and Jewish scholars to the same historical records of the post-exilic period than this doctrine of the Remnant which is put forward by the former. Indeed some Christian scholars trace the conception of the narrowing of the Promises to a much earlier period than the return from exile. Thus H. H. Rowley, in *The Biblical Doctrine of Election* (p. 71) traces it right back to the choice of Jacob and the rejection of Esau. W. J. Phythian-Adams in *The Way of At-one-ment* has this passage (p. 14): 'From Moses to David —and after that, apostasy, schism, and corruption; defeat, conquest, exile, servitude! This dreadful antithesis was what the Jewish Remnant saw all too plainly when they looked back upon the History of Israel.' The 'Jewish Remnant' is supposed by the author to be looking back from the standpoint of the last century B.C. Doubtless a sensitive Jew would find elements of tragedy in that thousand years of history which separated him from David. But I do not think he would characterize in the words used by Canon Phythian-Adams a period which contained the great prophets, the many psalmists, the courage of the return, the upbuilding of synagogue worship, and the steady progress in teaching the people the meaning of loyalty to the will of God.

Not all Christian scholars go as far back as Jacob or David to see the covenant relationship with a people breaking down. But, as to the post-exilic period, the majority seem to be agreed. It is treated as a period in which only a remnant of the nation remained faithful. From a historical point of view it is, in any case, doubtful whether the use of the term 'remnant' is justified at all. It is drawn from a passage in Isaiah. After his advice had been rejected by Ahaz (related in Ch. 7) who refused his offer of a sign (vv. 10-13), Isaiah says (8. 16): 'Bind up the testimony, seal the teaching among my disciples. I will wait for the Lord, who is hiding his face from the house of Jacob, and I will hope in him.' After further denunciation of the two kingdoms for their lack of faith, the prophet enunciates his doctrine that a remnant only will survive destruction: 'In that day the remnant of Israel and the survivors of the house of Jacob will no more lean upon him that smote them, but will lean upon the Lord, the Holy One of Israel, in truth. A remnant will return, the remnant of Jacob, to the mighty God. For though your people Israel be as the sand of the sea, only a remnant of them will return.' (10: 20-22, cf. the similar vision in 4: 2 f.).

That these words of Isaiah were very literally fulfilled by the extremely few who returned from the successive deportations of Assyrian and Babylonian kings, may be readily conceded by both sides alike, but the Christian scholar invests them with a theological meaning which predicated and determined the future. Consequently he continues, and indeed intensifies, his concentration on a remnant in the post-restoration period. Thus H. Wheeler Robinson, in his essay on *The Theology of the Old Testament* in the symposium which he edited in 1938, *Record and Revelation*, writes (p. 348): 'The minority group within the later Israel (to which we owe the essential religion of the Old Testament) was based, even from the time of Isaiah's disciples, on the response of individual men, whose spiritual outlook is reflected in the Psalter.' Now, in so far as the religious leaders of any people at any epoch of the world's history are a 'minority group', it is obviously true to say of this period in Jewish history that its spiritual leaders did not constitute the majority of the nation. And, in so far as all inspiration must originate and blossom in the individual consciousness, it is obviously true that the same thing happened to Jews in the period between Ezra and the New Testament. But this is not what was meant by the words and action of Isaiah. To him the band of disciples was a group deliberately withdrawn from the current life of the nation at a precise moment in its history. It is pressing the analogy somewhat far even to identify spiritually this consciously selected group of Ch. 8. with those Israelites who would return from exile as related in Ch. 10. But, when they did return from exile, there appears no further evidence in the sources for the introduction of a 'minority group' withdrawn from the life of the nation and carrying alone the inheritance of Abraham, Moses and the prophets. For the characteristic of the period is the attempt to convert the whole surviving nation, whether in the land of Israel or in the Diaspora, to precisely that faith and way of life which was inherited from its forefathers as the special responsibility of the covenant people. It was just because there was no such withdrawal on the part of those with a sensitive religious conscience that Jesus found everywhere crowds anxious to listen to him, and that Paul and his fellow apostles found throughout the hellenistic world an organised synagogue life through which they could deliver their message.

This use of the conception of a faithful remnant is, of course, not a product of modern scholarship. It has a long tradition behind it, and could, indeed, be traced right back to the 'testimonies' of which there are the beginnings in the New Testament itself. For the Church has, from its separation from Judaism, emphasized every passage in the prophets denouncing the rebelliousness of the children of Israel, and quoted with relish every passage in which their destruction is foretold. But the issue is not whether the people deserved these condemnations at the time when they were uttered, but whether, in the period following the return, they did not take them seriously to heart. That is why the view which is taken of the period following the return is of the greatest significance.

Needless to say Jewish scholars follow the exactly opposite course in their view of this period of their history. Majority and minority developments are reversed. That which is to give rise to Christianity is made to occupy, as far as possible, a peripheral situation in the story. The centre is occupied by those elements which lead straight to post-Biblical rabbinic Judaism. It must, however, be added that there is a Jewish tradition, going back at least as far as Maimonides, which sees Christianity as the divine method by which the Gentiles should learn the first elements of monotheism, before passing to its purer form of Judaism; and that Jewish thinkers, such as Franz Rosenzweig, have taken more seriously the spiritual claims of Christianity than any comparable Christian writer has been prepared to take those of Judaism—if we except men like George Foot Moore or Travers Herford, who have confined their scholarship to the period of the Mishnah and Talmud.

Those who believe that the field of divine activity lies in the actual history of nations and communities, and the actual lives of men and women, must ultimately, whether they be writing from a Jewish or a Christian standpoint, face the facts which each now presents separately. For, in their positive statements of their own faith and its roots, both are right, while in their negative attitude to the other, both are obliged to deal evasively with the substantial evidence which the period affords.

The period from Zerubbabel to the first century of the common era was not a period of decline. It was a period of such abounding vitality that it not only produced the nationalism which troubled three centuries of Jewish history, but also gave legitimate birth both to the Judaism which survived the destruction of state and Temple, and the Christianity which made Jewish monotheism a world religion. Both are truly rooted in it; and the effort of these two 'disparate twins' each to prove the illegitimacy of the other, is the tragic consequence of the separation between them.

That it was—and still is—a grievous tragedy it would be impossible to deny. And yet we should not judge too harshly those who effected the separation. It was an illimitable spiritual adventure which was opened before the Jewish people by the claims of the followers of

Jesus of Nazareth that the messianic age had come or was about to come. They were made at a time when the whole position of Jewry was precarious, hedged in as it was by the unimaginative Romans and the seductive Greeks. And, on the other side, the new-named Christians were so impatient, so 'brash', so *exalté* by the excitement of the spiritual power which they were releasing in the Gentile world, that it is not for us to judge either side for their inability to remain united, and to hold in unity the dual conviction that God had chosen a single people to draw nations to him by the example of its loyalty to his will, and that he had chosen men from all peoples to share in the salvation brought by his messiah.

In this book a picture is painted of the character of the returned community. There follows the record of the natural development of this community to provide the spiritual material for the growth of both rabbinic Judaism and Gentile Christianity.

To get this development with its dual and paradoxical consequences into a right perspective is the task of this work. But, in these days of specialisation, it is of particular importance to realise that it is only the *first stage* of understanding the contemporary situation. The Christian Biblical scholar rarely carries his interest beyond the period of the New Testament. If he sufficiently masters the nature of the new Jewish community established by the work of the rabbis to realise that the religion of Judaism is a parallel, and not a predecessor, to that of Christianity, then he has already become exceptional. But even a perspective that carries him down to the fifth century is still inadequate. For the Jewish people lived an artificially limited life from the time of the fall of the Maccabean kingdom right down to the emancipation of the nineteenth century.

Really to assess the work of those who saw in Torah the whole way of life, we have to wait and see what happened when Jews were free to express their religious inheritance in the open citizenship of a modern democracy. But we cannot transfer the quality of life to be considered simply from the fifth century to the nineteenth and twentieth. We have to know whether this or that which we approve and emulate, or condemn and criticize, today is the product of religion or of history, of persecution or of free choice. To present the whole picture in one volume proved impossible. Here the foundations are laid, from 500 B.C. to A.D. 500. The Christian story has not been presented in such detail, or carried so far, not because it is less important, but because a Christian, writing for Christians, could legitimately assume that the story of the Church, through Nicaea and Constantinople, is well known.

Throughout this book I have naturally used the word 'Torah' and not 'Law' to describe Judaism. For nothing has contributed more to the misunderstanding between the two religions than the fact that the Septuagint translated the word 'Torah' by the narrower word *nomos* and the English still further reduced the meaning by rendering *nomos* as *law*. For *law* is narrower than *nomos*, and *nomos* is narrower than 'Torah'. George Foot Moore, one of the greatest Christian scholars of rabbinic Judaism, thus defines Torah:[1] 'It is a source of manifold misconceptions that the word is customarily translated "Law", though it is not easy to suggest any one English word by which it would be better rendered. "Law" must, however, not be understood in the restricted sense of legislation, but must be taken to include the whole of revelation—all that God has made known of his nature, character and purpose, and of what he would have man be and do. The prophets call their own utterances Torah, and the Psalms deserve the name as well. . . . In a word, Torah in one aspect is the vehicle, in another and deeper view it is the whole content of revelation.' Another scholar, R. Travers Herford, says bluntly:[2] 'It does not, and never did, mean Law. It means, and always has meant, Teaching.'

[1] *Judaism in the First Centuries of the Christian Era*, Harvard, 1927, I, p. 263. There is also an excellent analysis of how the word came to acquire this full meaning by H. Wheeler Robinson, in *Record and Revelation*, Oxford, 1951, pp. 316-319.

[2] *Talmud and Apocrypha*, Soncino Press, 1933, p. 7, note.

Book One

THE COMMON FOUNDATION

Chapter One

THE COMMUNITY OF THE RETURN

1. THE RETURN FROM EXILE

In the period which stretches from the Babylonian exile to the destruction of Jerusalem in A.D. 70 the first decisive steps were taken which were to lead to the creation both of rabbinic Judaism and of the world-wide Christian Church, and were to ensure the survival of the Jews as a people, and the character of the Christian Church as a separate body.

The vital moment in this long period was that in which a certain number of the descendants of those inhabitants of the kingdom of Judah who had been deported by Nebuchadrezzar in 597 and 586 B.C. took advantage of the new policy initiated by Cyrus, the conqueror of Babylon, to return to the homeland of their ancestors in a succession of caravans of which the first set forth about 537 B.C. It was vital because by their action they showed their determination to continue the association of the Jewish people with the history, the religion, and the land, of Israel.

The moment *marks* the transition from 'the religion of Israel' to 'early Judaism', but a single event could not, of course, *create* that transition. Its roots lie deeper in the past, and a much longer period was needed in the future both to give those roots solidity and to determine the nature of the growth which would spring from them. The whole of the period of between six and seven hundred years which separates the exile from the destruction of Jerusalem is involved in the understanding of how Judaism and Christianity came into being as a result of the action of some Jews in returning to the land of their ancestors.

Cyrus had initiated a general policy of returning to their original shrines the gods who had been removed by his Babylonian predecessors, and he also allowed the descendants of those deported to return to their countries. In the first chapter of Ezra it is implied that he was especially moved by respect for the God of the Jews, but this must not be taken as serious history, for he treated all gods equally. Nevertheless, this Jewish return was, in its consequences, unique for it brought into existence a new kind of national and religious community. In the days of King David an inhabitant of Ephraim was his 'subject' even if he followed the polytheistic practices of his Canaanite predecessors. David, on the other hand, would have claimed no special authority over descendants of the Exodus who happened to live in the kingdom of one of his neighbours. After the return this situation was reversed. A member of the community was only a member so long as he professed religious loyalty to the God of the community. On the other hand, he remained a member of the community, and was linked to the community, whether he lived in the ancestral land or anywhere else. We may doubt whether Ezra was really given authority over all Jews west of the Euphrates, at any rate in such extensive terms as are implied in the words:[1] 'And you, Ezra, according to the wisdom of your God which is in your hand, appoint magistrates and judges who may judge all the people in the province Beyond-the-River, all such as know the laws of your God; and those who do not know them, you shall teach. Whoever will not obey the law of your God and the law of the king, let judgment be strictly executed upon him, whether for death or for banishment or for confiscation of his goods or for imprisonment.' But it is not impossible that he was given some authority over them in religious matters, for there was at least a voluntary recognition on the part of Jews outside the Land of Israel that they should turn to Jerusalem for guidance.[2]

We have sufficient allusions to Jewish life at this time to get a general picture of what this new kind of community looked like. Of the two halves the Babylonian was certainly the wealthier and probably the better educated, but the Judean was the more numerous. The deportation had not been penal but a matter of policy, and those deported were given their autonomy under their own authorities, and land on which to settle in the richest part of Mesopotamia. The chance discovery of over seven hundred tablets has given us the archives of the extensive business firm of Murashshu, trading at Nippur, many of whose clients were Jews,[3] and it shows us Jews occupied with all kinds of farming, as well as with commercial and public activities. The Jews in the homeland seem to have been less prosperous, for their poverty is referred to on a number of occasions by Ezra and Nehemiah. They had maintained their religion, and

[1] Ezra 7. 25-26.

[2] The Jews of Elephantine asked for such guidance and were refused approval of their temple. See A. H. Godbey, *The Lost Tribes a Myth*, Duke University, 1930, pp. 590 ff.

[3] Salo W. Baron, *A Social and Religious History of the Jews*, 2nd Ed., Columbia University, 1952, I, pp. 109 ff.

had made no clear distinction between themselves and those from the northern kingdom who also wished to remain loyal to Jahweh, although this may not have passed without earning the condemnation of Ezekiel,[4] long before it became a subject for decisive action after the return. They also, like the Babylonian Jews, had considerable local autonomy and their own authorities. The descriptions of the devastation of the land which abound in Jeremiah and Ezekiel should not be taken too literally; but the hill country of Judea has always been a stony and infertile part of Palestine, and we can well accept that the life of those who remained in the homeland lacked the amenities of the exiles, settled on rich lands around Nippur. It was natural, then, that when a series of caravans arrived from Babylon, the wealthier and better educated newcomers tended to take the lead in both social and religious life, and to exercise a determining influence over future developments.

It might at first sight appear an almost fatal weakness in the whole story of this development that it is impossible to give a straightforward account of the return itself, or to set it exactly in the double picture of the Babylonian community which was quitted, or the Judean community which was joined, by the returning exiles. Scholarly opinion is so divided about every detail that a full account would involve continuous examination of rejected hypotheses and continuous, and very detailed, references in support of the precise course of events suggested. But, while this would be necessary if the present purpose were to write a detailed political history of the Jewish people at this time, it is completely unnecessary if the objective is the understanding of the roots of the two religions which sprang from that history. For we are confronted with the almost absurd paradox that, while for the lesser objective our sources are considerable but hopelessly confused, for the greater the position is relatively clear *since none of the sources deal directly with the subject at all*, and to the two most vital factors there are not even the most indirect allusions.

We possess a considerable body of material in the prophets, in many psalms, and in a range of historical writings, to tell us about the Babylonian community, and the position in Judea. But the two factors on which no information is given are, firstly, how the scattered literature and folk-lore of a people came to be a collected and fixed body of 'Holy Scriptures', and, secondly, how there came into existence the synagogue. For the synagogue was to be the centre in which this literature was sifted and accepted, and it was to devote

[4] If the delegation which came to enquire of Ezekiel in Ch. 20 is to be so interpreted. But see note 5 below.

itself to an entirely unprecedented form of religious activity: the popular worship of God without sacrifice, and the instruction of ordinary Jews in the implications of the Scriptures as applied to the art of living according to his will.

We are almost certainly right in placing within the period of the Babylonian exile the germinal activities which led to these two results, for the exile provides a background on which they appear as reasonable and comprehensible developments. We know that certain Jewish communities living outside Palestine had created copies of the Temple at Jerusalem as the central expression of their national religious life, and it is even possible that one Babylonian Jewish community did the same.[5] But in the main, the Babylonian exiles, influenced by the reforms of Josiah,[6] rejected the idea that a temple in which sacrifice was offered to Jahweh could be built anywhere except in Jerusalem. They were, therefore, compelled to evolve religious activities in which the traditional forms and rituals played no part. The most reasonable explanation of the origin of the synagogue is that it resulted from this need for improvisation. For the exiles desired to give expression to their religious loyalty, and needed mutual support and assistance in retaining that loyalty for themselves and their children without the attraction of the great national festivals at Jerusalem.

The essence of the synagogue is that it is local, that it requires neither priesthood nor ritual, and that it contains the elements of both worship and instruction. It thus perfectly met the needs of the exiles. Moreover, when we look more closely into the two elements mentioned—worship and instruction—we begin to see the answer to the question as to how the scattered literature of a people came to be collected and fixed into 'Holy Scripture'.

2. THE EMERGENCE OF HOLY SCRIPTURE

ARCHAEOLOGY is continually revealing the extent of the written records maintained by the many little kingdoms and city states which flourished between the Nile and Euphrates valleys. Where those

[5] Certain scholars interpret Ezek. 20 as the prophet's reply to the community of Kasiphia (cf. Ezra 8. 17) which had built such a temple. See A. Lodz, *Les Prophètes d'Israel et les Débuts du Judaisme*, Paris, 1935, pp. 244 f. But see also note 4 above. Scholars today are so divided about the Book of Ezekiel that the choice between these two interpretations may depend on whether the chapter is thought to have come from Babylon or from Jerusalem.

[6] 2 Kings 22 and 23.

records were kept on clay tablets many have survived, and so we have the advantage of being able to see how some of the records of the Hebrews must have looked before they were edited and revised; for the Hebrews shared many of their early myths and rituals with their neighbours. Whether they also inscribed their records on clay we do not know, but the use of skins certainly antedates the exile,[7] and there is nothing unreasonable in the supposition that those who were deported took with them copies of much of their national literature. In addition they must have possessed, like all ancient peoples, hymns and legends which were still unwritten, but which had come to possess relatively fixed and standard forms. Out of this material were blended the folk-lore, the rituals, the sacred songs, the laws and customs, and the annals of their history, which make up our present Old Testament. From the frequent remark in our present historical books that the rest of the acts of such and such a ruler are to be found in his particular annals,[8] we can assume that they took with them more than has found its way into the Scriptures.

People who are in the midst of events may keep a record of them, but they rarely regard the record as a matter of special interest. They are concerned with what is going to happen next. But when 'history has stopped', then the past becomes significant. We can, therefore, reasonably assume that much editing and transcribing of these records took place during the exile. Scholars are much divided as to the state which the different elements of the Old Testament had reached at the time of the end of the independent kingdoms. The old theory (the Graf-Wellhausen hypothesis) posited two comprehensive versions of the story, one official to the northern, and one to the southern kingdom, and a series of successive editions, some before, some during and some after the exile, in which these two compilations were combined. In addition there was the independent re-edition of much of the earlier material (i.e. up to the Exodus) known as Deuteronomy, which was usually associated with the reforms of Josiah. Finally the exile itself contributed a fresh revision of law and history with much more emphasis on the role and power of the priesthood. There was no thought at that time that the Synagogue would replace the Temple.

Today most scholars would posit a much more fluid situation. Different editions of the same story may not have been successive, but come from different religious centres, reflecting different interests, some aggressively 'modernist', some old-fashioned and conservative.

[7] cf. the Scroll described in Jer. 36. 2 or the title deeds which he buried in a jar in the field at Anathoth in 32. 9 ff.

[8] e.g. 1 Kings 11. 41; 2 Kings 10. 34; 23. 28, etc.

From our point of view it does not matter which hypothesis is correct; for that which distinguishes the records of Israel from those discovered elsewhere in the Middle East is just that, in some way or other, they were continually gone over and edited, and that this process seems to have begun quite early and continued until after the return. For no scholar claims that our present books have come to us in their original form or denies that the exile played a very important part in their collation and preservation; and both of these are points which sharply distinguish these records from all others.

To take the second point first—the activity of the exiles. The method by which the records were put together enables us to see that in the early days of the Israelites they, like their neighbours, associated prosperity with the strength of their national god. When in the days of Eli they faced a decisive battle with the powerful Philistines, they took the Ark into battle with them, so as to involve their God in their defence. When they were defeated and it was captured, they were sure that 'the glory has departed from Israel'.[9] Sennacherib reflected the same belief when he sent his messengers to ask Hezekiah whether 'any of the gods of the nations ever delivered his land out of the hand of the king of Assyria'.[10] The exilic activity reflects a tremendous step forward from such ideas. That the exiles collected and edited their records after their complete defeat and the total destruction of their kingdom shows that, in their minds, it was not their God who had deserted them, it was they who had deserted their God. The lessons of the prophets had begun to sink in. It was they, by their idolatry and their wrong-doing, who had brought disaster on themselves. Their history had not, therefore, come to an end, nor had their God been defeated. Its lessons were still to be learnt, and in that learning lay their future deliverance.

It is here that we come to another unique point in the Jewish story: the editing had already begun, under the influence of the Hebrew prophets, and this explains the passage from the ideas at the time of Eli to those which prevailed in the time of Hezekiah. The point is made by Professor Salo Baron[11] that Judaism from an early period began to distinguish itself as a *historical* as opposed to a *natural* religion such as was common among the Semitic peoples. All the main festivals of Israel have their counterparts among their neigh-

[9] 1 Sam. 4. 21.

[10] 2 Kings 18. 33-35.

[11] *Op. cit.*, I, pp. 4. ff. Compare the remark of H. Wheeler Robinson in *Record and Revelation*, Oxford, 1951, p. 304: 'the philosophy of revelation is, for the Hebrew, primarily the philosophy of history'. On the transformation of the festivals see also H. St. John Thackeray, *The Septuagint and Jewish Worship*, The Schweich Lectures, 1920, pp. 41 f.

bours, but as nature festivals. Passover was probably a spring festival for centuries before the Exodus, and some of its ritual may go back to those early days. But Israel made it the festival of the deliverance from Egypt. In the same way the festival of first-fruits was associated with the giving of the Law, and the festival of Tabernacles, when the people dwelt in booths, with the period in the wilderness. As a historical monotheism the religion of Israel was intimately tied with the history of Israel, and the successive editings of that history were connected with the gradual development of the ethical and theological ideas of successive generations, each certain that, properly recounted, their story revealed the nature of their God, as at any moment they had come to understand it.

To the insistence on the activity of God in the whole history of his people, which gave importance to every scrap of that history which the exiles could collect, there could be added a second factor, which also would help to explain the passage from historical record to Holy Scripture. In a way which would be strange to a modern man, the individual Semite identified himself with the history of his people, so that the exiles sitting in the cities of Babylon could identify themselves with every incident which had revealed the hand of God in the lives of their ancestors. Their past history was a still living revelation of the purpose of God. It was, in a sense beyond what would be real to us, their own personal history. That this identification was a real factor we can see from many examples. In the psalms there is a constant passage from the singular to the plural, and from the future to the present or the past:

> 'O Lord God of Hosts hear *my* prayer: give ear, O God of Jacob! Behold *our* Shield, O God; look upon the face of *thine* anointed.'[12]

The most conspicuous example of this sense of identification is seen in the difficulties which modern scholars feel in deciding whether the servant poems in Deutero-Isaiah deal with the nation or with an individual. As Wheeler Robinson says 'the true answer would seem to be that it is both, or rather that there is a consciousness of both as so united in the speaker that he can emphasise now one side, now the other, without needing to draw a definite line.'[13]

Even today, in an orthodox Jewish household, the members partaking of the Passover are bidden to identify themselves with the actual generation which left Egypt. For in the order of service, after the recital of the events of the Exodus there follows: 'In every

[12] Ps. 84. 8-9.

[13] H. Wheeler Robinson, *The Cross of the Servant*, S.C.M. Press, 1926, pp. 32 ff. See also note 38 on on p. 88.

generation it is a man's duty to regard himself as if he had gone forth from Egypt, as it is written: "and thou shalt show thy son in that day, saying, Because of that which the Lord did unto *me* when *I* came forth out of Egypt".'[14]

Here, then, seem to be the steps by which the varied literature of Israel came to be 'Holy Scripture'. The increasing emphasis on history, rather than nature, as the scene of the divine activity and the source of religious fast and festival, emphasised the whole story of the people, and led to its continual restatement in terms consistent with contemporary belief. The Semitic identification of each individual and generation with the whole people made this story, and the lessons to be learnt from it, the centre of the new worship of the synagogue, and so gradually a canon of what might be read came to be formed.[15]

That the books of the Law came to be regarded as the central feature of this sacred literature is not surprising. What is surprising is that the Jews did not, as did the Samaritans, limit their body of Holy Scripture to the Pentateuch itself. Jews, Christians and Muslims alike have been for centuries so accustomed to the existence of a special body of literature to which they attribute a special sanctity, and which they separate from all other literature, that it is difficult for us to appreciate the fact that there was a period in the history of each religion in which this corpus of books was actually in process of formation. We cannot today recreate that strange combination of piety and discrimination by which each writing must have been approached, appraised, and then accepted or rejected. The solution of R. H. Charles that it was a result of the intolerable and intolerant legalism of the early Pharisees[16] is scarcely tenable, in view of the works which were accepted as 'Holy Scripture'. Ecclesiastes, The Song of Songs, or the Book of Job may later have had pious explanations or conventional additions attached to them. But did anyone attach such explanations or additions *before* they became Holy Scripture? Again, we shall see that many passages in the

[14] Ex. 13. 8. The passage occurs in the Haggadah at the end of the recital of the exodus and before the singing of the Hallel (Ps. 113 and 114).

[15] On the closure of the canon and its consequences see p. 93f.

[16] See for example his introduction to the volume *Pseudepigrapha* in his *Apocrypha and Pseudepigrapha of the Old Testament* (Oxford, 1913) pp. viii f, and *Eschatology, A Critical History of the Doctrine of a Future Life*. A. & C. Black, 1913. pp. 193-205. His view can be summarised in his own words as 'The law was supreme, inspiration was officially held to be dead, and the Canon was closed.' Though his work is now fifty years old, he remains the mainspring of those writers who lay stress on apocalyptic as against rabbinic Judaism.

Pentateuch itself caused considerable embarrassment to later rabbis.[17] It would be fascinating to know why they were not excised before the collections in which they were incorporated became sacrosanct.

It would be equally fascinating to know why books were left out, why we do not possess the Book of Jashar, which contained among its poems the invocation to the sun to stand still over Gibeon, as well as the lament of David over Saul and Jonathan;[18] or why the compilers of the canon rejected the records of the acts of Solomon which were written in 'the history of Nathan the prophet' and 'the prophecy of Ahijah the Shilonite', and, still more, in 'the visions of Iddo the seer concerning Jeroboam the son of Nebat'.[19] These, and many other similar works, are referred to as existing in writing at the time of the Chronicler, that is well after the return from exile.

Then there is the final problem. Why was the canon closed? Again we must say that the explanation of Dr. Charles, that it was narrow and fanatical hatred on the part of the Pharisees of the splendid continuation of prophecy by the apocalyptists, scarcely fits the facts, in view of the inclusion of the apocalyptic work of Daniel, on which the ink can scarcely have been dry when it was proposed for acceptance. Had a certain antiquity been necessary, closure would have been comprehensible. The makers of the canon of the *New* Testament sought to link each book with an actual eye-witness or contemporary of Jesus, and rejected those books for which no case for an apostolic origin could be plainly sustained. No such consideration can have governed the makers of the canon of the Old Testament; nor had they, as did their New Testament successors, a precedent by which it was natural, in making a canon, also to close it. In view of the lateness of Daniel and its character, the closure is perhaps the strangest and most insoluble problem of all. If, as Dr. Charles insists, and insists rightly, those who made it were ancestors of those who became Pharisees, why include Proverbs and leave out the Wisdom of Solomon and Ecclesiasticus? Why not have included, later if need be, the sober record of Jewish heroism in I Maccabees? It is not as though there was a sudden and lengthy period during which no religious literature was being produced, a period which could easily have become a dividing line. Nor was there a sudden change in its character, and the explanation of Dr. Charles, attributing everything to the narrowness of Pharisaism, leaves inexplicable the inclusion of Daniel, which was a novelty, and the exclusion of

[17] See below, Ch. 2, Section 4, p. 68

[18] Josh. 10. 13 and 2 Sam. 1. 18. Jashar is a mistake for *hasir*, song book.

[19] 2 Chron. 9. 29.

Jubilees, an extremely 'legalistic' work which is probably contemporary with it.

These unanswerable questions are raised in order that we may remember how unprecedented the whole story is. If, like Dr. Charles, we wish to condemn this or that aspect of their choice, and this or that attitude to Holy Scripture when it has been formed and accepted, we should humbly recognise that pioneers cannot always foresee all the consequences of their decisions, or anticipate the criticisms of later generations approaching their work from a standpoint totally different from their own.

3. THE SYNAGOGUE

THE creation of a canon of Holy Scripture, and the emergence of the synagogue as a part of the life of every Jewish community, are two consequences of the exile which go hand in hand. But with the latter, as with the former, there are antecedents which go back to pre-exilic days. Today a 'synagogue' brings to mind in the first place a building; but we cannot say when special buildings for instruction and worship first appeared, nor whether they have their origin in religion or in the necessities of public life. What dates from this period is not a building, but a local religious meeting.

It is possible that our first allusion to what was to lead to the development is to be found in the astonishment of the man of Shunem when his wife wished to make a sudden visit to Elisha owing to the death of her child. 'Why', asked the husband, 'will you go to him today? It is neither new moon nor Sabbath.'[20] This seems to imply that it would not have been unnatural for an ordinary person to visit a prophet on a recognised holy day, and it is possible that we have here a clue to the occasion on which some at least of the prophetic messages were delivered. People were accustomed to visit them on the Sabbath and on holy days and to hear what they had to say. We might carry this further from a reference of the Chronicler to the policy of Jehoshaphat. Jehoshaphat was a 'good' king of Judah, but the earlier annalist of his reign in the book of Kings records only that he suppressed one form of temple prostitution, while leaving local high-places undisturbed.[21] But since he makes the usual statement that the rest of his acts are to be found in the chronicles of the Kings of Judah, there may possibly be some real action behind

[20] 2 Kings 4. 23.
[21] 1 Kings 22. 43-46.

the much later account which our book of Chronicles has dressed in details which belong to the exilic period or later. According to this account Jehoshaphat sent princes, priests, and Levites to teach *in the cities of Judah* 'having the book of the law of the Lord with them'.[22] Finally, during the exile we have a statement in Ezekiel that he received a vision 'as I sat in my house with the elders of Judah sitting before me'.[23] Putting all these scraps together it is not unreasonable to suggest that *regular* meetings of the local community had their origin in the custom of occasional consultation and instruction at the local level with those who were particularly qualified to declare the divine will, whether priest or prophet.

It is clear that from the time of the exile the instruction of the people in the nature of their relationship with their God, and the duties which flowed from this relationship, occupied a central position in local religious life. In the previous section this was related to the gradual evolution of the text of the Holy Scriptures. The synagogue was likewise concerned with their translation into the vernacular (at that time Aramaic) and their interpretation, that is, with the development of the sermon and the midrash. In the account in Nehemiah of the reading of the Law by Ezra we have a clear indication that the people expected reading to be accompanied by translation and explanation,[24] and when this was done they made 'great rejoicing because they had understood the words which had been declared to them.'

Further evidence that interpretation dates from this time comes from the rabbinic tradition that 'Moses received the Torah at Sinai and transmitted it to Joshua, Joshua to the elders, and the elders to the prophets, and the prophets to the Men of the Great Synagogue.'[25] In this passage 'Torah' means the oral and not the written Law, since the latter was delivered openly to the whole people before the Mount. The 'Men of the Great Synagogue' is the rabbinic title given to the generation of the return under the leadership of Ezra and to their immediate successors. Actually the oral law was not exactly defined as such until some centuries later, but it grew out of the interpretation provided in the synagogue at this time. When fully developed, 'interpretation' was of two distinct kinds, *halakah*, or the actual definition of rules of conduct, and *haggadah*, or moral exhortation. In the latter capacity it is the origin of the parables of the gospels, as of the sermon in church. At this period both

[23] Ezek. 8. 1.
[22] 2 Chron. 17. 7-9.
[24] Neh. 8. 7-9 & 12.
[25] Aboth 1, pp. 1 f.

halakah and haggadah were covered by the word *midrash* or investigation.

The orderly fulfilment of Torah was the supreme objective of the 'Men of the Great Synagogue.' Tradition ascribed to them the statement: 'be patient [in the administration of justice], rear many disciples, and make a fence about the Torah.' Lest this should make life narrow, the last of them, Simeon the Just, summed up his teaching in a further triad: 'the world is based upon three things: the Torah, divine service and the practice of kindliness.'[26]

Two more points may be added to this side of the work of the synagogue. We hear nothing at this period of any special class exclusively devoted to the work of interpreting and administering the codes. These were later to be functions of a special class of 'scribes', but from the Chronicler and the author of the book of Nehemiah (possibly the same man) we see that in the beginning these tasks were undertaken by the still undifferentiated group, the Levitical priests. Secondly we see from the first of the sayings of the 'Men of the Great Synagogue' that the administration of justice was already recognised as one of the functions of the local religious leaders. Later it became an essential part of the work of a rabbi. The synagogue was both school and court.

When we turn to the other side of synagogal life, congregational worship, we are confronted with a similar lack of direct evidence as to its beginnings. It is interesting to note that prayer and praise do not seem to have appeared to the great pre-exilic prophets as the natural alternative to the sacrifices which they denounced, and as the proper approach of the ordinary Israelite to his God. Isaiah, for example, says:

> When you spread your hands,
> I will hide my eyes from you;
> even though you make many prayers,
> I will not listen;
> your hands are full of blood

and his demand is:

> Cease to do evil,
> learn to do good;
> seek justice,
> correct oppression;
> defend the fatherless,
> plead for the widow.

[26] *Ibid.*

Micah similarly insists that the ordinary man knows what God requires of him:

> to do justice, and to love kindness,
> and to walk humbly with your God.[27]

In fact the first direct suggestion of prayer as the normal approach to God for ordinary men seems to come in the magnificent composition, usually attributed to an exilic author, which is put in the mouth of Solomon at the dedication of the Temple. In that prayer the king intercedes on behalf of 'those who are carried captive' and 'pray to Thee towards their land'.[28]

The silence of the prophets is reinforced by the silence of the various codes. There were many forms of sacrifice ordained to secure various benefits, but prayer is nowhere directly enjoined. Whatever may be the explanation of this silence, it is not that the religion of Israel in pre-exilic days did not find expression in prayer. Prayers are recorded of almost every notable figure, from Moses praying for Israel to Hannah praying for a child. These, however, are all prayers offered on special occasions, and our real source book for the Israelite at prayer is the Psalter. In a number of psalms we find what we would have expected to find in the prophets, the direct insistence that prayer is more pleasing to God than sacrifice, and with prayer goes praise. Here are some examples from psalms which are in themselves prayers:

> Sacrifice and offering thou dost not desire;
> but thou hast given me an open ear.
> Burnt offering and sin offering
> thou hast not required.
> Then I said, 'Lo, I come;
> in the roll of the book it is written of me;
> I delight to do thy will, O my God;
> Thy law is within my heart.'
> Ps. 40. 6-8.

> Thou hast no delight in sacrifice;
> were I to give a burnt offering,
> thou wouldst not be pleased.
> The sacrifice acceptable to God is a broken spirit;
> a broken and contrite heart, O God, thou wilt not despise.
> Ps. 51. 16, 17.

[27] Is. 1. 15 & 17; Micah 6. 8. Cf. K. Kohler, *The Origins of the Synagogue and the Church*, New York, 1939, pp. 16, f.
[28] 1 Kings 8. 33-34 & 46-48.

I will praise the name of God with a song;
I will magnify him with thanksgiving.
This will please the Lord more than an ox,
or a bull with horns and hoofs.
Let the oppressed see it and be glad;
you who seek God, let your hearts revive.
For the Lord hears the needy,
and does not despise his own that are in bonds.
Ps. 69. 30-33.

Throughout the history of Israel there were among the clergy and laity those who remained faithful to Jahweh according to the lights vouchsafed to their generation, and it is this section of the population which we encounter in the psalms. Two classes are especially prominent, the *anavim*, the humble and oppressed, and the *hasidim*, the saintly—an epithet which is usually used of the faithful priests and levites.[29] The psalms are full of the contrast between the 'proud', the 'oppressor', and the 'poor' and 'afflicted', and their authors have no doubt that God is on the side of the latter—even if his power is slow to manifest itself. Psalms 9, 10, 12, are but the first of a series running right through the Psalter with this theme. So likewise God prizes his saints, even if they suffer for his name:

Depart from evil, and do good;
So shall you abide for ever.
For the Lord loves justice;
he will not forsake his saints.
Ps. 37. 27-28.

Precious in the sight of the Lord
is the death of his saints.
Ps. 116. 15.

It is in these two classes that we find the backbone of the synagogal life of the exile and of post-exilic Judaism; and it is in the extension of the ideas expressed in such psalms that we shall find the origins of the synagogal liturgy.

While we know that among the prayers still in use in synagogal worship are some which are of pre-Christian origin, and while the early forms of Christian liturgy give us clear indications of the Jewish liturgy from which they were derived, we cannot exactly say when this or that prayer was introduced, and the same is true of synagogal organisation. We have no reason to believe that any particular form

[29] On these two elements see Kohler, *op. cit.*, pp. 22 ff. & 29 ff.

of leadership was prescribed, and it is more natural to believe that the whole of this central structure of Jewish life grew gradually, and was moulded by the needs of the changing situation.

4. THE TEMPLE AND THE SAMARITANS

IT may at first appear illogical to have treated of the Scriptures and the synagogue before discussing the rebuilding of the Temple. But, in fact, it is only by taking these into account that it is possible to see that action in its proper perspective. For it was in the examination and the editing of the Scriptures that the people were made conscious of their inheritance and their responsibility, and it was in the synagogue that its lessons were regularly discussed, taught and adapted to daily living. The visible restoration of the Temple, and its visible sacrifices, would have been meaningless had they not been thought to set the seal on something which was commonly understood and accepted by the people, both Judeans and returning exiles, who were to build and maintain it.

That which 'was commonly understood and accepted' was that they were still part of that people with whom Jahweh had made a covenant at Sinai, and to whom he had promised the land once inhabited by Canaanites and others. Their task was to renew that covenant by a faithful observance of his demands such as their predecessors had failed to render, and so to justify the restoration which he, by the hand of Cyrus, had made possible for them. Coupled with this positive attitude to their future responsibility was the recognition that the destruction of the kingdom and its capital, and the pains of exile, were the just consequences of their own sins, and were not due to any failure on the part of their God. It is this remarkable attitude which had made the exile creative—how remarkable it was we can see by contrasting it with the protestations of modern nations when they meet misfortune, and claim it to be the consequences of every kind of wrongdoing except their own. Judeans and exiles accepted their misfortunes as the fitting punishment of their sins; and the particular sins which their prophets had indicated as meriting such punishment were idolatry and social injustice. The splendid ritual of the Temple was designed to prevent a repetition of the former, just as the steady teaching of the synagogue was intended to combat the evils of the latter.

At the time when the northern kingdom was tottering to its fall, both Amos and Isaiah had warned the people that exile would be the penalty for the luxury and oppression with which both kingdoms were filled. In scathing terms Amos had denounced 'those who are at ease in Zion' and prophesied that 'therefore they shall now be the first of those to go into exile'.[30] Isaiah, in one of his most dramatic utterances,

Let me sing for my beloved
A love song concerning his vineyard,

denounced the utter corruption of Judah as well as Israel, and warned them that exile would be the result.[31] Prophet after prophet had likewise denounced the idolatry which was practised in both kingdoms, but in this case the lesson was pointed by the prophet of the exile himself, Ezekiel, whose bitterness exceeded that of any of his predecessors:

> Thus says the Lord God: Behold, I, even I, am against you; and I will execute judgments in the midst of you in the sight of the nations. And because of all your abominations I will do with you what I have never yet done, and the like of which I will never do again. Therefore fathers shall eat their sons in the midst of you, and sons shall eat their fathers; and I will execute judgments on you, and any of you who survive I will scatter to all the winds. Wherefore, as I live, says the Lord God, surely, because you have defiled my sanctuary with all your detestable things and with all your abominations, therefore I will cut you down; my eye will not spare, and I will have no pity. A third part of you shall die of pestilence and be consumed with famine in the midst of you; a third part shall fall by the sword round about you; and a third part I will scatter to all the winds and will unsheathe the sword after them.[32]

Happily for Israel, God was less vindictive than his prophet. But this utter condemnation of idolatry was not confined to the neurotic and fanatical Ezekiel. It is true that the great universalist, the Second Isaiah, by his frequent references to the fabrication of idols,[33] could almost be said to laugh idolatry out of court, but the attention he

[30] Amos 6. 1 and 7.

[31] Is. 5. 1-24. Cf. Zech. 7. 8-14 for a post-exilic reminder that social injustice brought about the exile.

[32] Ezek. 5. 8-12. The whole of the following chapter continues in the same vein, and passages of similar violence are to be found in many other parts of his prophecies.

[33] Is. 40. 18-20; and, if this prose passage is accepted as part of the original work, 44. 9-20. It may not be in its original place, but there must have been few men of his day with the breadth of outlook to make such exquisite fun of idols and their worship.

paid to the subject shows that he realised its importance. Moreover, he stressed the need for absolute purity in the worship of God, and spoke of this purity in ritual as well as moral terms.[34] Nor did he doubt that it was Israel's own sins which brought about the downfall of the Kingdom and the exile.[35] It is not surprising, therefore, that the chief lesson which was burnt into the hearts of the generation which returned was that their sufferings were the penalty for their social and religious faithlessness to the God of Israel.

We must be even more precise. It was not merely the open worship of strange gods which had caused an offended deity to cast them out; it was also the syncretism which existed in most of the popular, and some of the official, worship nominally directed to Jahweh himself. Reference was made in the previous section to the two accounts of the reign of the 'good' king Jehoshaphat. The author of Kings could call him 'good' in spite of his admission that 'the high places were not taken away, and the people still sacrificed and burnt incense on the high places'.[36] For the reform of such high places he leaves to the later reign of Josiah. But what he has to recount of that reign shows the terrible lengths to which syncretism had gone, even in Solomon's Temple at Jerusalem itself,[37] and make it not surprising that the Chronicler, when he came to revise the narrative and to accept the epithet 'good' of Jehoshaphat, could not allow that a 'good' king could ever have permitted abominations such as Josiah encountered in his reforms. He, therefore, was sure that Jehoshaphat must have destroyed the shrines which the previous author had said that he had left.[38] This single instance of how annals, originally recording a historical development, were turned into 'Holy Scripture' giving a static but consistent record of God's moral demands and men's understanding of them, enables us better to understand the tremendous conviction with which those who returned insisted that Moses himself had laid it down that there must be only one shrine at Jerusalem where sacrifice was offered, and that no loophole whatever must be left through which the previous abominations could infiltrate themselves into it again.

This is the background from which to approach with understanding the task which Ezra set himself—or which he was given by those who despatched him from Babylon. It was not merely a question of ensuring the continuation of worship at the altar in Jerusalem; that, in

[34] Is. 52. 11.
[35] Is. 40. 1-2, 42. 24-25.
[36] 1 Kings 22. 43.
[37] 2 Kings 23. 4-14.
[38] 2 Chron. 17. 6.

all probability, had never ceased. The urgent necessity was to ensure that worship was offered to God in terms which were acceptable to him. To ensure that, every possible trace of the impurity of syncretism had to be removed, every possible detail of the divinely revealed order had to be maintained. That, to him and his contemporaries, was the only way in which the sin which led to the destruction of Jerusalem and the exile could be purged. Idolatry and its impurity had to be utterly rooted out.

There has been much discussion among scholars as to the actual content of 'the book of the law of Moses which God had given to Israel'[39] which Ezra read to the people in 'the square before the Water Gate'. At one time it was assumed that it was that part of the 'priestly code' which is embodied in Leviticus, and that this was an exilic composition. It was then objected that the people would not have accepted an entirely new code, and that it must have been something familiar. But if the caravan with which Ezra came was at least the fourth[40] to arrive from Babylon, then it is perfectly possible that those who had preceded him, or had been all the time at Jerusalem, were already aware of the fact that there was in Babylon an authoritative text of the Mosaic code (they would not have thought of it as a 'new' code) which they had not heard, and that they understood that it would be necessary to know it before they could properly restore the Temple and its worship. It may, then, have been a form of the priestly code which he read.

To meet its categoric demand for purity and conformity, two difficult problems had to be tackled. In pre-exilic days there was no clear distinction between 'priests' and 'levites'. While the descendants of the Solomonic high priest, Zadok, ministered in the Temple at Jerusalem, there were many other families of priests who ministered to the shrines of Jahweh which were scattered through Judah and Israel before the reformation of Josiah. In the mind of Ezra these priests were tainted with idolatry, for they had taken part in the worship which Josiah's reformation denounced as impure.[41] They were therefore excluded from any ministration at the new shrine at Jerusalem, and gradually reduced to the level of temple servants, while at the same time the dignity of the Zadokite high priest was increased. The degradation of the local priests to the status of a separate and inferior class of levites must have caused a great deal of bitterness in the families involved, but it was a matter of relatively

[39] Neh. 8. 1.

[40] The first being that of Sheshbazzar (Ezra 1. 5-8), the second that of Zerubbabel (Ezra 2. 1-2), and the third that of Nehemiah.

[41] Ezra 2. 59-63.

limited interest. Of much wider significance was the choice of attitude towards the Jahweh worshippers from the northern kingdom—in other words the whole complicated problem of the Samaritans.

Josiah appears to have destroyed all the local sanctuaries which he could reach in the old Northern Kingdom at the same time as he had destroyed those within his own kingdom of Judah[42]—how he was able to do this we have no means of knowing—so that perhaps we can assume that he also introduced into these same territories a purer worship and the idea of attendance at Jerusalem for the major festivals. Certainly we know of northerners bringing offerings to that city in the last days before its destruction.[43] But the contemptuous phrase of the editor of Kings that 'they feared the Lord and also served their graven images'[44] probably accurately represents a situation in which there were no rigid distinctions, and pure Jahwism with some faded off into pure idolatry with others.

Until the reforms of Ezra came into view, it seems to have been left to individual discretion how to act. The frontier between the province Beyond-the-River and the autonomous area round Jerusalem was a vague one. The Chronicler speaks of the first to return to devastated Jerusalem as being a number of exiles, 'and some of the people of Judah, Benjamin, Ephraim and Manasseh';[45] and the first Passover was eaten by 'the people of Israel who had returned from exile, and also by everyone who had joined them and separated himself from the pollutions of the peoples of the land to worship the Lord, the God of Israel'.[46] A further piece of evidence comes from the building of the walls by Nehemiah. Among those who built were 'Melatiah the Gibeonite and Jadon the Meronothite, the men of Gibeon and of Mizpah, who were under the jurisdiction of the governor of the province Beyond-the-River'.[47]

All this would be perfectly consistent with the parallel existence of a contrary attitude manifested in the political opposition and unpleasant intrigues which Nehemiah encountered from Sanballat, Tobiah and their companions.[48] Nor need we be surprised that these intrigues distressed many of the Judean landowners who were linked to Tobiah by marriage, as well as his son-in-law who was a priest at the Temple.[49]

[42] 2 Kings 23. 15-20.
[43] Jer. 41. 4-8.
[44] 2 Kings 17. 41
[45] 1 Chron. 9. 2-3.
[46] Ezra 6. 21.
[47] Neh. 3. 7.
[48] Neh. 2. 10, 19; 4. 1, 7, 10f.; 6. 1.
[49] Neh. 6. 17-19, and 13. 4-9.

The situation, however, needed clarification when the building of a new Temple out of the ruins of its predecessor was seen to be the intention of the newcomers, and was actually initiated by Zerubbabel.[50] What we are told is that as soon as that project became known, a group of northerners described as 'the adversaries of Judah and Benjamin' appeared upon the scene. They 'approached Zerubbabel and the heads of fathers' houses and said to them, Let us build with you; for we worship your God as you do, and we have been sacrificing to him ever since the days of Esarhaddon king of Assyria who brought us here. But Zerubbabel, Jeshua, and the rest of the heads of fathers' houses in Israel said to them, You have nothing to do with us in building a house to our God; but we alone will build to the Lord, the God of Israel, as King Cyrus, the king of Persia, has commanded us.' Then the people of the land discouraged the people of Judah and made them afraid to build.'[51]

Until modern scholarship had uncovered a great deal of new material about the Samaritans,[52] it was always assumed that the 'adversaries of Benjamin and Judah' and 'the people of the land' were identical, and that both were synonyms for the Samaritans, and that these, in their turn, were a mixed breed of Israelites and others who had been imported by Esarhaddon. Moses Gaster, whose authority in this field is great, doubts whether at this time any relics of these foreign immigrants survived in the country, and considers that they were most likely to have been temporary garrison troops. But he also makes it clear that it is extremely unlikely that such a request as is here described was ever made by the religious leaders of the Samaritans.[53] He believes that we may have the story upside down. What really happened, he thinks, was that these leaders invited the Judeans to worship at their shrine (whether at that time it was at Bethel or already on Mount Gerizim is perhaps uncertain) and that the Judeans inevitably refused—inevitably since to accept would have meant to deny the whole of their history since David, and reject all the writings of their prophets and psalmists, since these were regarded as heretical and schismatic by the Samaritans. The Samaritans were established, the Judeans were not, and Gaster regards it as impossible that they should have wished to have anything to do with a new religious centre in Jerusalem. On the other

[50] Ezra 4. 1-3.
[51] Ezra 4. 4.
[52] See especially Moses Gaster, *The Samaritans, Their History, Doctrines and Literature*, Schweich Lectures for 1923, Ch. 1.
[53] Moses Gaster, *Samaritan Oral Law and Ancient Tradition*, Search Pub. Co., 1932, pp. 21 f.

hand, perhaps it is possible that some of the foreign elements did survive in the country, or that not all the descendants of the previous Northern Kingdom were of one mind and that it was either or both of them who, already rejected by the Samaritan religious leaders, wished to join the Judeans and were refused.

This would not only allow of some basis for the incident recounted in Ezra, but would also explain certain chapters in 'Trito-Isaiah' which L. E. Browne has suggested as relevant to this question as to who should be accepted within the restored people.[54] That, as Browne believed, the debate concerned *all* the Samaritans Gaster has shown to be impossible. But that, in the period between Zerubbabel and Ezra, there must have been a debate on the limits of the restored community cannot be denied. For they had to decide whether to implement the splendid promise held out by Deutero-Isaiah, which had concluded with an invitation to any 'foreigner who had joined himself to the Lord':[55]

> And the foreigners who join themselves to the Lord,
> to minister to him, to love the name of the Lord,
> and to be his servants,
> every one who keeps the Sabbath,
> and does not profane it,
> and holds fast my covenant—
> these I will bring to my holy mountain,
> and make them joyful in my house of prayer;
> their burnt offerings and their sacrifices
> will be accepted on my altar;
> for my house shall be called a house of prayer
> for all peoples.
> Thus says the Lord God,
> who gathers the outcasts of Israel,
> I will gather yet others to him
> besides those already gathered.

There is no doubt that individual foreigners who accepted in full the obligations of a native Israelite were readily accepted, and this splendid invitation could legitimately be regarded as covering only such individual conversions. But the issue which confronted the

[54] L. E. Browne, *Early Judaism*, Cambridge, 1920, pp. 70 ff. Trito-Isaiah is not a single author.

[55] Is. 56. 6-8. The division between Deutero- and Trito-Isaiah is usually made at verse one of this chapter, whereas it is at verse 9 that the tone changes unmistakably. Vv. 1-8 form a superb and fitting conclusion to the previous poems; they have no link with v. 9 following.

first generations after the return was somewhat different; it could be considered as coming under the heading of 'reunion' rather than conversion. There were whole groups which sought recognition that they were *already* members of the covenant people. It is in such a group that Browne sees the source of a passage which is to be found in Isaiah 63. 7 to 65. 1. The passage opens with a recitation of God's loving-kindness to Israel, and of Israel's rebelliousness. God had turned against them, but then 'remembered the days of old'. The speaker therefore prays with confidence for a fresh outpouring of his mercy. Then occur the strange lines:

> For thou art our Father,
> though Abraham does not know us
> and Israel does not acknowledge us;
> Thou, O Lord, art our Father,
> our Redeemer from of old is thy name.
>
> . . . . . .
>
> We have become like those over whom thou hast never ruled,
> like those who are not called by thy name.[56]

The question as to who it is that Abraham does not know nor Israel acknowledge is a difficult one to answer. Browne's suggestion that they are of the mixed non-Israelite stock who had been settled in Samaria is plausible. Certainly, in spite of the recitation early in the prophecy of God's mercies upon Israel, it would seem that the phrases could not cover people of Israelite descent. The final verse contains the divine answer to the suppliants:

> I was ready to be sought by those who did not ask for me;
> I was ready to be found by those who did not seek me.
> I said, 'Here am I, here am I',
> to a nation that did not call on my name.[57]

Whatever be the interpretation of this difficult passage—and almost every scholar holds a different view—Browne makes out a very good case for referring it to this period, and for tying it up with the increasingly exclusive policy followed by the Judean leaders, and the widening rift between them and their northern neighbours.

While we are considering the possibility of a group other than the official religious leaders of the Samaritans seeking contact with

[56] Browne, *op. cit.* pp. 79 ff.

[57] Is. 65. 1. If this really is the interpretation of the passage, it must, I imagine, be assumed that the series of negatives refer to the previous history of these people, since on this occasion they did ask, seek, and call on his name.

the Judeans, we might take into account also a mysterious incident recorded by Zechariah. 'The people of Bethel had sent Sharezer and Regem-melech and their men' to ask the priests at Jerusalem whether they should continue to fast in the fifth and the seventh months. These two fasts actually commemorated the fall of Jerusalem and the murder of its subsequent Jewish governor, Gedaliah, so that their observance certainly implies a feeling of unity with the fate of Jerusalem. Nevertheless, Zechariah replied sarcastically and, to our mind, impertinently that in the days before the fall of Jerusalem the inhabitants of Bethel had worshipped strange gods, as the denunciations of the prophets made clear. Their fasts are therefore a matter of no interest to Jerusalem.[58]

It may well be that these passages, and that of Ezra, do reflect incidents to which we have no other references, and that the decision which was ultimately given in all such cases was tragically narrow. Under the influence of Haggai, Zechariah, and presumably Ezra himself, the 'outsiders' were rejected. They had no part in the new community. Nevertheless, Browne's verdict on their attitude, which is indeed the usual verdict of Christian scholars on the period, is extremely exaggerated. According to him, the Jews 'refused to be a light to lighten even their nearest kinsmen. This unanimous decision was the beginning of Israel's refusal to be the Servant of the Lord.'[59] We have, however, sufficient examples in Christian history to enable us to understand more sympathetically a policy of rigid conformity at a time when danger threatened both within and without the community.

To return to the Samaritans, we know that the opposition of 'the people of the land', if by this is meant the Samaritans, did postpone for a considerable period the rebuilding of the Jerusalem Temple. We know also that, in building it, the Judeans were conscious of it involving a schism with the Samaritans, at least if we interpret the answer of Haggai, as is usually done, as referring to their possible presence in the restored Temple:

> Ask the priests to decide this question, 'If one carries holy flesh in the skirt of his garment, and touches with his skirt bread, or pottage, or wine, or oil, or any kind of food, does it become holy?' The priests answered, 'No'. Then said Haggai, 'If one who is unclean by contact with a dead body touches any of these, does it become unclean?' The priests answered, 'It does become unclean.' Then Haggai said, 'So it is with this people, and with

[58] Zech. 7. 1-7.
[59] Browne, *op. cit.*, p. 112.

> this nation before me, says the Lord; and so with every work of their hands; and what they offer there is unclean.'[60]

It may help us to sympathise somewhat with Haggai on this subject if we take into account a statement of Gaster that the Samaritans themselves used to boast that, being linguistically indistinguishable from the Judeans, they were able to slip into the Temple at Jerusalem and introduce and strew dead men's bones in its courts in order to pollute it.[61]

It is often assumed that, whatever form it took, the final schism between Samaritans and Judeans took place immediately after the return of the Babylonian exiles to Jerusalem. The difficulty of accepting this date lies in the Samaritan possession of the priestly code, and the fact that subsequent Samaritan religious activities parallel in many ways those which were adopted by the restored community in Judea, but were unknown before the exile. Like the latter they possessed synagogues, and had their own targumim. They developed methods of interpretation very similar to that of the early developments of the oral law among the Jews. In fact Gaster considers that we can get our best information as to the development of this law, before the time when our rabbinical sources become adequate, from Samaritan traditions.[62] All this would appear to imply a considerable period during which there were fairly close associations between north and south, unless we carry all these developments, including the priestly code, back to the period before the fall of Samaria, a solution which Gaster adopts. Failing this, there may be some truth in the statement of Josephus[63] that the final schism took place in the fourth century, just before the entry on to the Syrian scene of Alexander of Macedon, even if his reason for the schism (a mixed marriage between a priest at Jerusalem and a Samaritan) is judged unconvincing.

It is only a guess, but a not unreasonable one, that the real reason was simply that each side accused the other of being too lax. That certainly would be a fair deduction about the opinions of the Judeans from the description of the Samaritans already quoted from the book of Kings, and from the scraps of information in the books of Ezra and Nehemiah. But it is also true that the Samaritans accused the Judeans of being too lax. Ezra, in Samaritan literature, bears

[60] Hag. 2. 10-14.
[61] Gaster, Schweich Lectures, p. 37.
[62] Gaster, *Samaritan Oral Law*, Ch. 2.
[63] *Ant.*, XI. 8.

the title 'the accursed Ezra who has written words of wickedness'[64] and the Samaritans rejected every part of what the Judeans came to accept as Holy Scripture except their version of the Pentateuch. Certainly, if either side is to be accused of excessive narrowness and rigidity, the charge could be more fairly laid against the Samaritans. Nothing in their history suggests that Jesus, in the parable of the Good Samaritan, was intending to take a typical example of that community.

It would be interesting to know what leakage there was from Samaritanism to Judaism during subsequent centuries. Just as some passed from Judaism to what seemed to them the wider world of Hellenism so some must have passed from Samaritanism to the wider world of Judaism. But between the two communities as such there remained through the centuries a bitter and tragic enmity from which both suffered at any rate until the nineteenth century. Today those tiny relics of the sect which have taken refuge in Israel are at last welcomed and protected by a Jewish people.

We must return to the Temple, which was the occasion of the schism. Purged of any elements which might debase its ritual purity in Judean eyes, it established itself as the ceremonial centre of the Jewish people, whether in Israel or in the Diaspora. The high priests came to be the effective rulers of the land and the people. But from the standpoint of the development of Judaism, their influence was almost negligible. For, though the earliest leaders in the synagogue seem to have been priests, the Temple apparently took less and less responsibility for the general instruction of the people. Though its worship owed much to Temple liturgies, the synagogue grew up as an entirely independent institution. The same thing seems to have happened in the administration of justice. While the supreme judges of the country were to be found in the high priests and their families, the local courts in Judea, as well as the administration of justice in the Diaspora, appear to have been in the hands of the leaders of the synagogues.

5. THE TEMPLE AND JERUSALEM

WE have thus far reviewed the situation at the time of the return

[64] Gaster, *Samaritan Oral Law*, p. 258. The rabbis knew that the Samaritans were stricter in their observances. See Ber. 47b. p. 286, 'whenever the Cutheans (Samaritans) have adopted a *mizwah*, they are much more particular with it than the Jews'. This is confirmed by R. Simeon b. Gamaliel Git. 10a, p. 34.

from the standpoint of the development of Holy Scriptures, the establishment of the synagogue, and the restoration with a purified administration of the ritual of the Temple. But we must now face the problem of why the Jewish people in Babylon felt any need for a return at all. Their position was socially and economically satisfactory, their religion was a universalist monotheism which had outgrown tribalism or any belief that Jahweh could only be worshipped in his 'own' land, and the attitude of Cyrus was permissive not compulsory. Why then did they return? It is not enough to say that the code of Deuteronomy or the reforms of Josiah compelled a centralisation on the Temple at Jerusalem. Holy Scripture was still fluid, and it would not have been difficult to find reasons for a *new* central shrine in the homeland of Abraham, and to accept, as Ezekiel had often enough implied, that the sins of their fathers had caused their God to desert Jerusalem and its Temple for ever, or at any rate until the dawn of a new age.

The answer can only be the extraordinary place which was occupied by the actual city of Jerusalem in the mind and heart of the Jewish people, wherever they lived. This place had nothing to do with what might be regarded as normal ancestral piety. The Jewish people made no secret of the fact that they were not autochthonous in the 'Land of Canaan'. They took pride in the call and migration of Abraham. Nor was Jerusalem in any way associated with the patriarchs (the legend that the rock on which the Temple was built was the rock on which Abraham sacrificed Isaac is a later legend) or even with the original re-entry after the Egyptian exile. Bethel and Shiloh were more ancient shrines of Jahweh, even if the former had been prostituted by Jeroboam I to the worship of a golden calf.[65] So far as the rejection of these more ancient shrines is concerned, it might be argued that they lay north of the territory over which the returning Jews could exercise authority; but that would still leave unanswered the question as to why any city in the 'old country' should call to them so insistently to return. The northern exiles could, presumably, have returned also had they wished to. There had, in fact, been some going and coming between them and the remaining population of the kingdom of Israel, and the latter had secured a Jahwistic priest who established a shrine at the ancient pilgrimage centre of Bethel.[66] But we hear no more of this shrine, and after the schism with the Samaritans had become final, it was not at Bethel, but on what appeared to have been a new site, Mount Gerizim, that they had established their temple. We must also recog-

[65] Gen. 28. 19 and 1 Kings 12. 29, for Bethel; and Josh. 18. 1 for Shiloh.
[66] 2 Kings 17. 28.

nise that the veneration for Jerusalem ante-dates the exile, and the city competed with northern shrines for recognition even after the split of David's kingdom into two.[67] In fact, if any of the northern exiles did return, they probably accompanied one of the caravans to Jerusalem and remained there. Thus, from every point of view, the question is focused on to the single issue as to how and why Jerusalem exercised such a powerful attraction over the Jewish people.

The answer to this question will come only from the long perspective of subsequent Jewish history. But, at this stage, it is very important to register the fact that this feeling did exist, for its consequences continue right through Jewish history down to the twentieth century.

It is interesting that the first passage which records a special veneration for Jerusalem comes from the prophet Ahijah, whose own home was in the more ancient shrine of Shiloh[68], and who might, therefore, have been expected to resent the holiness ascribed to the new capital. In a denunciation of the idolatry of Solomon the promise occurs that, while rule over most of the tribes will be taken from him, Judah shall be left to his descendants with Jerusalem: 'the city where I have chosen to put my name'. Passage after passage makes clear that it is Jerusalem which gives the Temple its sanctity, not the Temple, Jerusalem. In the psalms, for example, the city, by the name of either Jerusalem or Zion, is mentioned much more often than the Temple:

> Sing praises to the Lord, who dwells in Zion!
> Tell among the people his deeds!
> Ps. 9. 11

> His holy mountain, beautiful in elevation,
> Is the joy of all the earth.
> Ps. 48. 2

> On the holy mount stands the city he founded;
> The Lord loves the gates of Zion.
> Ps. 87. 1f.

The same thing is true of the prophets. Whether for promise or denunciation, Jerusalem occupies a special place,[69] and the earliest foreshadowings of the messianic age proclaim that:

> Out of Zion shall go forth the law,
> and the word of the Lord from Jerusalem.[70]

[67] 1 Kings 12. 26 f.
[68] 1 Kings 11. 29 ff.
[69] E.g. Micah 3. 9-12; Is. 14. 32; Zeph. 1. 4, 3. 14; Jer. 3, 14. 17.
[70] The passage occurs both in Is. 2. 3 and Micah 4. 2.

In prophecies written after the sack of Jerusalem by Nebuchadnezzar the promise of restoration and of a messianic flowering of the reign of God sometimes go side by side. Jeremiah, for example, combines the promise of the new covenant foretelling a messianic age with the restoration of Jerusalem.[71] Even Ezekiel, whose denunciations exceed in bitterness those of either his predecessors or successors, illustrates both the points which have been made. He illustrates the fact that the city did not owe its holiness just to the Temple by the horrific vision in which the Lord quits the Temple because of the iniquity of the city;[72] and he associates the final restoration of the people with the elaborate reconstruction of the Temple and the city.[73] Joel and Zechariah repeat the pattern of the other prophets. While the former confines the restored Jerusalem to the chosen people,[74] the latter, in a messianic passage, prophesies that 'many peoples and strong nations shall come to seek the Lord of hosts in Jerusalem.'[75]

The most striking testimony to the extraordinary hold which Jerusalem exercised over the spirit of the people is to be found in the greatest of all their prophets, Deutero-Isaiah. Whether the 'servant poems' are attributed to him or not, he is the outstanding preacher of the universal sovereignty of God, and the least tainted by any spirit which could be called 'nationalistic'. Yet for him the proof that God has forgiven his people for the sins which had brought about the exile lay in the restoration of Jerusalem[76] and the return of the exiles to dwell there.

> Comfort, comfort my people,
>   says your God,
> Speak tenderly to Jerusalem,
>   and cry to her
> that her warfare is ended,
>   that her iniquity is pardoned,
> that she has received from the Lord's hand
>   double for all her sins.

The community which dwelt in and around Jerusalem was a small one; its territory was limited, its soil was not rich, and the city stood on no important trade routes. Life must have been without luxury so

[71] Jer. 31. 38-40.
[72] Chs. 9 and 10.
[73] Chs. 40-48.
[74] Joel 3. 17.
[75] Zech. 8. 22.
[76] Is. 40. 1-2. Cf. 51. 1-3 and 52. 1 f.

far as material matters were concerned; but it did not have to suffer the additional hardships of isolation. It was continuously linked with larger and wealthier Jewish communities elsewhere, and by all it was accepted as the mother community to which respect was owed. The collection and circulation of the Scriptures, with their continual emphasis on the link between God and people in Jerusalem, would have increased the veneration in which it was held.

We have little direct information about the nature and extent of the authority of the high priests who, from their position in the Temple, ruled over the city and its territory, but the codes of law contain an elaborate system of taxation, often in kind, for the benefit of the clergy, and some at least of the obligations owed by Jews dwelling in Judea were accepted also by Jews elsewhere. Whether, either in Judea or elsewhere, there was any form of compulsion we do not know. The New Testament would suggest that part was voluntary and part was not.[77]

It was probably the Temple half-shekel which formed the bulk of the payment from the Diaspora, and later evidence tells us that this could amount to considerable sums.[78] But, in addition, a large number of Jews must have made the pilgrimage to Jerusalem at least once in their lives, and their offerings, as well as their payments for lodging and the purchase of sacrificial animals, would have brought a good deal of money into circulation in the country.

It was not only money which flowed in from outside. The relations between mother and daughter communities stimulated the intellectual and spiritual life of both, and explain the very substantial literary output, as well as the religious developments, which took place between the early days of the return and the Maccabean or Herodian periods.

That which set the seal upon the relations between the Jewish communities at home and abroad was the sacrificial system, as it had been developed in the final, or priestly, codes. The books of the Law, as they now stand, have been so much altered and edited that the most primitive and the most sophisticated customs stand side by side. But it is evident that there is to be found in them a considerable development from an earlier and simpler form of sacrifice to a more elaborate one, and that this development was accompanied by a

[77] The Pharisees took credit to themselves for paying the tithe on 'mint and dill and cummin', suggesting that all did not pay it (Matt. 23. 23); on the other hand Jesus paid the Temple half-shekel (Matt. 17. 24-27) as though it were a legal obligation.

[78] Cicero, *Pro Flacco*, Ch. 28.

definite shift of emphasis.[79] The change itself can be traced by comparing the earliest arrangements for sacrifice we possess in the 'Book of the Covenant'[80] with those in the Book of Deuteronomy,[81] the 'Code of Holiness'[82] and the various editions of the priestly code.[83] The consequences of the change are illustrated by the ceremonies which are prescribed in various sections of the later codes for purifying the Temple itself and the altar, 'because of the uncleannesses of the people of Israel, and because of their transgressions [and] all their sins', for the Temple 'abides with them in the midst of their uncleannesses.'[84]

In primitive religion, including that of Israel, a sacrifice was offered by a man to secure some benefit for himself and his family.[85] Gift offerings were in the nature of bribes to secure the fertility of his flocks or his fields, other sacrifices effected communion with the god; and yet others liberated the life of the victim through the shedding of its blood, in order that such life might strengthen either the god or his worshipper. On the whole sacrifices were festal occasions. It was in the post-exilic period that a change occurred. While these earlier sacrifices still survived, the ideas of expiation for sin and the making of atonement were introduced into existing sacrifices,[86] and made the subject of further offerings.

The tragedy and humiliation of the exile had made the post-exilic Jews very conscious of the reality of human sin, and this reality was heightened by the emphasis of the later prophets, especially Ezekiel, on the utter holiness of God. This sense of sin rarely became morbid; the apocalyptic work known as 4 Ezra is almost unique in its extreme pessimism about human sinfulness. On the other hand the concept of what constituted sin was very wide, and embraced many actions or conditions which modern theologians and moralists would dismiss as tabu and ritual, as well as those moral offences on which Jewish and Christian testimony would be in agreement. This has led to a good deal of misunderstanding about the constant insistence

[79] W. O. E. Oesterley, *Sacrifices in Ancient Israel*, Hodder & Stoughton, 1937, pp. 216 ff.

[80] Ex. 20. 22-24. 18. See especially 20. 24.

[81] Deut. 12. 6 f. Here the absence of sin or guilt offerings is striking. The whole note is given in v. 7; 'there you shall eat before the Lord your God, and you shall rejoice, you and your households, in all that you undertake'.

[82] Lev. Chs. 17-26, especially Chs. 17 and 22. 17-33.

[83] See especially earlier versions in Ex. Ch. 29 and Num. 18. 1-7.

[84] Lev. 16. 16, from the ritual of the Day of Atonement. See Oesterley, op cit., pp. 219ff.

[85] *Ibid.*, Ch. 8.

[86] *Ibid.*, p. 218.

in the legal codes on the necessity for material actions, such as purification or sacrifice, as a means to remove the consequences of sin. To identify such actions with a formalism akin to belief in magic is to ignore the basic difference between *magic* in which a spell was held to give power over the controlling spirits, good or bad, of man's destiny, and *Torah* in which such material actions are ordained because it is the will of God that by such means the order of the universe, which had been dis-ordered by the action, should be restored. There is no ritual in the Bible which is held to give man power over God. Nor is it the action itself which produces the result, according to Jewish thought, but the obedience to God's revealed will of which the action is evidence.

Moreover, we have to remember that Judaism is completely un-dualistic. It knows no conflict between soul and body, between matter and spirit, and so does not make a natural distinction between moral and ritual offences. As Dr. Gavin says: 'man is an indissoluble unity of body and soul, of which each part is essential. Man is neither the one nor the other, but both. Sin is of the whole man, not alone either of soul or body'.[87] A few pages later he says that in Judaism 'the whole of religion concerned the whole of man and was deemed to be a whole revelation on the part of God which involved a whole-hearted obedience on the part of the whole of Israel'.[88] All this is reflected in the fact that the Jew found both repentance and sacrifice, both ritual cleansing and spiritual discipline, to be methods by which God desired the unity of his world, compromised by man's sin, to be restored. There is a further point to be observed in the development of the idea of sacrifice. In the pre-exilic period sacrifices were usually personal affairs, whether of the monarch or of the people. During the exile Ezekiel proposed that the daily offerings should be made by the prince, and at his expense.[89] After the return they became a national responsibility and were paid for out of the Temple treasury to which the whole people, in the Diaspora as well as at home, contributed. Moreover Ezekiel had said that the prince should make these offerings 'to make atonement for the house of Israel'. They were to be *national* in their scope and their intention. Belief in the validity of sacrifices on behalf of those who were absent passed insensibly into the idea of sacrifices on behalf of those who were unaware that such atonement with God was being made for them. In other words, sacrifices became vicarious,

[87] F. Gavin, *The Jewish Antecedents of the Christian Sacraments*, S.P.C.K., 1928, p. 11.
[88] *Ibid.*, p. 14.
[89] Ezek. 45. 17.

and the intentions of those who offered them, in this case the priests on behalf of the nation, were what mattered. It was accepted by God as effecting atonement on behalf of the persons needing atonement.

This whole post-exilic development culminated in the observance of an annual Day of Atonement. It is first mentioned in the Code of Holiness,[90] but it is fully described only in the priestly code.[91] It was the crown of the national year-long sacrifices for sin and guilt offerings on behalf of the whole people; and it was also the occasion for each single Israelite to confess his sins to God, and to ask forgiveness of any man whom he had wronged. For it was a cardinal principle of its discipline that God could forgive sins committed against himself, but would not forgive wrongs done by one man to another until the guilty had done all in his power, not merely to ask forgiveness, but to make restitution for the wrong which he had done.

On the Day of Atonement nothing was assumed to be already clean and in a position to serve as the vehicle for acceptable offerings on behalf of something else. First the Temple and the altar themselves had to submit to the rite of cleansing.[92] When they were cleansed, the priests had to be cleansed. Only then were they in a position to start the impressive ceremonial, which culminated in the sending into the wilderness of the scapegoat, on behalf of the whole people, who either attended at the Temple service or spent the day in confession and prayer in their synagogues. By all, the day was observed as a complete fast.

Jewish thought did not remain stationary at that point. As the sacrifices to make atonement for sin came to be offered for the whole nation, and not merely for the benefit of the man who provided the

[90] Lev. 23. 26-32.

[91] Lev. Ch. 16. Its date is laid down as the tenth day of the seventh month (v. 29). Now Ezra began to read the law to the people on the first day of the seventh month (Neh. 7. 73), and it is said that his reading was followed by the celebration of the Feast of Tabernacles, which began on the 15th. But there is no mention of the Day of Atonement intervening. It is, therefore, thought that this fast had not then been instituted. On the other hand it is mentioned that after the Feast the people 'assembled with fasting and in sackcloth . . . and stood and confessed their sins and the iniquities of their fathers . . . and for a fourth of the day they stood and made confession' (Neh. 9. 1-3). May this not have been the beginning of its celebration, its date being subsequently moved back a few days to precede the Feast? But see W. O. E. Oesterley, *op. cit.*, p. 226.

[92] Lev. 16. 17-19 and 33 f. Ezekiel had introduced the idea of a six-monthly cleansing (45. 18-27 following the Septuagint text). This did not find a place in the priestly code, which substituted the cleansing on the Day of Atonement (Lev. 16. 33).

victim, so we shall see later that the idea of atonement by a sacrifice on the altar passed to atonement by a life of particular holiness or a martyr's death. We shall encounter it in the post-Christian period in a good deal of rabbinic discussion on the merits of the sacrifice of Isaac. But the first recorded instance of the thought comes just within our period. The second Book of Maccabees records the martyrdom of the aged priest, Eleazar.[93] But when his death was worked up into the sermon or lecture which we have as the fourth Book of Maccabees, it becomes more than the noble example it had appeared to the earlier writer. As he dies a martyr's death the aged priest exclaims: 'Be merciful unto thy people, and let our punishment be a satisfaction on their behalf. Make my blood their purification, and take my soul to ransom their souls.'[94] The date of this work is thought to lie between 63 B.C., the end of the Maccabean period, and A.D. 38, when Alexandrian Jewry suffered a violent persecution from Caligula.[95]

As has already been emphasised, it is important, in considering this whole growth, to ignore a great deal of the primitive ritual, and even magic formulas, which accompanied its ceremonial aspects. There is too much tendency at a time when anthropologists are perpetually revealing all kinds of strange magical customs among primitive people, to assume that wherever these customs are encountered in more developed societies the same magical ideas must have been held by those who practised them. But this is highly improbable. Ritual and ceremonial are the most conservative elements in religion, and clergy in particular may continue to perform gestures or rites long after their original meaning has been abandoned or transformed into something completely different. The later rabbis were aware that many of the prescriptions in Torah had no visible logic or meaning; but they considered that God had inserted them simply in order that men might obey his will without always asking 'why?'[96] While we cannot say how early it was realised that many customs had no spiritual significance in themselves, we can, for our purposes, concentrate the whole intention of these developments in the Code of Holiness and the priestly codes into the idea that a major purpose for which God had chosen Jerusalem to be his chosen city, and the Temple to be his dwelling place, was that atonement might be continuously made there for the sins which Israel was committing wherever it lived, and for the guilt which successive generations had

[93] 2 Macc. 6. 18-31.

[94] 4 Macc. 6. 28 f.

[95] See R. B. Townshend in R. H. Charles *Apocrypha and Pseudepigrapha of the Old Testament*, Oxford, 1913, II, p. 654.

[96] *Rabbinic Anthology*, pp. 148 f.

incurred by their faithlessness and evil doing. It was a symbol of the unity of all Israel before God, reinforced by the observance in every Jewish community of the Day of Atonement as an annual and corporate expression of repentance. This general implication of the sacrifices at Jerusalem is brought out by the description of the rededication of the Temple by Ezra, that they offered 'as a sin offering for all Israel twelve he-goats, according to the number of the tribes of Israel'.[97]

Jerusalem was thus the living symbol of Jewish unity, and of Jewish responsibility before God. Every Jew, wherever he lived, could feel that offering was made on his behalf at this central shrine of his people, and that he, by his annual observance of the Day of Atonement, became a beneficiary of its obedience to the will of God revealed in Torah.

6. 'MY PEOPLE ISRAEL'

THE significance attached to the physical city of Jerusalem, and its role as centre for a widely dispersed religious group, emphasises the parallel significance of the fact that this 'widely dispersed religious group' was not simply a selection of individuals who worshipped Jahweh, but had a physical existence as a nation which, in turn, regarded this physical existence as an actual and essential factor in the fulfilment of a divine purpose.

Those who had stayed in or returned from Babylon, together with those who had remained faithful in the home country, believed themselves to be a chosen people, and this implied a responsibility towards those of their own people who had fallen away to the idolatry of their neighbours, as well as the careful preservation of a distinction from those neighbours. When Jeremiah speaks of the new covenant by which 'no longer shall each man teach his neighbour and each his brother, saying 'know the Lord', for they shall all know me, from the least of them to the greatest'[98] he speaks of it as a covenant which God will make 'with the house of Israel'. Until that time should come it was a principal task of the synagogue to see that in every place, and in each succeeding generation, *all* Jews were taught obedience to the commands of their God.

Before and during the exile, prophets had thundered against the people, denouncing them for their disloyalty and threatening them with divine chastisement. They had spoken of the faithful among the

[97] Ezra 6. 17.
[98] Jer. 31. 34.

people as being but a handful, a pitiful 'remnant', or even proclaimed with the psalmist:[99]

> They have all gone astray, they are all alike corrupt;
> there is none that does good,
> no, not one.

But they did not waver in their belief that God would not finally abandon them, and that the day would dawn when Israel as a people would repent, would return to their Redeemer, and would be accepted by him and restored to favour. Nowhere is this more movingly expressed than when, in the midst of the overthrow of the kingdom and the pusillanimous desertion of the people, Jeremiah could say:[1]

> Thus says the Lord . . .
> I have loved you with an everlasting love;
> therefore I have continued my faithfulness to you.
> Again I will build you, and you shall be built,
> O virgin Israel!

From the standpoint of the post-exilic community a passage of particular interest is the promise of restoration in Ezekiel, a restoration which the prophet sees ultimately as a necessity implicit in God's own nature—in the bitterness with which he expresses it one might almost say 'in his vanity'! It begins, in a mood of unusual tenderness for this prophet, with God saying:

> I myself will be the shepherd of my sheep, and I will make them lie down. . . . I will seek the lost, and I will bring back the strayed, and I will bind up the crippled, and I will strengthen the weak, and the fat and the strong I will watch over; I will feed them in justice.[2]

But at the end, like a cold douche, comes the reason:

> It is not for your sake, O house of Israel, that I am about to act, but for the sake of my holy name, which you have profaned among the nations to which you came. And I will vindicate the holiness of my great name . . . and the nations will know that I am the Lord . . . when through you I vindicate my holiness before their eyes.[3]

This passage contains an early statement of an idea which we shall frequently meet later, that Israel's obedience is the evidence which

[99] Ps. 14. 3.
[1] Jer. 31. 3 f.
[2] Ezek. 34. 15 f.
[3] *Ibid.*, 36. 22 f.

will attract the nations to Israel's God. This is a point which must always be borne in mind when rabbi or sage appears to be limiting his interest too narrowly to the chosen people to the exclusion of wider interests.

We have already seen the important place which was taken in the religious life of the restored community by the synagogue and its teaching. Because the centre of that teaching was obedience to the will of God in daily living, the books of the Law came to possess a greater importance in the eyes of the leaders of the synagogue than the moral exhortations of the prophets, and from this standpoint the book of Deuteronomy has an especial importance. Unlike the other books in the Pentateuch, it is in the main from a single hand, and reflects a single religious standpoint—although, as we should expect, scholars are divided as to its actual date and provenance. One even carries it back to the time of Samuel,[4] but most date it just before or during the exile. Again this does not matter to us, since it was unquestionably in existence at the period under discussion.

Although in the matter of the Temple the prescriptions of the priestly codes were followed rather than the simpler ordinances of the Deuteronomist, yet so far as the synagogue was concerned Deuteronomy was a mine of material of all kinds. Its importance is illustrated by the fact that it is the source of the great text in which, since before the time of Jesus, Jews have daily affirmed their religious loyalty. 'Hear, O Israel: the Lord our God is one Lord, and you shall love the Lord your God with all your heart, and with all your soul, and with all your might.'[5]

The value of Deuteronomy lies in the fact that the author has sandwiched his actual code between two great series of exhortations which he ascribes to Moses at the moment when the children of Israel were about to enter the Promised Land. These discourses contain a historical survey of the Exodus and the forty years in the wilderness, and also the clearest statements of the nature of the obligations undertaken by the people at Sinai, and the consequences which would follow on obedience or disobedience. He might almost be said to have taken as his text the 'word of the Lord' revealed to Amos: [6]

[4] On the whole issue see the essay by C. R. North in H. H. Rowley, *The Old Testament and Modern Study*, Oxford, 1951, pp. 48 ff.

[5] Deut. 6. 4. This verse is known from its first word as 'The Shema'. It is followed by the verses which have produced the custom of tying phylacteries on arms and forehead at prayer, and of fastening the mezuzah to the posts of the door.

[6] Amos 3. 2.

You only have I known of all the families of the earth;
Therefore I will punish you for all your iniquities.

According to the Deuteronomist the whole purpose of the divine call was that there might be a whole people living according to the divine law. This is repeated again and again, and is constantly reinforced by the insistence that *all* the commandments which have been given them are to be taught to *all* the people, and to succeeding generations. Israel has declared that it accepts Jahweh as its God; Jahweh has declared that he accepts Israel as his people.[7] No other nation has been thus chosen, therefore no other nation owes him similar obedience.[8] On the other hand, the demands of Jahweh are not for something beyond their reach. In two famous passages the author expresses, in terms which closely parallel the language of prophet and psalmist, the conviction that obedience is possible to ordinary men. 'What', he asks, 'does the Lord your God require of you, but to fear the Lord your God, to walk in all his ways, to love him, to serve the Lord your God with all your heart and with all your soul, and to keep the commandments and statutes of the Lord, which I command you this day for your good?'[9] In a second passage he speaks again of these 'commandments and statutes':[10]

This commandment which I command you this day is not too hard for you, neither is it far off. It is not in heaven, that you should say, 'Who will go up for us to heaven, and bring it to us, that we may hear it and do it?' Neither is it beyond the sea, that you should say, 'Who will go over the sea for us, and bring it to us, that we may hear it and do it?' But the word is very near you; it is in your mouth and in your heart, so that you can do it.'

The commandments and statutes which are contained in the Deuteronomic code between chapters twelve and twenty-eight cover the whole life of a people. The space given to ritual and religious duties is not exaggerated, and a great deal of it deals with the life of a humane society, practising charity and mutual responsibility, merciful and just in its relations with its members and its neighbours. There are neither exaggerated penalties nor the elaborate ritual and semi-magical provisions which are to be found elsewhere in the codes. It may well be called the kind of society which the prophets in their demands for social justice would have envisaged, so that we may say, with Professor Rowley, that 'what the creators of Judaism

[7] Deut. 26. 16-19.
[8] *Ibid.*, 4. 32-40, 7. 6.
[9] *Ibid.*, 10. 12-16.
[10] *Ibid.*, 30. 11-14.

aimed to do was to make the strict observance of the Law the organ for the spirit that prophets had called for, and the protection of prophetic religion from all the contamination of the influences that had so often prevailed in early days'.[11]

The people are promised that, if they obey God's commandments, they will live in prosperity and peace under divine protection; if they disobey, appalling punishment will be visited upon them until they repent. When they repent, they will be restored. It is a self-contained society which the author envisages; his concern is almost exclusively with his own people, and he has little to say of relations with others. But he has his own contribution to those who see in the choice of Israel a responsibility to the world as a whole, and this contribution, carrying one stage further that adumbrated by Ezekiel, is of considerable importance for the future of Judaism.

It has already been pointed out that the messianic vision is not divorced from the conception of the peculiar religious significance of Jerusalem and of the people of Israel. It is out of Zion that the law is to go forth, and out of Jerusalem the word of the Lord. Similarly in Zechariah's vision of the future,[12] when 'the inhabitants of one city shall go to another, saying, "Let us go at once to entreat the favour of the Lord, and to seek the Lord of hosts", it is to Jerusalem that they go; and when 'ten men from the nations of every tongue shall take hold of the robe of a Jew, saying "Let us go with you, for we have heard that God is with you", it is because they assume that the Jew is going up to Jerusalem. The Deuteronomist tries to impress on the people what it is which will bring such a situation about. These things will happen only when Israel lives according to the commandments which God has given:[13]

> Behold, I have taught you statutes and ordinances, as the Lord my God commanded me, that you should do them in the land which you are entering to take possession of it. Keep them and do them; for that will be your wisdom and your understanding in the sight of the peoples, who, when they hear all these statutes, will say, 'Surely this great nation is a wise and understanding people.' For what great nation is there that has a god so near to it as the Lord our God is to us, whenever we call upon him? And what great nation is there that has statutes and ordinances so righteous as all this law which I set before you this day?

[11] H. H. Rowley, *The Rediscovery of the Old Testament*, Library of Contemporary Theology, 1946, p. 122.
[12] Zech. 8. 20-23.
[13] Deut. 4. 5-8.

Though the words are attributed to Moses and set in the framework of the Exodus, it is to the restored community that this far-reaching challenge became an effective call to action; and, so far as we know, it was the first time in history that such a challenge was issued and accepted. The idea of ritual obedience goes back to the most primitive societies. Exact conformity with ritual necessity had, from the earliest days of civilisation, brought into existence a class of priests, witch-doctors, and similar people, who knew the right action to take in any circumstances, and who could take it on behalf of their community. But this was something much more than that. Right action was now extended to every aspect of a man's life, and it had to be undertaken by himself, and not by another on his behalf. It is strange that so many Christian scholars have judged this period as one of decline and of falling away from the high ideals of the prophets, instead of seeing in it the opening pages of one of the most magnificent adventures of the human spirit, the attempt to weave, as Professor Rowley has said, the teachings of the prophets into the warp and woof of the life of every member of the nation.

It was in carrying out this vast design that the annals and written records of the people came to be transformed into Holy Scriptures, so that they might serve as a medium for instruction. Dr. Gaster has suggested[14] that the idea of filling them out with interpretation must have already developed in some fields at least at an early stage, since such matters as the observance of Sabbath would soon demand closer definition. But, in the main, it was in this period that the noble concept was accepted that the Law—Torah—was not something given once for all, but a living medium through which God continually spoke to his people. We may feel it to be a pity that, in their collections of previous codes and customs, so much of ancient magic and primitive ritual has survived; and this survival undoubtedly led to some of that 'legalism' which marks the development of Pharisaic and Rabbinic Judaism. But Christian writers have allowed it to cover much more than its share of the total canvas; and, in addition, have not considered the other side. Had those who made the canon of Scripture decided to exclude the edited mosaics of ancient records, and to include only the carefully rewritten and consistent picture of the period of the exodus as provided by the Deuteronomist, they would have presumably done the same with the historical books. Joshua and Judges did not, so far as we know, receive a similar refashioning, and the book of Jubilees was not written in time to be considered for the canon as a substitute for

[14] *Samaritan Oral Law,* esp. Chs. 2 & 3.

Genesis and Exodus. But in place of the books of Samuel and Kings we should have nothing but the colourless and very bowdlerised version of the Chronicler. We have only to read the two accounts of the reign and character of David to see what we should have lost! It is far better that we should have a picture of God dealing with real men and women and with real historical situations, even if the absence of a doctrine of 'progressive revelation' forced them sometimes to equate the primitive and magical with the spiritual and moral as equally expressing the will of God. Later rabbis were, as we have seen, not unaware of the problem and made provision for it, explaining many curious customs as ordained by God in order that men might sometimes obey his will without having to know the reason why.[15]

[15] *Rabbinic Anthology*, pp. 148 f.

Chapter Two

THE CENTURIES OF COMMON GROWTH

1. THE SITUATION OF JEWRY UP TO THE MACCABEAN REVOLT

IN speaking of this period as that of *the birth* of Judaism, there is naturally no intention of divorcing these centuries from their predecessors, or of denying the continuity between 'Judaism' and 'the religion of Israel'. But, as the previous chapter will have shown, the restoration of the Jewish community after the disorder of the Babylonian exile invested the national religion with profoundly significant and original new factors which determined the nature of its subsequent growth. It is likewise in this period that conditions of thought and life were created which led to the emergence of Christianity as a world religion. Whatever subsequent influence it may have received from its Gentile environment, its roots were set in the Jewish experience of this period, whether in Judea or in the Diaspora.

Politically the centuries preceding the Maccabean period are among the most tranquil in the whole history of the people. There is no record of any event of importance, except possibly a deportation by Artaxerxes Ochus after some disturbances in 353, which may have planted Jewish colonies on the Caspian Sea.[1] But it was evidently not a period of stagnation, for the population must have increased considerably, both in numbers and prosperity, to have been able to provide the man-power which sustained the Maccabean rising and the subsequent kingdom. It is very possible that many Jewish families returned from Babylon at this time. Nevertheless the most interesting development of the period was not the growth of Judea, but the spread of the Diaspora.

In the second century B.C., the work known as the 'Sibylline Oracles' contains the statement that every country and every sea is filled with Jews,[2] and this is paralleled by many other statements testifying to their unusual distribution. What is of special significance is not the identity of the precise cities in which we can trace Jewish communities but the general areas of their distribution. We

[1] A. Lods, *Les Prophètes d'Israel et les Débuts du Judaisme*, Paris, 1935, p. 224.

[2] R. H. Charles, *op. cit.*, II, p. 383 (verse 73).

know, of course, that there were extensive settlements in Mesopotamia, for they had been established there by both Assyrian and Babylonian kings. From the time of Alexander there was an important community at Alexandria. These two of themselves would link the Jewish world to the two other great cultures of Persia and of Greece. But we can also assume that before the Maccabean period there were a number of Jewish communities in the cities of Asia Minor, that Jews had crossed into western Europe, probably by sea, and were to be found in many of the Mediterranean cities of both Europe and Africa. Most of these settlements were due to the fact that Jews were a fertile people, with a religion which ensured high standards of health and family life, and that the homeland was narrow. We have no reason to assume that they were due to any specialised role which Jews played in the economy of the time. Most probably they were ordinary 'proletarians' and artisans. But there is one exception. In Egypt at Elephantine, and in remote centres along the north of Asia Minor and the region of the Caucasus, Jews were established as 'colonies', that is, resident military settlements enjoying wide privileges in return for guarding the frontiers. In such centres Jews were not a minority, but the main or sole population, and it is in these centres that we can most naturally see the beginnings of the extension of Judaism to the environing population, since its acceptance would be the condition of obtaining the status of colonist. For the evidence that such proselytizing activity took place we do not have to go to documents, but to Jewish physical types, and to the prevalence among them of characteristics which are not semitic, but originate in all the regions surrounding the Mediterranean and Black Seas, whether in western Asia, northern Africa or Europe.[3]

In the immense majority of cases we are unable to establish not merely the date of foundation of a Jewish settlement, but, what would be more interesting, the nature of its Judaism. It is quite impossible to imagine that close links with every community were maintained from Jerusalem, or even from the great central communities of Babylon and Alexandria.[4] In those centres themselves we can be fairly certain how the religion developed, but the only outlying community of which we happen to have evidence shows the

[3] See M. Fishberg, *The Jews, A Study of Race and Environment*, Walter Scott, 1911, and A. H. Godbey, *The Lost Tribes A Myth*, especially the maps on pp. 256 and 316.

[4] It is curious that the vast mass of rabbinic literature contains almost no references to Jewish settlement outside Palestine and Mesopotamia and environing areas. See, for example, A. Neubauer, *La Géographie du Talmud*, Paris, 1868.

most curiously syncretistic combinations. That community was the military colony of Elephantine or Yeb, in which a whole collection of papyri of the fifth century B.C. were discovered some fifty years ago.[5] We do, however, have a general idea of the government of these communities, largely because the Romans were innately conservative, and the organisation which they accepted as their empire spread over almost the entire area, is likely to be that which was already in existence.[6] They were oligarchies, with a constitution whose elaboration depended on the size of the community, but the important thing is that each community was accepted as part of the whole Jewish nation, or people. They did not have separate privileges, but general privileges because they were Jews.[7] In some measure their religious life was regulated from Jerusalem, but we cannot tell with what authority, or in what detail. It is obviously impossible that they could have followed the detailed development of the oral law, but they must have possessed some tradition as to the teaching of the Scriptures and some kind of rules for the development of 'case law' from the general prescriptions of Torah.

We are, in fact, equally little informed about the details of the Jewish government in Jerusalem itself during this time. It also was oligarchical, with the high priesthood confined to a small number of families, and we can assume that from these families would be chosen the equivalent of the 'privy council' of a medieval prince, to assist and supervise public affairs. How the government at Jerusalem was related to the distant communities we do not know. Later we have a somewhat elaborate system of relationships, but for the beginning we can only assume such recognition as is involved in the payment of the Temple half-shekel, and the pilgrimages to Jerusalem. In any case the association must have been voluntary, since there existed no force which could have compelled continued association with Jerusalem in a community on the Black Sea or the mountains of north Africa.

2. THE CULTURAL ENVIRONMENT

DURING the period under consideration, two rich and ancient

[5] R. H. Pfeiffer, *History of New Testament Times*, New York, 1949, p. 170. See also article in *Encyclopaedia Judaica* for bibliography. A selection has been published by the S.P.C.K.: *Jewish Documents of the Time of Ezra*, edited by A. Cowley, 1919.

[6] J. Juster, *Les Juifs dans l'Empire Romain*, Paris, 1914, I, pp. 438 ff.

[7] *Ibid.*, p. 422.

worlds of culture and civilisation were moving towards each other and intermingling. Each was compounded of many separate elements. One was that which flowed outwards from the rich valley of the Euphrates and had witnessed over several millenia a succession of creative civilisations, culminating in that which had come into it from the east, the Persian. The other was younger but perhaps even more dynamic, the Greek. They met before Alexander's conquests, but the empires established by his successors set the seal on the meeting. Alexander employed physical settlement to establish the unity he desired, and in the wake of his own great city of Alexandria with its mixed population of Greeks, Egyptians and Jews came the Greek cities which were established all through the Aramaic and Syriac speaking lands of western Asia. They were to be a feature of Palestinian life until a century after the coming of Islam. Christian scholars sometimes speak as though Jesus and his disciples, as Galileans, belonged to a backward and remote area. But from Nazareth itself a long day's walk would have been all that was necessary to reach the Greek cities of Ptolemais (Acre) to the west, Sebaste (Samaria) to the south, or Tiberias to the east. Cities such as these, together with others like Bethsaida Julias or Caesarea, betray their origin by their very names. But in addition, along the important eastern caravan route across the Jordan, lay the whole Greek region of the Decapolis, and purely Arab cities like Palmyra or Petra show by their architecture itself the penetration of Greek culture.

Each of the worlds which thus met had long been de-nationalised. They had become cosmopolitan. The change is illustrated by Robert Pfeiffer by two quotations.[8] Aristotle had advised Alexander to practise 'hegemony' with the Greeks but 'despotism' with the barbarians. A century later Eratosthenes taught that one should judge and distinguish men according to virtue and wickedness alone, without reference to their race. Each world had begun to think of humanity as one, and so each was fully open to influences from the other. If the Nile and the Euphrates flowed into the Tiber, the springs of Helicon also watered the plains of Mesopotamia and the valley of Egypt. This cultural mingling reflected a similar phenomenon in the political world, and was, indeed, greatly aided by it. The national state and the city state had alike passed from the foreground of the political map, to give way to the empire, whose size rested merely on the strength of its ruler, and whose frontiers took no note of distinctions between peoples.

In older days an adult man was, in some measure, part of the

[8] *Op. cit.*, p. 99.

government of his society; and if this was most conspicuous in the Greek city state, it was equally true at the other end of the scale in the tribe of the bedouin. The empires, for the first time in history, created the individual properly concerned only with his own affairs, the private citizen who was neither serf nor politician. It was paradoxically the natural consequence of the growing feeling that the world was one, that each man in it became a separate unit in himself.

It was a period of widespread literacy, and men had the leisure to read. To meet their needs there arose a vast literature, speculative, didactic, and entertaining, which we encounter sometimes in Greek, sometimes in Aramaic, sometimes in other eastern languages, all reflecting its common attraction and its widespread distribution. One of the oldest moral tales surviving is *The Story of Ahikar*.[9] Our earliest version of it is in Aramaic of the 5th century B.C., and comes from Elephantine. We also have texts of it in Arabic, Armenian and medieval French, and references to it in the Greek philosopher Democritus, in Old and New Testament writers, and in the Quran. It is probably in part an original inspiration of the story of Tobit in the Apocrypha, and may have influenced, or indeed been influenced by, the presentation of Biblical proverbial literature.

Two aspects of this literature, and of the intellectual activity which lay behind it, are of particular interest to us, that which deals with the nature of God and his universe, and that which reflects on the nature and destiny of man. In each field we find a mingling of Greek and oriental factors which was made the easier by a widespread feeling that the gods whom the different nations worshipped differed from each other primarily in name. The one supreme god might be known as Zeus, Jupiter, Baal, Marduk, but it was the same divine power which was worshipped under all these names, and from the different systems in which he was acknowledged men could pass to the matter which supremely interested them, the nature of his communication with his creation.

Most of the pre-exilic writings of the Old Testament had not hesitated to use the most anthropomorphic language in their descriptions of Jahweh and they felt no need for any intermediary to distinguish his holiness and perfection from the world of concrete matter which he had, by his own action, brought into being. But Deutero-Isaiah felt it necessary to remind his hearers that:

> My thoughts are not your thoughts,
> neither are your ways my ways, says the Lord,[10]

[9] Charles, *op. cit.*, II, pp. 715 ff.
[10] Is. 55. 8.

and in almost every chapter Ezekiel insists that there can be no direct contact between the absolute holiness of God and the utter sinfulness of man. The earliest targumim as well as the Septuagint constantly soften down the anthropomorphisms of the Hebrew Bible, and so it is not surprising that the speculations of Persia and Greece which related creator to creation through intermediaries should have found an echo among Jewish thinkers. From the eastern source came the angels and demons of later Biblical literature, reaching their culmination in Christian gnosticism, and Jewish Cabbalah. From the western source came the Wisdom literature of Bible and Apocrypha, and its fuller expression in Alexandrian Judaism, which in time provided the background to the Christian adaptation of the Philonic Logos to explain the Incarnation of the second person of the Trinity.

The second great sphere of interest lay in the nature and destiny of man. Both Greek and Persian thinkers had come to believe in some form of immortality, whether in terms of a resurrection of the body or in terms of the survival of the soul, and Jews encountered these beliefs in both forms. The problem of survival raised that of the conditions of survival, and here the philosophers encountered the propagandists of the mystery cults which had long flourished in both east and west, cults which ensured to their devotees the password to the future life. Ritual, morality and theology became inextricably intertwined.

These intermingling interests found expression in appropriate literary forms, some of which we encounter for the first time in this period. For the 'intellectual' there was the philosophic speculation in prose or poetry, of which the most famous example is the great poem of Lucretius, *De Natura Rerum*. For the academies there were the lecture notes, such as we have from Aristotle. For more popular consumption there was the *diatribe*, a word which is now used usually to express political abuse, but was then a technical term graphically described by Pfeiffer in the following words: 'like modern evangelistic appeals to conversion, these street-corner addresses were intended to kindle the emotions of uneducated masses: they consisted of anecdotes, observations of life, puns, easily remembered maxims, contrasts, sarcastic or impassioned attacks on the sinners, calls to repentance.'[11]

An immensely popular form was what might be called the 'embroidered history' or the purely imaginative moral tale given a historical setting. The official histories of an earlier period varied from the splendid narratives which we encounter, for example, in

[11] *Op. cit.*, p. 143.

the Annals of David, to the bombastic inscriptions of Mesopotamian sovereigns, but they were alike intended to be taken seriously as history. By contrast the political setting of the story of Ahikar, who is described as secretary to Sennacherib, is of no significance to the tale. Equally popular was the collection of apothegms or 'proverbs', and it is interesting evidence of their ubiquity that in the Book of Proverbs are included two collections of sayings which the Biblical editor himself ascribes to non-Israelite maxim-makers, 'Agur, son of Jakeh of Massa, and Lemuel, king of Massa (which his mother taught him)'.[12] Another collection, which originated with an Egyptian sage, Amen-em-Ope, is also included, though in this case the borrowing is unacknowledged.[13]

The literary evidence, then, confirms what the fact of Jewish dispersion would lead us to expect. Jews were not isolated from the main currents of thought and expression of their times, and freely developed the interests, and employed the forms, which lay to their hand in their environment. Nevertheless, as we shall see in the next section, they gave these forms and interests qualities and characteristics which they drew mainly from their own inheritance. This fact is of extreme importance for the understanding, both of the Gentile interest in Judaism as we find it in the Diaspora synagogues, and of the spread of Christianity into the Hellenistic world. The content might often be new, but the form in which it was given was familiar, and this familiarity won acceptance for the content.

3. THE SURVIVING JEWISH LITERATURE

BOTH in the Holy Land and abroad the Jewish people lived in intimate contact with the dynamic turmoil created by this meeting of two civilisations. It left a permanent impression on various aspects of their thought, and it is embodied in the surviving literature of the period. While that which dealt with the ultimate destiny of humanity, and goes by the title of 'apocalyptic' or more properly 'eschatology', is best postponed to a later section,[14] for it is primarily a Jewish product and owes little to its environment, almost all the forms described in the previous section have their counterpart in the work of Jewish authors.

Even the diatribe, the popular lecture or 'evangelical' address, is represented by two very diverse works. In a very different style

[12] Prov. chs. 30 and 31.
[13] A. Lods, *op. cit.*, p. 83.
[14] See below pp. 91ff.

from the forthright utterances of his predecessors, the prophet Malachi argues with his opponents: ' "I have loved you", says the Lord. But you say "How hast thou loved us?" "Is not Esau Jacob's brother?" says the Lord. "Yet I have loved Jacob but I have hated Esau" ' and so on.[15] In another vein, the author of the 'Fourth book of Maccabees', writing at some undetermined period possibly as late as when divine honours began to be paid to Roman emperors, delivers a powerful sermon in defence of 'divine reason'. This might be defined as the conscious understanding of the nature of the obedience which we owe to God and the reason for it. His subject matter he takes from the story of the loyalty of the aged priest Eleazar and the mother and seven sons, all of whom preferred martyrdom to obedience to the demands of Antiochus Epiphanes.[16] Although in its description of inspired reason[17] it owes a great deal to Greek, and especially Stoic, thought, yet it is a wholly Jewish statement that religion is meant to be *understood* by man, akin to the great utterances of the Deuteronomist already quoted and standing in interesting distinction from the later Christian emphasis on 'grace' or 'faith'. One can fairly say that a Christian preacher on the same theme, and using the same eloquence and spiritual insight, would have inevitably ascribed the resistance of the martyrs to their 'faith'. In fact there is almost certainly a reference to their martyrdom in the great catalogue of the heroes of faith[18] in the eleventh chapter of the Epistle to the Hebrews.

That which occupies the smallest space in the Jewish literature is, not unnaturally, speculation about the nature of the Creator and the act of creation, for to the Jews these were subjects on which they already possessed a divine revelation. Almost the only example of the influence of the general environment lies in the attempt to avoid the candid anthropomorphisms of the Bible itself and of earlier Jewish thought. The targumim, as already said, used various periphrases to avoid speaking of God's performance of physical actions, and the Septuagint did the same. But the most interesting example of this tendency is the evolution of 'Wisdom' as God's agent in creation.[19] While there is no doubt that Jewish thinkers were much influenced by the Stoic conception of a divine emanation filling the

[15] Mal. 1. 2 f.

[16] Recounted in 2 Macc. 6. 18-7. 42.

[17] Charles, *op. cit.*, II, pp. 666 ff. Chs. 1-3.

[18] See especially vv. 35 f.

[19] One of the best discussions of the nature of the Hebrew 'Wisdom' is still that of James Drummond in his *Philo Judaeus: or the Jewish-Alexandrian Philosophy in its development and completion*, Williams and Norgate, 1888, I, pp. 213 ff.

universe, they were not intending by their introduction of Wisdom (Hokmah) to add something new to the Godhead, or to introduce something new in their belief about God's relationship with his creation. It was a literary device, a necessity of interpretation, not a new theology which was involved. And yet it enriched Jewish thought about the intimacy of the relationship between Creator and created, and it is not surprising that later rabbis took over much of what was said about Wisdom and used it directly to express the relationship of Jahweh with the Torah.[20] Though the connection may be accidental, the elaboration of the idea of Wisdom also coincided with, and was used as the vehicle for, a great increase in the Jewish delight in the wonder, beauty and mystery of creation, in the lives of animals and birds, and in the majesty of natural phenomena. It is typical of the approach which is common in the Wisdom literature that in the book of Job, God challenges Job to dispute his wisdom and justice by describing the wonderful working of his creation.

Partly because the books of Proverbs, Ecclesiasticus and the Wisdom of Solomon are all poetic, we must not look for a clear, logical and philosophically defined exposition of the nature of Wisdom in their pages. The best description of Wisdom is that it is an 'inseparable emanation of the Divine essence', and that 'all her activity is in reality the activity of God'.[21] When we come to Philo and the concept of the Logos we move from the poetic to the philosophic field, but in the Wisdom literature it is unwise to seek too close a definition of the implications of a term which permitted a wide variety of graceful and spiritual variations on the theme of God the Creator and Sustainer of his universe.

It was not in philosophic speculation, but in the field of moral living that the Jewish genius was most at home, and it is not unnatural that Jews showed a particular aptitude for the moral tale, whether in the form of 'embroidered history' or in direct fiction. Almost every figure of the early part of their records became the subject of moralisation—Adam and Eve, Enoch, Noah, Moses, and the eponymous ancestors of the twelve tribes. In the Book of Jubilees there is a complete rewriting of Genesis and the early part of Exodus akin to the rewriting of the period of the kingdoms in the Book of Chronicles. As with the latter work, the motive is to make the record of creation and the patriarchs correspond with the conception of Torah and of

[20] Compare Prov. 8. 22, 'The Lord created me at the beginning of his work, the first of his acts of old', with 'When God resolved upon the creation of the world, He took counsel with the Torah.' L. Ginsberg, *Legends of the Jews*, J.P.S. America, 1947, I, p. 3.

[21] Drummond, *op. cit.*, I. p. 221.

morality current at the time at which the author lived. The author of Jubilees actually makes two of the basic observances of Judaism, circumcision and the Sabbath, date back to the lives of the angels before the creation of man.[22] But most of the patriarchal figures are shown as concerned with the ultimate destiny of their descendants, and treat of eschatology. Of more interest are those moral tales in which history provides merely a convenient framework, whether it be actual or legendary in itself. In the books of Ruth and Jonah, writers who were concerned lest preoccupation with loyalty to the covenant relationship with Jahweh should develop into a narrow nationalism, reminded their readers of their links with the outside world and their responsibilities to it. In Ruth is told the story of the Moabite ancestress of the beloved national figure, David; and in Jonah we have a brilliant and moving satire on those who desired to keep the goodness of God entirely to his own people—a satire made more telling by the ascription of the painful experience of the hero to an extremely nationalistic prophet of the time of Jeroboam II.[23]

The same literary form was also used to strengthen the loyalty to Torah of those Jews who were living in the Diaspora; but whether the authors were Palestinian or not we cannot always tell. In any case we have a series of vivid tales, the moral of all of which is that it is by the will of God that Jews who are living among the nations have laws which are 'different from those of every other people',[24] and that if they remain loyal to these laws, God will protect them. This is the moral of the book of Esther and of the first six chapters of the book of Daniel, both of which found their place in the canon of Holy Scripture. It is likewise the moral of two books included in the Apocrypha, the fierce story of Judith and Holofernes, and the tender romance of Tobit, charmingly described as 'The Tale of a Grateful Ghost'.

The last of these tales, that of Tobit, has two further points of interest. It is full of Mesopotamian ideas, both of magic and of the role of angels and demons in human affairs; and it is the only story which deals entirely with private individuals and their personal affairs. In the rest the destiny of the whole nation, or at least the local Jewish community, was involved. But the family of Tobit was concerned only with itself. It is thus a link with that growing interest in man as a private person which has already been described as an important feature of the age.

[22] Jubilees 2. 18, 19, 21: and 15. 26-28.
[23] 2 Kings 14. 25.
[24] Esther 3. 8; Dan. 6. 5.

Man as person had not been wholly excluded from the interests of previous Jewish authors. Many of the psalms, pre- as well as post-exilic, are personal, and the literature of apothegms or proverbs was wholly directed to the conduct of individuals. But it proved less easy to fit the responsibility and destiny of individuals into the general framework of the moral order of creation. The second commandment in the Decalogue had spoken of God 'visiting the iniquity of the fathers upon the children to the third and the fourth generation of those who hate me',[25] and might not at that time have shocked the individual conscience, for the link between the individual and the community of which he was a member was much stronger then than now. But already in the thought of Jeremiah it seemed right that in the messianic age this bearing of the burdens of another should no longer be imposed on the individual. 'In those days they shall no longer say:

> The fathers have eaten sour grapes,
> and the children's teeth are set on edge.

But everyone shall die for his own sin; each man who eats sour grapes, his teeth shall be set on edge.'[26] Ezekiel attempted to carry the same doctrine over into the time of the present dispensation. Referring directly to the familiar proverb about sour grapes, he proclaimed that God forbad them to quote it: 'Behold all souls are mine; the soul of the father as well as the soul of the son is mine; the soul that sins shall die'.[27] The whole chapter is cast somewhat in the form of a 'diatribe', in which God argues with Israel, asking them 'Have I any pleasure in the death of the wicked, and not rather that he should turn from his way and live?'[28] God argues that if the son of a wicked man does righteously his soul shall be saved, if his son in turn sins he shall die. Likewise if a sinner repents he shall save his soul, and, contrariwise, if a virtuous man lapses, he shall be punished. This advances the matter somewhat, but it only goes a part of the way for there is no doctrine of immortality or resurrection in Ezekiel. Hence it is mainly interesting not for what it says

[25] Ex. 20. 5. This amplification of the prohibition of graven images is thought to belong to the Deuteronomic period. In *Record and Revelation*, p. 304, H. Wheeler Robinson speaks of this Jewish feeling as the strong sense of corporate personality amongst them, combining ancestors and descendents with the present generation in the unity of the bundle of life! See also p. 332. See also above, Ch. 1, section 2. p. 9.

[26] Jer. 31. 29 f.

[27] Ezek. 18. 4.

[28] *Ibid.*, v. 23.

but for the evidence it offers that the problem of the individual was already beginning to trouble the religious conscience of his generation.

For any systematic examination of the 'nature and destiny of man' we have to turn to post-exilic writers. Of these by far the greatest is the author of the book of Job. It is probably true that the more primitive a society, the more closely do good conduct and prosperity coincide. Apart from accident or disease, the man whose conduct most approximated to what his fellows esteemed to be good was likely to prosper, so that it was natural that it was only slowly that men began to face the question of unmerited suffering and, on the other hand, the comfortable and honoured death of the wealthy unrighteous. The earlier proverbs assert with the utmost blandness that the wicked perish miserably, but experience made it increasingly evident that they frequently did the opposite.

Qoheleth or Ecclesiastes found a solution to the problem in the scepticism and agnosticism of many Greek thinkers. God did not care (all the pious references to God in the book are interpolations), all was vanity, and his conclusion was the typical Greek motto '*mēden agan*'—do nothing in excess. In fact the only thing Jewish about him was that he was no abstract thinker, but was only interested in the concrete actualities of existence. A different solution was offered by the author of the great dramatic poem, Job. Opinions may differ as to whether he deliberately made the comforters of Job into caricatures of the conventional religious, or whether he had more respect for their opinions; they may differ also as to whether it was he himself who set his poem within the framework of an older folk-story which, in fact, denied his problem. But there is no difference of opinion as to the grandeur of feeling and the poetic power of his central statement of the problem of suffering humanity. Once we have eliminated the prosy interpolation of Elihu the Buzite,[29] and put the last three verses of Job's final speech in our present text where they belong, that is earlier in the chapter, [30] then we have a superb statement of man's challenge to have a right to understand the ways of God:

[29] Chs. 32-37. The interpolation was almost certainly made by someone who felt that, like Elihu, he was quite competent to answer Job's questions without what must have seemed to his prosaic and pious mind the wrong-headed and improper introduction of God—an intervention in which incidentally God shows himself much less interested than Elihu in answering Job's challenge. But some scholars think it was an alternative ending written by the poet himself. I doubt it.

[30] Ch. 31. 38-40 should be put between 34 and 35, or somewhere in that section of 'ifs'.

Oh, that I had one to hear me!
(Here is my signature, let the Almighty answer me!)
Oh, that I had the indictment written by my adversary!
Surely I would carry it on my shoulder;
I would bind it on me as a crown;
I would give him an account of all my steps;
like a prince I would approach him.[31]

But God has no sympathy to offer. His reply is one of biting contempt:

Who is this that darkens counsel
by words without knowledge?[32]

It is an astonishingly courageous statement of a problem insoluble in the author's terms. Job professes himself satisfied, but only because he accepts that he is too small and ignorant to understand God's ways:

Behold I am of small account;
What shall I answer Thee?
I lay my hand upon my mouth.
I have spoken once, and I will not answer;
twice, but I will proceed no further . . .
I have uttered what I did not understand,
things too wonderful for me which I did not know.
I had heard of Thee by the hearing of the ear,
but now my eye sees Thee;
therefore I despise myself,
and repent in dust and ashes.[33]

The problem is insoluble to the author because he does not believe in any conscious future life. Man goes down to Sheol, and that is the end.[34] It is strange that the Hebrew mind came so slowly to a belief in some form of conscious future life, whether by a resurrection of the body or by the immortality of the soul, for both ideas were current in their environment, whether Persian or Greek. But while it is scarcely found in any book of the Old Testament outside Daniel, it

[31] 31. 35-37.
[32] 38. 2.
[33] 40. 4 f., 42: 3, 5.
[34] The most familiar verses of Job: 'I know that my Redeemer liveth, (19. 25) and 'though he slay me yet will I trust him' (13. 15) have both been given a meaning by Christian piety which they did not have for Job, and the second is actually a mistranslation, as the American Revised Standard version shows.

was widely current among Jews by the second century B.C., for it is expressed in a variety of writings of that time. Thus it occurs in the Book of Jubilees, written early in the Maccabean period, and in the following century it received magnificent exposition in the Wisdom of Solomon and the book of Enoch.[35]

Ecclesiastes, the book of Job, and the various references to resurrection and immortality, arise alike from Jewish sharing in that sense of the *lacrimae rerum* which so oppressed the pagan world, and were to make Lucretius and Virgil unique among epic poets—the one passionately proclaiming a mechanical materialism, and turning it into great poetry by the fact that the one person he desired to convince was himself and that he failed to do so, and the other making an epic hero of a sad middle-aged man, the speaker of the words quoted above[36] which perfectly express one aspect of the spirit of the age. But it was not really the Jewish spirit, and a larger proportion of the literature of the period which has come down to us is concerned with day-to-day morality, and day-to-day obedience to the revealed will of God. In this field we have matter of the greatest interest, for it shows us that the Jewish spirit was still developing and intensifying its heritage, and that the concept of Torah as the already revealed divine will did not have the cramping effect which Christian writers have too often attributed to it. The morality of the apocryphal and pseudepigraphical literature is often deeper and more penetrating than that of the prophets, and its analyses of motives and purpose more illuminating than those of the written codes of law.

Two works are outstanding from this point of view, the Letter of Aristeas, and the Testament of the Twelve Patriarchs. Both are thought to date from the last pre-Christian century. The Letter of Aristeas is, on the whole, a somewhat dull and prosy compilation, allegedly giving the story of how the Septuagint came to be written at the invitation of Ptolemy Philadelphus. It is typically 'embroidered history'; but it has this special interest that it contains (so far as I know) the only discussion to be found in ancient Jewish literature of the moral problems inherent in the responsibilities of a sovereign. The prophets had told kings to rule justly, to trust Jahweh, and to behave righteously themselves, but they had either dealt with special cases such as Nathan with David or Elijah with Ahab, or they had spoken in general terms to the whole nation, including its rulers. The author of the Letter of Aristeas, perhaps moved by the glowing opening and deplorable conclusion of the Hasmonean

[35] Jubilees 23. 31; Wisdom 1. 1–5. 23; and Enoch, 91. 1–104. 13.
[36] *Aeneid*, 1: 462.

dynasty, showed that he had reflected a great deal on the meaning of Torah when applied to and by the ruler himself.

He introduced the subject by describing a series of magnificent banquets which Ptolemy offered to the translators on their arrival. Each night he posed before ten of his guests ten precise problems of kingship, and approved their answers.[37] From the many topics raised three may be especially mentioned. The *essential quality of a ruler* is described as being his own obedience to the laws of his kingdom, his refusal of bribes, his practice of sobriety, the honour he pays to righteousness, and his willingness to seek friends among men with these qualities.[38] *His central duty* is the welfare of his subjects and his most necessary possession their love and friendship. Thus his greatest achievement is that he should dwell in peace and that justice should be speedily administered.[39] Finally the author has considered what should be *the main instruments of government* by which these objectives could be realised. On many occasions he insists on mildness and benignity in administering punishment, not only because such is the character of God himself, whom a ruler should try to emulate, but because of its remedial effects.[40] But he goes further into detail. A king should never exact forced labour, but pay a fair wage for all work he commanded to be done.[41] His subjects would fight for him when they knew he would choose their officers wisely and that, if they fell, he would care for their dependents.[42] Those who opposed him he should seek to win over by his generosity of spirit;[43] and for the sake of all his subjects, he should take particular care and forethought to see that harm was not wrought in his name by those whom he appointed as officials over them.[44] It is unfortunate that, while the Letter was known to patristic writers, they were interested only in the mythical account of how the Septuagint came to be written, and that none of them transmitted to Christian Roman emperors the excellent precepts of Aristeas on the duties and problems of kingship.

The other work of particular interest is the Testaments of the Twelve Patriarchs, which was written just before the breach between John Hyrcanus and the Pharisees in 106 B.C. It represents in some

[37] The whole discussion covers vv. 187 to 294.
[38] Vv. 209, 211, 279.
[39] Vv. 245, 265, 291. With the last verse, compare vvs. 109 to 111 on a particular application of the principle of speedy justice.
[40] Vv. 188, 207 f.
[41] Vv. 258 f.
[42] Vv. 273, 281.
[43] V. 227.
[44] V. 271.

ways the highest level of moral understanding reached in the period, and it is curious that it had little circulation among either Jewish or Christian readers after the first Christian century. So far as the Christian side is concerned, it disappeared almost completely until Bishop Grossetête of Lincoln in the thirteenth century obtained a copy from Greece which is now in the Cambridge University Library.

It is in the Testaments that we have the earliest example of the joining together of the twin commandments to love God and our neighbour,[45] and in the teaching of love of one's neighbour there is a very remarkable development. There is nothing more difficult for human nature than to avoid meeting hatred with hatred, and this is reflected in the development of Jewish thought on the subject over many centuries. Nothing shocks modern minds in the life of David more than the instructions which he gave to his son Solomon on his death-bed.[46] Even those to whom David had promised forgiveness for injuries done to him were to be sought out and killed by Solomon. The same attitude is found in many of the psalms, which automatically assume that God will be anxious to destroy anyone whom the author regards as an enemy. There is indeed a different attitude in the famous proverb:

> If your enemy is hungry, give him bread to eat;
> and if he is thirsty, give him water to drink;
> For you will heap coals of fire on his head,
> and the Lord will reward you.[47]

But it would be a mistake to assume that this had become an established principle even with this maker of apothegms himself, for he is capable also of saying, with unpleasant cynicism, the exact opposite.[48] In the prophets the reconciliation of the nations in the messianic age is sometimes assumed, but that cuts less deeply into human prejudice than the demand that we forgive our personal enemies now.

In the Testaments we shall find both subjects treated with deep spiritual insight. On the Gentiles there are such passages as:

> There shall be given to thee a blessing and to all thy seed, until the Lord shall visit all the Gentiles in his tender mercies;

or:

> From your root shall rise a stem; and from it shall grow a rod of

[45] Test. Issachar 5. 2, 7. 6; Test. Dan. 5. 3.
[46] 1 Kings 2. 5-9.
[47] Prov. 25. 21 f.
[48] E.g. 24. 17 f.

righteousness to the Gentiles to judge and to save all that call upon the Lord;

or again:

> The Lord shall judge Israel first . . . and he shall convict Israel through the chosen ones of the Gentiles.

This is in itself an advance on the greater part of prophetic thought, although it is foreshadowed in many passages from Amos onwards. But it is less penetrating than the attitude demanded to personal enemies:

> Love ye one another from the heart; and if a man sin against thee, speak peaceably to him, and in thy soul hold not guile; and if he repent and confess, forgive him. But if he deny it, do not get into a passion with him, lest catching the poison from thee he takes to swearing and so thou sin doubly . . . and if he is shameless and persist in his wrong-doing, even so forgive him from the heart, and leave to God the avenging.[49]

In the same spirit is the remarkable teaching about the effect on the character of anger or envy, both of which will warp the judgement.[50]

The final work for consideration in this section serves as a transition to the following one, that of the oral teaching of Torah by the 'scribes' who succeeded Ezra. This is the work known to the Church as Ecclesiasticus, whose original title was 'The Wisdom of Jesus ben-Sira'. It is a work of the second century B.C., translated into Greek for use in Alexandria by the author's grandson. Jesus ben-Sira was a conscientious and conservative teacher of Torah in Jerusalem. From his work we can see that he belonged to the cultured aristocracy, and his pupils were probably from the same class. But his whole purpose was similar to that of the more humble and anonymous teachers who were slowly penetrating into every town and village in which a Jewish community dwelt. Like them he takes passages from Scripture, expounds and expands them, and uses them to give practical rules for living. Less profound than the author of the Testaments, less Hellenised than the author of the Wisdom of Solomon, he affords us an excellent example of the kind of teaching which was given to the young aristocrat of his day, and its urbanity and sincerity alike impress the reader. It is significant that the Christian fathers, by the title which they gave it, regarded it as the manual for the clergy *par excellence*.

[49] Test. Gad 6. 3 ff. Compare Test. Joseph 18. 2.
[50] Test. Dan 2. 2; Test. Simeon 3. 2, 4. 8 f.

4. THE TEACHING OF TORAH TO THE PEOPLE

With one exception, the author of Ecclesiastes, every one of the writers whose works were described in the previous section accepted it as axiomatic that there was a unique covenant relationship between Israel and Jahweh which found expression in the obligation of the Jewish people to govern its daily life according to Torah. This belief gave to their existence a central interest, at once theological and practical, at once national and individual, which distinguished the Jews of the period from all other nations. Nothing comparable is to be found anywhere else in their environment. The reality of this interest is shown to us not merely by the writings which we have already discussed, but by the Maccabean revolt.

The revolt was precipitated by the desecration of the altar of the Temple at Jerusalem. Nevertheless it is clear that the motive behind the refusal of Mattathias and his sons to offer sacrifice at Modin, in confirmation of that desecration, was loyalty to Torah. For their battle cry was not that the Temple had been desecrated but: 'whosoever is zealous for Torah, and maintaineth the covenant, let him come forth after me.'[51]

Some general picture of the position at the time we can piece together from two contrasted incidents. On the one hand the insurgents, as they passed through the country, found many Jews who, through fear of the decrees of Antiochus Epiphanes, did not even practise the rite of circumcision, as well as many who were prepared to offer the sacrifices which he demanded.[52] On the other, a group, independent of Mattathias and his sons, was so deeply impregnated with loyalty to Torah that its members refused to offer any resistance on the Sabbath, and were all massacred.[53] Such extreme loyalty was felt by Mattathias and his followers to be suicidal and they themselves decided that, if attacked on the Sabbath, they would resist. But the decision is said to have been their own; there is no suggestion that it was reached after consultation with teachers of Torah, or with any specific religious authority.[54]

The party which supported the Maccabees called themselves the 'Hasidim', which is defined as 'every one that offered himself willingly for the Torah'.[55] But it is wrong at this stage to identify them exclusively with the ancestors of the Pharisees; they were ancestors of

[51] 1 Macc. 2. 27.
[52] *Ibid.*, vv. 45-48.
[53] *Ibid.*, vv. 29-38.
[54] *Ibid.*, vv. 39-41.
[55] *Ibid.*, v. 42.

both Pharisees and Sadducees, as well, probably, as of other groups which only developed a separate existence later. That they commanded the general allegiance, or at least approval, of the nation we can legitimately assume from the success of the revolt and the fact that it was able to place a dynasty on the throne of Jerusalem which endured for a century.

Such a situation compels us to recognise that a substantial religious movement had been in existence for a considerable period of which but the most meagre records have survived. There are five questions to which we have to seek the answer: Who taught Torah? How were they organised? What was the content of their teaching? What was their method? What was the result?

As to the teachers of Torah, we have already seen that they were in the beginning the levitical priests,[56] but that gradually a separate class of 'scribes' emerged. We get some clue as to when the transition took place from the fact that *Pirqe Aboth* records that the last survivor of the tradition established by Ezra, that is 'The Men of the Great Synagogue', was a high priest, Simeon the Just,[57] who died about 270 B.C.

Up to that time, then, we can assume a fairly close connection with the priesthood. After Simeon's death the trail is for a while thin. Then the same source gives us a series of names of leading teachers of Torah in each generation linked together in couples (*Zugoth*). There is none among them whom we know to have been connected with the Temple or the priesthood. And yet they begin in a period in which the Seleucid overlords of Judea, in a scheme to regularise the administration of their client states, had centralised Jewish political and religious administration in a sanhedrin composed largely of Temple officials and presided over by the high priest.[58]

[56] See above, p. 14.

[57] The whole question of the existence and nature of 'The Great Synagogue' is immensely complicated. In so far as such a body actually existed, it has been attributed to a number of periods, mostly later than the return. There is the same uncertainty about the existence and date of this high priest Simeon, and his possible identity with the Simeon praised by Jesus b. Sirach (ch. 50). On the other hand, the general facts as stated in the texts are independent of the conclusions reached about these controversial issues. The teaching of Torah must have begun soon after the return, the passage from levitical priests to a separate group of scribes must have occurred about about the time indicated. On the question of 'The Men of the Great Synagogue' see G. F. Moore, *Judaism*, Harvard, 1927, III, pp. 7 ff., where there is a full bibliography; and on Simeon, see the same author in *Jewish Studies in Memory of Israel Abrahams*, New York, 1927, pp. 348 ff.

[58] See Emil Schurer, *The Jewish People in the Time of Jesus Christ*, Eng. Trs., T. and T. Clark, Edinburgh, 1896, Div. II, Vol. I, pp. 163 ff.

Moreover when Judaism split into sects this sanhedrin was primarily Sadducaic, whereas the teaching of Torah to the nation as a whole had come to be regarded as a Pharisaic responsibility, and the *zugoth* contain the names of the recognised leaders of the Pharisaic party right down to the period when Pharisaism became identical with rabbinism. Hence we can say that before the end of the second century the answer to the second question must be that we do not know how the teachers of Torah were organised, but it was apparently independently of the sanhedrin.

Nevertheless our authority for assuming some organisation rests securely on a statement in *Pirqe Aboth*. One of the watchwords which tradition assigned to 'The Men of the Great Synagogue' was 'to raise up many disciples', and this can be fairly interpreted as involving the creation of a continuing teaching body.[59] Such a body must have been concerned both with the selection of teachers and with the determination of the teaching. For Judaism was so largely concerned with *doing* that it would have been impossible to avoid questions being asked, and answers being given, as to how this or that observance was to be carried out. Individual, and possibly itinerant, teachers cannot have been free to give whatever interpretations seemed good to them. Writers could and did express their own views, and we have already seen that there was a wide measure of variety in the views expressed. But the anonymous givers of oral teaching cannot have had quite the same liberty. We have to preserve a balance between assuming too great an authority or uniformity on the one hand, and too little organisation on the other. That there was no generally accepted and uniform authority we know from the growth of differing sects during the Maccabean period,[60] but that there *was* some formal organisation with substantial prestige we likewise know from the fact that it is within this period that, in three separate stages, the canon of Scripture was established. Moreover, it is in the second century that the doctrine of the authority of the oral tradition was formulated, a doctrine whose acceptance or rejection marked the subsequent distinction between Pharisees and Sadducees, both of whom agreed in the obligation of loyalty to Torah.

In the list of names given in *Pirqe Aboth*, there is attached to each some phrase or phrases which are held to summarise the particular contribution of the successive transmitters of the tradition. These sayings enable us to affirm that from very early days they were

[59] *Pirqe Aboth*, 1. 1. For a discussion of the question see Travers Herford, *Talmud and Apocrypha*, Soncino Press, 1933, pp. 44 f.

[60] See below pp. 97 ff.

training men to be both judges and teachers. There may have developed some supreme 'Beth Din' which exercised authority in regard to the former;[61] but, for the latter, we can legitimately assume that form of 'training college' which existed in rabbinic days, and is still to be found in the Islamic university of Al Azhar. A teacher gathered around him a band of disciples and transmitted his teaching orally to them. But the teacher himself would be a member of a wider body, an 'academy' in which the development of Torah was discussed and accepted, and new regulations were approved. That, in fact, some such body did exist, we can legitimately deduce from the action of John Hyrcanus, who, when he quarrelled with the Pharisaic party, annulled all the regulations which had been issued by the Pharisees.[62] According to Josephus the Pharisees had 'delivered to the people a great many observances by succession from their fathers, which are not written in the law of Moses', and in this passage he introduces the factors of both succession and development.[63] That it required the ruler to annul them suggests that it was a very influential body which issued them. That a stage was reached at which there was a fundamental split within the ranks of those who accepted a common loyalty to Torah, argues that the line of development had come to involve such radical novelties that the more conservative felt that it had gone too far. These novelties were, in fact, embodied in the doctrine of the authority of the oral tradition referred to by Josephus. Its acceptance and evolution by the Pharisees determined the line of the subsequent development of Judaism.

The canon of Scripture had been determined before the split took place, although it was not until after the destruction of Jerusalem in A.D. 70 that the number of books to be accepted was finally fixed,[64] and even then hesitation about one or two of them could still be encountered. But this hesitation concerned only minor writings, such as the Song of Songs and Ecclesiastes—in fact it is remarkable that the latter book ever came to be accepted at all—and by the time of the Maccabees the five books of Moses, the historical books, the

[61] See Herford, *op. cit.*, pp. 94 ff.
[62] Josephus, *Ant.* 13. 10, 6.
[63] Herford, *op. cit.*, pp. 94 and 100 f.
[64] B.B. 14 b, pp. 70 ff. The Jewish order of the Scriptures differs from the Christian, just as the Roman Catholics differ from the Anglican and other Reformed Churches in the books which they accept as canonical. Jews and Reformed Churches reject the Apocrypha accepted by the Roman Catholics. The Jewish order is in three divisions: Torah *par excellence*, i.e. the Pentateuch; then 'the prophets', which include also the historical books from Joshua to Kings; finally, 'the writings' or 'Hagiographa', which include the rest of the books, as in the canon of the Reformed Churches.

major and minor prophets, as well as such books as Proverbs, Job and the Psalms, were recognised by all parties alike as being 'Holy Scripture'. The division, then, was not about what constituted the written Scriptures, but the manner in which they were to be related to the actual problems of daily living.

As has been stated in the description of the synagogue, the method by which this relation was effected was known as midrash, *investigation*, and it covered two fields which were later to be more sharply distinguished. One field was that of haggadah and dealt with general religious teaching, both theological and moral or ethical; and the other was halakah or the precise rules of conduct to be followed in daily life, and the precise basis on which judgment was to be given when a matter came before the courts.

At this period both fields were regarded as of equal importance, and in both work of lasting value was achieved. We can deduce this from a single, but very fundamental, instance. During the long period in which the prophets were proclaiming in the loftiest terms the absolute uniqueness of Jahweh and the appalling sin of idolatry, idolatry did in fact flourish in almost every class of the people. In stark contrast, there is in the whole of the New Testament no suggestion that the direct worship of other gods by Jews was a problem to which either Jesus or his apostles had to give the slightest attention. Monotheism had become the religion of the whole people. This was no mean achievement. Moreover the whole people had become familiar with the actual Scriptures. Again we can take the evidence of the New Testament. Jesus, Paul and others could quote freely from them and expect to be understood, whether in Palestine itself or in the communities of the Diaspora. Finally, while we cannot assume that all the people lived up to their professions, we do not find evidence of fundamental disagreement as to what righteous living involved. By exact Pharisaic standards, Peter may have been a gross Galilean peasant. But when, in a vision at Joppa, he was invited to eat from 'all kinds of animals and reptiles and birds of the air', he cried out: 'No, Lord; for I have never eaten anything that is common or unclean.'[65]

In our estimate of the period it is too easy for us to take for granted a situation which, at that time, had to be consciously created. To us, for example, it is a commonplace that religious living involves such virtues as prayer, repentance and forgiveness. But, if we take the evidence of the Alexandrian philosopher, Philo, we find that he has to argue that these are 'virtues' since they were all unknown to the

[65] Acts 10. 14.

Greek thinkers on whose works he so constantly relied for his interpretation of Judaism in universalistic terms.[66]

The second field of activity of the teacher of Torah was the definition of precise rules of conduct. In the beginning it was doubtless sufficient to teach people the actual rules which are to be found in the written Torah, just as the teacher as judge would decide questions according to the written text. But more would very soon be required; for inevitably the question would be asked on issue after issue; *how* are we to do this? Does such or such an action come within the meaning of the written law? Interpretation would soon become a necessity, and agreement as to which interpretation was to be followed would be the only alternative to chaos. Nevertheless official acceptance of interpretation was a slow growth. Disagreements could produce violence, as at a feast of Tabernacles when the public pelted an unpopular Hasmonean high priest with citrons in the middle of the Temple service;[67] but the remarkable point is that they so rarely did so. Rival interpretations were accepted as existing within a general agreement as to how life should be lived.[68] As we shall see, when dealing with the legal aspects of the work of the teachers of Torah, the issue that was fought out during this period was that of the authority for any interpretation at all. Once the idea was accepted that interpretations also originated with Moses, they assumed independent authority. But at this time the only agreed authority was the written word of Scripture.

The method by which the teachers worked was the same whether they were exhorting and teaching the people, or whether they were dictating practice or judging misdeeds. They cited the relevant verse or verses of the Scriptures, and then elaborated them in a commentary. So far as the latter task is concerned, we have only one surviving example in rabbinic writings.[69] It occurs in the Mishnah, but it is totally different from the rest of that compilation, suggesting that it is a survival from an earlier period. It is an interpretation of a

[66] See H. A. Wolfson, *Philo*, Harvard, 1948, II, Ch. xii. 4. 'Prayer, repentance and study as virtues', pp. 237ff.

[67] Josephus, *Ant*. 13. 13. 5. The citron (ethrog) is still carried at the feast of Tabernacles.

[68] On the Pharisaic acceptance of differences without schism, see L. Finkelstein, *The Pharisees*, J. P. S., Philadelphia, 1938, I, pp. 9 ff.

[69] Dr. Gaster has suggested that the study of the Samaritan midrash will give us a clearer idea of this period, since the innate conservatism of the Samaritans and their rejection of the Jewish oral law preserved the early Jewish method of interpretation, as it was before the two peoples split apart. See Gaster, *Samaritan Oral Law*, Introduction. Compare also *Midrash Sifre on Numbers*, ed. Paul Levertoff, S.P.C.K., 1926, Introduction.

passage in Deuteronomy which deals with the conditions of military service. Certain classes are exempt, and each class is more fully described and defined in the comment. A single passage will suffice as illustration. First comes the Deuteronomic verse, then the comment:

> *And the officers shall speak unto the people, saying, What man is there that hath built a new house and hath not dedicated it? let him go and return to his house.* It is all one whether he builds a barn for straw, a stable for cattle, a shed for wood, or a storehouse; it is all one whether he built, purchased or inherited it, or somebody had given it to him as a present.[70]

In ethical, moral and theological teaching precisely the same method was followed. A scriptural passage was quoted, and then elaborated; and of this we have innumerable examples in the writings of Philo. For his own purpose this was an extraordinarily clumsy method of procedure, since it meant that his teaching on any subject was given because some word in a verse happened to suggest the theme, and not because it enabled him logically to develop his whole thought on any single matter. But the fact that he chose it shows that it was the usual method in which Jewish teaching was given. In other words, in both tasks the teachers of Torah followed the procedure which is still normal in a Jewish or Christian sermon based on a text, or in a court where a decision is based on the interpretation of a previous one.

As midrash developed it became more elaborate and more profound; in its early days it was probably relatively elementary—except of course that, then as now, there must have been great personal differences between one preacher and another. Two relatively early examples of sermons on Genesis 1. 31 will, at least, illustrate the method:[71]

> Nahman said in R. Samuel's name: *Behold, it was very good* refers to the Good Desire; *and behold, it was very good*, to the Evil Desire. Can then the Evil Desire be very good? That would be extraordinary! But for the Evil Desire, however, no man would

[70] The Biblical passage is found in Deut. 20. 1-9. The midrash on it is in *Mishnah, Sotah*, Ch. 8, p. 213. The actual question is somewhat academic! In fact the concluding verses of the chapter record exceptions which largely nullify the matter, though they also record disagreement as to the basis for the nullification. Some hold that 'all go forth' if the battle is for a righteous cause, but Rabbi Judah (author of the Mishnah) held that for a righteous cause the exceptions applied, but did not apply 'in a battle waged in duty bound'. The distinction is a nice one.

[71] *Midrash Rabbah, Genesis*, 9. 7 and 8. on Gen. 1. 31. Ed. Soncino, 1 p. 68.

build a house, take a wife and beget children; and thus said Solomon: Again, I considered all labour and all excelling in work, and it is a man's rivalry with his neighbour.
R. Huna said: *Behold, it was very good* refers to the dispensation of happiness; *and behold it was very good,* to the dispensation of suffering. Can then suffering actually be very good? It is in fact so because through its instrumentality men attain to the life of the future world; and so said Solomon: And reproofs of chastisement [A. V. 'instruction'] are the way of life [Prov. 6. 23]. Say now, go forth and see which road leads man to the life of the future world? Surely it is suffering.

An example which may be late, but which affords an interesting comparison with the parables of the Gospels, is to be found in Midrash Rabbah on Numbers 5. 6. It is argued that the Biblical passage deals with proselytes, and then follows this parable:[72]

'The Holy One, blessed be He, greatly loves the proselytes. To what may this be compared? To a king who had a flock which used to go out to the field and come in at even. So it was each day. Once a stag came in with the flock. He associated with the goats and grazed with them. When the flock came into the fold he came in with them; when they went out to graze he went out with them. The king was told: 'A certain stag has joined the flock and is grazing with them every day. He goes out with them and comes in with them'. The king felt an affection for him. When he came out into the field the king gave orders: 'Let him have good pasture, such as he likes; no man shall beat him; be careful with him!' When he came in with the flock also the king would tell them, 'Give him to drink'; and he loved him very much. The servants said to him 'Sovereign! You possess so many he-goats, you possess so many lambs, you possess so many kids, and you never caution us about them; yet you give us instructions every day about this stag!' Said the king to them: 'The flock have no choice; whether they want or not, it is their nature to graze in the field all day and to come in at even to sleep in the fold. The stags, however, sleep in the wilderness. It is not in their nature to come into places inhabited by man. Shall we then not account it as a merit to this one which has left behind the whole of the broad, vast wilderness, the abode of all the beasts, and has come to stay in the courtyard?' In like manner ought we not to be grateful to the proselyte who has left behind him his family and his father's house, aye, has left behind his people and all the other peoples

[72] *Midrash Rabbah*, Numbers 8. 2. Ed. Soncino 1. p. 204.

of the world, and has chosen to come to us? Accordingly, He has provided him with special protection, for He exhorted Israel that they be very careful in relation to the proselytes so as not to do them harm; and so indeed it says, Love ye therefore the proselyte, etc. [Deut. 10. 19]. And a proselyte shalt thou not oppress [Ex. 23. 9; cf. also Lev. 19. 33 f.].

In spite of our difficulty in dating any precise midrash to any precise period, there is no doubt that the general direction which such teaching followed was akin to the general direction of the literature of the period. The basic materials in the written Scripture were widened and deepened, filled with greater spiritual insight and broadened by the more sensitive appreciation of individual problems.[73] One interesting illustration of this spiritual development is the embarrassment which teachers felt at those portions of the Scriptures which fell lamentably short of the moral living they desired to inculcate. They had not our solution of early and late texts at their disposal; they had to accept all alike as divine, and they reveal their deeper insight by their halting explanations, their embarrassed silences and their quick passage to more attractive themes.[74] Another illustration comes from the development of the synagogal lectionary. Certain passages, both from the Pentateuch and from later books were read on their allotted Sabbath, but they were left in the Hebrew, and neither commented upon nor translated, because they were not edifying. Two such passages referred to the unchastity of Judah with regard to Tamar, and that of David's sons with their sister.[75] In the same way two at least of the imprecatory psalms were never used in the liturgy.[76] So long as the whole of Scripture was regarded as of divine origin, there was no other solution but this embarrassed silence.

There is yet one other aspect of this whole question on which we are in no doubt about the results, once they were achieved, but on which we know nothing of the steps which made the achievement

[73] A valuable, but possibly too enthusiastic, description of the moral and religious values of the teaching of the period will be found in Travers Herford, *Talmud and Apocrypha*, II, Ch. 7, pp. 127 ff. One could not expect in any religious society that more than a tiny minority of preachers or congregants should reach the spiritual levels here described. But I know nothing to suggest that, as a description of the heights which could be reached at this time, the account is false.

[74] Cf. Herford, *op. cit.*, pp. 10, 154, 160, 163, etc.

[75] Gen. 38. 12 ff. and 2. Sam. 13, 1-22. On the rabbinic passages dealing with these readings, see A. Buchler, *The Triennial Reading of the Law and the Prophets*, in J. Q. R., O.S., Vol. VI, pp. 2 ff. These chapters were excluded from the Anglican lectionary only in the revision of 1871.

[76] Ps. 59 and 109. See Herford, *op. cit.*, pp. 159 ff.

possible. That is the education of children. Jesus at the age of twelve knew enough about his religion to enter into discussion with the rabbis of Jerusalem.[77] As an adult, he not only knew the Scriptures, but could read them,[78] and yet his background was that of an ordinary Galilean village. In the second and third Christian centuries we have long discussions as to the minutiae of education.[79] But we have no information as to when the education of childen was first thought of as involving more than a general exhortation to parents,[80] nor do we know how 'public' education was first organised. Nevertheless it must have been during the period under review, and we are probably right in assuming that the teaching of boys would have been one of the tasks of the teachers of Torah, and that the innumerable stories and parables of the midrash were meant to appeal to the childish mind as much as to the mind of the simple and ignorant among the adult population. So far as girls are concerned, it would have been a question of how far rules of Torah were observed by the mother in the home, for the religious duties of women were confined to the duties of the household, whether in the preparation of food, in the rules for ritual cleanliness, or in the home observance of the Sabbath and festivals.

If we are to assess the general content and effect of the literature created by the teachers of Torah, which fills innumerable volumes and covers practically the whole remaining evidence of Jewish mental and spiritual activity for many centuries to come, we have to be careful by what standards we are to judge it. As literature, it is not 'great' in any sense. Its critics claim, with some justice, that it is often prosy, dull, and trivial, and that its flashes of genius and spiritual insight are rare jewels in a mass of mediocrity. Certainly it cannot be compared with the majesty of the Scriptures, or with the artistic and philosophic output of Greece. But that was not its object. It is doubly a *popular* literature. It is a popular literature in the sense that it was meant to teach their religion to a whole people, and not merely its intellectual élite; and it is a popular literature in the sense that it was meant to determine a daily conduct for ordinary people, and to lay down rules for the normal administration of justice. To both these aspects we shall return at later stages of this work. But here it is worth stating that the proper comparison

[77] Luke 2. 46.

[78] Luke 4. 16.

[79] See below, pp. 307 f.

[80] Deut. 4. 10. On the spread of schools among the people see Moore, *Judaism*, I pp. 316 ff., and Eliezer Ebner, *Elementary Education in Ancient Israel*, New York, 1956, Ch. 2, pp. 38 ff.

by which to assess it, is not to measure it against Isaiah, Plato or Aeschylus, but to see what kind of popular worship it produced,[81] and what kind of folklore accompanied it in Jewry. For there is immense significance in the ideas which, even if reprehended by the official leaders, were held by the common folk. Jews have never lived so isolated from their neighbours that they were uninfluenced by their popular beliefs. But if there were differences, then it is to this vast output of midrash that we owe them.

There are such differences. One emerges readily from a comparison between the Old and the New Testaments. All through the Gospels we meet a belief in demons which is absent from the Old Testament. It has been rightly traced to the influence of the exile, and to the prevalent belief in demons of all kinds in Persian folklore. But the *Jewish* demons, unlike their Persian progenitors, are not independent of God, or of equal power with him. They are bound to acknowledge his superior authority, and to obey him when called upon to do so.[82] In Jewish folklore there is no power greater than that of God; nowhere is the power of evil equated with that of good. 'The folklore of the Jews is distinguished from that of other nations, primitive and even civilised, by its *monotheistic* and *ethical* background. There is hardly a belief, a custom or a superstition, a legend, a folk-tale or a folksong, even if imported from abroad, that does not reflect the Jewish conviction of the existence of one God or does not teach a moral lesson.'[83] When we reflect on the long battle which has been fought by the Christian clergy—and is still being fought in many parts of the world—against the cruelties and barbarities of pagan superstition in Europe and elsewhere, we shall get a better appreciation of the significance of the work of these forerunners of popular religious education than if we attempt to compare their works with the great literary or spiritual masterpieces of their own or other nations.

5. SYNAGOGUE WORSHIP

IT has already been said that the synagogue was a unique institution. Professor Guignebert describes it picturesquely as 'une sorte d'université populaire confessionelle',[84] but this was only one side, though

[81] See below, p. 304.
[82] Cf., for example, Mark 3. 23 f.; 5. 7; Luke 10. 17-19.
[83] Angelo S. Rappoport, *The Folklore of the Jews*, Soncino, 1937, p. 5.
[84] Ch. Guignebert, *Le Monde juif vers le Temps de Jésus*, Paris, 1935, p. 101 (Eng. Ed. p. 75).

a very important one, of its activity and significance. The other side was its non-sacrificial and congregational worship. We must expect an institution for which there was neither precedent nor comparison to develop slowly, and we must also expect many stages of its development to pass unrecorded. Nevertheless two facts suggest that the main lines of its activities had become fixed fairly early in the restoration period. One is that later rabbis usually refer its forms to the Men of the Great Synagogue,[85] indicating that they knew of no later origin for them; and the other is that synagogue worship was adopted by the Samaritans, and was not a matter of dispute when Jewry split into sects, indicating that it had become universally accepted at an earlier period.[86]

At the same time this universal acceptance does not mean that any uniformity had been established, even on important matters such as the reading of the Pentateuch over an annual or a triennial cycle,[87] and on matters of detail there were always divergences. The New Testament accidentally illustrates this by two incidents. Jesus was asked to speak to the congregation at Capernaum and *sat down* to do so. Paul was asked to do the same at the Pisidian Antioch, and *stood up*.[88] This lack of uniformity was doubtless due to the reality of the local control of synagogue worship. At the beginning its direction seems to have been in the hands of local priestly families, but it early passed to a council of laymen with all the advantages and disadvantages of such control. Some rabbis were to complain later that the services had become so 'popular' (in the bad sense) that a scholar should not quit his study to attend them,[89] and the decorum to which we are accustomed today was probably never a main objective of the worship of the congregants. But what was lost in decorum was probably gained in vitality. In any case it is but another example of the curious unity which pervades all Jewish life. While we shall see in the following section that teachers of Torah were also judges, we might think that this was *ab initio* an entirely separate activity. But a Jew who was denied justice on a weekday was entitled to interrupt

[85] Ismar Elbogen, *Der Judische Gottesdienst in seiner geschichtliche Entwicklung*, 3rd Ed. Frankfurt, 1931, pp. 241 ff.

[86] *Ibid.*, p. 244.

[87] Meg. 29b, p. 181.

[88] Luke 4. 20 and Acts 13. 16. On the continuation of these differences in the Middle Ages, see A. Buchler, *The Triennial Reading of the Law and the Prophets*, in JQR., O.S., V, p. 422, and especially the quotation from Abraham Maimuni, son of Maimonides.

[89] Ber. 8a, p. 41. On the increasingly democratic nature of synagogue worship, see Salo Baron, *A Social and Religious History of the Jews*, 2nd Ed., II, pp. 280 ff.

the prayers on the Sabbath to say so; and this right, though very rarely exercised, appears to go right back to the period under review.[90]

From very early times the services were open to 'outsiders'. Possibly this is due to the fact that in a number of situations they were held in the open air, and that special buildings were only gradually adopted, particularly in small congregations.[91] But it is one of the subjects on which we cannot but regret that our sources give us no information, for it is of the first importance in considering the relation of Jew and Gentile, and the sources and character of Jewish missionary activity. It may, as Guignebert thinks, have originated in the Diaspora,[92] but it was certainly established in Palestine by New Testament times, as we see from the experiences of both Jesus and Peter with Roman centurions stationed in Jewish towns.[93] It would be fascinating to know whether this sharp differentiation from Jewish Temple worship with its sacred tabus, or pagan mysteries with their secrecy, was accidental or deliberate.

While the beginnings of the synagogue in the Diaspora are shrouded in complete silence, we can, as we have already seen,[94] trace its origin in Palestine definitely to the reading of the Torah and instruction thereon. We can define it still further. It was a continuation of the policy of Ezra of securing the proper observance of the ritual and ceremonies of Temple worship against the laxity of the Palestinian population during the exile, or the alternative claims of the Samaritans.[95] The emphasis was, therefore, more on the ceremonial than the moral aspects of Torah, and to some extent this has left a permanent mark on biblical lectionaries for synagogal use. There were two readings, one from the Pentateuch, and one from

[90] This, at any rate, is the opinion of Salo Baron. See *The Jewish Community*, II, pp. 32 ff, and the notes which give the sources for his statements in Vol. III, p. 112. It would appear that the right might be considered comparable to the *Clameur de Haro* with which, as a Guernseyman, I have been familiar since my youth. The parallel is worth quoting because it shows that an unusual and irritating right can exist without being abused. I do not think the *Clameur* has been raised more than half a dozen times in my lifetime.

[91] From very early days in the restored community the Pentateuch was read twice weekly on market days throughout the towns of Judea. See B.K. 82 a and b, pp. 466 ff. and compare Elbogen, *op. cit.*, p. 241. At Philippi Paul on the Sabbath went to look for the Jewish congregation, and found it outside the city by the riverside (Acts 16. 13).

[92] Guignebert, *op. cit.* p. 99.

[93] Matt. 8. 5 and Acts 10. 1-8.

[94] See above p. 13.

[95] A. Buchler, *op. cit.* p. 424.

the historic or prophetic writings; but the latter were chosen only to illustrate the former, and the connection between them was often only verbal, or the mention of the same name.[96] Not more than a few verses were read, without regard to their setting in a longer passage, so that the spiritual meaning of the prophetic message or historical narrative was easily lost or, rather, entirely ignored. Had the reading of the Scripture, therefore, been the sole *raison d'être* for the establishment of the synagogue, the result might well have been a somewhat sterile repetition of Temple ritual and ceremonial prescription.

But it was not all. Temple worship, even in pre-exilic days, was not solely concerned with sacrifice, and its non-sacrificial aspects were much developed after the return. In pre-exilic days there were special liturgies on the occasion of the great fasts and it is possible that some of these survive in our prophetic literature and elsewhere; for scholars have suggested that the books of Nahum, Habakkuk, and Joel, as well as certain chapters of Isaiah and Micah, embody such liturgies; and the much later apocryphal book of Baruch specifically states that it was intended for use in the (Second) Temple on the fast of the ninth of Ab, the day of the destruction of its predecessor.[97] After the exile, *daily* services of worship were introduced into the Temple ritual, and these services included the prayer and praise which were to find their permanent place in the synagogue.

These services of the Temple were deliberately associated with the life of the community by a system which appears to go back to the early days after the return. The country was divided into twenty-four districts, in each of which there was established a representative body of priests, levites and laymen known as a *ma'amad*. These bodies served in turn for a week in the national worship. But it would seem that not all of them, especially of the laymen, were able to go to Jerusalem. There was therefore established a system by which they shared in the obligations of the *ma'amad* by a special week of prayer and fasting in their own synagogues.[98] We are told that on Monday they offered intercession for travellers by sea, on Tuesday for those

[98] The system is described in Mishnah, Ta'an, 26a, p. 136. See also Elbogen, *op. cit.*, pp. 237 ff. Compare Luke 1. 8. 'Now while [Zechariah] was serving as priest before God when his division was on duty . . . and when his time of service was ended, he went to his home.'

[96] See H. St. John Thackeray, *The Septuagint and Jewish Worship*, pp. 46 ff.

[97] Otto Eissfeldt quotes a number of such studies in *Record and Revelation*, p. 93. See also H. St. John Thackeray, *op. cit.* p. 82.

travelling across the desert, on Wednesday for sick children, and on Thursday for nursing mothers.[99]

As the Temple services were also attended by laymen living in Jerusalem and by Jews passing through the Holy City, this system ensured the closest links between national and local worship, and reinforces the description already given of the period, that every effort was made to bring the whole people into loyal conformity with the purpose of God revealed in Torah. The Temple thus provided invaluable material for the development of the ritual of the synagogue. As Elbogen eloquently says: 'From the exilic assemblies came the reading and interpretation of Scripture, from the priestly liturgy the confession of faith and the benediction, from the levitical choirs the psalms, and from the prayers of the *ma'amadoth* the petitions.'[1] All the elements of later Jewish worship, as well as the services of the Christian Churches, thus took shape in the period following the return.

Synagogue prayers in this early period were almost certainly short and simple. They have been continually elaborated with the centuries, but their essence has not been changed, and the two basic periods of prayer in the service have been neither altered nor abandoned. Of these the first centres in the confession of faith, the *Shema*, and the second in the great complex of praise, petition and thanksgiving known either as the *Amidah*, the 'prayer' *par excellence*, or (later) the *Shemoneh Esreh*. This simply means 'eighteen', the number of clauses which it reached after the final destruction of the Temple.

The *Shema* is the nearest approach to a 'creed' known to Judaism before the time of Maimonides, and consists of the verse from Deuteronomy:

'Hear, O Israel: The Lord our God is one Lord'.[2]

While this verse forms the essential affirmation of Judaism, the verses which follow have also been used from very early days.[3] In the period under discussion the Decalogue also had its place in this part of the service of the synagogue, as it had in the daily worship of the Temple. It was dropped later owing to its use by the Christians,

[99] Ta'an, 27b, p. 145. The passage dates from after the separation from Christianity, indeed from a time when Jews were somewhat fearful of the Church. For Sunday's fasting and intercession had been abandoned lest Christians should complain that their Holy Day was being insulted, and we do not know what had been the subject of intercession in early days.

[1] *Op. cit.*, p. 239.

[2] Deut. 6. 4.

[3] See Israel Abrahams, *Studies in Pharisaism and the Gospels*, Cambridge, 1917, Second Series, pp. 18 ff. and Elbogen, *op. cit.*, pp. 16 ff.

and their claim that it was the only authentic and divinely ordained section of 'the Law'.[4] The *Shema* was preceded and followed by benedictions of great depth and beauty. Dr. Oesterley offers a reconstruction of their earliest form as follows:[5]

> Blessed art Thou, O Lord our God, King of the Universe, who formest light and createst darkness; who makest peace and createst all things; who giveth light in mercy to the earth and to those who live thereon, and in goodness renewest every day continually the work of creation. Be thou blessed, O Lord our God, for the excellency of the work of Thy hands, and for the bright luminaries which Thou hast made; let them glorify Thee. Selah. Blessed art Thou, O Lord, who formest the luminaries.
>
> With great love hast Thou loved us, O Lord our God; with great and overflowing pity hast Thou pitied us, O our Father, our King, for our fathers' sake, who trusted in Thee, and whom Thou didst teach the statutes of life, be gracious unto us too, and teach us. Enlighten our eyes in Thy Law, and let our hearts cleave unto Thy commandments, and unite our hearts to love and fear Thy Name, that we may never be put to confusion. For a God that worketh salvation art Thou; and us hast Thou chosen from every people and tongue, and hast brought us near unto Thy great Name (Selah) in faithfulness, to give thanks unto Thee, and to proclaim Thy unity, in love. Blessed art Thou, O Lord, who choosest Thy people Israel in love.

The prayer which followed the Shema is of equal beauty in its adoration of God as Creator and Redeemer.[6]

The *Amidah*, or eighteen benedictions, probably consisted at this time of not more than six or so, but it already contained the essential elements of praise, confession, and thanksgiving.[7] Finally the morning service concluded with the *Alenu* prayer, which is particularly moving because its uncompromising hostility to the vain worship

[4] The Babylonian Talmud, Ber. 12a, pp. 66 f. says that it was stopped 'because of the insinuations of the Minim'. It is the Jerusalem Talmud which explains these insinuations as being that 'these only were given to Moses on Sinai'. See Elbogen, *op. cit.*, p. 242, and Oesterley, *The Jewish Background of the Christian Liturgy*, Oxford 1925, p. 81.

[5] *Ibid.*, pp. 48 and 49. The translation is that of Dr. Oesterley.

[6] *Ibid.*, p. 50.

[7] A full text and translation of the *Amidah*, giving the approximate dates to which each of its clauses is assigned, is to be found in C. W. Dugmore, *The Influence of the Synagogue Upon the Divine Office*, Oxford, 1944, pp. 114-129. See also his Index for discussion of the *Amidah* in the text.

of the heathen is followed by explicit references to the salvation of all mankind:[8]

> Therefore we hope in Thee, O Lord our God; that we may speedily see the glory of Thy might,
> When Thou removest the abominations from the earth, and the idols shall be utterly cut off;
> When the world shall be set right in the Kingdom of the Almighty; and all the children of flesh shall call upon Thy Name.
> When Thou wilt turn unto Thyself all the wicked of the earth, that all the inhabitants of the world may perceive and know
> That to Thee every knee must bow, every tongue swear.
> Before Thee, O Lord our God, let them bow and fall down; and to the glory of Thy great Name let them give honour.
> And let them take upon themselves the yoke of Thy Kingdom, and do Thou reign over them for ever and ever.
> For the Kingdom is Thine, and for ever and ever shalt Thou reign in glory.

At some unspecified time, but before the Christian era, the services of the synagogue came to be daily and not merely weekly; and during the same period they were interwoven into the daily life of the population by the fact that their central emphasis on the praise of God as Creator and Redeemer of his creation was repeated in the association of the benediction of the Giver with the use of his gifts in daily life. The idea which underlay this development was that everything which existed belonged to its Creator. It was 'sanctified' to human use by the recognition that it came from him, and this recognition was expressed by the pronouncement of a blessing before it was used.[9] A familiar example is the grace before meals. Before bread is eaten the participants will say: 'Blessed art Thou, O Lord, King of the Universe, who producest food from the earth.' Before wine is drunk comes the similar blessing on him 'who has created the fruit of the vine'.[10]

It is, of course, impossible to say what proportion of the population either attended the daily services of the synagogue, or were

[8] Oesterley, *op. cit.* pp. 68 ff. The translation is that of Dr. Oesterley.

[9] Ber. 35a, pp. 218 f. (which is also a good specimen of rabbinic methods of argument).

[10] Both are referred to in the Consecration Prayer of the Communion Service in the words: 'Who, *after he had given thanks*, took . . .' On the relation of this idea of the sanctification of material things to Christian sacramentalism, see F. Gavin, *The Jewish Antecedents of the Christian Sacraments*, Ch. 3. Berakha and Eucharist.

punctilious in the constant use of the appropriate benediction in their daily lives and occupations. But modern scholars, examining the question on the basis of contemporary attitudes, are certainly too apt to say that a population largely consisting of farmers and artisans could not possibly have performed the increasingly elaborate ritual of life put forward by the teachers of Torah. Undoubtedly there is truth in this statement, and the words ascribed to Peter at the Council of Jerusalem reinforce it;[11] but those of us who are fortunate enough to be able to do so, may look back at the theological reading and pious activities of our Evangelical or Scottish Presbyterian forbears, and realise that the modern age is not a measure for the religious activities and possibilities of all previous generations of mankind.

6. TORAH AS A LEGAL CODE, AND THE EMERGENCE OF THE ORAL LAW

As with so many other aspects of the life of a community, so also with the growth of its laws and the manner of their enforcement, the Old Testament records enable us to see the changes and developments of a thousand years of history. Because many Biblical scholars still regard it as axiomatic that in a primitive society law is always an aspect of religion, not much attention has been paid to this feature of the Biblical record. But, now that this view is challenged from many quarters[12] and that we can consequently look more objectively to see what this particular record tells us, we find ourselves confronted with a very interesting picture. Professor Daube has shown what fascinating survivals of laws, which may have nothing to do with religion, underlie many stories of the patriarchs.[13] But, whereas with most peoples what association there was between law and religion in the beginning becomes looser as the society becomes more mature, with the people of Israel the opposite happened. Whatever the beginnings, there is no doubt that the covenant relationship between Jahweh and his people came in time to cover the whole field of the making and administration of law. This development was already far advanced during the kingdom. With the return and the establishment of a high priest as supreme leader of the nation, the association became complete.

[11] Acts 15. 10.

[12] David Daube, *Studies in Biblical Law*, Cambridge, 1947, p. 1 and especially footnote 2 on pp. 62 f.

[13] *Ibid.* On Abraham and the cities of the Plain, pp. 155 ff.; on Jacob and his various tricks, pp. 191 ff.; on the death of Moses, pp. 25 ff; and see Index of Biblical Quotations.

At the same time the evidence prevents us from leaving the matter there. That the supreme court was identified with the supreme authorities of the Temple seems to have remained true until the Maccabean period. When under the Hasmoneans the Temple was identified with the throne, royal and priestly prerogatives were confused. But we have already seen that the association between the priesthood and the local life of the people was gradually weakened as the class of 'scribes' came to be separate from the class of 'priests'. We discover at the same time that scribes became increasingly concerned with the administration of justice. But we have no means of telling what relationship was established between the central organisations of the scribes and the central administration of throne or Temple. It would be rash to assume that every teacher of Torah was, from the beginning, also automatically a magistrate, or had a precise sphere of authority. But we have records of capital judgments being pronounced by some of the leading teachers of Torah during the Hasmonean period,[14] and the various sayings attributed to the Men of the Great Synagogue and their successors in Pirqe Aboth show us that the administration of Torah as law was recognised as part of their whole curriculum of teaching. Thus the first of the three sayings attributed to the Men of the Great Synagogue themselves is 'Be deliberate in judgment', and to three of the later scribes are also attributed sayings concerned with judicial tasks. Joshua b. Perahyah (c. 120 B.C.) said: 'When thou judgest any man, incline the balance in his favour.' To Judah b. Tabbai (c. 80 B.C.) is ascribed the saying: 'Make not thyself like them that would influence the judges; and when the suitors stand before thee, let them be in thine eyes as wicked men, and when they have departed from before thee let them be in thine eyes as innocent, as soon as they have accepted the judgment.' His contemporary, Simeon b. Shetah, added 'Examine the witnesses diligently, and be cautious in thy words, lest from them they learn to swear falsely.'[15] I assume that the last phrase means 'do not ask leading questions'. That these men were also human we learn from the fact that the last two named both offended against their own precepts and were challenged by their contemporaries for doing so.[16]

The general line of all these sayings is consistent. They plead

[14] On the reliability of traditions which ascribe particular actions to particular individuals during the period in which records were not written, see Oesterley, *Jewish Background*, pp. 20 ff.

[15] Ab., 1. 1, 7, 9, pp. 5-7. The translations are from Danby's edition of the Mishnah, pp. 446 f.

[16] Mak. 5b, p. 27, and San. 46a, pp. 300 and 302.

for an impartial and humane administration of justice, along lines which are very parallel to those advocated by the Letter of Aristeas for the conduct of a ruler, and they indicate that questions concerned with the practical administration of the law were always present in the minds of the teachers of Torah. It seems a reasonable hypothesis that the application of the laws which are to be found in Torah to cases before the courts is the origin of the controversy about the existence and authority of the oral law. It is the normal, indeed, inevitable, experience of every community that a written code of laws is in need of constant expansion and revision, expansion to cover cases which had not been directly dealt with by the framers of the laws, and revision as standards of moral behaviour alter or improve. The Jewish community can have been no exception and we do, indeed, have two instances at least where it seems likely that profound modifications of clear Biblical laws took place quite early in the period after the return. One is in regard to the death sentence and the other to the *lex talionis*.

The question of the *lex talionis* is of peculiar importance for the Christian reader, because it is so commonly assumed on the strength of the Sermon on the Mount that savage Jewish legalism could be contrasted with Christian love, not merely up to the time of Christ, but in all subsequent periods.[17] Studies of comparative law suggest that behind the doctrine of 'an eye for an eye' there probably lay not merely uncontrolled vengeance, but legal provisions which were even more cruel.[18] At the time of its formulation therefore, it indicated an advance in clemency. At what date it in its turn was abandoned, and the principle of the compensation of the sufferer was inserted in place of the sterile punishment of the aggressor, we cannot exactly say. Professor Daube has pointed out that the principle of compensation is just as primitive as that of punishment;[19] and Travers Herford argues cogently for a very early date for the change, on the ground that the rabbis of the first and second Christian centuries, who certainly accepted the idea of compensation in place of punishment, ascribed the change to no particular name or date, and therefore accepted it as 'traditional'.[20]

The other subject is the death sentence. On one particular applica-

[17] Matt. 5. 38-42. It is interesting to study the comment on this passage in C. G. Montefiore, *The Synoptic Gospels*, Macmillan, 1927, II. pp. 69 ff. Travers Herford ascribes an earlier date to the substitution of compensation for punishment than does Montefiore, see note 20.

[18] Daube, *op. cit.* pp. 105, 168 f.

[19] *Ibid.*, pp. 102 ff.

[20] *Talmud and Apocrypha*, pp. 119 ff. Compare H. Loewe in *Rabbinic Anthology*, p. lxxiii.

tion of the sentence—to a presumed adulteress—we have a stern law in Numbers Ch. 5. This prescribes that the woman shall prove her innocence by 'drinking the waters of bitterness'. In a discussion in Sifre on Numbers,[21] we are told that it was this or that rabbi who modified this or that clause. For instance, Rabbi Simeon b. Johai directed that the evidence of the bitter waters should be neglected. But on the basic question as to whether, if guilty, the woman should be put to death, it is just assumed that she would not be[22] without any authority being quoted. In other words it had already become traditional.

In section four a case was quoted where interpretation was necessary to show how Biblical law was to be carried out; here we have two instances of how, in fact, a Biblical law was *not* to be carried out. These are but a few cases of what must have been an almost daily occurence in the execution of justice, and there must have grown up a substantial body of 'case law' in the period during which we cannot divide the teaching and practice of Torah into different party allegiances. But the strong Jewish emphasis on the divine origin and divine authority of Torah was bound, at some time, to make some decision necessary as to the status of these practical decisions, and their relationship to the divine authority of the laws which they either interpreted or modified. It was on this rock that Pharisees and Sadducees split. The Sadducees were prepared to concede a divine authority to such laws as were actually written in the Torah and to admit that, where they exactly covered some case before the court, they had to be carried out. On all other matters they claimed the right inherent in any people to build up its own code. The Pharisees were not prepared to make any such distinction, and claimed the same divine authority for what was written and for what, under the guidance of their leaders, was to be the actual practice of the court.

From our available sources we cannot further fill out the picture of the development which led to this division of opinion. We lack the necessary evidence. This, however, matters the less in that we have a very adequate field for the study of the problem in the history of the use of the Bible as a legal and penal authority by the Christian Church and the relationship of this to the development of European law. The sanctity attached to the scriptural word was the same in

[21] Para. 19. Ed. P. Levertoff, S.P.C.K., 1926, p. 25.

[22] The Biblical prescription is not, of course, cancelled in so many words. By the method on which more will be said later, the conditions under which she could be pronounced guilty of death are made such that the penalty could never be inflicted.

Church and Synagogue, and the battle over strict conformity or developing interpretation was exactly reproduced.

Influenced by the complete condemnation of the Pharisaic doctrine of interpretation which is attributed to Christ himself,[23] churchmen at least as late as the eighteenth century adopted a broadly Sadducaic attitude, that is to say that on issues which they considered to lie within their competence they demanded that the divine law, as embodied in the text of the Scriptures, should be exactly administered by the courts.

It is true that there were many harsh practices in the legal procedures of Christendom which owed nothing to the authority of the Old Testament, whether applied literally or not. Jewish law knew nothing of physical torture as practised even by the Church in the courts of the Inquisition; and the hideous mutilations familiar to the Christians of Byzantium would have horrified the most severe rabbi. Nevertheless Karl Ludwig von Bar, the great historian of European criminal law, writes thus of the influence of the medieval Church on the Courts: 'In the Middle Ages the expressions of the Mosaic Law were construed singly and literally, and where offences against religion and morality were concerned, it is in many respects harsh and cruel. The idea of the "talio" (originally unknown to Germanic Law) often reappears exactly in its original form in the South German statutes. This contributed not a little to making the criminal law harsh and cruel, since its alleged divine origin seemed to preclude any compromise or mitigation.'[24] On the subject of the last sentence he remarks in another passage that theologians even contested the right of rulers to remit the death penalty or to punish adultery with less than death by invoking the divine authority of the Bible.[25] Nor was the situation any better after the Reformation. Describing the attitude of the Reformed Churches, he speaks of 'the fanatical tenacity with which, after the Reformation, criminal justice allowed itself to revel in blood and gruesome penalties with an almost universal approval. Amidst an increasing progress and culture, the law remained, until well into the 1700s, the bulwark, as it were, of cruelty and barbarity.'[26]

The cruelty of the witch trials of the seventeenth century[27], the passionate defence of slavery by some churchmen in the great

[23] Mark 7. 6-23, culminating in 'You leave the commandment of God, and hold fast the tradition of men.'

[24] *History of Continental Criminal Law*, Continental Legal History Series 6, London, 1916, p. 108.

[25] *Ibid.*, p. 228.

[26] *Ibid.*, p. 93.

[27] Based on Ex. 22. 18, 'You shall not permit a sorceress to live.'

debates on Abolition at the beginning of the nineteenth century, and the defence of the segregation and humiliation of the coloured person by Afrikaans-speaking Christians of South Africa in our own day,[28] are all witnesses to the effect of rejecting the idea of a continuous interpretation of the words of Scripture as the basis of a living legal code. What is of equal interest for our subject is the way in which the more sensitive churchmen of the medieval and post-medieval periods attempted to find a line of escape without appearing to impugn the authenticity of the Bible as God's word.

The great work of Richard Hooker *On the Laws of Ecclesiastical Politie*, published at the end of the sixteenth century, provides an admirable example. It is of particular interest because Hooker was writing to confute the literalism of the Puritans, and their denial that the Church could have any laws save those to be found in the Scriptures. Hooker had, therefore, every reason to develop some theory of 'interpretation' similar to that which sixteen hundred years earlier had drawn the Pharisees away from the traditional attitude represented by the Sadducees. Yet Hooker cannot escape from the basic Sadducaic standpoint; he is ready to admit that 'it were in vain to make laws which the Scripture hath already made, because what we are already there commanded to do, on our part there resteth nothing but only that it is executed.' His argument for freedom is only that 'a number of things there are for which the Scripture hath not provided any law.' But this is not enough, for Hooker does not wish to practise all that is 'there commanded'. The result is that, as Professor Seaborne Davies says in a study of the influence of the Bible on English legal development, he escapes by subtle and *ad hoc* distinguishing. He distinguishes between 'laws natural', which always bind, and 'positive laws', whether God or man be the author, which are either permanent or changeable according to the matter concerning which they were first made. And again, he says 'there is the role of "reason" which is not only supplementary to the Scriptures, but necessary for their understanding and application.' There are laws in the Bible given with restraint to the land of Jewry, and so on.[29] What is noticeable is that there is no basic and general principle by which to escape from the dilemma of obedience or disobedience to the accepted 'word of God'. It is all casuistry,

[28] Based on Gen. 9. 25; 'Cursed be Canaan [son of Ham, reputed ancestor of the negroes]; a slave of slaves shall he be to his brothers.'

[29] Quoted from D. Seaborne Davies, *The Bible in English Law*, a lecture delivered before the Jewish Historical Society, 1954. The passages cited above are from his discussion of Richard Hooker's *Laws of Ecclesiastical Politie*, Bk. III.

devoted to smoothing away what had become intolerable to the sensitive conscience, and it always ended by claiming that God is concerned in his creation with the prohibition and punishment only of the grosser offences, murder, theft and adultery, while all other matters he leaves to the judgement of man. The result has been that real amelioration of the law became possible in most Christian countries only when the lawyers had the courage to declare outright that the Mosaic code was not the acceptable basis for the laws of their country.

With these historical examples in mind, we can return to the problem facing the Jewish community in the Maccabean period. The modern solution, by which a divine origin is denied to all legal systems, was clearly precluded by the belief held by all opinions among the Jews that Torah, with its legal code, was of divine origin. There remained only the alternatives adopted by Sadducees and Pharisees. The consequences of the Sadducaic attitude we can see clearly from the history of European law. That of the Pharisees stands out as infinitely more spiritual as well as infinitely more creative. Whereas in Europe humanising and moderating influences had usually to fight the authority of religion, in rabbinic Judaism it was religion which was itself the humanising and refining agent. Whereas in Europe the activity of the Churches in moulding the law of the nations was gradually more and more restricted, because progress could come only as detail after detail of the legal system was rescued from the dead hand of clerical literalism, in rabbinic Judaism the religious mind was perpetually free to range over the whole field of the legal life of the community. This conclusion is not purely theoretical. Christians in the Middle Ages and later, who regarded Jews with traditional abhorrence, were still ready to accept the verdicts of Jewish courts or to submit their problems to the decisions of Jewish rabbis rather than their own priests.[30]

Doubtless in their elevation of the oral law to a place beside the written Torah, Jews did at times 'multiply commandments' unnecessarily, and many of these commandments dealt with ritual and ceremonial matters. But such issues were peripheral to the main purpose, which was to lay upon those whose task it was perpetually to keep the administration of justice at the highest level, the spiritual responsibility involved in the claim that God himself sanctioned and required their action. Torah was something which lived and grew with Israel. It was not through frivolity, but to give immense solemnity to the responsibility which the rabbis felt to be laid on

[30] Compare my *The Jew in the Medieval Community*, p. 257 and M. Zborowski and E. Herzog, *Life is With People*, New York, 1952, p. 172.

their shoulders, that they proclaimed that 'there is greater stringency in respect to the teachings of the scribes than in respect to the Torah'.[31]

7. THE MACCABEAN REVOLT AND THE MEANING OF HISTORY

THE tremendous developments which have been described in previous sections were made possible by the relative tranquillity which the Jews had enjoyed under the Persians. When Persia was succeeded by the empire of Alexander the Great and his successors, this tranquillity still continued. Palestine in due course became part of the kingdom of the Ptolemies, and the main change was that its rulers came from Egypt instead of from Mesopotamia. From time to time armies must have passed through the country; but Jerusalem, surrounded by its mountains, was left on one side while they passed up and down the coastal plain, to whose possession the Jews did not aspire until the time of the Maccabees.

This tranquillity was shattered, and shattered for ever, by the ambitions of the house of Seleucus which ruled in Syria. After two successful battles in 200 and 198 B.C. the Seleucid, Antiochus III (the Great), conquered Palestine from the Ptolemies. But a new world power was already threatening Syria from the north. The Romans had defeated Philip V, king of Macedon and ally of Antiochus, in the year of the latter's second victory over Ptolemy. In 190 they entered Asia, compelled Antiochus to recognise their dominant position in the eastern Mediterranean, and imposed on him a vast indemnity which led him to the systematic plundering of the treasures of the temples in his dominions including that of Jerusalem. His successor, Antiochus IV (Epiphanes), added to his financial necessities a strong desire to impose Hellenism on his Syrian subjects. To many, especially of the more prosperous, the imposition was not unwelcome, and this was as true among the Jews as among others. There grew up a party, including members of the wealthy families from which the high priests were chosen, which was prepared to abandon the traditional austerity of Jewish moral and religious practice in favour of the seductive laxity of Hellenism. The combination of the most extensive power to bribe with the most enthusiastic desire to hellenise brought the reward of the high priestly office to a certain Jason (Joshua), brother of the existing high priest Onias. Onias, deposed, fled from the country and was later murdered by Jason's successor. For Jason did not long retain the office he had

[31] Mishnah, San. 88b, p. 587.

usurped. Antiochus always needed money and another helleniser, Menelaus, outbid him, selling the Temple vessels to raise the money to do so, and allowing the king to strip the gold from the Temple doors and decorations. A year later Jason led a *coup d'état*, seized Jerusalem, and indulged in wholesale massacre both of the supporters of Menelaus and of the loyal Jews who had opposed both venal high priests equally. Antiochus first sent an army to recapture the city and then in 167, convinced that Judaism itself was the enemy and that there would be disorder in Jerusalem and Judea as long as it existed, he proscribed all Jewish practices. He ordered swine to be offered on the Temple altar and so precipitated the revolt of Mattathias and his family, who are known by the names of the Maccabees (from his son Judas Maccabeus) or the Hasmoneans (from the grandfather of Mattathias, Hashmon).

There is no need to describe in detail the dramatic rise and sad decline of the dynasty.[32] Even before its rise Rome had asserted its dominance in Syrian affairs and it was by the favour of Rome that the Hasmoneans reigned and were succeeded by the Herods, until the cruelty and incompetence of the latter led to direct Roman rule. It was Roman brutality which, in turn, led to the two disastrous revolts in which all Jewish independence was extinguished. We are not, however, concerned with the political story but with the effects of the profound political change on the religious life of the people.

The effects were twofold. In the next section we shall see how the strains and stresses of independence, and the compromises which it entailed, led to conflicts of opinion which resulted in a number of rival 'sects' differently interpreting the meaning of life under Torah; here we are concerned with the appearance of a new type of literature to which the name of apocalyptic has been given.[33] The essence of apocalyptic is that it seeks to explain the nature of history and, in particular, the end to which under God's over-ruling purpose all history is to come.

The very idea of a historical perspective is one which we cannot expect to emerge until a society has reached a considerable degree of

[32] There are excellent critical surveys of the period in Pfeiffer, *op. cit.*, Part I, and in Guignebert, *op. cit.*, Bk. I, Ch. 3.

[33] The words 'apocrypha' and 'apocalyptic' have the same root-meaning of 'something hidden'. But the Apocrypha involves that which should be put (or hidden) away by man, as not being 'Holy Scripture'. It is the same as the Hebrew 'Genizah', the depository in which worn-out sacred works were 'hidden away' lest they should come to harm, and rejected works hidden away lest they should do harm. In Apocalyptic, it is God who is supposed to have hidden his purpose from vulgar scrutiny, and revealed it only in parables and symbols to chosen vessels.

moral development, and we do not know when the feeling that all human life moved to a predestined end under divine guidance emerged among the people of Israel. We can, however, see its origin in the tendency to substitute a historical for a natural significance in the annual rhythm of feast and fast. The festival which looked forward to the future was the celebration of the New Year in the autumn. The 'day of the Lord', to which it looked forward originally as a rebirth of nature, was enlarged to include the rebirth of the nation, in other words its rescue from the continuous political defeats, humiliations and uncertainties which beset the chosen people.[34] The first surviving reference to this transformation is in the form of a violent protest by Amos against what was already obviously held as a popular belief. His contemporaries looked forward to a 'day of the Lord' in which Jahweh would raise his people to a position of supremacy among the nations of the world and destroy all their enemies. Amos transformed this popular conception of a 'day of the Lord' and raised it to the level, which it was henceforth to preserve in Jewish religious thought, of a moral judgment on human conduct:

> Woe to you who desire the day of the Lord!
> Why would you have the day of the Lord?
> It is darkness, and not light;
> as if a man fled from a lion,
> and a bear met him;
> or went into the house and leaned with his hand against the wall,
> and a serpent bit him.
> Is not the day of the Lord darkness, and not light,
> and gloom with no brightness in it!
> 'I hate, I despise your feasts,
> and I take no delight in your solemn assemblies.
> Even though you offer me your burnt offerings and cereal offerings,
> I will not accept them,
> and the peace offerings of your fatted beasts
> I will not look upon.
> Take away from me the noise of your songs;
> to the melody of your harps I will not listen.
> But let justice roll down like waters,
> and righteousness like an ever-flowing stream' . . .
> says the Lord whose name is the Lord of Hosts.[35]

[34] On the possible link between the day of the Lord and the annual ritual of the festivals see S. Mowinckel, *He that Cometh*, Blackwell, Oxford, 1956, pp. 133 ff.

[35] Amos 5. 18-24.

The prophecy of Amos is a sustained condemnation of the unrighteousness, not merely of Israel but of all human societies, and an assertion of the authority of God over all peoples alike:

'Are you not like the Ethiopians to me,
O people of Israel?' says the Lord.
'Did not I bring up Israel from the land of Egypt,
and the Philistines from Caphtor and the Syrians from Kir?'[36]

Nevertheless in the concluding verses of his prophecy he distinguishes between Israel and other peoples, and promises the little remnant that survives the day of the Lord that it will blossom out again into a nation over which God will reign as the righteous king of a righteous people.[37]

The same thought is to be found in the other prophets of the eighth century, Hosea, Micah and Isaiah. When the mass of the nation had been destroyed for its iniquity the survivors would repent, and through them the nation would be restored. The feeling —for it is scarcely more—that God's moral judgment on human conduct involved also God's initiative in forgiveness and reconciliation was a natural consequence of a belief in a basic purpose and moral order in the creation. In this way the conviction grew that the final period of history would be one of the victory and rule of God.

Down to the exile it would be wrong to insist too much on the word 'final'. The rule of God, expressed through a righteous king and a righteous people, was to be expected in the future—perhaps the near future—but this involved neither a change in the order of history nor its coming to an end. It is in this 'natural' order of things that the

[36] *Ibid.*, 9. 7, and compare the woes on the nations surrounding Israel in 1. 3—2. 3.

[37] Many great Christian scholars of the Old Testament have considered that these passages in Amos, as well as similar passages in other pre-exilic prophets, are post-exilic interpolations (see R. H. Charles, *Eschatology, Hebrew, Jewish and Christian*, A. and C. Black, 1913, where these scholars are listed under each of the prophets, pp. 88 ff.), and that the authentic prophecies of the period consisted *solely* of denunciation. I find this very difficult to accept as a general principle, though it is obviously true in individual instances. These prophets have not been preserved because they were 'Holy Scripture'; they became Holy Scripture centuries later because they had been preserved from among the mass of oracular utterances spoken to the people of Israel with the preface 'Thus saith the Lord'. It is already sufficiently remarkable that in any nation men should preserve such wholesale and forthright condemnations of their vices. If, in addition, these condemnations held no promise of the possibility of amendment and restoration, then I find their preservation totally incomprehensible. It has again become the fashion to describe pre-exilic prophecy as wholly denunciatory, but this is in the interest of Christian apologetic and not of scholarship.

'messianic' idea was born. A remnant of the nation would repent, would be restored and under a king—or a succession of kings—of wise and righteous character would attain a hitherto unimagined power and prosperity. The whole picture is 'this-worldly' and the king, when mentioned, a normal human being. But generation followed generation without any deep spiritual change resulting from the disasters which history had brought upon the nation. Prophets saw the reforms of righteous kings like Hezekiah or Josiah swept away by their successors, and king and people lapsing into the idolatry, social injustice and immorality from which they had been temporarily shaken. So the idea grew that something more than the natural sequence of events, or something more than a human king, or something more than human repentance, or than all three, was needed before such a restoration could be secure and permanent.

Meanwhile a totally different factor had entered the religious picture which was to have considerable influence on developing ideas of this longed for rule of God. That was the growing concern with the nature and destiny of the individual, and the slow growth of belief in some other world in which the injustices of this were remedied and into which the human personality entered at death. As concern with history worked towards the introduction of superhuman or supernatural characteristics in the time of restoration, so concern with the individual introduced the idea that the restoration of the nation was linked to that other world in which the righteousness of the individual was vindicated, or was even postponed until that other world should be born.

There was yet a third religious development which was to influence religious thought about the future. This has already been discussed as it affected the introduction of a Day of Atonement into the worship of Temple and synagogue. It was the thought of vicarious expiation for the nation's sins as a necessary preliminary to the restoration. Its deepest expression in the Old Testament is to be found in the Servant Songs included in the text of Deutero-Isaiah, and this is equally true whether the servant is the nation purified or some individual linked to his people's fate and redeeming them by his patient bearing of suffering.[38] Opinions differ as to the extent to

[38] Is. 42. 1-4, 49. 1-6, 50. 4-9, 52. 13—53. 12. An early study which is still worth consulting because it contains the traditional Jewish exegesis together with opinions of three great 19th century scholars, one Jewish and two Christian is *The Fifty-Third Chapter of Isaiah according to Jewish Commentators*, by S. R. Driver, A. Neubauer, and E. B. Pusey, Parker, Oxford, 1857. See also *The Cross of the Servant*, S.C.M. 1926, by H. Wheeler Robinson, *The Suffering Servant* by C. R. North, London, 1948 and Ch. 7, 'The Servant of the Lord' in *He that Cometh* by S. Mowinckel.

which an identification was made, before the Christian period, of the action of the Servant and the ushering in of a 'messianic age', but at least the idea of willing endurance of a preliminary time of distress and suffering took its place in the expectations of the future. It would be foolish to expect that Jewish thinkers saw all these things clearly and at once, and that they were able to mark out in advance a logical and co-ordinated development to meet the demands of these deeper insights. Nor can we expect any sudden or complete change of emphasis to arise from the apprehension of these new horizons. The centre of their thought remained the chosen people and its destiny as a people. Evidence of awareness of the new perspective comes fitfully and in all fields and we cannot assume that succession in date means succession in ideas.

One of the most beautiful expressions of the culmination of history is the book of Joel, which is usually dated to some time within the Persian period. Another of the same date is found incorporated in the book of Isaiah.[39] In both, but especially in Joel, there is contained the idea that something new will have to happen before the hostile nations are completely destroyed and the remnant of Israel completely restored. For Joel that new thing will be that

> 'I will pour out my spirit on all flesh;
> your sons and your daughters shall prophesy,
> your old men shall dream dreams,
> and your young men shall see visions.
> Even upon the menservants and maidservants
> in those days, I will pour out my spirit.[40]

This idea that something new has to happen first becomes clear in the prophets of the exile, Jeremiah and Ezekiel. But there is a difference in the way in which they proclaim it. It has already been seen that both examined the problem of the individual from the standpoint of the same popular saying that the fathers had eaten sour grapes and the children's teeth were set on edge.[41] But the answer to the problem is widely different in the two prophets. Jeremiah declares God's answer to be that *he* will make a new covenant with them, and that *he* will put his law within them, and *he* will write it on

[39] Chs. 24—27, and 34—35. See *The Book of Isaiah*, G. H. Box, Pitman, 1908, pp. 111 ff.
[40] Joel 2. 28 f.
[41] See above, Ch. 3, section 3, p. 53.

their hearts.[42] Ezekiel, however, destroys the basis of the existing order of divine-human co-operation, by a complete atomisation of society. No man will have any responsibility for another but only for himself: 'the righteousness of the righteous shall be upon himself, and the wickedness of the wicked shall be upon himself'.[43] Mutual responsibility will no longer exist. Moreover the individual himself will be atomised, in that the only essential will be his *last* action—if good, 'life', if evil, 'destruction'. What was involved in this is uncertain, for there is no evidence that Ezekiel was familiar with the doctrine of survival in any form, but the division is clear—as Qoheleth says: 'as the tree falls, so shall it lie'.[44] Moreover God will do nothing further about it. The prophet can only tell the people: 'get *yourselves* a new heart and a new spirit'.[45] Ezekiel's future age does not, therefore, grow organically out of this age. It is achieved only by casting aside previous realities. According to Jeremiah, however, God promises to restore Israel because 'I have loved you with an everlasting love'. There is a world of

[42] Jer. 31. 33. The idea of a 'new covenant' expressed by Jeremiah, was not taken up directly by any subsequent Jewish writer. It would seem that the words were held to be fulfilled in the new impetus given after the return to the direct teaching of Torah to the people; no one seems to have thought of it in terms of a different Torah and, indeed, the words do not imply that such was in the prophet's mind. There appear to be few references to the passage in rabbinic writings. *Midrash Rabba, Song of Songs*, Ed. Soncino, pp. 26 and 325, refers it to the learning of Torah by the people. *Ibid. Ecclesiastes*, p. 51, refers it to the Age to come, when people will learn and not forget. Joseph Albo, in *Sefer ha-Ikkarim*, J.P.S. America, 1946, III, pp. 181 f., discusses it with apparent reference to Christian interpretations, and adopts the view of the *Midrash on Ecclesiastes*. H. Freedman in a modern orthodox commentary follows the same line: Soncino Bible, *Jeremiah*, p. 211. The Christian interpretation naturally refers the conception of the 'new covenant' to the Incarnation. Although this particular passage does not seem to have been used by Paul, he quotes Isaiah 59. 20 f. where there is a similar reference to a covenant 'which I have put into your mouth'. It is, however, quoted by the author of the Epistle to the Hebrews (8. 6-13), who reads into the words of Jeremiah a good deal more than the prophet says. For Jewish scholars are right in saying that the emphasis in Jeremiah is *not* on a different Torah, but on a new way of making Torah effective. In Hebrews the emphasis is the opposite. God is made to say that it was the old Torah which was 'obsolete'. Rabbinic scholars drew deductions from texts which are just as strange to our pedestrian attitude to what an author meant, but I doubt whether Jeremiah can be fairly cited as an authority for the abolition of Torah.

[43] Ezek. 18. 20.

[44] Eccles. 11. 3.

[45] Ezek. 18. 31.

difference between this and the cold contempt of God in Ezekiel:

> Say to the house of Israel, Thus says the Lord God: It is not for your sake, O house of Israel, that I am about to act, but for the sake of my holy name, which you have profaned among the nations to which you came.[46]

Broadly speaking the ideas of Ezekiel developed into apocalyptic, those of Jeremiah into many and deeper channels. But we must not assume any hard and fast division into two schools of thought.

Many contributory elements were involved in the speculations about the future which provided an escape from the miseries of the present, and some part of all these elements is to be found in almost every Jewish group of the post-exilic period. But gradually a distinction became manifest which separated those who followed the line of apocalyptic, however great their loyalty to Torah, from those who followed the rabbinic line, however great their interest in apocalyptic. This distinction lay in the attitude adopted to the moral order which had hitherto governed the relationship between Jahweh and his creation. To the predecessors of the rabbis the age of perfection was an age of fulfilment of Torah—even if it was to the extent that it was so universally known and accepted that no one needed to define its observance. But to the apocalyptists something new was substituted and this involved the admission, even if only by implication, that Torah had failed and could not, or could no longer, bring the will of God to its fruition. God could bring about the fulfilment of Torah only with man's co-operation. It was a covenant relationship. But he could flash about the heavens, hurl thunderbolts, and ride on clouds, without that co-operation. If he demanded any assistance it was from legions of celestial beings. Man is no longer a subject; in the apocalyptists, whatever their apparent respect for Torah, he is merely the object of uninhibited divine autocracy.

It is in the Maccabean and Roman periods, when the profound suffering and weakness of the nation reached a new depth, and

[46] Ezek. 36. 22. It is not until the rabbinic period that the full spiritual significance of the holiness of *the Name* of God finds its true expression and becomes something 'the depth of whose meaning modern scholars have not plumbed to this day' (J. Klausner, *The Messianic Idea in Israel*, p. 118). The doctrine of 'the sanctification of the Name' and its opposite, 'the profanation of the Name', occupy a vital place in the rabbinic concept of the need for Israel to remain loyal to Torah in the face of Gentile temptation or provocation.

expectations of earthly deliverance were non-existent or short-lived, that these expectations of an apocalyptic 'day of the Lord' became prominent. Many were unable to wait with the patience of the main body of teachers of Torah for the gradual emergence of a righteous nation, and demanded a quicker and more radical, if more superficial, 'issue out of all their afflictions' by predicating the same impatience and pessimism on to the Almighty. God would overthrow the whole historical process by direct intervention on a cosmic scale. The result was a new body of writings of which the Book of Daniel is an early example, and the only example to be included within the canon.

This literature has three peculiar features. It is all pseudepigraphical, the name adopted being usually that of one of the patriarchs; the overthrow of history is usually communicated to the author in turgid and confused visions; and usually (though not always) there is a supernatural figure who acts as the divine agent of the cataclysm. On the other hand, like all other Jewish literature, it accepts the rule of Torah as being the destined obligation on Israel, though its interest in its development is, with the single exception of The Testament of the Twelve Patriarchs, banal and superficial. The reason is not far to seek. Not Torah, but the end of history was its main interest.

It is only, as it were, by accident that this literature has made any permanent contributions to the history of either Judaism or Christianity. The real Jewish expectation of the end of history was the righteous reign of God over his creation, and this belief already existed in its most spiritual form in the writings of the canonical prophets. Christians have, indeed, taken over the idea of a final judgment from apocalyptic writers; but the attempt to interpret the life and teaching of Jesus simply in terms of his eschatological beliefs has not been accepted by the Churches.[47] The character of Jesus of Nazareth and the Christian experience of the meaning of the Pauline phrase (repeated in his letters 240 times) 'in Christ' are very different from that to be found in the messiah of the apocalypses.

There is, therefore, no need to examine in detail the separate works

[47] The fullest attempt to fit the teaching of Jesus into an 'Interimsethik', that is the brief moment before history came to an end with his second coming, is to be found in Albert Schweitzer's *Quest of the Historical Jesus* (*Von Reimarus zu Wrede*), A. and C. Black, 1954, but Dr. Schweitzer's own life is the most effective condemnation of his scholarship in this work. The 'living Christ' of Christian contemporary living has nothing in common with the supernatural figure of apocalyptic.

coming under the general heading of apocalyptic eschatology[48]. There is a general sequence of events which apocalyptic presupposes, though all of them will not be found in any single work, and they may not always occur in the same order. After 'visionary' accounts of the centuries which have already passed, presented in a confused mass of symbols from cows to talking vines, the real interest begins with the cataclysmic end of history in the immediate future. Joseph Klausner has described the ensuing sequence thus: 'the signs of the Messiah, the birth-pangs of the Messiah, the coming of Elijah, the trumpet of the Messiah, the ingathering of the exiles, the reception of proselytes, the war with Gog and Magog, the Days of the Messiah, the renovation of the world, the Day of Judgment, the Resurrection of the dead, the World to Come'.[49]

We know so little of the actual conditions in which the canon of Scripture was first formed, and then closed, that we cannot really tell why this literature is all anonymous. The explanation of Dr. Charles that 'the Law was supreme, inspiration was officially held to be dead'[50] breaks down not merely by the inclusion of the pseudepigraphical and apocalyptic work written under the name of Daniel within the canon, but, still more, by the fact that this is the very period in which inspiration came to be 'officially held' not to be dead, but to be still living in the unwritten Torah. In principle the inspiration of these works could also have been accepted, though most readers will be profoundly thankful that this mass of, for the most part, uninspiring verbosity was permanently rejected.[51] We owe our knowledge of its existence almost wholly to the Eastern Christian Churches, though its influence can be seen in the New Testament and among the earlier patristic writers.

Its survival, as its original creation, arose out of its presentation of a divine action to remedy the defects of human history; and the fact that it was the Christians who preserved it emphasises that it was the idea of a divine agent as supervisor or actor in the final

[48] Analyses of their contents and teaching are to be found in *Eschatology. Hebrew, Jewish and Christian*, by R. H. Charles; *The Doctrine of God in the Jewish Apocryphal and Apocalyptic Literature*, by H. J. Wicks, Hunter and Longhurst, 1915; and *The Ethics of Jewish Apocryphal Literature*, by Maldwyn Hughes, Robert Cullery, 1909. An unfavourable view of this literature is to be found in *Talmud and Apocrypha* by R. Travers Herford. The texts have been collected and critically introduced and edited by various scholars in *Apocrypha and Pseudepigrapha of the Old Testament* by R. H. Charles, Vol. II, *Pseudepigrapha*.

[49] Klausner, *op. cit.*, p. 385.

[50] Introduction to the *Pseudepigrapha*.

[51] The Abyssinian Church alone preserves much of it in its canon.

cataclysm which provided the main attraction. At the same time the material which this literature offers on the subject of this divine agent is extremely meagre. He does not always appear at all; and when he does, he is merely the instrument of a situation which has already been created independently of his existence. He does not make the righteous, or augment their number. He does not decide who is righteous and who is not; obedience to Torah decides that, and the lines on which he shall judge (when judgment is considered to be part of his functions) are laid down for him in advance. If he is to be ruler over a 'messianic' kingdom, that kingdom has no clear-cut existence. Sometimes it is eternal, sometimes of limited duration. Sometimes it is of this world, sometimes not. Everything is vague; and all that can be said is that there grew within a section of Jewry, during the centuries which followed the Maccabean revolt, a belief in a speedy supernatural deliverance with which was often associated a supernatural person. The roots of the belief lay in an earlier expectation of a human king of the house of David who should restore the political fortunes of his people; but its flowering was due to the pessimism which doubted whether any Jewish king would be strong enough to overthrow the vast empires which surrounded their little strip of disputed territory.

That which caused these works to be written, and to be preserved, was their glamour, and neither their ethics nor their theology. Their false visions—false because nine-tenths of the history their pretended authors 'foresaw' had already happened—their imagery and hyperbole, made little men feel partners in great events. Jews, impatient in distress, wrote them; Christians, impatient in distress, preserved them. The midrash, and the preaching of the teachers of Torah which lay behind it, was humdrum stuff compared with the tinsel phantasies of apocalyptic; in the same way it provided in its cosmic hurly-burly an exciting substitute for the intellectualism of Christian theology, and the exacting standards of Christian living. It is a literature of short cuts, banal and trite when stripped of its 'oriental imagery'. Some of its ideas became incorporated into basic Jewish and Christian thinking, just because of the tension between the actual and the ideal which it presented in sweeping and graphic strokes. But at bottom Judaism was right to reject, and Christianity to forget, it. To the Christian understanding of Jesus as Messiah, or to the Jewish expectation of the reign of righteousness, justice and peace as the culmination of history, it could make no real contribution.

8. THE EMERGENCE OF SECTS

THE pressures to which Jewry was subjected in the second century B.C. led not only to the rise of apocalyptic eschatology but to the emergence of divisions based on differing interpretations of Jewish duty. The key to the understanding of these interpretations lies in the realisation that more than two hundred years of the teaching of Torah had made ordinary Jews more conscious of the claims which religion made upon them, personally and nationally, than had ever been the case before. It is significant that the victims of the persecution of Antiochus Epiphanes are the first ordinary men and women to become religious martyrs, so far as we know, in the history of mankind.[52] To say that the nation had become conscious of the claims of Torah does not, of course, mean that all individuals accepted those claims. In fact, the first party to be discussed is that of those who consciously rejected them. Nevertheless, they are rightly included with the others, because the emphasis is on their *conscious* rejection.

The hellenising party, largely confined to members of the wealthy and politically ambitious families, positively desired the substitution of Greek for Hebraic values. They saw in the Greek cities which began to dot the Galilean and Judean countrysides, centres of a superior civilisation they desired to copy. These families provided successive high priests during the period which preceded the Maccabean outbreak. Forced into opposition during the time when supreme power and loyalty to Torah were combined in the ruling dynasty, they still remained alert to every opportunity to reassert hellenic values. When the half-Idumean dynasty of the Herods succeeded the Hasmoneans they came into their own. Greek cities were increased. Herod himself, though he rebuilt with Greek magnificence the national shrine at Jerusalem, was quite prepared to build also temples to Augustus, and he and his dynasty spent vast sums on embellishing Athens itself with pompous buildings. The hellenisers may have prized their Jewish autonomy for political purposes, but culturally they wished to be Greeks. When, politically, Rome succeeded the neighbouring hellenistic dynasties of the Ptolemies and Seleucids, they eagerly sought the friendship of the Roman emperors

[52] This is not to belittle the death of Socrates, or to deny that in even earlier centuries unknown men may have died for their convictions. But the special claim for the martyrs of Antiochus lies in the fact that they were found among ordinary men and women. They were not outstanding personalities, like Socrates, who could appear to endanger the 'powers that be'.

and Roman aristocrats. It is important to distinguish these 'hellenisers' in the Holy Land itself from the hellenistic Judaism of the communities of the Diaspora. The former were seeking to substitute Greek values for those of their own religious and social tradition; the latter were honourably seeking to interpret their Judaism to the environing Greek world.

There were, of course, Palestinian Jews who sought also this interpretation. The most famous of them is Josephus. Certainly he never wished to be anything but a Jew and claimed, indeed, that after searching experience of all forms of Judaism he had adopted the religious view of Pharisaism. Nevertheless, his acceptance of Judaism was linked to his belief in its universal significance and venerable antiquity rather than to its national peculiarities. He wrote at great length about these aspects of his faith for the benefit of Greek and Roman readers; and his *Antiquities of the Jews* is one of our most valuable historical sources for the whole of this period. In the turmoil of the times in which he lived, it was not possible to express such views in an atmosphere of academic calm. He was unwillingly caught up in the rebellion of A.D. 66, and was even appointed rebel governor of Galilee and organised its defences. His defeat and surrender were probably among the happiest experiences of his life.

Few could maintain the foot in both camps which Josephus attempted, and he may be said to have succeeded only by becoming a prisoner of the Romans and so withdrawing from public life and national responsibility. But there were others who, long before his time, had to face the same issues and succeeded in producing what appeared a working compromise. These were they who became known as Sadducees. Like the out and out hellenisers, they also came largely from the wealthy and aristocratic families living in and around Jerusalem. During the Maccabean period, whether the rulers themselves adopted a piety greater than theirs or a worldliness in excess of what they would have considered 'good form', they formed a stable element in the background of an administration which was obliged to accept relations with the non-Jewish world around them. When the Hasmoneans fell and were succeeded by the Herodians, they were firmly established in the possession of the high priesthood and the controlling influence in the religious life of the nation, at any rate in so far as this was expressed in the worship of the Temple and in the courts which were centred in it. They were a party easy to understand by comparison with many periods of English post-reformation history. They were essentially the supporters of 'the Establishment', loyal, conservative, hostile to innovation, deploring 'enthusiasm'. Their split from other loyal accepters of Torah came either from their dislike of innovation—as when they rejected the Pharisaic doctrine of the unwritten Torah—or from the prudence which deplored excess. They were as indifferent to the quietism which led to Essenism as they were hostile to the fanaticism which led to zealotry.

On the other hand it has not been sufficiently recognised that they fully accepted the authority of the written Torah and the covenant relationship between Jahweh and his people. They are no more justly described as 'quislings' than would be our own eighteenth century bishops and clergy who combined loyalty to the Established Church with extreme conservatism in politics and full recognition of the authority of the government in matters which enthusiasts sought to bring under the aegis of religion. In loyalty to Torah there was no distinction between Sadducees and Pharisees. Indeed, during the long period from the return to the break between the two parties, the predecessors of both alike were concerned with carrying into effect the teaching of Torah. They broke with each other; neither broke with their common past. The ancestors of the Sadducees were probably more concerned with the Temple, but the rules for Temple worship were an essential part of Torah. In their teaching they may have been more conservative, like the author of Ecclesiasticus, and less interested in speculative questions such as the nature of free-will, or the immortality of the soul. Like our eighteenth century clergy, they may have esteemed worldly virtues, prudence and moderation too highly. But it is a grave mistake to imagine that they did not take their religion seriously, or thought of it only in terms of ritual. In fact it has been suggested that the most beautiful and spiritual of all the pseudepigraphical works, the *Testaments of the Twelve Patriarchs*, is a Sadducaic eirenicon addressed to the Pharisees in the interest of peace and unity—qualities which had been pitifully absent in the original patriarchs as each of them confesses.[53]

[53] Rudolf Leszynsky, *Die Sadduzaer*, Berlin, 1912, p. 237. This book is the fullest and most sympathetic study of the Sadducees. Leszynsky also claims Sadducaic authorship for the *Book of Jubilees*, and the original versions of the *Book of Enoch* and the *Psalms of Solomon*. He considers the Damascus Fragment also to originate with a group of Sadducees who fled to Damascus during the Pharisaic hegemony under Queen Alexandra Salome, and finds confirmation of this flight in Josephus (Ant. 13. 16. 2), p. 167. On the other hand, Louis Finkelstein, in *The Pharisees*, J. P. S. America, 1938, regards them as worldly and formal in their religion, considering prudence a higher virtue than faith and worldly success the most evident mark of divine approval. See, for example, the discussion of the *Book of Proverbs*, I, pp. 203 ff.

So far as the written Torah itself went the Sadducees desired its strictest fulfilment and challenged the readiness of the Pharisees to make adjustments and modifications. But they would not accept the unlimited obligations implied in the Pharisaic doctrine of a living tradition. Firmly fixed as to what Torah demanded, and accepting that this was conceded by the Roman authorities in the freedom which they granted to Temple worship and to Jewish courts, they found no difficulty in principle in accepting their autonomy under Roman rule, and in co-operating with the Roman power in 'secular' affairs.

There were two groups within the nation which could not accept this doctrine of political prudence and co-operation. The one demanded unlimited political freedom, the other unlimited freedom for the development of Torah. There was a third group which sought to retire entirely from the struggle by something akin to an ascetic and monastic movement; they were the Essenes. The two groups which wished to continue the struggle, but on grounds different from those adopted by the Sadducees, were those who are commonly called the zealots, and the Pharisees.

Zealot, as a proper name, should be confined to the followers of John of Gischala, and not used before their emergence in A.D. 66,[54] but it is a term which has passed into common usage to describe a type of religio-political activity, and it is most convenient to keep it, but without a capital Z, and not with the implication that it is linked precisely to the movement of John of Gischala.

With the appearance of zealotry, as with so many other issues during these fascinating centuries, we are dealing with something new and unprecedented in human history, at any rate so far as our western society is concerned. For zealotry was a *popular* religio-political movement, seeking to overthrow or mould a political society in accordance with a religious inspiration which had been received *directly* by its members. Their own individual consciences compelled them to take political action and they were indifferent to the approval or disapproval of their political or religious leaders.

Although the movement was without precedent, it was not without roots in the history of Israel. Samuel rebuked Saul as the acknowledged spiritual leader of his time,[55] but Nathan rebuked David at the behest of his own prophetic conscience,[56] and from the time of Nathan onwards no prophet claimed an official position as the

[54] See Lake and Foakes-Jackson, *The Beginnings of Christianity*, Macmillan, 1920, I, pp. 421 ff.

[55] 1 Sam. 3. 20 f.

[56] 2 Sam. 12. 1-14.

authority for his moral warnings. Jahweh had communicated directly with him, and he could not remain silent. In the great prophets of Israel we have a unique series of men who took with the utmost seriousness the burden which was laid upon them. But we must remember that these men were not unique in Israel because they were 'prophets'. Throughout they were exceptions. Amos reveals the actual situation by vigorously protesting that he was *not* a prophet in the sense that his contemporaries would have understood the word.[57] In Israel, as in the surrounding countries, there was a common belief that men could be filled with the divine afflatus and speak 'as the spirit gave them utterance', and Paul was not the only religious leader who was embarrassed by the results.[58] The ordinary prophet of ancient Israel was more akin to the dervish (at his worst) than to Elijah or Isaiah.

The Hebrew prophets of the canon never preserved more than a precarious eminence among those who professed to speak in the name of the Lord. While they denounced royal immorality, there were plenty of other prophets to indulge in flattery of the reigning sovereign. When they themselves 'foretold' as well as 'forth-told', they had also to compete with lesser imitations. In the post-exilic period a man like Joel could still remain at the highest ethical and spiritual level in speaking of the day of the Lord. But it is almost certain that there were at the same time ecstatic soothsayers travelling the country and indulging in eschatological pronouncements in the name of the patriarchs of Israel who, by their intemperance and their exaggeration, rightly incurred the hostility of those who were seeking to effect a real moral transformation of the people. If this were so, it would explain a curious passage in Deutero-Zechariah, in which a feature of the day of the Lord will be that 'if anyone again appears as a prophet, his father and mother who bore him will say to him, "You shall not live, for you speak lies in the name of the Lord"; and his father and mother who bore him shall pierce him through when he prophesies.'[59] The suggested treatment is so drastic, and the prophet's denials in the following verse that he *was* indulging in prophesying so vehement, that there was clearly a serious situation for which our lack of information provides us with no contemporary explanation.

[57] Amos 7. 10-14.
[58] 1 Cor. 14. 1-5.
[59] Zech. 13. 3. Various dates are suggested for the passage, mostly towards the end of the Persian or the beginning of the Greek period of domination. This is the period to which the beginnings of the pseudepigraphic eschatologies are ascribed. But compare Deut. 13. 1-5.

If, in fact, we have here the earliest examples of what is now the familiar phenomenon of 'millenarianism', then contemporary attitudes to the Doukhobors in Canada or Jehovah's Witnesses in various countries, as well as the behaviour of some at least of the adherents of those beliefs, would explain rabbinic hostility to the pseudepigraphical literature, and at the same time warn us that this literature had secured a real grip on some sections of the population, and led them into a state of dangerous turbulence. Hence the rise of zealotry, especially in the districts far from the influence of Jerusalem, of which Galilee is the chief.

If the contemporary problems created by Jehovah's Witnesses and similar movements enable us to understand one aspect of zealotry, the religious wars of the seventeenth century will throw light on another. There is no doubt that the core of zealotry was profoundly and sincerely religious; but it is also true, both that zealots committed hideous acts against normal morality and humanity, and that they attracted to themselves outlaws and bad characters who increased their violence. With the possible exception of the Scottish Covenanters, and some of the Swiss Protestants, the same was true of both Roman Catholic and Protestant armies in seventeenth century Europe. Hideous cruelties were committed in the name of religion by those to whom religion was nothing but a pretence.

That there is a close association between the zealots and the apocalyptists is unquestionable, but it is difficult to say whether, before Bar-Cochbar, any Jew actually thought of himself as the messiah, though all the zealot leaders probably thought of their role as being connected with the Times of the End and the messiah's appearance.[60] In Mattathias and his sons political activism found prudent and competent leaders and the establishment of the Hasmonean dynasty was the result.[61] But it fell into a serious moral decline before it perished, and there was no possibility of zealotry seeing anything but an enemy in either the Herodians or the Roman procurators. It became a movement of secret rebellion, nourished on fantastic messianic hopes and attracting to itself many undesirable elements in the population.

The account of the first beginnings of the Maccabean revolt tells us of the existence of another group who found difficulty in re-

[60] Compare the prudent speech of Gamaliel before the sanhedrin in Acts 5. 33-39.

[61] It is interesting that in the *Testaments of the Twelve Patriarchs*, the messiah is expected from the line of Levi, not of David, Mattathias being a levitical priest. See T. Reuben 6. 7-12; T. Levi 8. 14 and Ch. 18; T. Judah 24. 1-3, etc.

conciling the existing situation of the nation with their loyalty to Torah, but who found a different solution for their dilemma. One of the main springs of the revolt was an incident thus pathetically recounted:

> [The Syrians] put to death certain women that had caused their children to be circumcised. And they hanged the infants about their necks, and rifled their houses, and slew them that had circumcised them. Howbeit many in Israel were fully resolved and confirmed in themselves not to eat any unclean thing. Wherefore they chose rather to die, that they might not be defiled with meats, and that they might not profane the holy covenant: so then they died.[62]

This was not the end of the story. Others who felt similarly sought the prudent solution of flight to the many desolate and uninhabited regions to be found especially on the eastern slopes of the Judean hills. But the Syrians pursued them and came upon them on the Sabbath day. They refused to resist, saying 'Let us die all in our innocency: heaven and earth shall testify for us that ye put us to death wrongfully.'[63] Nothing could be more moving than this simple opening to the still unfinished record of the courage of ordinary men and women confronted with the alternatives of death or disloyalty to their faith.

It was out of the existence of such convictions, combined with the widespread expectation of a day of the Lord falling in cosmic disaster on humanity, that was born a movement of ascetic quietism, of withdrawal from the places or, at least, pursuits of common life. We know it as Essenism, and new light has perhaps been thrown on the habits and beliefs of the Essenes by the discovery of the 'Dead Sea Scrolls' in Wadi Qumran and the exploration of the near-by monastery at Khirbet Qumran. Our main source for the teaching of the Essenes had previously been descriptions of their doctrines given us by Josephus, Philo and Hippolytus,[64] but we learn both from Philo and from Pliny in what great respect this ascetic and monastic sect was held by its contemporaries. There is, however, a considerable mystery about its doctrines and it is not even certain that we should claim uniformity for all Essene communities. We

[62] 1 Macc. 1. 60-63.

[63] *Ibid.*, 2. 37.

[64] Josephus *Ant.* 15. 10. 4-5; 18. 1. 5. *Bell. Jud.*, 2. 8. 2-13; Philo, *Quod omnis Probus Liber sit*, 12, and *De Vita Contemplativa*, I, also fragment preserved in Eusebius, *Prep. Evan.* Bk. 8; Hippolytus, *Refutatio Omnium Haeresium*, 9: 18-28. All are quoted in full by Kohler. See following note.

may well be better informed when more work of interpretation has been done on the Scrolls.[65]

The dominant idea of the Essenes was the holiness which God through Torah demanded, and they sought to fulfil all its demands, even with works of supererogation. They immersed themselves in a daily bath of purification, and one of the most surprising discoveries in the monastery at Khirbet Qumran is the existence of two large water tanks—almost the size of swimming pools—which would well suit this purpose. To get water above the shores of the Dead Sea is nowhere easy, and the replenishment of these tanks must often have been a difficult problem. They either abstained entirely from sexual intercourse or limited it to Wednesday, having calculated that this was least likely to profane the Sabbath by a birth. Such are some of the formal aspects of their quest for ritual holiness; but their reputation rested on deeper matters, their simplicity and integrity, their ascetic lives, their refusal to participate in animal sacrifice, their insistence on supporting themselves by the work of their hands, their gentleness and refusal to take an oath, their avoidance of all worldly ambitions. Not all lived in the desert; some were to be found also in the towns and villages of Judea; but we do not know enough to know whether the monastic life was a higher order of Essenism or a retreat in which all members of the sect partook.

What is of particular importance for the future in the Essene movement is not any particular belief held by the Essenes, but their basic belief that the will of God could be most completely fulfilled only by withdrawal from the common life of men. Scholars have sought to find the sources of this aspect of the Essene community in either the Buddhist monks or the Pythagorean ascetics, and there was so much intermingling in the hellenistic world that indirect influences from both are possible. But, in its essentials, it was a Jewish community based on a special interpretation of Torah; and its particular interest

[65] There is a very important article on the Essenes by Kaufmann Kohler in *The Jewish Encyclopaedia*. See also Guignebert, Bk. 3, Ch. 2. A full, discussion of earlier authorities is in Schurer, Eng. Ed. Div. 2. Pt. 2., pp. 188 ff. Two theories have been put forward as to the origin and doctrines of the sect. Certain writers, Schurer among them, have claimed that they were syncretists, bringing alien elements into Judaism from the Jewish environment to east or west. (cf. *Hellenism* by N. Bentwich, J. P. S., America, 1919, pp. 104 ff.). Others, and especially Kohler, have seen them as a natural development of the teaching of Torah, and an example of that '100%ism' of which Pharisaism provides a more solid and continuing example. In fact, Kohler sees the foundations of Pharisaism and Essenism as indistinguishable elements in the position of the Hasidim in the second century B.C. This view is supported by Guignebert after careful consideration of the sources.

is that it is the only *Jewish* community which identified its loyalty to Torah with withdrawal from the common life. Throughout its history Judaism has always resisted the temptation to identify the fulfilment of the demands of God with a way of life which was not open to ordinary men, following the avocations which their situation in this world made essential for humanity. The Essenes had no successors. A Karaite community in medieval Jerusalem created a movement called the 'Mourners for Zion' based on the asceticism and monasticism of the Christian orders in the city. But rabbinic Judaism continued its chosen path of seeking to fulfil the will of God in the daily life of ordinary men.

To include the Pharisees in this study of sects and parties would be misleading. For, though the Pharisees themselves seem to have been a definite society with limited membership and rules of admission, their sphere of activity was the whole people and their influence extended through the whole people. While all those discussed in this section, with the exception of the hellenisers of Palestine, were in one way equally the heirs of the teachers of Torah whose work began with the return, in another way it was the Pharisees alone who came to bear the whole weight of the tradition, and to ensure its continuation through the disasters of the first and second Christian centuries. Likewise the 'amme ha-aretz', the common people, were not a 'sect'. It, therefore, seems most appropriate to treat of these two subjects in the following chapter, where the common people, the Pharisees, and Jesus of Nazareth and his followers, form the essential elements in the picture.

9. THE JEWS IN THE DIASPORA AND THEIR MISSIONARY ACTIVITY

So far we have been considering almost exclusively the situation of the Jewish population in the Holy Land itself; but during the whole period under review substantial Jewish communities were living outside the home country, and at some time during it they came to be the majority of the Jewish people. As was said in the first section of this chapter, the origin of these communities is shrouded in complete mystery. The Bible tells us nothing of movements which might lead to them apart from the deportations which followed the collapse first of the northern, then of the southern, kingdom and the flight of some from the latter to Egypt. But Deutero-Isaiah, writing during the Babylonian exile, unquestionably implies that these were by no means the only Jews living abroad. In speaking of the future ingathering of the nation he uses these terms:

I will bring your offspring from the east,
and from the west I will gather you;
I will say to the north, Give up,
and to the south, Do not withhold;
bring my sons from afar
and my daughters from the ends of the earth.[66]

Even though the evidence for a widespread dispersion is convincing, yet we get no clue as to how all but a few of the dispersed communities came into existence, and we know little of the occupations Jews followed in the cities of their choice. With certain exceptions, however, we are safe in saying 'cities' and not 'lands';[67] for agriculture was the occupation of slaves or natives, and only in mass settlements such as those established in Babylon would it be normal for those who came from abroad to follow agricultural pursuits. This would not mean that Jews were wholly divorced from the land for the ancient, like the medieval, city grew much of its own food. But it would mean that the basis of Jewish life abroad would be the artisanate or commerce, and that they were much more likely to be found as minority communities in the polyglot cities of the ancient world than in the more homogeneous country districts or small market towns.

If we are in the dark as to the origin of most of the Diaspora, we do possess a fair picture of the organisation of a diaspora community. In spite of a mass of honorific titles such as was common to all public life in antiquity, the communities were 'democratically' organised, if on a somewhat narrow and oligarchic basis. Their chief officers were laymen, and elected.[68] They were self-governing, possessed considerable judicial, fiscal and administrative autonomy, and controlled all matters of entry into the community, and the personal rights and status of their members.[69] So far as the territory of the Roman empire was concerned, the justification for this special status was the concession of Julius Caesar, which formed the basis of all subsequent privileges, 'that Jews might live according to their

[66] Is. 43. 5-6. Post-exilic prophecies make similar statements; e.g. that contained in Is. 11. 11-12. See also texts quoted in Juster, *op. cit.*, I, p. 180, and Schurer, *op. cit.*, Eng. Ed., II, 2, pp. 220 ff.

[67] See the map on p. 316 in A. H. Godbey, *The Lost Tribes a Myth* for early traces of Jewish dispersion and, for example, his discussion of Solomon's horse-trading activities in Asia Minor, p. 272 f. On the available information see *Hellenism* by N. Bentwich, pp. 34 ff.

[68] Juster, *op. cit.*, I, pp. 440 ff.

[69] *Ibid.*, pp. 424 ff.

Torah'.[70] This carried two important implications. It recognised Torah as part of the public law of the empire,[71] and it accepted a Jewish community living anywhere within the Roman *limes* as part of a single Jewish people. In both these respects, but particularly in the latter, it was unique among the concessions made by Rome to the diversity of peoples and customs in her dominions.

While our picture of the local Jewish community is relatively clear, there is complete confusion once we attempt to describe the relations between communities and between the Diaspora and the authorities in Palestine.[72] The one certain point is the payment of the Temple shekel (succeeded by the *aurum coronarium* paid to the patriarch at Tiberias after the destruction of Jerusalem in A.D. 135) until its confiscation by the Christian emperor, Theodosius II, in A.D. 429.[73] From the evidence of the *Codex Theodosianus* it looks as though this payment were but the financial aspect of a complete dependence of the diaspora community on the centre; for, though the evidence is late, it would, if valid, apply to the period under discussion.

The *Codex* contains a series of edicts of Christian emperors, at first defending the patriarchate against the encroachments of Christian fanaticism, and then abolishing first the office and finally the *aurum coronarium* itself. One edict speaks of 'those [Jewish] authorities who are, in the opinion of the most noble and illustrious patriarch, competent to decide questions of their religion', and another lists 'chiefs of synagogues, patriarchs, elders and other synagogue officials who are under the jurisdiction of the illustrious patriarch'.[74] The patriarchate itself was abolished by Theodosius II in 415, but even after that blow to Jewish autonomy there is a reference to 'Jewish primates who are nominated by the sanhedrins of the two Palestines or who dwell in other provinces'.[75] All this seems to imply a hierarchical organisation of Jewry and its control from the centre,[76] something in fact very like the organisation of the

[70] See passages cited *ibid.*, I., p. 252, n.l.

[71] A Roman magistrate, for example, could not summon a Jew to court on one of his holy days or the sabbath, C.T., 8.8.8.

[72] Juster, *ibid.*, pp. 391 ff.

[73] C.T., 16.8.29. The payment is vouched for in the period under discussion by the fact that Cicero defended Flaccus, Propraetor of Asia in 62 B.C. against the charge of having stolen it. See Th. Reinach, *Textes des Auteurs grecs et latins*, Paris, 1895, p. 238.

[74] C.T. 16.8.8. and 13. The 'patriarchs' mentioned in the second edict are thought by Juster to be regional Jewish chiefs, *op. cit.*, p. 402.

[75] *Ibid.*, 16.8.29. The two Palestines are the Roman provinces into which the country was divided.

[76] See Juster, *op. cit.*, I., pp. 391 ff.

Christian Church with its patriarchs, provinces and dioceses, and we can safely assume that, did this exist in the fourth Christian century, it would have existed from the beginning of Roman rule. For it is impossible to suggest a period after the first war with Rome at which the emperors, however friendly disposed, would have wished deliberately to increase the authority of the Palestinian Jews over Jewish communities elsewhere. It was Palestine not the Diaspora which was a recurrent menace.

What prevents our acceptance of the evidence that these edicts offer is the almost complete lack of any trace of the exercise of the powers they imply in the vast literature, Christian as well as Jewish, of the centuries involved. We are told that Paul was converted while on an inquisitorial mission from the high priest to the Jewish community of Damascus;[77] we are told that, fifty years later, the rabbinic authorities of Palestine sent out letters to the synagogues of the Diaspora formally rejecting the messianic claims made on behalf of Jesus of Nazareth and providing for the exclusion from the community of Jews who accepted them.[78] And this is all. We never hear of any local official being appointed by a patriarch; no Talmudic discussion covers an issue which had arisen from the relations between the centre and the Diaspora; there is no record of any dispute, of any patriarchal decision being received, rejected, or challenged. In our information about diaspora communities there are no references to the centre; in our information from Palestine and Babylon there are no references to questions of public or religious policy arising from the existence of Jewish communities in the west. From early days the Christian Church had possessed *three* independent patriarchates, Antioch, Alexandria and Rome. To these in the fourth century Constantinople was added. But there was never any question of more than *one* Jewish patriarch; and yet Jews were as widely distributed and (at any rate before the fourth century) probably as numerous as Christians.[79] It seems impossible to believe that anything comparable to the Christian organisation existed from a single centre in Jewry, and yet left no trace among our records.

We *must* assume that there were personal contacts between the centre and the local rabbinate, for we must remember that no

[77] Acts 9. 1-2.

[78] Justin, *Dialogue*, 108. See my *Conflict of the Church and the Synagogue*, pp. 79 ff.

[79] Juster lists 350 places in which literary or epigraphic evidence tells of a Jewish community, *op. cit.*, I., pp. 179 ff. Contrast the meagre information collected by A. Neubauer in *La Géographie du Talmud*, Paris, 1868.

halakic decisions and no midrashic interpretations were officially committed to writing before the third Christian century;[80] and the general historical picture is of the existence of a consistent Judaism throughout these centuries. Even allowing for the influence of Hellenism, which will be discussed in the next section, we have no evidence of profound differences between one Judaism and another. Certainly there is no evidence for such in the New Testament. Wherever the apostles went they found organised synagogue life, and this life corresponded in pattern to what Jesus had encountered in Galilee. Moreover Paul, speaking to Galatian Jews in Asia, Corinthian Jews in Greece, or Roman Jews in Italy, could use the normal methods and material of rabbinic belief, exegesis and argument. That up to A.D. 70 there must have been a considerable number of pilgrims in Jerusalem annually, and that the diaspora communities maintained synagogues in the city,[81] would certainly have helped to maintain unity by personal contact. But these contacts must have been much reduced with the destruction of the Temple in A.D. 70, and still more reduced with the destruction of the city in A.D. 135, for there was nothing particularly sacred about the Judean and Galilean cities where subsequent rabbinical centres were established.

Even the existence of these personal contacts is an assumption. So far as the evidence goes there is an astonishing silence. A handful of the rank and file scholars whose discussions fill the pages of both Talmuds are explicitly said to have been born in cities outside Palestine or Babylon,[82] but of only one leading figure is this true.

[80] It appears to be generally recognised that written notes of halakic decisions and midrashic interpretations must have existed some centuries earlier; nothing less would have secured continuity in a situation where communication with the centre was always a lengthy matter and frequently precarious. If there were nothing in writing, the sudden death of a rabbi could have brought the religious and judicial life of a whole community to a standstill. But such notes would not have been authoritative, and their value would have been transitory. We must still assume that the main relationship was based on the presence of pupils from the Diaspora at the academies of the Palestinian and Babylonian teachers.

[81] E.g. the synagogues of Freedmen, of Cyrenians, Alexandrians, Cilicians and Asians referred to in Acts 6: 9.

[82] It should, however, be said that biographical details are uncommon in any case, and that of relatively few participants is the place of birth known. That, however, is only one aspect of the silence. We do not learn from the participants in the Talmudic discussions that they had themselves been faced with halakic decisions in diaspora communities, or that they had heard of disputes as to decisions while they were in some diaspora community. We do not get such phrases as Rabbi X. said that in Marseilles

The great Palestinian scholar of the beginning of the second Christian century, Rabbi Meir, was born somewhere in Asia Minor. Moreover in all rabbinic literature there is mention of only two scholars who established a rabbinic academy in a diaspora community. These exceptional men were R. Mattithia ben Heresh, who established himself at Rome, and R. Judah ben Bathyra who taught at Nisibis.[83] But we do not know if a centre of learning continued in either city after their deaths. We hear of occasional visits, for example to Rome,[84] but we do not hear of any consistent visitation, either by the patriarch, his deputies, or distinguished scholars, to the communities of the west, north and south, although there were continual goings and comings between Palestine and Babylon.

In the face of this silence it is only possible to suggest that the authority of the patriarch was honorific rather than actual, and that informal relations based on diaspora scholars attending the schools of the rabbis at the two great centres (as Paul attended the courses of Gamaliel) were balanced by the general willingness of Jewish communities to take responsibility for their own lives in matters alike civil and religious.[85]

A second vital point on which we are equally uninformed is to be found in the relation of these Jewish communities to their Gentile environment. Again the New Testament is decisive as to the facts, but as to what brought the facts into existence we have no information. The synagogue *did* attract widespread interest and a variety of degrees of adherence among the Gentile neighbours of the hellenistic Jews,

they did so and so. Rabbi Y. said that, when he was in Constantinople, the Jewish community was uncertain about so and so. There were two known commentaries on the Mishnah, the Talmuds of Babylon and Jerusalem. Is it possible that there were others, and that all trace of them has been lost in the perpetual harrying to which Jewish communities were subjected by Christendom and, later, by Islam? The conditions which enable a Genizah to render up its treasures centuries later obtained nowhere in the damper climate of Europe; and the burning of Hebrew books was an occupation followed in many European cities of the Middle Ages. After all, only one copy of the Babylonian Talmud itself has survived the medieval holocausts.

[83] San. 32 b, p. 204.

[84] Yom., 53b and 86 a, pp. 253 and 426.

[85] Salo Baron, in the 2nd Ed. of his *Social and Religious History of the Jews*, likewise leaves the question open, while inclining to the autonomy and variety of communal organisation, II., p. 201. In his earlier work, *The Jewish Community*, I., pp. 122 and 142 he speaks of the possibility of itinerant preachers being appointed from Palestine, and of tours of the communities of the Diaspora by the patriarch. But in neither case can he adduce evidence that these were regular or routine practices.

and these Jews were prepared to welcome such interest and adherence. Paul might have had new things to say about the *status* of the Gentiles who accepted his message; but he did not have to argue that Gentiles had a right to hear it—they were there already listening to him in the synagogue or in whatever other places Jews foregathered.

This situation had grown up over centuries. In the historical narrative of the Old Testament there is little reference to the conversion of non-Israelites. On the other hand the successive editions of the legal codes recognise that a 'stranger' could be joined to the community of Israel; birth was not the only means of entry. A 'stranger' could eat of the Passover, if he accepted circumcision.[86] The worship of the God of Israel was, however, thought of at first as limited by the extent of the land of Israel. David, an outlaw pursued by Saul, accused his enemies of driving him away 'that I should have no share in the heritage of the Lord, saying "Go, serve other gods"';[87] and when Naaman wished to continue to worship the God of Israel after his return to Damascus, he begged, 'two mules' burden of earth' from Elisha so that he might continue to worship the God of Israel on soil that properly appertained to him.[88]

This exclusive connection between the God of Israel, the children of Israel, and the soil of Israel, was broken by two developments. The first was the universalism of the great prophets and their vision of the time when many nations would gather together for worship in Jerusalem; and the second was the dispersion of a large section of the children of Israel themselves into foreign lands. Both developments encouraged a missionary attitude to the foreign environment of Judaism. The natural theatre for such activities was the Diaspora, for the compulsory circumcisions of Idumeans and others, though no worse than the compulsory baptisms of Jews by the medieval Church, do not enter into the discussion.

We hear directly and indirectly of a number of converts to Judaism during the period before the destruction of the Temple. Sometimes the references are casual, as in the inclusion among the first deacons of the Jerusalem Church of 'Nicolaus, a proselyte of Antioch'[89] and sometimes we possess a substantial narrative. By far the most famous converts were the royal family of Adiabene who early in the first century of the Christian era became Jews.[90] Adiabene was a small

[86] Ex. 12. 48.
[87] 1. Sam. 26. 19.
[88] 2 Kings 5. 17.
[89] Acts 6. 5.
[90] The Adiabeneans are referred to a number of times in *The Jewish War* of Josephus.

Mesopotamian kingdom, but it is doubtful if many of the population followed the example of the royal house. Or the implication may be indirect: the works of Philo imply a considerable number of Gentile hearers, for his discussion of Greek philosophy would have been of limited interest to a purely Jewish audience.[91]

The preceding paragraphs have dealt with actual conversion and acceptance into the people of Israel. We must, however, make a distinction which arose naturally out of the increasing regulation of society in the period under review: acceptance of the attraction of Judaism, and acceptance of the legal status of Jews, came to be two different possibilities, and need to be sharply distinguished. The former was a matter of no interest to the authorities of the Roman Empire or the local governments within it; the latter had serious political and economic implications. The charter granted by Julius Caesar to Hyrcanus II allowed Jews within the empire to live in loyalty to Torah, and this had the important implications, first of imposing on the public authorities respect for the sabbath and holy days where Jews were concerned, and secondly of excusing Jews from a number of onerous public duties in which the worship of other gods might be involved. The chief of these duties was the decurionate, the system by which responsibility for local government was assumed, at their own expense, by families of a certain level of wealth. As local government included games and temple worship, it was an expensive honour, and a good deal of the hostility which Jews encountered in city states arose from the jealousy which their freedom from this burden aroused. It is not surprising that public law accepted as Jews only those who were born Jews. No other might claim exemption.

While evasions certainly did take place, for Roman officials were no more omniscient than their modern counterpart, this general situation brought into existence within Roman territory[92] a class known in the New Testament as the 'godfearers'.[93] It consisted of people (mostly men) who were attracted by the monotheism or puritanism of Judaism but did not take the step of becoming Jews. Maybe circumcision was a substantial deterrent, but there was the additional fact in many situations it would give no protection to their new monotheism. In any case the worship and teaching of the

[91] On Jewish converts at this period see B. J. Bamberger, *Proselytism in the Talmudic Period*, Hebrew Union College Press, 1939, Ch. 2. There is also a very valuable critical review in the first chapter of the whole literature of the subject.

[92] It may have existed elsewhere, but we have not the information to affirm or deny it.

[93] E.g., Acts 10. 2 and 22; 13. 16.

synagogues were always open to those who were not members of the community, so that formal conversion might well appear to them unnecessary. The situation was different when such an informal status was inacceptable, and we shall have to revert to the subject when we consider the Pauline mission. Before that we can accept that there was a situation with no clearly defined boundaries, but with knowledge and acceptance of Jewish ethics and theology among a wide circle of Gentiles.

10. PHILO AND HELLENISTIC JUDAISM

THE background to the whole of this chapter has been the vast hellenistic world within which the Jews were but one people among scores of others, and Judaism but one of the innumerable religions practised by those who were influenced by the hellenistic culture which spread in the train of the armies of Alexander the Great. Change of ruler, from the Ptolemies of Egypt to the Seleucids of Syria, and from these to Rome meant nothing in the cultural field; for eastern Roman society, in language as well as thought, was thoroughly hellenised.

Inevitably the Jews and their religion were profoundly influenced by the pressure of this all-embracing environment. At the surface level, it is evidenced by the number of Greek words which have passed into common Jewish usage. Sanhedrin is but the Greek *sunedrion*, a transformation which, as we shall see, may have important implications on the nature of the court which tried Jesus of Nazareth.[94] Not only is 'synagogue' an obvious Greek word, but the homely Yiddish word 'Schule' is also Greek, though possibly only at second hand. More unexpected is to find that the word piyyut, the synagogal hymn, derives directly from the Greek *poietes* a poet; and one could continue the list indefinitely.

Of more importance is the effect upon the idea which a word expresses when it is translated into another language. Basic words like *theos* (God), *kurios* (Lord), and above all *nomos* (law) had subtly different implications from their Hebrew originals. There were innumerable *theoi* in the hellenistic heavens, *kurios* was the common term for the saviour of the mystery religions, and *nomos* reflected but a limited portion of the much richer Hebrew word *Torah*.[95] The whole problem is admirably stated by the grandson who translated from Hebrew into Greek the work of the conservative

[94] See below, p. 163.
[95] Cf. Pfeiffer, *op. cit.*, p. 182 f.

teacher of Torah in Jerusalem, Jesus ben Sirach: 'things originally spoken in Hebrew have not the same force in them, when they are translated into another tongue: and not only these, but the law itself, and the prophecies, and the rest of the books, have no small difference when they are spoken in their original language.'[96]

This subtle change was recognised in later Judaism by the fact that after the first translation of the Hebrew Bible, that made into Greek in Alexandria and familiar to us as the Septuagint, the scholars of rabbinic Judaism used to refer to any such translation as *an interpretation*, and were more concerned with the explanation of the text than its exact wording. In fact such a text, when it was officially used in divine worship, was not merely read but elucidated to bring out the original Hebrew meaning. To the Jews of the Diaspora such translation and comment were necessary, because Greek was their mother tongue, and because in all their contacts with their non-Jewish neighbours they would constantly hear such words as *theos*, *kurios*, *nomos*, being used in their normal, Greek, context. They needed to be reminded that these words carried different overtones when they were used as the vehicle for conveying the truths of Judaism. It is, however, interesting that apart from the Scriptures themselves Jews freely used a multiplicity of languages, and had no such exclusive veneration for Hebrew as Muslims were later to have for Arabic, a veneration carried to such a point that it was seriously discussed in the entirely non-Arab Muslim state of Pakistan, whether Arabic should not be made an official language of the state. Certainly for a Muslim the ritual use of the Quran in any language but Arabic would be unthinkable.

The question which has constantly exercised scholars is the extent to which the penetration of the Greek language involved a penetration of Greek ideas into Judaism. So far as odd details are concerned, there is no question but that the familiarity with Greek shown by Jewish scholars enriched their vocabulary of ideas as well as of words;[97] but at that point the influence appears to stop. Such a conclusion would be consistent with the evidence offered by the New Testament, a collection of works entirely written in Greek, and primarily addressed to Jews and converts living in hellenistic communities, and yet, with small exceptions, wholly Palestinian in its thinking and manner of expression. Even Paul, who has been held to have been deeply impregnated with the ideas of the mystery

[96] *Ecclesiasticus*, Prologue. On the whole question see Saul Lieberman, *Greek in Jewish Palestine*, Jewish Theological Seminary, 1942.

[97] Lieberman, *op. cit.*, especially chs. 2 and 3. *The Greek of the Rabbis* and *The Greek of the Synagogue*.

religions, does not speak in a manner which would have been incomprehensible to a Palestinian or Babylonian Jew in his letters—that these Jews might have disagreed violently with the remarks of the apostle is not the question. They would have disagreed, but they would have understood his method of argument, and have known *why* they disagreed. The evidence of Paul is important, because we have no other writer of the time who moved over such a wide variety of Jewish communities, touching in succession those of Palestine, Syria, Asia Minor, Greece and Italy. In all he seems to have spoken, and to all he seems to have written, in the same way. There is nothing in the method of argument in his letters which betrays a close acquaintance with hellenistic thought, or implies that his hearers were familiar with such thought and needed to be addressed in its terms or with its ideas. If he points his arguments by using examples which would have been familiar to a particular group among his hearers—for example his analogy of ransom from slavery in his argument on the atonement—he was doing exactly the same thing as the rabbis of Palestine.[98]

So far as our evidence goes, there is only one Jewry of the Diaspora of which this estimate would not be wholly true. We have no evidence of independent Jewish activities in such great centres of hellenistic culture as Athens, Ephesus, Antioch, or elsewhere; but we have already encountered, in discussing the literature of the period, the activities of the Jews of Alexandria. There Jews introduced new vehicles of literary expression, previously unknown in their records, and made use of material which went beyond the superficialities of language or just the exchange of ideas culled from daily life; and it was there that the Scriptures themselves were translated into Greek.

The supreme exponent of Alexandrian thought was the philosopher Philo of whose life we have no details, but who must have lived from around the second or third decade B.C. to some time after A.D. 40. Philo certainly had the intention of rendering Judaism an attractive universal religion by expounding it in terms which might win the acceptance of the philosophically minded Gentile. As a historical fact we know that his work was wholly rejected by the rabbis who, a generation after his death, came to shape the Jewish religion in the discussions formulated in Mishnah, Talmud and Midrash. There is no reference to him in all this vast literature. But—and this is one of the most fascinating of the enigmas which surround him—the curious thing is that he frequently chose as the vehicle for his thought, not the new forms elaborated by his Alexandrian predecessors, but precisely that form which was being employed simultaneously by the

[98] E.g., Lieberman, p. 37 ff.

Palestinian teachers of Torah, that is the Midrash upon some passage of the Scriptures. In its Palestinian development the Midrash can be regarded as the sermon on a scriptural text; the number of interpretations which might be deduced from a given verse or fact was unlimited, and the widest fancy of allegory or deduction was not merely allowed but expected.

This was the normal vehicle which Philo chose for the exposition of his philosophic ideas; and it would be difficult to imagine one which was likely to be more confusing, or would make it more difficult to get a consistent picture of his thought on any subject.[99] It is possible that much of what he has written has taken this form because, in fact, his words were originally delivered on appropriate sabbaths in the Alexandrian synagogues before the usual diaspora congregations of Jews and God-fearing Gentiles. In any case one must assume that he felt that he was merely performing in the Alexandrian environment the same task as was being performed by other religious leaders in the mother country. Whatever the reason, it has done great harm to his reputation as a philosopher, so much so that one critic dismisses him as 'a preacher with a flair for philosophy',[1] and few have taken the trouble necessary to track down his ideas through the many works of his which have survived, and build up a single picture out of the results.[2] But when this is done, as it is by Professor Wolfson of Harvard, the result is astonishingly consistent. There are, of course, many fields in which Philo left the meaning vague; he admitted himself that he was not primarily a jurist when it came to the precise understanding of laws; and at times his opinions appear conflicting, as one would expect in view of the range of his knowledge and his interests, and the period over which he must have been

[99] E.g. in H. A. Wolfson's *Philo*, Harvard, 1948, in the single section 'Relations between God, The Logos and the Ideas' (a section of a dozen pages chosen at random to illustrate the point), the author has to quote no less than eleven different works of Philo, often including quite separate passages in the same work, to get the full content of Philo's thought. Nor would the titles be any help in directing the reader to these sources of his ideas about the Logos. They include such subjects as *De Plantatione*, *De Somniis*, *De Cherubim* and *De Fuga et Inventione*.

[1] See the discussion in Wolfson, *op. cit.*, I., pp. 95 ff.

[2] Three works on Philo are of particular value, *Philo Judaeus, or the Jewish-Alexandrian Philosophy in its Development and Completion*, by James Drummond, Williams and Norgate, 1888, *Philo Judaeus of Alexandria*, by Norman Bentwich, J.P.S., 1940 and, above all, the recent and most comprehensive study, already cited, by Harry A. Wolfson, published under the title *Philo, Foundations of Religious Philosophy in Judaism, Christianity and Islam*, as the second volume in his immense project: *Structure and Growth of Philosophic Systems from Plato to Spinoza*.

writing. But so far as all the main points in his system are concerned we can be confident that we know what he wished to say.

The method by which Philo worked was that of allegory. As Dr. Wolfson says: 'Everything in Scripture, from names, dates and numbers to the narration of historical events or the prescription of rules for human conduct is to him subject to allegorical interpretation'.[3] But this must never be taken as an indication that he thought that an allegorical interpretation could be made a substitute for literal obedience when it came to an actual law, or to literal acceptance of the veridical character of an historical narrative.[4] Those who took such a line, and they existed in Alexandria, he condemned as 'people who live as if they were mere souls unconnected with the body'.[5] Philo would have unequivocally rejected such a method of allegorising as is used by Paul in his letter to the Romans: 'he is not a real Jew who is one outwardly, nor is true circumcision something external and physical. He is a Jew who is one inwardly, and real circumcision is a matter of the heart, spiritual and not literal'.[6] The allegorical meaning which underlay every word of Scripture had been implanted in it, not to act as a substitute for acceptance and obedience, but to give to those who were intellectually and morally fitted for it the opportunity to understand the universal principles which underlay the whole universe.

Allegory is, therefore, the foundation on which he builds his philosophical adaptation of the work of the Greeks, especially Plato and Aristotle, though he was evidently familiar with many others and in close touch with the philosophical thought of his own day.

While Philo shows himself very widely read in Greek philosophy he could receive no help from it in the establishment of his main purpose, the presentation of Judaism as the universal religion of reasonable men. The God of Plato and Aristotle was very far removed from the active and intensely 'personal' God of the Scriptures. It had occurred to no Greek philosopher to see in revelation a source of knowledge, let alone a source of knowledge higher than reason. Nor did any Greek philosopher, in his search for the ideal society, identify it with any existing state or claim for any existing code of laws a divine origin and an eternal validity. In all these fundamentals Philo is original, and is entitled to the full credit for the

[3] Wolfson, *op. cit.*, I., p. 116.

[4] Creation in six days, or the extraction of Eve from a rib of Adam, he would treat as allegorical in essence, but such events as the migration of Abraham expressed both historical and allegorical truth.

[5] *On the Migration of Abraham*, 16.

[6] Rom. 2. 26 f. On the other hand Philo would have been quite at home with Paul's argument about Hagar and Mount Sinai in Gal. 4. 24 ff.

means which he evolved to express his ideas; in all secondary matters he draws freely and impartially on his sources, now preferring one now another.

The key to his basic problem lay in the success with which he could present for philosophic consideration the conception of a God, himself active in his creation, and yet related to it in a manner which could be approved by reason. It is here that his much discussed 'logos doctrine' occupies the key role; and it is important for the understanding of his whole method of work to realise that the 'logos' is not an idea culled from abstract thinking and having, as it were, a life of its own. It is, after all, but the Greek for 'word', and is thus a plain deduction from his allegorising of the Scriptures, being precisely 'the word' of God which occurs on almost every page of those Scriptures; and the Philonic doctrine of the 'logos' is simply the product of analysis of what was already conveyed by the Scriptures in the phrases 'the word of the Lord' or 'God spake'.[7]

The 'word' becomes in Philo the link between the remote and impassible ultimate first cause of Aristotle, the divine idea of Plato, and the concrete historical world in which we live. It is therefore vital to his whole system. Once he had produced an acceptable concept of the 'word', then at a single stroke he established both the reasonableness of the Jewish idea of an active God, and the Jewish claim to a particularly significant place in human history. From this foundation he could go on to defend, what philosophers would be reluctant to admit, the existence of miracle, that is the independent activity of God in his creation, and revelation, that is the direct communication by God of his will to his creation. This simple statement will show the measure of the originality of Philo; for the Greek god either did not communicate, or communicated only through the human reason and its capacity for abstract thought. It will also show why we cannot point to a single, neat, consistent picture of the 'word' as Philo used it. For it has to cover the whole area in which God is related to man. Philo accepted the belief that, in his own nature, God was incomprehensible; but he had to claim that it was from the side of this incomprehensible God, not from the side of human reason, that understanding grew of the world we live in. The 'word' is therefore always

[7] G. F. Moore, in *Judaism*, I., pp. 416 f, tends more to identify Philo's idea of God with the 'Pure Being' of Greek philosophy, so that all activity had to be performed by the intermediary 'Logos'. This would be more convincing if Philo's system was worked out in a consistent series of philosophic treatises. But, in fact, Philo was thoroughly Jewish in being as unsystematic as the rabbis of Palestine, and his God is certainly more than 'Pure Being' and was under no compulsion to communicate with creation by an intermediary.

within God; but, since creation, it is also the agent of God; and it is likewise in man, enabling him to understand and carry out the will of God. On the other hand, it is not as it became in Christian theology an independent intermediary between God and man, a 'second God'.

The 'word', linking God and history, made it possible for Philo to expound the history of the children of Israel in terms of the pursuit of virtue which was the goal of Greek philosophers. For the 'word' implanted in that concrete and actual history the universal ideas which philosophers sought and the human reason deduced. That is why patriarchs could become virtues, historical incidents had symbolic meanings, numbers could convey a subtle truth, and so on. For there was one consistent agent of ultimate reality working in the whole of it, the 'word'. In the same way, it was logical and natural that the 'word' should have been expressed in a divinely ordained law at Sinai; and, thus revealed, this law became the highest source of knowledge, judging reason as well as being judged by it.[8]

It may be that this whole line of argument appears unreal to the modern mind; but that is not of importance in assessing the significance of Philo, who was dealing in the categories of his own day. From a historical standpoint he was the creator of religious philosophy. Yet we have to recognise that he had singularly little influence on the development of Judaism. As has been already mentioned, no reference to him is to be found in the vast masses of rabbinic literature; and it is also true that there is little in the way of reflection of his ideas. One reason for this may be purely local and fortuitous. In the middle of the first Christian century, that is immediately after the probable date of his death, the Jews of Alexandria passed through a period of conflict and persecution.[9] Foreign Jews were forbidden to enter the city[10] (which may be the reason why the Christian Church does not seem to have been founded there until later), and Alexandrian Jews took a long time to recover the prosperity and tranquillity they had enjoyed during the lifetime of Philo. But there must be a deeper reason for the lack of interest in his ideas exhibited by his co-religionists; and it seems probable that this should be found in the fact that Christian scholars have exag-

[8] The latter, primarily in the sense that reason could explain the symbolic meaning of a law which, in its literal application was either impossible or apparently unworthy. Here Philo took a different line from the rabbis, who claimed of such laws that they were inserted in order to test human obedience to what was inexplicable to human reason.

[9] See H. I. Bell, *Jews and Christians in Egypt*, British Museum, 1924, pp. 16 ff. See also p. 10, n.l. for a full bibliography on the subject.

[10] See Marcel Simon, *Apropos de la Lettre de Claude aux Alexandriens* in Bulletin de la Faculté de Lettres de Strasbourg, 1943.

gerated the importance among diaspora Jewry and its Gentile sympathisers of the kind of problem with which Philo dealt. What they call 'hellenistic Judaism' was neither so separate nor so widespread as they suggest. The Jewries encountered by Paul were more Palestinian than Alexandrian in their outlook; and it is evident that the success of the apostolic mission arose, not from its provision of a satisfying philosophy, but from its ability to offer, in acceptance of the Crucified Redeemer, an answer to the *Weltschmerz* of the times. It would seem truer to say that the mass of Jewry, including the rabbis of Palestine, were not much interested in the problems Philo strove to solve, rather than that they rejected his views as heretical.

It was far otherwise when the Christian Church, as a body separated from its parent, had to develop its own interpretation of history. Christianity became as inevitably an orthodoxy as Judaism was an orthopraxis, and here Philo offered the essential basis on which Clement of Alexandria, Origen, and all their successors right through the Middle Ages, were to build up a Christian theocentric philosophy. He is more than the bridge between them and the antique pagan philosophers, he is the actual source of their ideas. The 'word' became the Second Person of the Trinity and with this development they could use the whole range of Philo's ideas. Professor Wolfson thus sums up his significance for the whole period down to the *Tractatus Theologico-Politicus* of Baruch Spinoza, written in 1670: 'Taken altogether, these principles of medieval philosophy constitute a radical departure from ancient pagan Greek philosophy—they radically change its theory of knowledge by introducing into it a new source of knowledge;[11] they radically change its metaphysics, by introducing a new conception into the nature and causality of God who is the main subject of metaphysics;[12] they radically change its physics, by introducing a new conception into the working of its laws;[13] they radically change its ethics, by introducing a new source of morality.[14] The changes thus introduced .... into Greek philosophy are as great as those introduced by Plato,

[11] Philo's doctrine of revelation as the highest source of knowledge. See Wolfson, I., p. 48, II., p. 28.

[12] Philo's doctrines of the unknowability of God (*ibid.*, II., pp. 110 ff.) and his personal activity in creation (*ibid.*, I., pp. 209 ff.).

[13] Philo's conception of the ability of God to perform 'miracles' (*ibid.*, I., pp. 298 f.).

[14] Philo's conceptions of the significance of the human will, which was not previously a subject of philosophic interest (*ibid.*, I., ch. viii) and his introduction of the new religious virtues of prayer and penitence (*Ibid.*, II., pp. 237 ff. and II., pp. 253 ff.).

and greater than those introduced into it by any other philosopher after Plato'.[15]

The works of Philo have been preserved for us by the Christian Church and it is to Christian, not Jewish, development that they provided an indispensable foundation. Later they were to provide a similar foundation for the development of a philosophy of Islam; and it is only in the period of Jewish-Arab symbiosis a thousand years after his death that his own people, albeit unknowingly, were to build up in a Muslim environment a philosophy of Judaism of which he is similarly the founder. To have been the inspirer of such a line of development is surely a sufficient justification for the words of his greatest interpreter, Professor Wolfson, that 'he was a philosopher in the grand manner, not a mere dabbler in philosophy'.[16]

This chapter was already in proof when I received *Hellenistic Civilization and the Jews* by the late Professor V. Tcherikover of Jerusalem (J.P.S. America, 1959) which will be an essential work of reference on the period for many years to come.

[15] *Ibid.*, II, p. 456.
[16] *Ibid.*, c. I., p. 98.

Book Two

THE EMERGENCE OF CHRISTIANITY

Chapter Three

AROUND A.D. 30

1. THE PALESTINE OF A.D. 30

ALTHOUGH this section bears, for convenience, the word 'Palestine' in its heading there was no such name on the political map of A.D. 30. It is used simply because there is no single name which covers the whole area in which we are interested. If we were dealing with the period between the two wars with Rome, we could use the name 'Judea'; for, during that period there was created a province of Judea, independent of Syria, which covered the whole area of our interest. But, at the time with which we are concerned, we have only the general supervision of the legate of Syria to give unity to the country. Under this general supervision were the two tetrarchies of Herod Antipas and Philip, the Greek league of the Ten Cities (The Decapolis), the Roman procuratorship of Judea (comprising also Samaria), and finally, a number of autonomous cities of Greek or Herodian foundation which were scattered through the country.[1] We should also add that the province of Syria came down to and included the Carmel range, and that the Kingdom of the Nabatean Arabs, later to be formed into the Roman frontier province of Arabia Petrea by Trajan, stretched across what is now the Negev to the coast, and formed the eastern neighbour of all the governments mentioned as far north as Damascus.[2]

The population was as heterogeneous as were the governments; and since important trade routes crossed the country both from north to south and from east to west, no section of it could easily live in complete isolation from the rest.[3] A Jew of Judea, who had

[1] *The Westminster Historical Atlas of the Bible*, Philadelphia, 1946, Plate XIV, p. 82, together with its descriptive text, gives the best picture of the political and geographical situation at this time. There is a map of the Greek cities in my *History of Palestine:* A.D. 135-1948, Oxford University Press, New York and Gollancz, 1949, p. 52.

[2] In the time of Paul the Nabateans occupied Damascus itself. See 2 Cor. 11. 32.

[3] That even the supposedly 'exclusive' Pharisaic Jew expected to live in amicable daily contact with the Gentile world has been shown by H. Loewe in *Judaism and Christianity: The Age of Transition*, The Sheldon Press, 1937, pp. 113ff.

business with the Roman governor at Caesarea, had to traverse all Samaria in his journey. A Greek trader of the Decapolis, or a caravan of the Nabateans, might pass through Galilee and a portion of Syria to reach the port of Ptolemais (Acre); and a Galilean pilgrim to Jerusalem had to pass through either Samaria or the territory of the Greek cities which split the tetrarchy of Herod Antipas into two portions.

The governments which made up the area were, indeed, small compared to others within the Roman system; but we must not speak as though they were a 'backwater' in an otherwise civilised world. Jesus was born in a 'small corner of a vast empire'; but that 'small corner' pulsated with life from many sources, and prospered from its position. The Roman system was harsh but not intolerable to the majority; and at least it secured external peace, internal order, and safety on the roads. Even after the tax collectors had taken their share, and even though that share was probably excessive, there remained more wealth in the country *as a result of its own activities* than there has been at any subsequent stage of its history. Palestine became again a wealthy country after the conversion of the Roman empire to Christianity, but that was because emperors and pious pilgrims lavished money on its supposed 'holy places'; it was a wealthy country during the Latin Kingdom of the Crusaders, for it was supported by gifts from all over Christendom, much in the same manner as Israel today is supported by Jewish communities throughout the world. But the Palestine we are dealing with was wealthy by its own effort not by any external act of favour, except in so far as the Temple half-shekel contributed by Jewish communities elsewhere increased the demand for material for sacrifice.

In the hey-day of the Renaissance it was common for painters to depict Biblical scenes in the rich costumes, and amid the gorgeous architectural settings, which were appropriate to classical or contemporary Italy. From the latter part of the nineteenth century onwards, it became equally common to depict the same scenes in costumes and settings appropriate to the nineteenth-century appearance of the country. All personages were dressed in the costumes of impoverished fellaheen and the landscape background was provided by bare, empty and eroded hills. Both representations are equally inaccurate though elements of both are true. There *was* gorgeous classical architecture and there *were* rich silks in first century Palestine; there *were* deserts and there *were* poor peasants (though they did not necessarily dress like contemporary Arab fellaheen). But so far as the general impression is concerned, it is the nineteenth-century picture which is wrong. Whittier's exquisite description of the hills of Galilee dwelling in 'the silence of eternity' is poetic licence not historical realism. The land must have been thickly populated and intensively cultivated.[4]

We can form no reliable estimate of the size of the population of the country before A.D. 70; and if we could we should be hard put to it to divide it up among Jews, Samaritans, Greeks, Romans, Levantines, Arabs, and others. But there were certainly too many people, and there was certainly too much prosperity, for emptiness and eroded hills to be the most obvious features of its landscape, or impoverished peasants to be the main element of any crowd or street scene.

In the political mosaic of the country Jerusalem occupied a special position, parallel perhaps to that of the Greek cities, Delphi and Olympia. To Jews throughout the empire and beyond its frontiers it was a holy city, unique and under divine protection. To its Temple they paid their half shekel and, at least once in their lives, they tried to visit it in pilgrimage. Within its boundaries many Jewish communities had their special synagogues, so that a pilgrim from any part of the empire would find congenial company and such help as he might need. But to those of the country itself who were not Jews it was a city of relatively little importance. It was not the capital of any administration, and it lay remote on a secondary route from the desert to the coast which crossed the Jordan just before its entry into the Dead Sea, a route less frequented than those south of the Dead Sea, or further north by Scythopolis and Galilee. In normal times the priestly and aristocratic families who controlled the city had little to complain of in the way of Roman interference. There was a small garrison in Fort Antonia north of the Temple area but for the rest matters were in their own hands. The times of danger were the times of pilgrimage at the High Holy Days. Then crowds from Galilee and abroad filled the city, religious fanatics competed

[4] There are excellent descriptions of the variety of costume and activity to be encountered in first century Palestine in A. C. Bouquet's *Everyday Life in New Testament Times*, B. T. Batsford, 1953. But to show how strong is the influence of the contemporary stereotype of an impoverished country, there is a vast landscape in the illustration of an olive press on p. 77, but it is entirely empty except for a few olive trees and some bushes. Likewise the street scene on p. 111 would be more realistic with less decayed Arab medievalism and a strong dash of the Venetian painters who delighted in classical columns and handsome entablatures. The typical city of first century Palestine was brand new, expensive and probably vulgar and highly gilded. On the other hand, the extent to which it is possible to link contemporary custom with the narrative of the Gospels is fully, perhaps too fully, illustrated by Eric F. F. Bishop's *Jesus of Palestine*, Lutterworth Press, 1955.

for popular attention, and the Roman Governor himself came up with adequate troops and occupied Herod's old palace on the western hill.

From the Roman point of view the most irritating and difficult section of the population would have been the Pharisees and their followers; for their whole attitude to life and conduct must have been impenetrably strange to the normal Roman mentality with its easy tolerance and still easier morality. But though they were irritating Pharisees were not dangerous; if seriously moved they might request martyrdom; but they did not propose murder. The dangerous elements were those infected with the poisonous hotch-potch of apocalyptic eschatology who, it appears, were especially numerous in Galilee. This element was always liable to be turbulent. Since it was convinced that supernatural aid would remove any disparity of power between it and the Roman legions it might break out at any time into violence. Such incidents are referred to in all the narratives dealing with the period; and it is natural that it was at the major festivals, when a vast crowd filled the city of Jerusalem, that the Romans on one hand, and the Temple authorities on the other, were most apprehensive that a spark would set the tinder alight. This special situation lies behind both the trial and condemnation of Jesus and the arrest of Paul.

At this period it is probably true to say that the bulk of the Jewish population—the amme ha-aretz of the rabbis—accepted Roman rule, albeit unwillingly. It needed another thirty years of harshness mixed with brutality to bring them to the suicidal point of rebellion. The two most influential parties, the Sadducees and the Pharisees, might differ from each other, but, so long as the former preached conformity and the latter resignation, they did all the Romans could desire. Both disapproved of the 'zealots', and their disapproval inevitably limited the influence which zealotry could exercise on ordinary men with a living to earn.[5]

2. RELIGIOUS PERSPECTIVE

It has already been said in the Introduction that the period described in the previous chapter is one on which Jewish and Christian scholars offer divergent and basically contradictory judgements. In the Christian tradition it is thought of as a period of decline, with progress only in peripheral and minority movements. In the Jewish

[5] For a fuller account of religious and political relations with Rome see Chapter 5.

tradition it is, on the contrary, considered a period of basic advance during which there was a gradual weeding out of dead wood—which was to be the tinder for the conflagration of A.D. 66–70—while the essential elements in Judaism took shape and gathered the strength which was to ensure the survival both of the Jewish people and of their religion in spite of the double disaster of the rebellions against Rome.

The account which has been given of the period in the previous chapter is one which inclines wholly to the Jewish view of its character, and rejects that traditional in the writer's own religion. A period so rich in developments, many of them unprecedented, in the religious history of mankind could not with any justice be characterised as one of decline. We have only to list some of its achievements to see that this is so: the inauguration of a popular worship based not on sacrifice but on prayer, praise and instruction; the acceptance by the religious leaders of an obligation to bring the whole people into practising a way of daily living pleasing to God; the establishment of Holy Scriptures *including history*, and the recognition that this involved a duty constantly to interpret those Scriptures so that they were applicable to the changing conditions of life; the belief that God spoke through these interpretations with the same authority as he had originally spoken in the calling of the nation at Sinai; the discovery of man as fully personal; the deepened understanding of the nature of sin and of the holiness of God; belief in a future life, whether by resurrection or immortality. The list does not pretend to be complete, but it is sufficient to confound the statement that this half millenium was a period of decay, of narrowed vision and of lessened spiritual insight. But, while the verdict seems inescapable on a purely historical analysis of the available facts, it carries with it important theological overtones, not all of which can be considered in the present study. One, however, must be fairly faced: *a positive attitude to the religious developments which followed the return from exile inevitably carries with it a positive attitude to the subsequent growths which emerged organically from those developments at the time of the Incarnation, and in the centuries which followed the separation of Christianity from its Jewish parent.*

To the Christian this is the period of 'the Pharisees', and by distinguishing them somewhat from 'the rabbis' some Christian scholars achieve a half-hearted commendation of post-separation 'rabbinic' Judaism; but to the Jewish scholar the period in which he would speak of 'Pharisees' has already passed. By A.D. 30 Judaism has already entered the rabbinic period of the Tannaim, which was opened by the successors of Shammai and Hillel (who died about A.D. 10) and lasted until the publication of the Mishnah, about A.D. 200. Moreover again the Jewish scholar is right, so far as historical evidence goes. There is a tremendous break in the political history of Jewry in the first century; but there is no such break in the growth of the Tannaitic tradition, though, of course, there are changes of emphasis within Tannaitic Judaism; and it is only in the middle of the second century that we can begin to speak of it as a single Jewish 'orthodoxy' or 'orthopraxis,' covering the bulk of the Jewish people at home, in Babylon and in the western Diaspora. But it was the early Tannaim with whom Jesus argued, it was by early Tannaim that he had been taught as a boy, it was the leaders of the first generation of Tannaim who did not intervene to frustrate his arrest and condemnation, although Acts records them as doing precisely that later on behalf of Peter and of Paul.[6] For the Gamaliel of Acts was the grandson of Hillel, and the ancestor of the patriarchal line.

The evidence, then, supports the Jewish historian who traces an unbroken sequence of development from patriarch to patriarch, from the House of Abraham to the House of Hillel. There is no point at which we are justified in saying that 'the election has departed from Israel'. If we accept an 'election' at all, then it is still with the Judaism which can trace an unbroken succession through lawgiver, prophet and rabbi to modern times. For, before the end of the period of the Tannaim, Jewry, with the loss of independence, entered into a period of abnormality which was further accentuated in the time of their successors, the Amoraim, by the loss of any central authority within the nation; and this period continued until emancipation in the nineteenth and twentieth centuries. This abnormality means that we cannot pass a valid moral judgement on the teaching of the Tannaim until we see how it worked out when Jews were able to express their religious convictions in a free society nearly two thousand years later. For a judgement at any earlier period can always be justly challenged by the statement that the situation was abnormal.

To say that there is no break in continuity does not, of course, mean that we can pass no judgement on this or that incident, nor does it prevent us from distinguishing between a development which seems to us regrettable and one which seems to us admirable. Nor, yet again, does it mean that we must regard all periods as identical in outlook. We can, for example, legitimately distinguish the period with which we are at the moment concerned, that around A.D. 30, from that a hundred years later. For in A.D. 30 the early Tannaim represented but one group, albeit our hindsight shows them to be the most important, within the nation. They were a minority, and in

[6] Acts 5. 34, 23. 9.

conflict and controversy with other Jews (including Jesus and his first disciples) and, like other religious parties in such a situation, they tended to emphasize distinctions and to insist on rigid conformity. There is evidence that the sterner doctrines of Shammai prevailed with the majority of the 'Pharisees' at this time and that the milder doctrines of Hillel won their decisive victory later.

Thus far, then, the evidence seems in favour of the point of view of the Jewish scholar. But it need not carry us to the further point of agreeing that the movement represented by Jesus and the Christian Church was peripheral to the main line of legitimate religious development from Sinai up to and through the centuries after the return in which historic Judaism was born. This view of Jewish scholars had unexpected support from the school of Christian historians who saw the origins of the Christian movement in apocalyptic eschatology. To this view Jewish scholars, knowing how decisively the main rabbinic tradition rejected eschatological speculation, willingly consented. Indeed, so long as Christian scholars themselves sought the origin of the Church on the margin of the Sinaitic revelation, why should they dissent? Curiously enough it enabled them to take a more tolerant view of Christianity than Christians did of Judaism. Secure in their possession of the central stream of revelation and inspiration they could easily hand over the marginal incidents of their history 'to be a light to lighten the Gentiles'. That 'the righteous of all nations would share in the world to come' was said by a Jew long before it was said by a Christian.

I am profoundly convinced that the origin of Christianity is not to be found in any peripheral movement of pre-Christian Jewish history. It certainly does not lie in apocalyptic eschatology, even though the earliest explanation of the career of Jesus was couched by his followers in eschatological terms, and in some measure such terms pervade the whole of the New Testament. But if it is not to be found in the apocalyptists, neither is to be found in the popular candidate of the moment, the Essenes. There is no question but that the interpretation of the mass of new documents which have come to us from Wadi Qumran and its neighbourhood will immensely enrich our knowledge of the varieties of Judaism current at the time with which we are concerned. But Essenism, with or without the new documentation, will not explain the birth and rise of Christianity.[7] For Christianity did not arise from the periphery of religious life in the centuries which followed the return from exile, but from its centre *just as rabbinic Judaism did.*

[7] See *The Scrolls and the New Testament*, edited by Krister Stendahl, S.C.M. Press, 1958.

I said above that '*a positive attitude to the religious developments which followed the return from exile inevitably carried with it a positive attitude to the subsequent growths which emerged organically from those developments at the time of the Incarnation and in the centuries which followed the separation of Christianity from its Jewish parent.*' I believe that to be true, and to be true of post-Christian Judaism. But *it is equally true of Christianity*. And that is the paradox that the historians of both sides must ultimately face.

When it is not perverted by the attempt to force it into the straight jacket of a non-existent remnant, the Christian interpretation of the period as one in which man as person came more and more into the centre of the picture is a true one. We have seen how Jeremiah and Ezekiel were troubled by the destiny of the individual man, and saw the necessity for the divine justice to be vindicated in the treatment of the individual as well as of the nation. We have the unique outpouring of personal devotion in the psalms. The individual is the main subject of the Wisdom literature. The pessimism of the author of Ecclesiastes is purely individual. Above all, we have the book of Job. None of this is peripheral. Concern with man as person is as authentically the hall-mark of the period as concern with teaching a whole community a national way of life pleasing to God, and of constantly deepening the understanding of what that way of life should be.

In this concern with man as person, nothing is taken away from the power or meaning of the working out in history of the revelation of Sinai. But, if that be true, it is equally true that something is added. The moment when the people of Israel stood before the Mount was not the beginning of human concern with the moral problems of men in society. There lay behind Sinai centuries, perhaps millenia, of experience, experience which was at the same time and indistinguishably human discovery and divine revelation. At Sinai that long and slow growth blossomed into its full flowering, even though men took centuries to realise what had happened and still cannot define exactly wherein that moment consisted. But the results gradually became clear and part of the unchallengeable facts of history—the growth of the children of Israel into a people unlike all other peoples, and channelling through their life as a people the divine power available to human societies.

Now another stage was reached in the full unfolding of the extent of divine-human co-operation, when, within the Sinaitic community and 'in the fulness of time', God could similarly reveal the full meaning of man as person, and Jesus of Nazareth stepped on to the stage of history.

This did not replace Sinai, nor could, on the other hand, Sinai simply absorb it and continue unchanged. It did not contradict Sinai, but in the life and teaching of Jesus the earlier revelation and the new revelation stand together in creative tension with each other. One of the sayings of Jesus whose authenticity we have least grounds to dispute—since it is inconceivable that the Church, engaged in full controversy with Judaism, should have invented it—is that he came 'not to destroy Torah and the prophets, but to bring them to their full meaning'.[8] The divine plan for human society is given its full meaning when the divine plan for man as person is revealed within it. In Jesus the ultimate unity is not destroyed; Paul still struggles to maintain it; but in the complex setting of first century life the two halves broke apart, and the beginning of the second century witnessed two religions confronting each other—Judaism and Christianity.

Nevertheless they are inextricably linked together *as equals*, for the tension is not some Barthian metaphysic imposed upon history from outside, but a simple and inescapable fact of ordinary human life—the perennial and inevitable tension between man as social being and man as person, as an ultimate value in himself, as one made in the likeness of God. Man as citizen must be concerned with the attainable, as person he is concerned with the unattainable; as citizen he must perpetually seek a compromise, for he is dependent on his neighbour's acceptance; as person he must often refuse compromise; as citizen he is concerned with the impersonal, and must not let personal considerations warp his judgement; as person he approaches every other person as one 'for whom Christ died' who must be made to subserve no other ends. The tension extends through the whole of life and to matters of everyday concern, and it will endure so long as this world endures. For man cannot live without society, and true society is made of men and not of robots. It is for that reason that the story of Israel is not *Heilsgeschichte*, something set apart from the ordinary processes of human life and reasoning, but ordinary, everyday, history. For the same reason the Jews today remain incapable of being fitted into our modern demand for a distinction between a religion and a people. There are Jewish groups who have accepted that distinction and proclaimed themselves the one or the other. In that they take their place among the peripheral groups which

[8] Matt. 5. 17 (my translation). When we translate 'plerosai' as 'fulfilled', we convey the impression of something which has completed the function for which it was intended—as New Testament writers constantly speak of prophecies being 'fulfilled'. In Elizabethan English, however, 'fulfilled' also has the meaning 'filled to the full', as in the Anglican post-communion prayer 'that we may be fulfilled with thy grace and heavenly benediction.' This meaning exists also in the Greek word 'plēroō', and is, I am sure, the right meaning here.

adhere around every core. But the core remains unchanged; the Jews are neither a religion nor a people, but both.

The destiny of what we must now call 'the Gentile Church' is equally determined by the revelation on which it rests: the ultimate value of man as person 'for whom Christ died'. Throughout all its long and varied history it is the power of the risen Christ to make new men of 'Jew and Greek, bond and free'—living today Paul would certainly have added 'white or coloured'—which is its glory and its strength. That divine power, which came to its full expression in the Incarnation, it rightly traces back through history, wherever it sees men as persons accepting the will of God and being changed thereby, as the author of the Epistle to the Hebrews saw them all through the history of Israel in his tremendous gallery of the heroes of faith.[9]

Just as the separation of the Church does not deprive the Jewish people of their inheritance in the story of the people of Israel, so the rejection of the Church by the Jewish people does not rob the Christians either of their inheritance. But they *share* the inheritance with each other, even though neither is willing to admit the legitimacy of the other.

When in due course we come to approach the controversies between Jesus and the Pharisees of the gospels, it is in terms of this perpetual tension that we must approach them. It is not a conflict between divine revelation and human religion; it is not an example of 'the good being enemy of the best'. Nor can it be resolved by the permanent separation of the two religions, or by the absorption of either into the other by individual conversion. It can be resolved only by recognition that it can never be resolved, and so must be accepted as part of the basic conditions of human life.

3. THE PHARISEES AND EARLY TANNAIM

In the introduction to his remarkable study of the sociological aspects of Pharisaism, Dr. Louis Finkelstein has these sentences: 'The Pharisees constituted a religious Order of singular influence in the history of civilisation. Judaism, Christianity, and Mohammedanism all derive from this ancient Palestinian Society; and through their influence in the preservation and advancement of learning, it has become the cornerstone of modern civilisation. . . . Fully half the world adheres to Pharisaic faiths.'[10] Such a claim will certainly

[9] Heb. Ch. 11.

[10] Louis Finkelstein, *The Pharisees: The Sociological Background of their Faith*, Jewish Theological Seminary, New York, 1938, p. ix.

astonish, and even shock, the ordinary Christian reader, whose knowledge of the Pharisees rests on the New Testament; and it is, indeed, so all-embracing that even Jewish scholars have felt that it went too far.[11] But, provided one remembers that one does not shelter under a cornerstone, nor can one, in fact, have a building with only one corner, it is a salutary reminder that by the middle of the second century B.C. the newly organised sect of the Pharisees had come to be the sole authentic heirs of the line of development which opens with the Babylonian exile and the return, and which is still giving the world the worship of synagogue, church and mosque, the conception (at any rate in the western world) of holy Scriptures, whether Old and New Testament or Quran, as well as making a substantial contribution to both education and law. Whether those contributions, which do not *originate* with a separately organised body known as the Pharisees, were advanced or debased by contact with Pharisaism is obviously a subject meriting the most careful enquiry. Before, however, we can undertake this, something must be said of their origin and development.

Pharisaism as a separate body first appears in the Maccabean period, though our earliest accounts of its structure derive from Josephus[12] a hundred or more years later. One reason for the establishment of a separate body has already been given[13]—the division of opinion about the authority of the decisions which were a practical necessity for the elucidation and application of the written Torah. But the form which the new organisation took seems to have originated in a different manner. For the Pharisees were as closely and carefully organised as the Essenes, and the number of actual 'members' or 'fellows' (Haberim, the word used in modern Israel to describe members of a Kibbutz) seems never to have exceeded a few thousand. But they radically differed from the Essenes in that their concern lay, not with each other, but with the whole people of Israel. If the Essenes shared some of the characteristics of a monastic order, the Pharisees in some aspects more resembled the National Union of Teachers,[14] although the basis of the order was personal observance of Torah.[15] The particular sphere of Torah in which their conformity

[11] See, for example, M. R. Cohen, *Reflections of a Wondering Jew*, Glencoe, 1ll., 1950, p. 137.

[12] *Bell Jud.* 2. 8. 14, *Ant.* 13. 5. 9 and 18. 1. 2 ff. Other passages from Josephus are collected in Schürer, *The Jewish People*, Eng. Trs. II: 2, pp. 2 ff.

[13] See above pp. 80 ff.

[14] cf. Travers Herford, *Judaism in the New Testament Period*, Lindsey Press, 1928, p. 76.

[15] See Bek. 30b, pp. 191 ff. Finkelstein, *op. cit.*, I, pp. 77 ff.

was obligatory and basic to the whole association, was that of scrupulous observance of the laws of tithing and of ritual purity, and this does something to explain why they have been the subject of such disagreement between Jewish and Christian scholars, and why both have come only slowly to the examination of their contribution to Judaism in a wider setting.

Wherever Christian Fundamentalism rules, the characteristics of Pharisaism are, naturally, described on the basis of the controversies in the gospels and the terrible denunciation of Matthew 23, repeated as it is in various passages in Luke. But there is now an impressive gallery of Christian scholars who from one standpoint or another have challenged the traditional picture.[16] It begins with the sixteenth century Frenchman, Jean Bodin, and gets its most notable expression, before modern times, in the great Cambridge Hebraist, John Selden, and the still greater Dutchman, William Surenhuis, who edited the translation of the Mishnah into Latin at the end of the seventeenth century. Thereafter the subject seems to have aroused little interest until the beginning of the twentieth century. Travers Herford published his series of books between 1912 and 1933;[17] and at the same time the American scholar, George Foot Moore, was preparing his two great volumes, *Judaism in the Tannaitic Period*, published in 1927. This time, the work was paralleled by that of two Jewish scholars, working in collaboration with each other, Claude G. Montefiore and Israel Abrahams, who made a detailed examination of the gospels, with the minimum of apologetic or polemic intention, and with an obviously sincere desire to relate the material which they contained to their understanding of the Judaism of the period.[18]

It would, however, be untrue to make any automatic association between the intimate knowledge of Pharisaism and a revision of the traditional Christian judgement. John Lightfoot, the contemporary of Selden and the most profound rabbinic scholar of his day, held purely conventional views of the aridity and lack of value of rabbinic Judaism. In modern times the encyclopaedic learning of the English scholar R. H. Charles, or the German Emil Schürer, was combined with strict adherence to the traditional view. For the latter, as for the

[16] There is a brief description of the development of this challenge in my *Judaism and Christianity*, pp. 142 ff. But, except for individual studies, the subject has not to my knowledge been systematically explored.

[17] *Pharisaism*, 1912, *The Pharisees*, 1924, *Judaism in the New Testament Period*, 1928, *Talmud and Apocrypha*, 1933.

[18] Montefiore's *The Synoptic Gospels* appeared in two volumes in 1909, with a revised edition in 1927, followed by *Rabbinic Literature and Gospel Teaching* in 1930. The two volumes of Israel Abrahams, *Studies in Pharisaism and the Gospels*, appeared in 1917 and 1924.

former, the whole matter is summed up in the statement that in Pharisaism 'the accurate observance of the ceremonial law is regarded as the true essence of religious conduct',[19] so that the fact that their teaching about God and man was a proper development of that of the Old Testament seems to these scholars a matter of small importance.

It is put in a truer perspective by the Dominican scholar, M.-J. Lagrange, who emphasises the authenticity of this development by noting that 'there was no controversy at all between Jesus and them on these fundamental points. He rather commends their authority as teachers when they comment on the law of Moses.'[20] But at the same time, he quotes Schürer with approval, and assents to his general judgement on the decline of Judaism as represented by Pharisaism.

Now, whether the Pharisees regarded their teaching about God and man as more important than that about ritual purity or not, there is no question but that the general 'modern' approach, whether Jewish or Christian, would so do. We must, therefore, get some idea of their teaching on the former subjects before we can estimate, in terms we should understand, the reasons for their insistence on the latter. Nevertheless we must not forget that, in some measure at least, their views on the former subjects were not necessarily held only by themselves, whereas it was in the latter field that their distinctiveness lay. We must, however, treat of these former subjects also because the Pharisees contained a large proportion of the nation's teachers and of the local leaders in the worship of the synagogues. They were perpetually occupied with the most varied questions of every day morality, and in the synagogue they developed a medium of great richness in piety and devotion.

This dual, and sometimes paradoxical, aspect of Pharisaism is presented in so balanced a picture by Charles Guignebert[21] that it is worth quoting in full:

'As for the Scribes, they may appear to be mere casuists and hair-splitters, but this is really a superficial view, which only considers the letter of their religion and not the feeling underneath. These

[19] Schürer, *op. cit.*, II, 2, p. 25.

[20] Lagrange, *Le Judaisme avant Jésus-Christ*, Paris, 1933, p. 278. 'Aussi n'y aura-t-il aucune controverse entre Jésus et eux sur ces points fondamentaux. Il a plûtot recommandé leur autorité comme docteurs quand ils commentaient la loi de Moïse.'

[21] Guignebert, *Le Monde Juif vers le Temps de Jésus*, pp. 95 f., Eng. tr. p. 71.

subtile dialecticians, obstinate and vain, full of absurd pedantry about trivial details of ritual and observance, were nevertheless at heart deeply pious, exponents of a religion characterised by a broad humanity. It is difficult to form a convincing picture of their attitude with its contrasting elements, for the modern world has nothing like it. But we should do well to bear in mind that far from being crushed or oppressed by the minuteness and complexity of their practical exegesis of the Torah, they were exalted and delighted by it. The Torah, which they made so burdensome, was no burden for them. On the contrary they rejoiced in it, finding in its every word the visible sign of Jahweh's love for his people. To the pious Jew, living in constant contact with the Law, which was in a sense his very life, the fulfilment of any one of these prescriptions, which seem to us so wearisome, was an act of infinite gratitude to God, who had deigned to vouchsafe this Law to Israel.

Delight in the Law is then the keynote of the lives of the Rabbis, and we must add to this, pride in the Law, pride in being singled out by Jahweh's special grace for the unique privilege of actually knowing the divine will and therefore being able to live according to it. They possessed in the Torah the very embodiment of that will; there they could examine his every act of justice and love, and contemplate the visible proof of his favour, and their hearts glowed with a perpetual gratitude. We must insist that the real concern of the Scribes was not juridical, but religious. It was not a matter of simply interpreting and administering a code but of setting forth the divine revelation and correlating the will of Jahweh with the realities of daily life. This explains the many Rabbinical precepts which are not the outcome of legalistic scruples but of pious meditations and moral considerations.

When we examine the non-ritual aspects of their religion we must be careful not to attribute to them a 'systematic theology'. Even the hellenistic Jew, Philo of Alexandria, possessed no such worked out system. His theology has to be discovered 'here a little, there a little' from his many writings. It is the same with Pharisaism. In 1880 a great German scholar, Ferdinand Weber, wrote a book entitled '*System der Altsynagogalen palästinschen Theologie*'. An equally great English scholar reviewed it with commendation of its vast learning, but with regret that it contained two defects: 'there was no "Altsynagogale palästinische Theologie" and it had no "System".' Today, as in classical times, there is no Jewish systematic theology. The Jews never sought to prove the existence of God and deduced his character from his activities, not from metaphysical speculation. It is typical of Jewish thought that the Pharisees are credited with discussion of the eternal problem of 'fixed fate and free will', but they accepted both.[22]

There is the same absence of philosophic or theological clarity in their explanation of their concern with the delicacy of attention to ritual purity and exact conformity with the prescriptions of Torah which the Christian world has regarded as their main characteristic. But the key phrase in their outlook is that quoted by Guignebert: 'the joy of the commandments'. Behind this conception lay the belief that is expressed in various ways in rabbinic writings that the world was made for Torah, not Torah for the world.[23] While this may seem strange to us, it is admirably illuminated by George Foot Moore in the sentence 'religion was not an afterthought of God'.[24] The same idea underlies the deepest aspects of the Philonic concept of the logos, which has, in turn, provided much of the foundation for the Christian doctrine of the pre-existence of Christ.[25] God, in the very beginning, when he was contemplating creation, contemplated a whole way of life for his creatures whereby the pattern of creation should be brought to its fulfilment. We come here to a point of particular interest in specifically Pharisaic teaching of the relation between the written and the oral Torah. Torah contained *the whole* of God's design for creation, and the whole of Torah was divine.[26] This Pharisaic belief is frequently used by Christian scholars to justify the charge of 'literalism' when they find them paying such attention to matters of ritual and ceremonial observance which, unquestionably, originated in the written Torah. But, while we may disagree with the way in which they used their discretion, there is no question but that the rabbis considered that they *had* discretion to select from Torah, to lay aside what we should regard as 'earlier' or cruder commandments, and to concentrate on particular interpretations which they did not necessarily claim were the original intention of the law in question.[27] They were, moreover, aware that

[22] Josephus, *Ant*. 13. 5. 9. Compare the statement (Aboth, 3. 15, p. 38) 'Everything is foreseen, yet freedom of choice is given.'

[23] See the quotations in *Rabbinic Anthology*, pp. 168 ff. The whole of this section is well worth reading for an understanding of the richness and 'piety' of the rabbinic conception of Torah.

[24] *Judaism*, I, p. 268.

[25] Wolfson, *Philo*, I, Ch. 4.

[26] 'Nothing was kept back in heaven.' Cf. Moore, *op. cit*. I, p. 112.

[27] Moore, *op. cit*., I, pp. 358 f. Compare also the discussion in David Daube, *The New Testament and Rabbinic Judaism*, pp. 259 ff; and B.M., 59b, p. 353.

there were greater and lesser commandments, and that, in the last resort, 'the righteous man liveth by his faith'.[28]

There is yet one other point to be mentioned before we come to discuss the particular scope of Pharisaic activity in matters of ritual, and it is a point that reminds us once again that the whole period is full of unprecedented events, whose consequences we can see in history, but whose origin escapes us. All are agreed that the Pharisees insisted on the basic religious significance of exact obedience to the prescriptions of Torah; but they accepted for many generations the existence of two conflicting schools of interpretation of how that obedience was to be put into practice, and ascribed to both schools a divine authority. On many issues the School of Shammai held very different views from the School of Hillel, but both were accepted as divine.[29] Dr. Finkelstein explains these differences by contrasting the aristocratic origin of Shammai with the plebeian origin of Hillel,[30] but this does not appear to give any reason why both should be accepted as of divine authority by both sides. One would have expected the majority to prevail, and the minority to be ignored, or even expelled. But, even when the Hillelites had prevailed, the decisions of the Shammaites were still recorded. The explanation of differing social origin—even if we accepted the curiously un-hellenic view of Dr. Finkelstein which automatically associates wealth with boorishness and poverty with good manners—does not seem to touch more than possible superficial differences of personality, whereas we are confronted with a much more fundamental peculiarity. It would appear more probable that it is a continuation of that particular attitude of mind which has preserved for us, within the same canon, two contradictory stories of the anointing of Saul by Samuel, and has left side by side the 'edited' story of the monarchy in Chronicles and the version from which the editing was done in Samuel and Kings.[31] In

[28] See discussion in Mak. 23b-24a, pp. 169 ff. On this passage the 613 commandments are first reduced by David to eleven, then by Isaiah to six, then by Micah to three, then by Isaiah again to two, finally by Habakkuk to the one quoted. The passage is discussed in I. Abrahams, *Pharisaism and the Gospels*, I, pp. 23 f.

[29] Er. 13b, pp. 85 f. where a Bath Kol so pronounces them.

[30] *Op. cit.*, I, pp. 83 ff. See also II, pp. 619 ff.

[31] It may be that we are here confronted with a 'Semitic' as opposed to a 'Hellenic' attitude, even if not expressed in terms of wealth and poverty. For the example of the two stories of Saul and Samuel shows that it was deeply rooted in the traditions of Israel, and this would be confirmed by any professor with Jewish students in his class—their instinctive reaction to a solution is not obedient acceptance, but to propose an alternative. We have also the interesting parallel of Sharia Law in Islam, which is

any case we meet in the early Tannaim a phenomenon which is to be a constant in Judaism, and in sharp opposition to the classical Christian tradition—the belief that the greater the truth the more varied will be the interpretations which can be properly drawn from it, a belief which does much to explain why there is no single or systematic orthodoxy in the Jewish tradition, and why the equivalent to heresy in Christianity is non-conformity in observance.

We come, at last, to the three subjects which the Pharisees developed as specifically Pharisaic teaching, and which they transmitted to their successors, the Tannaim. The first of these is the necessity to 'build a fence about the Torah'; the second is the absolute duty to pay the tithes prescribed in Scripture; and the third is the necessity, independently of Temple worship, to preserve a state of ritual purity. The three are interdependent, they are the basis of that separateness which some have seen as the origin of the word 'Pharisee', and they are the three subjects around which the controversies of the gospels revolve.

In relation to all three of the issues in question it is important to remember that the Pharisees had no power to compel acceptance of their decisions on these matters. This absence of compulsion was one of the reasons why the beginnings of Pharisaism lay in pious men binding themselves together by a common pledge that they would be punctilious in exact obedience to those matters of Torah which involved personal daily conduct, especially the second and third points mentioned, scrupulous payment of tithe and observance of ritual purity. Having pledged obedience for themselves they sought to persuade others to a like discipline, since, as we shall see, there was an inevitable separation between the observant and the non-observant.

The prescription to 'make a fence about the Torah' is attributed to the Men of the Great Synagogue themselves;[32] and we might find a justification for its antiquity in the conditions under which Jews returned to Jerusalem, and in the similar conditions which have affected Jewish life in the Holy Land ever since: that they were living

certainly Semitic, whether by direct Jewish influence or not. In the Sunni form of Islam, there are four schools of interpretation which are equally authoritative (Cf. P. K. Hitti, *History of the Arabs*, 3rd Ed. Macmillan, 1943, pp. 397 ff.), and, since there is no Bath Kol in Islam, there are special regulations as to how a suit is to be tried between adherents of two different orthodox interpretations (M. Khadduri and H. J. Liebesny, *Law in the Middle East*, Washington, 1955, I, p. 341).

[32] Ab., 1. 1. There are many fanciful explanations in *Aboth de Rabbi Nathan*, Chs. 1 and 2; but a simple and convincing analogy is given in Yeb., 21a, pp. 123 f.

in an exposed situation, not separated at all from other peoples, but continually compelled to mingle with them, even in their daily lives. If they were to be strengthened in their loyalty to Torah, then that loyalty had to be made so much a part of daily living that it could not be forgotten. There are three particular ways in which the 'fence' was thus strengthened: in relation to Jewish dress, with its prohibition of mixed materials and its special ritual garments; in exact obedience to the laws of the sabbath; and in the fullest definition of the dietary laws. Especially in the two latter fields there was a constant tendency to 'multiply commandments'.

To understand the attention paid to the sabbath we must remember that the world owes the idea of a weekly day of rest *entirely* to Judaism. The nineteenth-century struggle of Christian social reformers to secure regular rest for factory workers relied on the fourth commandment in the decalogue, not on any passage in the New Testament. Jews living in Palestine at the period with which we are concerned were in constant contact, and continual business association, with Gentiles to whom the whole idea was ludicrous and self-indulgent, as almost every Latin satirist testifies.[33] The request: 'surely you can do *that* on the sabbath?' whether from friend, business client or in relation to commercial competition, must have involved the ordinary Jew in constant temptation. Once his religious guides had begun to yield an inch, contemporary conditions would soon have made it an ell. But the determination to preserve the sabbath was not merely a negative or practical one. Its values were positive and spiritual. The Jewish home was, to a large extent, consecrated by the home observance of the sabbath. The Jewish woman, with little place in the worship of the synagogue or the lecture hall of the rabbi, was priestess of the sabbath observance at her own table.[34] The sanctity of the sabbath played a large part in preserving the Jewish spirit through the centuries of dispersion and restriction which the Jewish people were soon to undergo.

To some extent the same wider significance must be attributed to Jewish ritual laws about the use of food. They were designed to preserve positive values, not to enforce separation. In fact, just as any Jew might invite a Gentile to share his sabbath, so also he might invite him to share a meal. But the Jewish table was, in rabbinic eyes, a 'home altar'. It was to preserve this atmosphere at meals to which

[33] See, for example, quotations from Ovid, Persius, Petronius and Juvenal in Reinach, *Textes des Auteurs Grecs et Latins*, pp. 248, 264, 266, 291.

[34] Something of the mysticism of the sabbath, and of the precious part it plays in Jewish life is exquisitely described by A. J. Heschel in *The Sabbath: Its Meaning for Modern Man*, New York, 1951.

others were admitted that much of the precise definition of food was designed.[35]

In all these matters of 'fencing', we shall get a proper perspective if we compare the equally careful and close-knit 'fence' which the Christian Church in its elaborate Christology erected around the historic Incarnation and the doctrine of the Trinity. The Christian fence was a theological one, the Jewish one of conduct, thus emphasising the difference between the orthodoxy of the one religion and the orthopraxis of the other. But the motive was the same: to preserve that which was holy in itself, and also central to the religion concerned.

Secondly the Pharisees were especially punctilious in the payment of tithes on agricultural produce. There are in the Pentateuch two contradictory passages dealing with these payments. In Numbers the tithe is given to the levites who have no territorial inheritance in the division of the land 'in return for their service which they serve, their service in the tent of meeting'.[36] We encounter this tithe in the pledge given by the heads of families to Nehemiah, where it is arranged that it shall be collected by a levite and a priest, visiting each tithe payer.[37] But in Deuteronomy there is a different allocation of the tithe. The essential is that it is to be eaten *in Jerusalem* or sold and used to buy food *in Jerusalem*. It is to be eaten primarily by the owner of the tithe although, at the end of the passage, is the somewhat vague reference 'and you shall not forsake the Levite who is within your towns, for he has no portion or inheritance with you'. In addition there is a further triennial tithe to be consumed in Jerusalem, and in this the levite, together with 'the sojourner, the fatherless and the widow' shall share.[38] In neither Pentateuchal passage is there any statement as to how the tithe is to be collected and the plan evolved by Nehemiah did not work, since within a few years the levites are to be found going out of Jerusalem to work in the fields because they were unsupported.[39]

A modern scholar would scarcely be charged with impropriety if he dismissed the Deuteronomic passage as an obviously academic and totally unpractical and unreasonable set of provisions. But this common-sense solution was not available to any school of thought at the time. In consequence its fulfilment troubled sensitive consciences long before the separate organisation of the Pharisees. The

[35] See the excellent discussion of this in I. Abrahams, *op. cit.* I, pp. 55 f.
[36] Num. 18. 21.
[37] Neh. 10. 35-39.
[38] Deut. 14. 22-28.
[39] Neh. 13. 10.

book of Tobit is, by general agreement, pre-Maccabean,[40] but one of the examples of the piety of Tobit is that, though he lived in Babylon, he paid *both* tithes in full conformity with the Deuteronomic prescription as well as the tithes prescribed in Numbers[41]—three tithes in all.

This was the situation which confronted the Pharisees from the inception of their movement but it confronted them in a particular way. They were an urban rather than a rural grouping. They bought food more often than they grew it, so that they could not control the paying of the tithe themselves. But they became accomplices in disobedience to Torah when they bought or ate food which had not paid tithe; and (sellers, then as now, being what they are) they hesitated to rely on the seller's word that he had fulfilled the dual and onerous burden imposed on him. Their solution was to pay the levite's 'tithe of a tithe' on everything which they bought,[42] and to refuse to eat in any house where they felt there was no guarantee that tithe had been paid. They would thus invite an Israelite suspected of non-observance to their own houses, but they would not eat in his.[43]

The third issue, that of ritual purity, differs from those already discussed in that the Pharisaic attitude seems to have been largely of their own devising, and was not something which they had inherited from the more pious and scrupulous of previous generations. The written law contains a great many provisions about ritual purity in objects, and about the ability of an object which was itself unclean to communicate uncleanness to other objects or to persons who came into contact with it. Considered separately, some of these regulations must appear to us meaningless, except on the then reasonable basis that God asked obedience, not necessarily agreement based on understanding, from men in the performance of what he had prescribed in Torah. Nevertheless, taken as a whole, we have to recognise that these regulations preserved the health of many Jewish communities living in the insanitary conditions which the Gentile world too easily tolerated.

The Pharisaic stand rested on two presuppositions. One was the power of communicating uncleanness. Of what use was it to pay attention, for example, to the proper tithing of your food if the vessel

[40] See D. C. Simpson, in R. H. Charles' *Apocrypha and Pseudepigrapha*, I, p. 183

[41] Tobit 1. 6-8.

[42] Num. 18. 26.

[43] This is exactly the situation reflected in the gospels. The Pharisees were shocked that Jesus ate with 'publicans and sinners', but they would invite him to their own houses (Lk. 5. 30, 7. 36).

you cooked it in was unclean? As with tithing, the only solution was separation from the sources of uncleanness. This solution would be accepted also by any pious Jew. The second presupposition seems to have been explicitly Pharisaic, and Jewish scholars, who recognise that it was a subject much under discussion in the second century, are astonished that Mark implies that the Pharisaic developments were already well known in the first half of the first.[44] The development in question is the transference to the ordinary layman of rules of ceremonial washing traditionally associated only with the priesthood and attendance at the Temple worship. Ablutions were, of course, already accepted as proper in such matters as sexual relations; but the constant hand-washing spoken of by Mark was, so far as the written Torah is concerned, required only in relation to the Temple. The basis of Pharisaic action seems to have been the conception of the whole people as 'a kingdom of priests and a holy nation',[45] a description of the people at the solemn moment of their arrival at Sinai. The Pharisees thus took what Moore calls a 'supersacerdotal standpoint',[46] which could only be justified by the 'joy of the commandments' which lay at the root of their whole policy of multiplying 'mitzwoth', or opportunities to fulfil the will of God.

At the period with which we are concerned the early Tannaim were still only one group within the nation, and were at the formative stage in developing their teaching and practice. But it has been made clear that it was the whole nation with which they were concerned; they were not a group like the Essenes caring only to live their own lives in rigorous obedience to Torah as they understood it. After A.D. 70 the Essenes disappeared, and the whole burden of the future of the life of the nation was taken on the shoulders of the Tannaim. When we come to that period we shall see them modifying and developing their teaching so as to make it a way of life which the whole nation could follow, and did, indeed, follow for a millenium and a half with only one substantial schism.

When we come to examine the relations between Jesus and the Pharisees we shall be in a better position to estimate what must be put down to individual failing, what arose out of 'primitive' essays in development, and what arose out of the basic tension between the community and the individual person. That the controversies took place no serious scholar would doubt; but, if we are to understand them, we need to supplement the picture of Pharisaism which

[44] The passage is in Mark 7. 3 f. There is an interesting discussion of the question in I. Abrahams, *op. cit.*, II, pp. 199 ff.

[45] Ex. 19. 6.

[46] Moore, *op. cit.*, II, p. 76. Compare Finkelstein, *op. cit.*, I, p. 278.

has been given in this section by an examination of the gospels in which the controversies were recorded and the nature, both of popular messianic expectation, and of the claims of Jesus as Messiah, which lie behind the gospels. For both the dates at which the gospels were written, and the eschatological beliefs and expectations of the early Church, have had their influence upon the records.

4. JESUS OF NAZARETH AND THE RECORDS OF HIS LIFE

It is a common place of scholars to say that 'the Church made the gospels'. But, while that is true, it is only half the truth. The other half is that 'Jesus of Nazareth made the Church'. If we had to add that 'the gospels made Jesus of Nazareth', then we should be confronted with a vicious circle from which there would be no escape. And this is, in fact, the way in which the vicious circle is completed by various scholars who deny the Christian interpretation of the life of Jesus of Nazareth. Because I am concerned throughout this chapter with the relationship between the two religions, it is worth pointing out that the same set of three sentences can be applied to the older religion. Once we accept the fact of the continual revision of the Torah over many centuries, then it is evident that we could say that 'Judaism made the Pentateuch'. But that also is only half the truth. The other half is that 'Sinai made Judaism'. Here again we could join some Christian and rationalist scholars by completing a vicious circle and saying that 'the Pentateuch made Sinai'. There is only one escape from the vicious circle, and it is identical in the two religions; it is the belief, shared by both, in a divine initiative in human history *independent of the human interpretation of that initiative.*

That which made the Church was the life, death and resurrection of Jesus of Nazareth, *as it actually happened*, and not just as it is described by the evangelists or their successors, or as it is interpreted by Paul and his successors. In the same way that which made Judaism is what God did at Sinai, and not just the interpretation of that event by prophetic or priestly writers at any period afterwards. This is no condemnation of our interpretations. Indeed interpretation, according to the best knowledge and deepest insights of any generation, is a continual duty of both Synagogue and Church. But those interpretations are made necessary in the beginning, and grow and change with succeeding generations, just because the original event which is interpreted is an act of God and not an act which men, of themselves, brought into existence and control. Nor was it a single act, completed in one moment. The two religions live today because each act released a continuing activity of God; and so the human interpretation of that activity is a continuing process, corporate and individual, by which men in succeeding generations draw from an inexhaustible and life-giving stream which is outside themselves and exists independently of themselves. But because the act is in history, our past descriptions need to be continually related to our present experience, our past language and ideas to our present language and ideas. Theologian and historian are inextricably interlocked in any true account of either faith—except on the basis that neither religion embodies essential truth.

The particular question which we have to ask in the present section is: what was the nature of the revelation which came with Jesus of Nazareth, which those who accepted him expressed in the belief that he was the Messiah? It is not a question which can be answered by an examination of what men, at that time, expected the Messiah to be. The divine activity *is* limited by the human capacity to understand it; it is *not* limited by the human expectation of the form it shall take. Again I want to press the analogy of Judaism and of Sinai. If there had not been some expectation of 'deliverance' among the children of Israel reduced to degrading slavery in Egypt, then they would not, by any human calculation, have been ready to follow Moses into the uncertainties and dangers of the terrifying wilderness which (as they would have known from ancestral memories) separated the fertile Nile delta from the land of Canaan. But we can be certain that what actually happened to them in their passage through the wilderness was something totally different from their expectation. That the time was ripe for a revelation of the divine purpose for men in community such as befell them at Sinai was a historical fact even though at that moment it was known only to God. With our hindsight we can perceive the lineaments of the divine-human co-operation which made it possible and, indeed, appropriate. Even so there are nearly a thousand years between the day when Moses ascended the Mount and the time when teachers spread through all the nation to tell men what the divine Torah meant in terms of daily human living.

The expectation of a Messiah around A.D. 30 corresponds historically with that 'expectation of deliverance' at the time of the Exodus; but, as with that earlier event, it did not determine what the Messiah should actually be. And, as with the earlier event, the reality was almost wholly different from the human expectation. Jesus was not the Messiah as envisioned by the prophets. Not only was a personal Messiah not an essential feature of the messianic age as they foreshadowed it, but, even where he is spoken of, there is one basic difference from the reality of the Incarnation. No prophet envisaged a Messiah who would be rejected by his own people, or would depend for recognition on the personal surrender of each one of his followers. It is noticeable that in the first gospel, which consistently attempts to relate the life of Jesus to that which was 'spoken of by the prophets', the evangelist, or the collector of testimonies used by the evangelist, was able only to adduce the most trifling and anecdotal incidents as the fulfilment of prophecy—the place of his birth, his entry into Jerusalem on an ass and so on.[47] Those who have followed the subject in later times in the many disputations recorded in the history of the Church must admit that the evidence of prophecies recognised to be messianic is extremely meagre; and those who have examined the matter from the other side, that of Jewish polemic and apologetic, will not be astonished at the ease with which most of them were refuted by Jewish scholars.[48] A Messiah whose mission was to the 'outcasts in Israel', who was rejected by the leaders of the people, who made atonement by his death, all this was foreign to such messianic expectation as is found in the prophets.

The distinction between the prophetic expectation and the actual life of Jesus of Nazareth is not confined to the difference in what he *was*; it is even more significant in relation to what he was not. Though the figure of a personal Messiah was not a constant in prophetic visions of the future, all alike expected *a messianic age*, and that the new age would be visibly and universally different from the present age. But Jesus did not usher in the expected messianic age. As we shall see, the lack of any visible change in the conditions of life was one of the problems which exercised the first generation of Christians and made their apologetic to the Jewish people particularly difficult.

[47] The virgin birth, Matt. 1. 23 to fulfil Isa. 7. 14; birth in Bethlehem, 2. 6 to fulfil Micah 5. 2; flight into Egypt, 2. 15 to fulfil Hosea 11. 1; massacre of the Innocents, 2. 18 to fulfil Jer. 31. 15; settlement at Nazareth, 2. 23 to fulfil? (it is uncertain to what the author refers); settlement at Capernaum, 4. 15 to fulfil Isa. 9. 1-2; secret teaching, 12. 18, to fulfil Isa. 42. 1-3; teaching in parables, 13. 35 to fulfil Ps. 78. 2; triumphal entry, 21. 5 to fulfil Zech. 9. 9; praises of children in the Temple, 21. 16, to fulfil Ps. 8. 2; the betrayal, 26. 54 to fulfil? (it is uncertain to what the author refers); the thirty pieces, 27. 9 to fulfil 'Jeremiah', but actually Zech. 11. 13. When testimonies try to go deeper, they are evidence of the failure of this type of reference. The healings by Jesus (Matt. 8. 17) are said to be due to the need to fulfil Isa. 53. 4-5, a shocking misunderstanding of both Jesus and Deutero-Isaiah.

[48] See my *Conflict of Church and Synagogue*, Altercations, in Index for the early period, and *Judaism and Christianity*, pp. 128 ff. for the medieval period.

If Jesus was not the Messiah as he was expected by the prophets, still less did he fulfil the role allotted to a Messiah (where one is expected) in the literature of apocalyptic eschatology. The fact that one or two titles, such as 'the Elect One' or 'the Son of Man' are to be found in this literature as well as in the New Testament offers a parallel even more superficial than the testimonies of the prophets. It is a strange fact that the intervention of this bombastic and often ethically degenerate literature between the nobler ideals of the prophets and the actual coming of Jesus of Nazareth has its parallel in the earlier revelation also. We cannot tell to what extent the records preserve information as to what the Israelite slaves expected, but at least we can say that there are few, if any, lengthy passages in the historical books as devoid of ethical content or spiritual insight as those which describe how the children of Israel escaped from Egypt. Whether we look at the story of the plagues, at the hardening of Pharaoh's heart, or at the spoiling of the Egyptians, there is nothing to suggest that one of the great moments in the spiritual odyssey of mankind was approaching—and this is true whether we speak of evolving folkways or of the action of God in history. But it is just the sort of turning of the tables on their oppressors that slaves might have spoken of together in the secrecy of their hovels.

In a recent book[49] Dom Gregory Dix has put forward the view that we should take much more seriously than is usually done the claim of Jesus to be the actual Davidic heir to the throne of Jerusalem. In his view not only did Jesus so regard himself, but the whole populace also so regarded him, both in Galilee and in Judea. The connection of the Messiah with the Davidic house is, indeed, an established, though not universal, belief. But, even were Dom Gregory's point accepted,[50] it still would give no real indication as to the nature of the

[49] *Jew and Greek, a Study of the Primitive Church*, A. and C. Black, 1953, pp. 20 ff.

[50] Though the point is made very persuasively by Dom Gregory, there are a number of difficulties in the way of accepting it. Such a claim would, of course, be hereditary and there is no suggestion that Joseph was such a claimant, while there were many others than himself who were 'of the house and lineage of David'. In fact Bethlehem was once so full of them that 'there was no room at the inn'. In so far as Jewish memory linked David to existing physical descendants of his, they seem to have been found in Babylon not in Palestine (see *Jewish Encyclopaedia*, article '*Exilarch*'). Moreover it is difficult to believe that Jesus was universally accepted as a 'Comte de Paris' without its coming at once to the ears both of the Herodians and the Romans, both of whom would have made short work of such a claimant. There is in fact a considerable difference between Jesus being *a* son of David (a title which he certainly accepted) and his being *the* Davidic claimant to the throne.

life of Jesus. He entirely rejected the role of heir apparent to an earthly throne.

Nevertheless to say that Jesus was not the Messiah expected by the prophets, nor the Messiah of apocalyptic eschatology, nor the political heir to the throne of David, does not mean that the answer to the question 'art thou he that cometh?' should be negative. Nor does it mean that we can explain the Incarnation, after the fashion of Dr. Barth, only as an 'intersection' of the plane of history by a wholly other, wholly unforseeable, wholly incomprehensible, vertical plane which strikes the historical plane in the manner of an 'exploding shell' leaving a void, or crater like that of an exploding bomb, at the point of intersection.[51] Jesus came, on the plane of ordinary history, and 'in the fulness of time'—our time, the time of history.

It was said in the previous section that it was the growing consciousness of the separateness of men as persons which brought the time to its fulness; but this does not imply that it constituted the whole reason for, and meaning of, the Incarnation. The followers of Jesus were right to see that aspects of the meaning of his life and death were to be found in the Servant poems of Deutero-Isaiah,[52] that the increasing attention paid to the solemn ritual of the Day of Atonement prepared the way for an understanding of his death, and that the consciousness of sin which was revealed by that ritual, and by the sense that men were vicariously responsible for each other, found a deeper answer in the victory of the cross. It was factors such as these, and not the straight messianic expectation of the period, which ensured that men should be able to begin the process of understanding and interpreting the new outpouring of divine initiative.

The New Testament does not present us with a systematic and complete Christology. It records rather the beginnings of interpretation, and gives us a precious record of how the apostolic teachers gradually

[51] The sensitive choice of metaphor is Dr. Barth's not mine. See *Epistle to the Romans*, trs. Sir E. Hoskyns, p. 29.

[52] The Servant Poems of Deutero-Isaiah were not at this time linked with the expectation of a Messiah, at any rate by the Pharisees or the Zealots. It is possible that, when we have fuller information about the sect of Wadi Qumran, we shall find that a suffering Messiah had a place in their expectations, and was interpreted in terms of particular experiences of persecution within the sect. In historic Judaism we begin to find traces of it around the third Christian century, when the sacrifice of Isaac (the Akedah) was said to have atoning value for his descendants. See my *Conflict of the Church and the Synagogue*, pp. 116 f. I. Abrahams in *Festival Studies*, Goldston, 1934, pp. 92 ff. discusses the medieval use of the idea. See also the interesting discussion of it by David Baumgardt in *Commentary* for March 1950.

emancipated themselves from the conventional language of messianic apocalyptic, and from the attempt to fit the life of Jesus somehow into the pattern of what people expected of a Messiah. It is not the fault of New Testament writers that their work became a canon of inspired Scripture, leaving to subsequent generations a *damnosa hereditas* which gives permanent validity to their first crude interpretations of an event so portentous that we have not yet exhausted its significance.

Because they believed Jesus to be the Messiah, they sought in their apologetic to fit him into the pattern of the Messiah foretold by the prophets.[53] Though they brought the Suffering Servant into the scope of messianic expectation, it was still difficult to fit the career of Jesus into the traditional form. In Peter's second speech,[54] in Paul's two letters to the Thessalonians, and in much of his complicated argument in Romans we have the solution which held sway for at least twenty years. It was that there had been a *preliminary* coming of the Messiah to call men to repentance—a merciful dispensation of God, because (in their thought at that time) the main function of the Messiah, when he appeared in his full dignity, was instantly to divide men into sheep and goats[55] and take the former to the new heavens, while the latter passed into the evelasting fires of hell. There are no half-tones in the repulsive picture which Paul presents to the Thessalonians. When Jesus appears as Messiah he is 'revealed from heaven with his mighty angels in flaming fire, inflicting vengeance upon those who do not know God, and upon those who do not obey the Gospel of our Lord Jesus. They shall suffer the punishment of eternal destruction and exclusion from the presence of the Lord and from the glory of his might, when he comes on that day to be glorified in his saints, and to be marvelled at in all who have believed'.[56] This is the Messiah whom men shall see 'sitting at the right hand of Power and coming with the clouds of Heaven'[57] as the words are put into the mouth of Jesus in his trial before the high priest's council. The remarkable thing about this whole picture is not merely that it stands in total dissonance from the actual life of Jesus, but that it goes beyond what any contemporary expected of the Messiah. It 'outherods Herod'. Even apocalyptic rarely presented the Messiah as

[53] See Peter's first speeh in Acts, Ch. 2. From a literary point of view the speech may be a Lucan composition, but that it rested on a very vivid memory of what had actually been said on that memorable occasion seems evident both from what it contains and from what it omits.

[54] Acts 3. 20.

[55] Acts 3. 23.

[56] 2 Thess. 1. 7-10.

[57] Mark 14. 62.

'coming on the clouds of heaven' breathing instant threats and slaughter; its inconsistency with the Suffering Servant must be obvious to any one. But the idea has left its traces all through the gospels. Wherever Jesus speaks of the moral distinction between good and evil, there is apt to be added in conclusion a permanent division into sheep and goats and a threat of aeonian fires for the latter. Nowhere is the incompatibility of the two pictures more evident than in the lovely and tender passage where Jesus says that a good or kindly deed done or denied to the humblest creature is done or denied to him, and is made to add that, when he comes 'in his glory', it will be to say to those who denied him 'depart from me, you cursed, into the eternal fire prepared for the devil and his angels'.[58] An odd idea of 'glory'!

Whence does this horrifying picture, this appalling misunderstanding of the life of Jesus of Nazareth, come? The right answer seems to be that it arose from the picture of 'the day of the Lord', to be found mainly in the pre-exilic prophets, and the transference of an action which originally was attributed to Jahweh himself to his Messiah.[59]

What gives these twenty years their importance, however, is not the expectation which they had of an almost immediate return of Jesus to fill the conventional messianic role, but the use which they made of the intervening time. Even though they regarded it as short, yet it was the time given them to preach repentance and faith in the Jesus whom they had themselves known. For an essential part of the apostolic preaching was the insistence that they had been actual witnesses to his life, death and resurrection; and it was during this period that the memories of his actions and his teaching came to be embodied in the material out of which our gospels are made. And in the process of this activity the actual Jesus came to dominate over the imaginary Jesus of apocalyptic and the prophetic day of the Lord. They discovered that the continuing action of the living Christ was wholly seminal and in no wise eschatal.

It was in the course of their preaching that they came to take the step which was to make the Church universal; they preached to

[58] Matt. 25. 31-46. Compare Matt. 8. 12, 13. 41 f. Luke, 13. 27 f. showing how the idea of rejection passes with the evangelist into that of everlasting damnation. Note also in this particular passage that the words of Jesus, essentially addressed to individuals, are forced into a framework of a judgement on the nations. (v. 32).

[59] The issue is fully discussed and convincingly demonstrated by T. F. Glasson in *The Second Advent*, 2nd Ed. Epworth Press, 1947, especially Chs. 17 and 18. That the early Christians frequently transferred Old Testament passages from Jahweh to the Messiah is shown by the list of quotations, *ibid.*, pp. 159 ff.

Gentiles and admitted them to membership in their community. The unlimited scope and responsibility which was given them by the Gentile mission, and the necessity for constantly teaching and repeating the actual events of the life of Jesus, gradually led them to abandon the idea that the Incarnation had been merely a preliminary to a more important manifestation which was to come. When Paul saw the cross as itself the messianic throne, the need for a second coming had passed. We can see this from the development manifest in Paul's own letters. In the circular letter to the Churches of Asia, which we have from the copy which was preserved at Ephesus,[60] a pre-existent Christ takes the place of a returning Christ,[61] and, the Incarnation completed, Christ *now* 'sits at the right hand of God' in the heavenly places, and God has *already* 'put all things under his feet'.[62]

In John the change is complete. There is no mention of a second coming whatever and, though there is word of a final judgement, it is not Christ whose mission it is to judge.[63] The Johannine teaching is that 'he who has the Son has life'.[64] It is something which he has now, life is still to be lived in time, but in a new dimension; it is not something postponed to another world or a 'future life'.

All these stages were passed through in the apostolic age and within a Christian body which was not separated from its parent, Judaism. Jesus the fulfilment of prophecy and the agent of the day of the Lord becomes gradually the Jesus of the gospels and the Christ of subsequent Christian experience. The 'new life in Christ' becomes the centre of Christian preaching, the other aspects fall into the background, to return only when apostolic writings became in the second century a new sacred canon of Scripture.

5. THE JESUS OF HISTORY

If the ultimate evidence for what happened at Sinai is to be found in the whole of the subsequent history of the people of Israel, it is equally true that the ultimate evidence for the life of Jesus of Nazareth lies in all the subsequent history of the Christian Church, a fact

[60] That the Epistle to the Ephesians was more than just a local letter we can see from 1. 15. Paul would not write to a Church which he himself had created 'because I have heard of your faith in the Lord Jesus'.

[61] E.g. 1. 4.

[62] 1. 20 and 22.

[63] John 3. 17 f., and 12. 47 f., but compare 5. 22 'the Father judges no one but hath committed all judgement to the Son', which appears to refer to the actions of Jesus during his earthly life, and 5. 27 in which Jesus judges as Son of Man, but here and now.

[64] 1 John 5. 12.

which seems often to be forgotten by New Testament scholars. The New Testament, which records only the experience of a single generation, can never provide an adequate basis either for our appreciation of the life of Jesus or for the development of a Christology. To the schools of contemporary interpretation which follow each other with bewildering rapidity (and sometimes devastating result on the English style of theological writing) might well be addressed the warning given by the author of the Epistle to the Hebrews: 'Remember your leaders, those who spoke to you the word of God; consider the outcome of their life, and imitate their faith. Jesus Christ is the same yesterday and today and forever. Do not be led away by diverse and strange teachings.'[65]

The *interpretations* which New Testament writers have given to their experience is of only secondary significance and, in almost every case, they are interpretations which have lost all or most of their validity in the totally different circumstances and thought forms in which we express our spiritual experience today. The only matter of lasting importance is that their *experience* is the same as that of every subsequent generation of Christians down to the contemporary world, the experience of 'new life in Christ'. What was communicated alike by Paul and the writers of the gospels was a new and unique experience of a direct, positive and creative relationship between God and man 'in' or 'through' Christ. In the categories of their previous thinking, whether Jewish or Greek, there had been only two alternatives, 'God' and 'man'. They found it exceedingly difficult to intellectualize this experience and there is no systematic Christology among the New Testament writers, nor did they find and define a precise new place into which to fit Jesus Christ; but there is complete unanimity among them that somehow he belongs 'on the Godward side' while sharing also our human nature. It took the Church four centuries to work out a satisfactory definition of this paradox in intellectual terms; but the experience of the 'new life in Christ' was not dependent on their definitions. Nor is the experience of Paul and his converts dependent on the often complex and unsatisfying arguments he uses in his attempts at intellectual explanation in his letters. What had 'converted' him, and what converted them, was a new experience of the power of God flowing into their lives,

[65] Heb. 13. 7-9. One would like to specify among the 'diverse and strange teachings' such ephemeridae as the introduction into almost every sentence of such words as 'eschatological'—whether 'realised' or not, 'kerygmatic', 'typological', 'existential' and the ideas associated with 'ritual kingship' or 'Biblical theology'. Doubtless they have their place, and have contributed something to our understanding of the beginnings of Christianity. But none of them is an 'open sesame' to the experience of the Christian Church.

because 'they had accepted Jesus as saviour' by an act of faith. Though the New Testament uses the term, we have to be careful of our meaning when we use the term 'mediator' or 'mediation' in this connection. For, almost inevitably, the idea involved in these words is of a new stage interposed between man and his Creator. And this is far from the thought of Paul and his contemporaries. For they would not accept the existence of the first of the two stages implied. It is not that *we* have access to Christ and *he* has access to God; but we *in Christ*, have direct access to God and receive his power into our lives directly. The language, and the idea behind it, have to be linked to another constant in Pauline thought, that 'we are members of Christ'; we are part of that *corpus mysticum* in which the risen Christ and his Church are united and, in that capacity, 'have access to the Father'.

All this is the language of experience and not of reason, but exactly the same is true of the Jewish doctrine of Torah, which is as incomprehensible to the average Christian as the foregoing paragraph might be to the average Jew. Nevertheless, though the language is of the same quality, and the religious truth is equally profound in both, there remains the profound difference between the two religions that arises from their two centres, in man as member of community, and in man as person. Though Paul and his contemporaries would not regard a person as an isolated human being apart from the Church, yet the Church was not a 'natural' community, as was the Synagogue, but a body of persons who, separately as persons, had been converted, or predestined,[66] to faith in Christ. Even from the standpoint of the Church we come back to man as person. For the Church is not the whole world, even though it is gathered from the whole world without distinction of Jew or Greek, bond or free. It called, as Judaism did not, for personal surrender, and we are therefore thrown back on the question as to the basis and object of that surrender, and can find one answer only, the life of Jesus of Nazareth and its continuance in the risen Christ.

When we come to study our evidence for that life, we find at the outset an interesting piece of confirmation of what has been written above. It is the accepted idea of New Testament scholars, common to all their many schools of interpretation, that any Aramaic source behind our Greek texts began with a series of 'logia' or sayings. In other words, the Jewish Christians in the beginning recorded in their memories or on paper what any religious Jew would have recorded of his teacher—his sayings and not an outline of his life. We have

[66] Paul sometimes uses the term 'predestination', e.g. in Rom. 8. 29 f., but I doubt if he would have accepted the use made of it by Augustine or Calvin.

the parallel in 'Sayings of the Fathers' (Pirqe Aboth), which is among the earliest documents of rabbinic Judaism. But that soon proved inadequate in this particular case; and the sayings were quickly supplemented by a narrative of his life, beginning with the tremendous events of the last week, the crucifixion and resurrection. The corpus of Pauline epistles begins little more than twenty years after the crucifixion, and yet it is the rarest thing for Paul to quote the sayings of Jesus, and he never quotes a gospel parable to illustrate a lesson which he wishes to impress on his converts. He is concerned with certain events in the life of a Person which, he is convinced, possessed a cosmic significance.

In the gospels the picture is the same. The person of Jesus dominates his teaching, much of which, as we now know, can be closely paralleled from the teaching of the rabbis. This is told us explicitly by Mark in the first recorded teaching, that in the synagogue of Capernaum: 'and they were astonished at his teaching, *for he taught them as one who had authority, and not as the scribes*'.[67] I doubt whether the remark is intended to be derogatory of scribal teaching, or to imply that the substance of the teaching of Jesus was in conflict with that taught by the scribes. It was simply that Jesus expressed in his person an authority which no scribe would wish to claim, and that the impress of this authority was inescapable wherever he went and whenever he spoke or healed.[68] The vivid pictures which the style of Mark is so well calculated to convey succeed one another throughout his gospel, and always at the centre is the same thing, a man with an astonishing personal ascendancy and authority. It is this picture of a glowing and compelling personality which links together the synoptic and the fourth gospels,[69] and which is common to all the apostolic writings.

[67] Mark 1. 22.

[68] E.g. Mark 1. 24, where a man with an unclean spirit recognises his authority; 27, where the bystanders similarly recognise it; and so throughout the gospel.

[69] Every time I read it, I become more convinced that the fourth gospel is by John the apostle, written with the strange perspective of extreme old age. Our picture of John has been so distorted by Christian art, and, for example, by the picture of an emotional adolescent portrayed in Dorothy Sayers, *The Man Born to be King*, that we entirely forget that the name given him and his brother by Jesus was 'Sons of Thunder', and this the gospel perfectly reflects. In the egocentricity, the violence, and the unfairness which break through in the portrait of Jesus in the fourth gospel (e.g. 8. 44, 55; 10. 8 and in many of the passages where Jesus makes his messianic claims in a deliberately mystifying fashion), we have exactly the John of Luke 9. 49-50 and 51-56; or of Matt. 20. 20. But in the overpowering impression of a Person we have surely the memory of an eyewitness.

Nowhere in the gospels is the impression of a unique personality more prominent than in the constant stories of the healing power of Jesus. Jewish scholars have sometimes drawn attention to the contrast between the profound belief in demonic possession to be found in the New Testament and the Christian Church, and the more rational attitude to sickness in Judaism; and it is true that for many centuries Jews were pioneers in all medical matters. Kings, popes and bishops, who expelled and persecuted Jewish communities, were apt to make exceptions for their own doctors. But, while the language may lend itself to superstitious interpretation, we must remember that the words 'psychology', 'neurosis' and 'psychosomatic' had not yet been invented, nor the facts they represent distinguished in the study of the human body and the human personality. The intimate connection between physical and spiritual sickness was recognised by Jesus in one of his earliest recorded healings by the question: 'Which is easier, to say to the paralytic, "Your sins are forgiven", or to say, "Rise, take up your pallet and walk"?'[70] Throughout his career what we should call the neurotic and psychotic recognised the force of his personality and its authority over themselves, and today we are beginning to recognise that almost all diseases have a relationship of both cause and effect to the personality of the sufferer.

The most convincing evidence for the authenticity of this picture is that there is nothing in previous history which prepared men to expect it. We can dismiss the constant eschatological overtones inserted into the gospels, and present elsewhere, because we can see exactly where they came from and why they have intruded into the New Testament. But no expectation of a Messiah prepared men to expect someone whose Person dominated his teaching and determined his influence in the way which the gospels record. In all the writings of Paul there is a vivid contrast between the laboured, and sometimes unsuccessful, argumentation with which he attempts the intellectual explanation of his beliefs, and the utterly spontaneous and whole-hearted conviction which possesses and uplifts him once his subject is the power which flows into his life, and into the life of the Church, from the Person of the risen Christ. For this there is no source in previous Jewish history; there is only one possible source, that this was, in fact, the basis and meaning of the Incarnation.

The second point which impressed the contemporaries of Jesus, and is reflected in his own sayings, is the universality of his recognition of men as persons. There is no hesitation in the belief of the teachers of Torah, and of their successors in the Pharisees and Tannaim, that they were concerned with the whole people of Israel.

[70] Mark 2. 9.

But they taught through the synagogues and the rabbinic academies, and expected the people to come to them. There was an underlying tendency to look down on and despise those who rejected their teaching, or did not trouble to become familiar with it. As has already been explained,[71] there was a valid reason for a certain element of separatism, but it is also true that there was a long and painful struggle before the rabbinic leaders overcame the belief of their followers that those less strict than themselves, or even totally non-observant, were right outside the covenant relationship between God and the people of Israel.[72] There is nothing improbable in the idea that John may have overheard a follower of Shammai exclaim 'This crowd, who do not know the law, are accursed.'[73] For Jesus, on the other hand, it was these people who were the especial concern of his ministry, as is attested not merely by his sayings, but by his actions. 'I was sent only to the lost sheep of the house of Israel', 'those who are well have no need of a physician, but those who are sick', the parables of the ninety and nine sheep, or the lost piece of silver, attest this as clearly as his eating with 'publicans and sinners', or his staying with Zacchaeus.[74] But it is not on single sayings or incidents that we need to rely. The whole character of the Galilean mission, and of the appearance of Jesus in Jerusalem, bear the same testimony. He did not wait for people to come to him; he went out to them, and wherever he went 'the common people heard him gladly'. His teaching and his healing powers were available to all who sought him, and all who came to him he treated as persons in their own right.

Just as man as person was the object of his teaching, so also man as person was the subject. His teaching was not 'eschatological,' and even the phrase coined by Professor Dodd, 'realised eschatology', misinterprets it. For, in some form or other, eschatological belief implied the 'passing away' of an 'age' and its substitution by a 'new' age; and the phrase 'realised eschatology' merely transfers this passage from the absolute future to a future implied in a change which begins in the present, but which belongs in its fulness to a future. Jesus certainly saw his coming as a fulfilment;[75] but a fulfilment, as already suggested,[76] means 'bringing to its full meaning' as well as 'bringing to an end or completion', and it is the former meaning which is consistent with the general tenor of his teaching. For he

[71] Supra, p. 140.
[72] See below pp. 271 f.
[73] John 7. 49.
[74] Matt. 15. 24, Mark 2. 17, Matt. 18. 12, Luke 15. 1, 3-8, 19. 2.
[75] Mark 1. 15, Luke 4. 21.
[76] See above, p. 131.

taught that the reign of God existed here and now, and that it depended on our personal attitude whether we were within or outside its scope,—'if it is by the finger of God that I cast out demons, then the kingdom of God *has come upon you*', or again 'The kingdom of God is in the midst of you'.[77]

There is nothing in the history of the last two thousand years to suggest that the world of Sinai, based on man's natural but inevitable relationships, in the family, the village, the city and the state, had in fact passed away, and that a new age, based on men's choice of relationships, has taken its place. If Jesus saw the two forms of relationship as mutually exclusive alternatives, one of which must pass to give way to the other, then we can only say that he was wrong. The Church, which will be considered in a later section,[78] was a new society, based on a new principle, but it did not replace the existing divine order. When Jesus opened his ministry in Galilee, his first proclamation comes to us in words that do inevitably suggest the passing away of the old: 'the time is fulfilled, the kingdom of God is at hand; repent, and believe in the Gospel.'[79] But it is legitimate to question whether the words originally used would have borne the same connotation. Behind the word 'repent' is the Greek *metanoeité* which has the implication 'change your outlook', and behind that in turn is the Aramaic word which goes back to the Hebrew of the Old Testament 'turn back to God'. Neither have the implication of 'be sorry for your past sins' which 'repent' conveys to us. Moreover the words 'is at hand' can mean 'at hand' in the spatial as well as the temporal sense, whether we take the English, Greek or Aramaic.[80] What Jesus proclaimed was, then, 'turn back to God and His kingdom is all round you', and this meaning is borne out by his other teaching, as well as by many of the parables of the kingdom. The kingdom—or kingship—of God is not something new; it is something which has always been there, but which had, in the teaching of Jesus, reached a fuller meaning than men had hitherto given it.

[77] Luke 11. 20, 17. 21. The Revised Version gives this as a possible translation, but prefers 'within you'.

[78] See below, pp. 178 ff.

[79] Mark 1. 15.

[80] The philological question is too complicated to treat in full, but the general position is as follows. There is no doubt about the word for 'repent'; its Aramaic equivalent means properly return (to God); but it is impossible to be certain what Aramaic word lies behind the Greek 'eggus' which refers to both time and space like the English 'near'. The word used in the Syriac Version of Mark refers only to time, but this is not conclusive, since the Syriac is itself a translation of the Greek. On the other hand, there are words Jesus could have used with both meanings. In Luke 10. 9 'eggus' (in form eggiken) is certainly spatial and not temporal.

Certain New Testament scholars have suggested that Jesus delivered a *new* Torah,[81] and there is little doubt that Matthew collected his teaching together as 'The Sermon on the Mount' to parallel the giving of the Law from Mount Sinai, and to serve as a basis for a Church lectionary.[82] But that Jesus did not think of his teaching as being a 'new' Torah in opposition to, or distinction from, the 'old' is shown by two passages whose authenticity is guaranteed by the fact that it would be inconceivable for the Church to have invented them in the middle of the controversy with the rabbis which led to the separation of the two religions. On one occasion Jesus said 'Think not that I have come to abolish the law and the prophets; I have come not to abolish them but to fulfil them.'[83] On another, when he was denouncing what he regarded as errors in Pharisaic Judaism, he said 'the scribes and the Pharisees sit on Moses' seat; so practise and observe whatever they tell you, but not what they do; for they preach but do not practise.'[84]

The positive attitude of Jesus to Torah is best discovered in the series of sayings in the Sermon on the Mount which begin with 'You have heard that it was said to the men of old . . . but I say to you'[85] Here Jesus uses the familiar rabbinic formula by which what we would regard as crude and 'primitive' enactments were modified by the citation of some other passage of Torah which corrected them. But he uses the formula with a difference consistent with what has already been said of his mission. A scribe would not say 'but *I* say unto you'; he would say 'but learn also to say'. If we take the separate subjects on which Jesus speaks in these sayings, they have one common characteristic: they ask of men that they should go beyond what any community could embody in its laws. The question of the validity of law in itself does not arise, it is the attitude of the individual person with which Jesus is concerned. We could summarise them in deliberately banal language by saying that 'if a community is to be just, its members must be generous', and we can see that this is true in the everyday affairs of any society.

Finally we have to consider his own choice as to the nature of his mission, his conception of the relationship between God as person and man as person. At the beginning of his ministry we have the story

[81] See, for example, W. D. Davies, *Paul and Rabbinic Judaism*, S.P.C.K., 1948, ch. 7.

[82] G. D. Kilpatrick, *The Origins of the Gospel according to St. Matthew*, Oxford, 1946, ch. 5.

[83] Matt. 5. 17.

[84] Matt. 23. 2.

[85] Matt. 5, 21-end. See D. Daube, *The New Testament and Rabbinic Judaism*, London University, 1956, pp. 55 ff.

of the Temptation, and the rejection of any imposed solution on the world's ills. Jesus rejected successively in his own mind the political, the 'philanthropic' and the miraculous (or eschatological) opportunities which he believed to be available to him. He refused to seek political authority and to provide the world compulsorily with a just government; he refused to use his powers to solve automatically the world's problems of poverty, homelessness and suffering; and he refused to provide it with a religion whose divine authority should be objectively provable and beyond question.[86] Here, at the very beginning, the whole apocalyptic and eschatological scheme of things is rejected. He refused to make any change from outside in the world as it was, or to inaugurate any 'new age', political, social *or religious*.

It is, however, in the events with which his life terminated that the full meaning of his personality and his mission, in terms of the divine-human relationship expressed in terms of personality, reaches its fulfilment. The Mystery of the Cross remains the centre of the Christian faith as an expression of victorious suffering which is both human and divine, and distinguishes most clearly the religions of Sinai and Calvary, as they have developed on the scene of history. Nevertheless it is again an error to seek an interpretation based on the entry of something absolutely new into the plane of history—the vertical bomb of Barth exploding and making a crater-vacuum in the historic scene. The Cross fills to the full an insight as to the divine nature already present in Jewish lawgiver and prophet. In spite of the strong influence of Aristotle in the development of Jewish theology during the period of symbiosis with Arab speculation approximately a thousand years later, the God of Judaism is neither the 'prime mover who is himself unmoved' of Aristotle, nor the completely transcendent and impassible Allah of Islam.

It was a commonplace with the prophets that God was moved to joy and sorrow by the obedience or disobedience of his people, and they were not strangers to the idea that he suffered with their suffering. The strongest link between Philo and the rabbis, who knew nothing of his existence, was the common conviction that God was himself implicated in every aspect of his creation. Philo expressed it in the doctrine that the logos originates in God's divine conception of creation; the rabbis expressed it more naively in the quaint conceit that God himself spent a certain amount of every day in the study of Torah.[87] Moreover, the belief that God would redeem his children is fundamental to Judaism. Whatever may or may not have been the influence of mystery religions on Paul, he had no need to step a pace

[86] Matt. 4. 1-11, Luke 4. 1-13.
[87] Wolfson, *Philo*, I, ch. iv, A.Z., 3b., p. 79.

outside his Jewish tradition to see in the Cross the instrument by which God, always implicated to the full in his own creation, effected that redemption. Paul's statement to the Corinthians that 'God was in Christ reconciling the world to himself'[88] was one with which Jews might have disagreed, but it was one which they would have understood.

It is important for our understanding to recognise that the action of Jesus in the last weeks was deliberate, and the result only of his own initiative. He was not being actively pursued by the authorities, either Jewish or Roman; and, if he had considered his life in danger within either the Roman territory of Judea or the Herodian tetrarchies, he could easily have retired to the well organised Jewish communities of the Diaspora, and there continued his mission of preaching and healing. But it is evident that he knew that that aspect of his task was completed, even though his mission had lasted at the most for three years, or, more probably, for little more than one.

The question which we have to ask is: with what purpose did he make this last journey to Jerusalem? The gospel narratives tell us that he expected it, in worldly terms, to be unsuccessful, and to lead to his own death. But we must still ask: at whose hands and why? And here the gospels themselves give us very little help. For the events which succeeded each other between the time when Jesus disappeared with his guard within the doors of the high-priestly palace and when he appeared again from the palace of the Roman governor, could only be pieced together by hearsay. None of his followers were present. Hence we have a series of difficulties, about which whole volumes have been written, in that, firstly, the narratives of the trial or trials show profound disagreements with each other, secondly that the procedures adopted are incomprehensible from our knowledge of both Jewish and Roman law, and thirdly that nowhere was a crime alleged which would have led, by judicial procedure, to a capital sentence following immediately upon a proper trial.

Christian scholars have, perhaps, been too unwilling to listen to the objections which Jewish scholars have long made to these narratives. It is true that our knowledge of Jewish judicial procedure comes from documents written down more than a hundred and fifty years later. But we have to remember that the Mishnah of A.D. 200 codified practices which were already well established and had long been discussed; and that the original collection of these practices had been made by Johanan ben Zakkai immediately after the war of 70, not on the basis of working out a new procedure, but on that of collecting all he could of what had been the practice before the war

[88] 2 Cor. 5. 19.

with Rome. By the evidence of the Mishnah not only was a sudden trial by night completely illegal, but no evidence was produced at the trial of Jesus which would have justified a capital sentence. From the standpoint of a court, the statement that Jesus would destroy the Temple and rebuild it miraculously was merely an idle boast and not actionable at all; the second charge, that by claiming to be the Messiah he was committing blasphemy, is more complicated. In itself it was not blasphemy, which was defined as definitely cursing the Name of God;[89] and it would be difficult to find evidence, even in the fourth gospel, on which he could have been tried on the alternative charge of inviting the worship of himself. This would have been the capital offence of encouraging idolatry, and so akin to blasphemy.

We may, however, with advantage turn at this point from the gospel narratives to Jewish tradition about the death of Jesus. Though the references are extremely few and extremely vague Talmudic tradition knows nothing of a death sentence at the hands of the Romans, but substitutes death by stoning at Jewish hands, after a properly conducted trial for inducing Jews into idolatry—'deceiving Israel'.[90] From a Jewish standpoint the Christology of the earliest Church, acclaiming Jesus as 'Lord' and 'Son of God',[91] was idolatrous, and the fine distinction between the legal offences of 'blasphemy' and 'inducing idolatry' may well have been missed by those not familiar with the language of the law-courts.

[89] Hyman E. Goldin, *The Case of the Nazarene Re-opened*, New York, 1948, pp. 420 ff. This is a rather curious book which has, so far as I know, been completely ignored by Christian scholarship. This may be because its first three hundred pages contain a crude cross-examination of the evangelists, on the basis of the verbal inspiration of their writings. A liberal scholar finds it impossibly tedious and a fundamentalist is not likely to read it. But in the next two hundred pages is a very detailed and documented examination of the trials themselves which should not be ignored, in spite of the imaginary form in which it is cast (the hearing of expert witnesses at a trial), because its examination of Talmudic and Roman law, and of Christian attempts to reconcile them with the trial narratives, is the most exhaustive with which I am acquainted, though one might add that—as with other witnesses in that trial—he does not always agree in his evidence with the other Jewish scholar quoted below in note 92.

[90] R. Travers Herford, *Christianity in Talmud and Midrash*, Williams and Norgate, 1903, pp. 83 ff.

[91] It is well to remember that the Church also found that these definitions infringed the unity of God and were inadequate. A great deal of the struggle with Arianism arose because the Church was determined to reject any attribution of a 'lesser' Godhead to Jesus Christ, as this would involve an infringement of the unity of the Godhead.

What may have happened is this. Nobody knew what had passed behind the closed doors of the palaces of Jerusalem; but Christians, Gentile or Jewish, must often have reproached Jews with 'having killed the Messiah'. A probable Jewish answer could be that he was justly executed for claiming to be what his followers said he was—Lord, and Son of God. There is no reason why Christians should not have accepted this as a statement of fact while they would, of course, have denied that the judges were right in denying the truth of these two titles. Our narratives of the trial would, then, be the joint product of Jewish and Christian arguments as to why Jesus was condemned—as he unquestionably had been—and they were accepted because there was no one to tell them what had actually happened behind the closed doors. Moreover, by the time that the narratives were composed, the supposition that there had been a trial for some offence concerned with the deviation of the new religious group from traditional Jewish practice was a plausible one.

Nevertheless it is not plausible in terms of the conditions which existed during the life of Jesus, for it is commonly agreed among scholars that Jesus himself lived and died a Jew, and that he did not openly claim during his lifetime a messianic role such as would justify a charge of encouraging the worship of himself. Moreover, if we approach the events of the last days from the standpoint that Jesus went deliberately to Jerusalem, we shall with difficulty accept the idea that he went in order that his person and his teaching should be judicially condemned by the religious authorities of his nation. His disagreements with religious leaders had been conducted openly in the course of his mission; there was nothing further to be gained by such a religio-judicial procedure. But, if it be a correct interpretation of the Incarnation that the centre of it was the full revelation of man as person, and of the divine-human relationship in terms of God as person and man as person, then a different light is shed on the meaning of those last days.

Two aspects of his ministry had been completed. But there still remained an essential task to be accomplished. He had appeared before the people as teacher and as healer; he had spoken to them of their personal relationship to God; he had treated all alike as persons; now he had to take himself the role of person at its crucial point, where the individual confronts society and claims from it his freedom of conscience, his freedom of action, whether such be convenient to society or not. It was not the religious authorities which Jesus went up to challenge in Jerusalem; it was the political, whether Jewish or Roman.

Such an interpretation is made easier by the double meaning of the word *sunedrion* which is used in the gospel narratives for the body before which he appeared. Although later Judaism took the word into common usage and Hebraised it as *sanhedrin*, as it had done with other Greek words, and applied it to the supreme religious court of Judaism, the word itself simply means 'council'. It does not necessarily mean a religious court and there is evidence that there existed in Roman client states, such as Judea, a body equivalent to the inner council of a medieval prince, and the same word would be used to describe it. Much of the gospel narrative falls into place if we make the assumption that the *sunedrion* before which Jesus was summoned was the inner council of the Roman appointee, the high priest. As such it would consist of such of his friends and supporters as he chose to summon on any particular occasion. It would be bound by no rules of procedure, and was a political body, not a court of justice. This fits perfectly into the setting provided by Matthew and Mark of a meeting held at night, and to the evidence of all the gospels that whatever happened took place privately in the palace of the high priest, and not in the chamber of the sanhedrin.[92] Such a solution would also explain the silence of the Pharisees. They were opposed to the teaching of Jesus, but there is a long step between religious opposition and judicial murder, and the intervention of Gamaliel to defend Peter and of other Pharisees to defend Paul, though not sharing their views, is evidence in their favour.[93] If the whole business was carried through secretly between late evening and the following mid-day they may well not have known of its happening. It is worth adding that none of the synoptists accuse them of participating in the arrest, trial or condemnation of Jesus. They disappear from the picture at the beginning of the last week.[94]

Jesus, then, went up openly to Jerusalem. He allowed his followers to make of his entry a festal occasion, in which those who wished to might see a suggestion of the entry of the Messiah—it is doubtful if we can put it much more strongly than this—and he, equally openly, drew attention to his presence by driving the horde of temple traders in the outer courts of the Temple from their habitual position. He then quietly resumed his teaching and preaching, doing it openly in

[92] This interpretation of *sunedrion* is put forward by S. Zeitlin in *Who Crucified Jesus?*, Harper, 1942, pp. 76 ff., and though much of the argument would not carry conviction to a Christian reader, that is no reason for rejecting this particular suggestion.

[93] Acts 5. 34, 23. 1-9.

[94] Mark 12. 13-17, Matt. 22. 45. In Luke the action is throughout that of the temple authorities. It is not always realised that 'scribes' belonged to both parties, so that 'scribes' in association with priests would be scribes of the Sadducaic party.

the Temple precincts. As he is made to say by John: 'I have spoken openly to the world; I have always taught in synagogues and in the temple, where all Jews come together; I have said nothing secretly.'[95] But he had become a 'national figure', and, even though the political nationalists had no use for him, he could still draw the crowds of pilgrims at Jerusalem as he had the crowds of Galilee. And this was, from the standpoint of the political authorities, his unforgiveable sin. The Romans would not care what he taught, but would merely see a man who was capable of attracting an immense following among a turbulent subject people. From their point of view a man who cleansed the temple might suddenly decide to 'cleanse' Jerusalem of the Roman eagles. Therefore, before they could use him as a pretext for further repression, his own authorities seized and surrendered him to the imperial power for condemnation as a political danger. This is, surely, far more impressive, as well as far more convincing, than a false trial for non-existent blasphemy, or the unconvincing details of Pilate's pusillanimous pity which we have in the gospel narratives. As person he staked his life for conscience' sake against the '*raison d'état*' and refused, though Gethsemane tells us at what a cost, to save himself or reassure his followers by flight.

That the Christian, recognising in Jesus divinity as well as humanity, believes that Jesus saw far more than this in the crucifixion is as true as that the Jew sees more in Torah than a 'law of commandments and ordinances'.[96] He sees in the voluntary death of Jesus on the Cross the method which God had chosen for that redemption of creation to which both Jew and Christian alike look forward, the at-one-ment by which the unity of creation, and the unity of creation with its Creator, is restored. It is one of the historical curiosities of the development of Christian doctrine that the death of Jesus is so often compared to the sacrifice of the Paschal lamb, whereas the real comparison is the ritual of the Day of Atonement and the offering of the scapegoat. But the choice is merely a historical curiosity; the doctrine behind the choice is that of the full atonement by which God accepts his creation and fulfils its purpose.

Undoubtedly the idea of atonement, just like the idea of mediation, has often been expressed very imperfectly in Christian thought. What was said earlier of Paul's conception of the unity of the redeemed in the mystical body of Christ[97] did not prevent many Christians from seeing the double step between man and God through Christ which Paul would have indignantly rejected. But a living religion is always

[95] John 18. 20.
[96] Eph. 2. 15.
[97] See above, p. 153.

in movement, and because it is in movement, it will at any one moment always contain paradox and even contradiction—which is why it is so easy for 'outsiders' to misunderstand it. Deeply but often obscurely felt universals are rarely logically fitted into the pattern of immediate and particular concerns. Nowhere is the misunderstanding easier than between Jews and Christians, because of the extraordinarily disparate literature which the fathers of Church and Synagogue have bequeathed. In the one we have all the scaffolding and raw material of their discussions; in the other we have a metaphysic and mystical awareness of the deepest truths, which seem insincere when combined with the fumbling and inadequate personal experience with which they were worked out in the history of the Church.

6. JESUS AND THE PHARISEES

IF we are to understand the actual conflicts between Jesus and the Pharisees which are recorded in the gospels, we must first obtain an accurate picture of the place which he occupied in Jewish life as it presented itself in its range and variety of opinion and activity around A.D. 30. We must hold the balance between identifying him completely with any particular Jewish party or sect, and dissociating him completely, as a unique phenomenon, from the religious tendencies and groupings in contemporary Judaism.

His neighbours in Nazareth, where so far as we know his life was spent until the beginning of his public mission, would have been made up of *amme ha-aretz*, the rank and file Jews who observed the main traditions of Judaism, but who ignored the refinements of Pharisaic practice, and who were too occupied with the difficult task of earning enough to meet the harsh demands of Roman taxation to identify themselves closely with an active nationalism determined on rebellion. Nevertheless Galilee was a centre of such nationalism, and Jesus must have been familiar with it throughout his life. In the same way he must have been familiar with the assimilationist tendencies of those who lived in the Greek cities dotted through the province, although there is no record in the gospels that he ever visited or preached in such cities. But his religious training in school and synagogue would have been given him by those who, in an earlier period, we should have described as 'teachers of Torah', and at this time they can be identified with members of the Pharisaic party and, more precisely, with the 'scribes' who are usually mentioned in the gospels together with the Pharisees. For the word 'scribes' covered at this period those who, in some way, were authorised to give religious instruction and leadership, and would have included not merely the teachers of children but the rabbis and religious officials of the synagogues. At the same time we must not think of them as a salaried or 'ecclesiastical' class, such as the Christian clergy or the Jewish rabbis of today. Even the great rabbis of Jerusalem were either men of independent means or earned their living by following a trade or other occupation. Shammai, for example, an outstanding influence at this time, was by profession a mason.

Jesus was not a 'scribe', that is to say that he had not turned to any human authority, as he had turned to John for baptism, to set the seal upon his personal conviction of his mission. When, at the beginning of that mission, people noticed that he spoke with authority, that is clearly not 'authority' in the technical sense.[98] But when, after 'the cleansing of the Temple', an official group of those who controlled its life and worship came to him and asked him 'by what authority are you doing these things, or who gave you this authority to do them?'[99] it almost certainly was a technical question meaning 'What rabbi whom we should recognise ordained you, and with the support of whose teaching have you conducted yourself in this way?' —a question which Jesus refused to answer, challenging them to assess the career of the other great independent preacher of his day, John the Baptist, by the same yard-stick.

The fact that Jesus was not a 'scribe' or rabbi has important implications. The teaching of Judaism is somewhat rigorously divided into halakah—the manner in which the actual precepts of Torah are to be carried out—and haggada or moral and spiritual encouragement and instruction. The former could be given only by one who had received authority to do so though, at this time, there were a number of groups from which that authority might emanate. It could not be given by an individual of his own volition. But the latter was free, and there was no 'authority' which could forbid Jesus to preach in public or to accept invitations to preach in the synagogues. With one exception the Church has recognised that the teaching of Jesus is not halakic. It has not embodied in canon law an instruction that when a man seeks to take the coat of a Christian he shall surrender his overcoat also. The most striking example of this acceptance of the teaching

[98] A number of Jewish scholars, basing their argument on the fact that the same Hebrew word means both 'authority' and 'parable' have suggested that the latter meaning is the right one here. I do not find the argument convincing, since the narrative throughout witnesses to the unusual authority which the personality of Jesus exercised wherever he went. Moreover, the parable is a familiar form of teaching for scribes.

[99] Mark 11. 28.

of Jesus as an ideal and not a rule demanding legal obedience lies in the attitude taken towards pacifism. None of the great Churches of Christendom have pronounced themselves pacifist. The one exception lies in the field of matrimonial relations. Many Churches have pronounced the statements of Jesus about divorce (even though their text is uncertain)[1] to be halakic, without realising the implications of this in terms of the Judaism current at the time of his ministry. For, though a number of bodies were pronouncing differing halakah at that period, it was only within corporate bodies that this halakah was valid, and it needed to cover the whole field of religion. We have, for example, learnt much about the discipline of the Dead Sea community of Qumran from their manual of discipline. For Jesus to pronounce halakah was, then, for him to found a Jewish sect; but this sect had, on this basis, only one 'law'—that there should be no divorce—since on no other subject are the words of Jesus given halakic value.[2] It is, therefore, surely much more probable that here, as with non-resistance or love towards one's enemies, he was stating an ethical ideal in speaking of relations between man and wife. We shall, later, discuss the relation of Jesus to the Church, but it can be said here that the idea that he was founding a new Jewish 'sect' with its own halakic laws does not correspond with anything else that the gospels tell us.

Jesus, like John, was an independent preacher and teacher. Because of the variety of groupings within Judaism, it was still possible for such men to emerge and to be received according to their merits; for no single group could yet claim a monopoly of teaching and interpretation and automatically exclude someone who did not emerge from their own ranks. We know, in fact, that in addition to John and Jesus various people appeared and disappeared during the period with messianic claims or messages of an apocalyptic kind.

Because Jesus was an independent preacher, and because his main controversies were with the Pharisees, it is important to observe the limits within which those controversies were set. They did not touch on any of the fundamentals of Pharisaic Judaism. There is no record that the Pharisees found anything to criticize in his teaching about God and his relations with men, or man and his relations with his neighbours. They did not attack his teaching about 'the kingdom', although this was an issue on which the nationalists would have found him completely wanting. Nor did Jesus attack the Pharisees for their teachings on these subjects.

[1] Matt. 5. 31 f.; Mark 10. 11 f.; Luke 16. 18.

[2] Except possibly on the abolition of clean and unclean meats. See below, p. 170.

It is important also to scrutinize carefully the records of his contacts as they are to be found in the gospels. The fourth we cannot make use of for such a study, for it assumes that 'the Jews' were hostile from the beginning to a Jesus who proclaimed without restraint his messianic and divine nature, and both of these assumptions are almost certainly unhistorical. But even within the synoptists there are significant differences, for they succeed each other in date during the period when the controversy between the followers and rejecters of Jesus as Messiah was growing in intensity, and the stage was being made ready for the separation of the two religions. This was not a single event, but took place in different ways and at different times in different places. At the place and time when the fourth gospel was written, for example, it is complete. 'Jew' is a synonym for 'enemy of Jesus', and one could almost assume from the narrative that Jesus and His disciples were not Jewish.[3]

As to the synoptists, the easiest way to see their differences is to compare them where all, or more than one, are relating the same incident from the same source. Matthew and Luke both report the content of the preaching of John the Baptist. Luke tells us that it was 'the multitudes that came out to be baptized' that John called a 'brood of vipers'. But Matthew reserves this phrase for the 'Pharisees and Sadducees'.[4] When Jesus was accused of casting out demons by Be-elzebul, Mark says that the accusation was made by 'scribes who came down from Jerusalem', and these scribes might have been either Pharisaic or Sadducaic. Luke is not interested, and simply ascribes it to local bystanders. Matthew, who has already stated on another occasion that the Pharisees charged Jesus with using satanic powers to effect his cures, substitutes 'Pharisees' in this passage, and entirely omits the visitors from Jerusalem.[5] There are also more subtle distinctions. In the cure of the paralytic in Mark Jesus asks the astonished scribes 'Why do you question thus in your hearts?' while Matthew assumes their hostility and rephrases the question as 'Why do you think evil in your hearts?'[6]

In reviewing the actual incidents recorded in the gospels we have to distinguish three fields. There are the denunciations of ecclesiastical

[3] For a full study of the period of separation see my *Conflict of the Church and Synagogue*, Ch. 3. My attention has been drawn to the fact that the Greek for 'Jews' and 'Judeans' is the same. On this basis it may be that the hostility is not that by Jews to the first Christian, but of Judeans to a prophet from Galilee.

[4] Luke 3. 7 and Matt. 3. 7.

[5] Mark 3. 22; Luke 11. 15; Matt. 9. 34, 12. 24.

[6] Mark 2. 8; Matt. 9. 4. A fuller study of these passages is to be found in my *Jesus, Paul and the Jews*. S.C.M., 1936.

self-congratulation, pretention, insincerity and actual hypocrisy, in which Pharisaism was no more and no less involved than any other form of institutional religion; there are denunciations which are difficult to interpret because they are at some point contrary to facts which we know about either Jesus or Pharisaism; and there are arguments which genuinely and unmistakeably turn on the tension between the teaching of Jesus and the Pharisaism of his time.

To the first category would belong some of the charges made in the wholesale onslaught on the scribes and Pharisees collected together in Matthew 23,[7] or the distinction between the prayers of the Pharisee and the publican 'who went up to the temple to pray'[8] recorded by Luke. So far as the environment of Jesus was concerned, the charges could have been made with equal justice against members of the Sadducaic party, and we know from countless rabbinic utterances that the Pharisees and their successors adopted exactly the same attitude of condemnation to such actions or attitudes as did Jesus.

To the second category belongs especially the passage in Mark 7. 1-23 which bristles with difficulties.[9] In the opening verses the Pharisees together with 'some of the scribes who had come from Jerusalem', question Jesus about the indifference of his disciples to the rules of hand-washing before meals. Mark gives an editorial note that all Jews perform elaborate washings on a number of occasions, which adds to the complications of the passage, because there is no other evidence that *at this period* these formal washings were incumbent on laymen. Jewish scholars would like, therefore, to suggest that it is an interpolation dating, at earliest, from the end of the century. But this otherwise reasonable hypothesis is wrecked by the fact that the basic question (though not the note) is a part of Mark which is used by Matthew[10], and we seem to be left with the only possible explanation that even as early as this *some* particularly strict Pharisees were trying to make the ordinary laity conform to

[7] E.g. vv. 5-7, 27 f.

[8] Luke 18. 9-14. There are, of course, other parables and sayings which make the same point.

[9] By far the best treatment of this chapter, with reference to all the many Christian and Jewish interpretations of its different sections, is in C. G. Montefiore, *The Synoptic Gospels*, 2nd Ed. Macmillan, 1927, I, pp. 129-166.

[10] Matt. 15. 1-20. Though Matthew gives a somewhat smoother narrative than Mark, all the problems of Mark remain in his text. Some of the points occur in yet another variant in Luke 11. 39-41. For an argument against the possibility that this kind of ritual purity could be asked for at this period see A. Buechler, *Die galiläische Am-ha-Ares des Zweiten Jahrhunderts*, Vienna, 1906, p. 212.

rules of cleanliness originally laid down for the Temple service. This, in itself, is quite possible, and might well incur the condemnation of Jesus. But his reply, as given by Mark, is 'You leave the commandment of God and hold fast the tradition of men', and this seems an impossible reply to attribute to him, for the basic commandments about ritual cleanliness are in the written Torah and are not an addition of Pharisaic Judaism. Jesus is made to appear to distinguish between the 'commandment of God' as though it dealt only with ethical and moral issues, and 'the tradition of men' as though they were concerned only with formal and ritual matters. But this is not true and Jesus must have known it. Both contain both.

A similar difficulty besets the next issue which Jesus raises, that of 'Corban'. He is made to accuse the Pharisees of inventing a new law by which a man, who had made a rash vow which prevented him from fulfilling his duty to his parents, could not annul it. But the facts are the opposite. It is the written Torah which makes no provision for the annulment of vows, and the Pharisees who introduced an annulment to cover precisely such cases.[11] It would, perhaps, be easy to say that Mark, unfamiliar with the niceties of rabbinic Judaism, had got the terms of the controversy mixed; but the difficulty goes deeper than that. For, since Jesus and Pharisaism agreed on the subject, it is difficult to know why and with what motive any argument about it occurred.

The final section (14-23) goes back to the hand-washing, but extends the question. Ritually unclean hands would, in conditions where Torah requires ritual cleansing, make otherwise 'clean' food 'unclean'; but now Jesus is made to attack the whole principle of any distinction between 'clean' and 'unclean' foods, a distinction which is clearly to be found in Torah itself, and is not an addition of Pharisaism. The words of Jesus are: 'There is nothing outside a man which by going into him can defile him; but the things which come out of a man are what defile him.' The link with hand-washing is a very tenuous one, for the distinction between permitted and prohibited foods is something of much greater significance. But, even if we remit the remark to another occasion, it still needs elucidation. For here, even more than with divorce, if Jesus was making a halakic pronouncement he was breaking entirely with the Judaism of his day, in whatever form it expressed itself. Some Christian commentators have taken the passage in this way; but, as a halakic

[11] Montefiore, *op cit.*, pp. 148 ff. especially p. 150. This page is also evidence of Dr. Montefiore's unusual breadth of sympathy in that he suggests a possible escape in an argument with a particular Pharisee who did not accept the general Pharisaic attitude to annulment.

commandment, it is in stark opposition to the various statements made by Jesus about the validity and permanence of Torah.

In this passage, as in that concerning divorce, it seems much more likely that Jesus is stating an ultimate truth, not trying to direct the immediate activity of the judicial or social authorities. What he here says is not, in fact, capable of that exact definition of meaning which is necessary for a court or for a social enactment. It is parallel to the statement that if a man looks lustfully at a woman he is committing adultery in his heart. For there *are* many things which go into a man and defile him, things of the same quality as those which come out of him and defile him. The lustful look goes in before the adulterous thought comes out; temptation goes in before theft or murder come out. It was not with such nice distinctions that Jesus was concerned, but with the basic affirmation that material objects could not cause religious defilement. And yet we cannot, from the Christian standpoint, accept as adequate to the thought of Jesus the comment which Mark adds to the saying: 'Thus he declared all foods clean.' He was dealing with something much deeper. We might, without exaggeration, call the comment a superficial misunderstanding of his words. All meats are *not* clean, and it is not surprising to find that the Jewish record on this subject, in spite of their adherence to a considerable body of precise and even pedantic ritual restrictions, is, historically, much better than the Christian. It is to the credit of Judaism that no Jew, without doing violence to his religion, has for nearly two thousand years killed or chased an animal for sport; it is to its credit that Jewish households have paid meticulous attention to the cleanliness and healthiness of their food, when both were dangerously neglected by their Christian neighbours; it is to its credit that the Jewish method of slaughter attained under rabbinic instruction a humaneness which we are only today beginning to equal.[12] And all these things Judaism owes to the original brief sentences in Torah distinguishing clean and unclean meats, and providing for the use of meat for food.

The words of Jesus on this subject, as in similar cases where he pronounces an ultimate truth, are not intended to be in conflict or contradiction with the laws by which society must live. But they point the goal and thereby indicate the direction in which the moral

[12] Floods of propaganda have been poured out on the subject of Shehita, but, in my opinion, there has been no valid criticism of the action itself, but only in certain cases of the preliminaries (i.e. the method of putting the animal in the position for the act of slaughter). Today, with an efficient stunning system coming into practice, it may be necessary for orthodox Jews to re-examine these aspects of what still remains, in the opinions of competent experts, as painless a manner of slaughter as can be devised.

conscience of society may be deepened and its laws developed or altered. They were 'interpretations' of Torah, as were the developments of the Pharisees; but they were based, as was the rest of his teaching, on man's personal submission to them, rather than on the strengthening of the social discipline of a community.

It will be seen that these twenty-three verses of Mark provide something of an enigma for the interpreter. From a literary point of view we could lift the whole passage without disturbing the sequence of Mark's narrative; but we cannot regard it as a late interpolation because of its presence in the first gospel. It might well, however, be a collection of incidents which had been put together before Mark made use of them, and put together by someone whose knowledge was too vague or memory too faulty for the truth underlying them to be sufficiently clear for us to be sure of our interpretation of them. That Jesus made the statement that material objects cannot cause religious defilement we can accept without difficulty; that he had a controversy with some individual or group of Pharisees on the washing of hands is quite possible, but his arguments have been confused. As to Corban, we can only say that this was a point on which Jesus and the Pharisees were at one, and the nature of the original incident is wholly lost.

The same uncertainty besets the interpretation of sections of Matthew's comprehensive denunciation in chapter twenty-three of his gospel. We have seen that some verses of it apply to any ecclesiastical system. Some of it is, frankly, incomprehensible, for example the laboured argument that killing the prophets and building their tombs argues identity of purpose.[13] Nor have we any evidence from rabbinic sources for the fine distinctions in swearing by the gold of the Temple or the Temple itself, by the altar or the sacrifice upon it, which Jesus attributes to them. But if we were to substitute 'woe unto *those* Pharisees *who*' for 'woe to *the* Pharisees because *they*', that is, if we took out the generalisations and applied it to 'those whom the cap fitted', then we should have an attitude which is not only borne out by the best Pharisaic thought itself, but is consistent with the whole tenor of the teaching of Jesus. The dangers inherent in any system such as that which the Pharisees were erecting are the loss of a moral sense of proportion on the one hand and the provision of a substitute in observance for genuine religion on the other, and the rabbis were well aware of this. But, doubtless, they did not always live up to their professions, and had among their number those who cloaked 'extortion and rapacity' beneath a great outward show of piety, or those who 'tithed mint and dill and cummin' and neglected

[13] Matt. 23. 29 ff.

'justice, mercy and faith'. That Jesus, with his emphasis on personal sincerity in the approach to God, would have denounced such perversions we may well believe, but they are not denunciations exclusively of Pharisaism, since the rabbis denounced the same perversions with equal vigour.

The real key to the relations between Jesus and the Pharisees is to be found neither in the wholesale denunciations of Matthew, nor in the difficulties of the chapter already discussed, but in the simple narrative of Mark. Like the nationalists with whom both disagreed, but unlike the Sadducees or Essenes, both Jesus and the Pharisees were concerned with the same field, that is, the whole people of Israel. We are justified in claiming this identity because, though the Church soon spread to the Gentile world, all the evidence is that Jesus never entered the Gentile cities which he must have continuously passed on his travels, and confined himself to people who were 'members of the Synagogue', in name if not in fact.

It is because both were concerned with the same field that they were inevitably concerned with each other, and that the constituted synagogal authorities (the scribes) and their warmest supporters (the members of the Pharisaic brotherhoods) immediately took a keen interest in the success of this new independent preacher. What they saw soon began to puzzle them. But there is no hostility in Mark's first record. He preached on a sabbath in the synagogue at Capernaum; and 'they were astonished'. He healed a psychotic with a word of authority, 'and they were all amazed'.[14] There is nothing hostile in his own attitude either, and when he healed a leper he told him to keep quiet about the healing and carry out the proper regulations for registering his cure.[15] After a tour in the countryside he returned to Capernaum and a paralytic was brought to him. This time the scribes—and we can legitimately say that some at least of them must have been in the synagogue on his previous visit—were disturbed. It made them 'question in their hearts' when he told the man that his sins were forgiven as the channel by which he healed his paralysis. But, as already mentioned, their questioning was natural and at the end they are included by Mark in those who glorified God.[16]

Next comes an action which puzzled them still more. He accepted a tax-collector as a personal disciple and took a meal with him and his friends—a meal on which it was most unlikely that the proper tithes had been paid.[17] They asked his disciples to explain this sur-

[14] Mark 1. 22 and 27.
[15] *Ibid.* 1. 44.
[16] *Ibid.* 2. 6-12.
[17] See above, p. 141.

prising conduct in a religious leader. Jesus heard them and gave the required explanation: 'Those who are well have no need of a physician, but those who are sick; I came not to call the righteous but sinners.'[18] It was an original idea to them, perhaps, but he gave a friendly and reasonable explanation even though it probably seemed to them a risky one.

The next recorded incident is of a somewhat different character. Thus far the justification for the action of Jesus had been that it was effective—the sick were made whole by his treatment—and that it brought him into contact with those to whom he wished his message to come—an erstwhile tax-collector had actually thrown up his work and become a disciple. But now they observed something odd which was of a different character. It was not the conduct of his mission but the behaviour of his disciples which attracted unfavourable attention. They observed no weekly fasts.[19] The mission would not be affected if his disciples, like both Pharisees and the followers of John the Baptist, disciplined themselves by fasting regularly. That these weekly fasts do not occur in the written Torah is certainly irrelevant. Jesus was not asserting the authority of Torah against Pharisaic 'traditions of men' when he defended the disciples. Mark gives his reply in two parts. First there is a light-hearted answer which avoids any point of principle. The campaign is, after all, only beginning, and Jesus compares it to wedding festivities in whose joyousness fasting is legitimately omitted. Fasting, he adds, will come later when he himself is no longer with them (the form of this sentence may have been moulded later to become a first warning of the Passion). But then there is added by Mark a different answer, and one which is quite inappropriate to this type of issue. Jesus is made to say: 'No one sews a piece of unshrunk cloth on an old garment . . . and no one puts new wine into old wine-skins.' As it stands this cannot describe the relations either of Jesus or of the Christian Church to Judaism. There is no such break as the words imply. Weekly worship, for example, was taken over direct from the synagogue. The decalogue and the great commandment alike come from the Old Testament. In their original context the words must have been used for an individual situation, where Jesus saw that a complete break was necessary. The rich young man had to have *either* his riches *or* his discipleship; he could not fit the new life on to the old.

Whatever form the original discussion took, it must have left an increasing disquiet in the minds of the scribes and Pharisees of Galilee. Jesus claimed a dangerous independence of judgement in dangerous

[18] *Ibid.* 2. 17.
[19] *Ibid.* 2. 18 ff.

times. Doubtless there were many other discussions, many other clashes of which we have no record. But it is not surprising to find that what appears to have been the final crisis was connected with sabbath observance. It has already been shown that the developments of Pharisaism arose out of a genuine concern for the public welfare.[20] Even in their homeland Jews were surrounded and interpenetrated by Greek societies; and many of their own wealthy classes had succumbed to the temptations of Greek civilisation. The Pharisees saw in a measure of precisely determined separation the only guarantee of survival. Jesus had already shown his indifference to these measures if they cut him off from the 'publicans and sinners' whom he wished to reach. It was more serious when he showed that he was prepared to ignore the fences about the sabbath—its basic observance was never at issue—and to justify his action by the generalisation that 'the sabbath was made for man, not man for the sabbath'.[21] The saying itself is in accordance with Pharisaic ideas. Whether they had been so epigramatically expressed at the time of Jesus we do not know; but almost identical words are attributed to more than one later rabbi.[22] It is not the saying that is decisive proof of disagreement, but the situation which has led to it. There has been a preliminary skirmish when his disciples are detected pulling and eating grains of corn as they pass through the fields.[23] The recorded reply of Jesus—a reference to David's conduct—is clever rather than convincing, and evades again all question of principle.[24] But immediately afterwards the real challenge comes. It had, apparently, been prepared: 'He entered the synagogue, and a man was there who had a withered hand. And they watched him, to see whether he would heal him on the sabbath, so that they might accuse him'.[25] Jesus sees that it is a deliberate challenge, looks round at them 'with anger, grieved at their hardness of heart', asks whether 'it is lawful on the

[20] See above, p. 140.

[21] *Ibid.* 2. 27.

[22] I. Abrahams, *Studies in Pharisaism and the Gospels*, First Series, Cambridge, 1917, Ch. xvii, pp. 129 ff.

[23] *Ibid.* 2. 23 ff.

[24] I wonder whether on this occasion, as when Jesus dealt with the question of fasting, he was covering the ignorance of Pharisaic discipline of his disciples. They had not been with him more than a matter of months, and were drawn from the Galilean working classes. He was certainly not opposed to fasting, for he had preceded his ministry by a long fast; later he spoke to his followers on two occasions about fasting (Matt. 6. 16 and 17. 21). Fasting appears at the very beginning of the apostolic ministry (Acts 13. 2 f., 14. 23); and so does observance of the sabbath.

[25] Mark 3. 1 f.

sabbath to do good or to do harm, to save life or to kill', and heals the man.

This incident, apparently so trifling in itself, led to a final breach. The Pharisees could not accept his attitude. The times were too dangerous, and it admitted too great a licence to 'private judgement'. Once admitted on a minor matter, there would be no knowing where it would stop. The very popularity of Jesus increased the threat to the national loyalty to Torah which the provisions for strict sabbath observance were meant to aid and ensure. They could not but go into opposition and seek to undermine his influence. The passage ends with the strange alliance, to which Mark alone refers, between Pharisees and Herodians.[26] That, from their standpoint, they were not acting with undue haste is told us by the following verses, relating that the reputation of Jesus had so spread that crowds came to him 'from Galilee, also from Judaea and Jerusalem and Idumea and from beyond the Jordan and from about Tyre and Sidon'.

Mark says simply that they 'held counsel how to destroy him'. That this was not a determination to kill him is shown in the subsequent narrative. Their intention was to discredit him. 'Scribes'—we do not know if they were Pharisaic or Sadducaic—came down from Jerusalem to study the situation, and declared that 'he is possessed by Be-elzebul and by the prince of demons he casts out the demons'.[27] We can associate with their campaign other untoward incidents. His friends and family tried to restrain him as being 'beside himself'.[28] When, a little later, he returned to Nazareth and preached there in the synagogue, he had a hostile reception 'and could do no mighty work there'.[29] There, however, the matter seems to have rested. Mark reports further preaching tours with the accustomed crowds, the sending out of the twelve, and one of the rare visits to a non-Jewish region (possibly to avoid the interest of Herod) before the Pharisees appear again.[30] This time they ask him for a sign, and he refuses to answer. A little later, as he is on his way to Jerusalem, some Pharisees ask him about divorce.[31] During the last week, Mark's strange alliance makes its last appearance with a question, while he

[26] *Ibid.* 3. 6. Mark couples the two disparate groups together again in the warning against their 'leaven', in 8. 15.

[27] *Ibid.* 3. 22.

[28] *Ibid.* 3. 21 and 31.

[29] *Ibid.* 6. 5.

[30] *Ibid.* 8. 11-13. This is omitting ch. 7 from the chronological sequence. In any case it would add nothing fresh.

[31] *Ibid.* 10. 2 ff.

is teaching in the Temple, about the tribute money.[32] But the initiative has already passed to the temple authorities and this is the last mention of the Pharisees. So far as they were concerned, the die had been cast much earlier, in the disagreement over sabbath observance. The later incidents appear unplanned, except that Mark suggests that the final question was due to the temple authorities, and not to Pharisaic initiative at all.[33]

The most that we are entitled to say of the Pharisaic leaders is that, when the temple authorities planned, not to discredit him, but to kill him, they did not intervene; but even so, we must remember that we have no means of judging what powers or opportunities for intervention they may have possessed. Their attitude rested on that sabbath in Galilee, not on political considerations. In the end it was more decisive. The crucified Jesus rose again; but the breach between his followers and the Synagogue proved unbridgeable and, after an uneasy century, the two sides stood forth before the world as two wholly separate religions.

It is essential to realise that the Pharisees could no more have just surrendered to Jesus than he could to them. Of course the healing by a word of a diseased hand was in itself only a trifle, but it was done deliberately as an assertion of the primacy of each man as person. Yet Jesus never attempted, so far as all our evidence goes, to discuss with the Pharisees how to reconcile the needs of man and community. William Temple once said: 'Revelation is an event; its interpretation is our responsibility', and this applies alike to Sinai and to the Incarnation. Jesus did not attempt to interpret his mission, or to reconcile it with that ordering of the community which he likewise proclaimed as divine. For the task of reconciliation is not a single act, or to be achieved by subordinating either side to the other. It is a continuous process and cannot be solved by any neat formula. Within the divinely chosen community he proclaimed the divine concern with each man as person. It is for men to hold the two in a continuously destroyed and continuously recreated balance. Jesus did not attempt to resolve the tension for us; he challenged us only to recognise that it existed.

[32] *Ibid.* 12. 13 ff. On this occasion Matthew copies Mark by linking together Pharisees and Herodians; but their combination in Jerusalem, outside the tetrarchy of Herod, is odd.

[33] The sequence is: 'the chief priests and the scribes and the elders came to him . . . and they tried to arrest him, but feared the multitude . . . and they sent to him some of the Pharisees and some of the Herodians (Mark 11. 27; 12. 12, 13).

7. JESUS AND THE CHURCH

THAT disciples should gather round a teacher was the normal practice in Judaism—indeed it is inevitably a normal practice in any religion. It is, however, another example of that authority which his contemporaries recognised in Jesus that all the evangelists except Luke emphasise that the initiative came from him in the calling of his first disciples. It was *he* who chose *them;* he did not wait for them to come to him although, of course, we cannot tell whether he had already marked them out among those who had listened to his teaching.[34] But, however the association began, and however normal the presence of a band of followers around the Master, the subsequent story contains features which were unique. After the crisis had been reached with the Galilean Pharisees, Jesus withdrew into the hills and formed an inner core of twelve whom he appointed 'to be with him, and to be sent out to preach and to have authority to cast out demons'.[35] It would be interesting to know whether this was an unprecedented action, or whether such short missions to the countryside by chosen disciples was the manner in which the leading teachers of Torah spread their teaching into the rural communities. But we can safely say that the instruction to heal the sick was peculiar to Jesus. In Talmudic times, and later in Polish Hasidism, we find evidence of healing powers in individual saintly rabbis but it was never a regular part of rabbinic ordination or the rabbinic commission.

In the second part of his public ministry, however, the basic novelty of the relationship between Jesus and his picked followers becomes unquestionable. He viewed them as a continuing community, especially charged, not only to carry on his work, but to explain his person and his mission. The Galilean period ended with the dramatic feeding of a huge crowd which had come to listen to him, and with the failure of the disciples to understand the power by which he did such things. Jesus took them away to the 'villages of

[34] Matt. 4. 18-22, 9. 9; Mark 1. 16-20, 2. 14; John 1. 35-51. Luke gives less emphasis to the call, setting it later in the Galilean mission, though he follows Mark in the account of the call of Levi (5. 11 and 27).

[35] Mark 3. 13. The mission of the twelve is related in much greater detail in Matt. 10. 5-42 and in Luke 9. 1-6. Luke also relates a second mission of seventy disciples (10. 1-20) and attributes to them much of the address attributed by Matthew to the sending out of the twelve. A good deal of the material of these addresses seems more naturally to belong to a later stage of the ministry, or to the period after the Resurrection, e.g. the references to conflicts with synagogal authorities and Gentile rulers in Matt. 10. 17 f.

Caesarea Philippi'; and on the way he asked his disciples, 'Who do men say that I am?' When Peter, challenged as to the opinion of the disciples themselves, replied 'You are the Christ' he evidently felt that the time had come when he could explain to them more fully the nature of his mission and his person, while he still insisted that they were 'to tell no one about him'.[36]

There will still be times when he will preach and heal, there will still be arguments with the Pharisees and others, but from the moment when he began the journey to the region of Caesarea Philippi the main emphasis has changed. The centre of the picture becomes his own destiny and its continuing effect upon his followers; and it is that 'continuing effect' which is the *raison d'être* of the Christian Church; for, through his followers, the effect is to be communicated to the whole world.

Mark tells us bluntly that during that journey 'he began to teach them that the Son of man must suffer many things, and be rejected by the elders and the chief priests and the scribes, and be killed, and after three days rise again. And he said this plainly.'[37] The same statement, in almost identical words, recurs again in Mark's description of the days spent on the road up to Jerusalem, with the addition that his actual death would be at the hands of the Gentiles.[38] In the form in which we have it the bald account must date from after the Resurrection; for if Jesus predicted the final events with complete accuracy, it could only mean that he knew his victory to be a mechanical, rather than a moral, certainty. But this robs the whole Passion story of any semblance of reality, reducing its real tragedy to a staged melodrama enacted for our benefit. We do not need to rely on such an argument for asserting that Mark gives us an *ex post facto* interpretation of the conversations between Jesus and his disciples. The Passion narratives in all the gospels make the truth abundantly clear. The arrest, condemnation and crucifixion of Jesus left the disciples utterly bewildered, heartbroken and without hope for the future. When the Resurrection was first reported to them they refused to believe it. All this could scarcely have been the case had the actual sequence of events been repeatedly explained to them in advance. There is, in fact, a wistful pathos about the words 'and he said this plainly', which links up with one of those touches in the fourth gospel which remind us that, however stylised, genuine memories lie behind the author's work. Three times he speaks of the disciples remembering

[36] Mark 8. 27 ff.
[37] *Ibid.* 8. 31 f.
[38] *Ibid.* 10. 32.

afterwards what Jesus had foretold.[39] It is no artificial reading between the lines to interpret these memories as 'we see now that he did tell us, but then we did not understand'.

It is to the fourth gospel that we naturally turn for a fuller understanding of the intimate relations between Jesus and his disciples, and of those expositions of his nature and purpose which were essential to them, but would have been incomprehensible to some and misunderstood by others of the crowds that followed him. Two points we owe particularly to John. The first is the repeated insistence of Jesus that his mission, and therefore the Church which continued it, was something of the very warp and woof of creation, and planned from the beginning. In his activity in creation he was therefore identical with God.[40] The complement of this linking, as it were, backward to God is the linking forward to the disciples.[41] The Church will continue to be the veritable body of Christ, drawing its life from him. Much of the language and some of the actual expressions we may owe to the author and through him to Philo, but the content must surely have come from Jesus himself. For it would be difficult to explain why he should have remained silent on these topics in the intimacy of discussion with his disciples.

Yet, when every suggestion is made, the content of these days of withdrawal must remain as much a mystery as the forty days which, it is recorded in Exodus,[42] were spent by Moses on Mount Sinai. We can say that for both Jesus and the disciples they were days of preparation for the Passion, and so days of foundation for the Church in which the work of the Passion was to be perpetuated. The parallel drawn with the period spent by Moses on the Mount is not accidental. We may not accept the literalism of Jewish orthodox belief that the actual laws of the Pentateuch constitute the perfect and divine plan for human life in community; we may regard them as the human interpretation of the revelation made to Moses. But in the revelation itself to Moses of the 'heavenly Torah' as it existed in God's mind there was that perfection. So likewise with the Incarnation and with Calvary. There is in the account of it a human interpretation; but in the event itself, as it existed in the divine purpose and in the activity of Jesus, there was that perfection. In each case that which was enacted was enacted 'once for all'. Nothing could be added or taken from it. On the other hand, no Jew believes that Jewish society has

39 John 2. 17, 22 and 12. 16.

40 For example John 3. 11-21, 31-36; 5. 17, 19-24, 43-47; 8. 54-58; 10. 14-18, 31-38.

41 For example John 5. 25-29; 6. 32-35, 50-59; 7. 37-39; 8. 12, 31.

42 Ex. 24. 18.

ever expressed the perfection of Torah; no Christian believes that any Church has expressed the perfection of Calvary. The relationship between the two revelations cannot therefore be gauged by the human failures of the followers of either to achieve perfection; it must be judged by the revelations themselves, and so we come to the fundamental question: did Jesus teach that by his action in founding the Church he was replacing Sinai, and that the old Israel was thereby rejected to be replaced by a new Israel?

That this was so has certainly been assumed by the Christian tradition as a fact so evident that it needed only confirmation, rather than proof, from the gospels themselves. New Testament 'proof' was to be found in the Pauline epistles, which will have to be considered later. That the general assumption has led to extravagant interpretations by both Roman Catholic and Protestant theologians has been convincingly demonstrated by Jules Isaac in *Jésus et Israel*,[43] but even such a sober and conservative scholar as Dr. Newton Flew, while admitting that 'Jesus nowhere speaks of the disciples whom he is gathering as the nucleus for a new Israel', holds that such a rejection is implicit in various places in the gospels.[44]

The issue cannot really be settled by the interpretation of particular verses or parables. It is so fundamental that it would require the most categoric statement by Jesus to justify the Christian assumption. If we considered that Synagogue and Church were both committed to identical tasks, then we could justify the rejection of Israel and the substitution of a new body by the claim that Israel was unworthy to continue. This is often done by exaggerating the sinfulness of one or more generations of Jewry. But, in fact, that is nonsense. There is no evidence that the particular generation which witnessed the Incarnation was exceptionally wicked. And if we are to deal in generalisations, then the Christian Church would stand under the same condemnation.

If on the other hand we take the historical evidence, then we cannot help observing that Judaism and Christianity have chosen different tasks as the fields in which they believe themselves to be obeying the divine will. Judaism has dealt with the whole life of a

[43] Editions A. Michel, Paris, 1948, Proposition XV, pp. 277 ff.

[44] *Jesus and His Church*, Epworth Press, 1951, p. 36. Dr. Flew adds 'But His actions speak more clearly than any words', but nowhere in the following pages does he adduce evidence that the creation of a new body automatically disposes of the old one. When he sees a 'secure foundation' for the rejection of Israel in the verse 'fear not little flock; for it is your Father's good pleasure to give you the kingdom (Luke 12. 32)' one cannot but ask why to give the kingdom to X *must* mean to take it away from Y. The kingdom is not a fixed or limited quantity.

'natural' community. Christianity has been built by the voluntary adherence of men and women individually from every variety of natural community, and has ignored (in principle) natural boundaries. We could, then, claim that Judaism has been rejected only if either the natural community had lost all importance, or the activity of the Church did, in fact, cover its moral needs and problems. Neither is true. By both its theory and its practice the Christian tradition has again and again made it clear that it does not identify the Church with the natural community. The distinction which it makes between the 'secular' and the 'religious' fields of life, and which has its roots in the New Testament itself,[45] is basic evidence of this; the withdrawal from common life in Christian asceticism, and innumerable examples from every century of Christian thought, would confirm that this separation is fundamental to Christian thinking even on social and political issues. But, on the other hand, the natural community, so far from vanishing, has assumed ever increasing importance in the life of the world and of every single person within it. Life has become so complex that 'the state' is continuously extending its responsibility at the cost of the freedom and independence of the individual.

While, for the purpose of analysis, a sharp distinction has been made between the divine action in society and the divine call to man as person, and the one has been identified with Sinai and the other with the Incarnation and Calvary, this is not in itself evidence that the two are meant to be separate or that, in actual life, the fields in which the two operate can or should be kept distinct. It was no accident that Jesus was born a Jew, and the same individual is at one and the same time person and citizen. Moreover in practice it is evident that Judaism is constantly preoccupied with man as person since a true society is not built of robots, and that Christianity is constantly affecting society since no man, however personal his concerns, lives in a vacuum. In fact it is true to say that, though they operate from different centres within the total sphere of human activity, there is a good deal of 'Christianity' in Jewish life and thought, and a good deal of 'Judaism' in Christian life and thought.

This constant interaction has made possible, and even plausible, the traditional Christian claim that it has taken over or 'inherited' all that is of permanent validity in Sinai. Rejecting the elaborations of the Law, it claims that it has retained the moral imperative especially as interpreted by the prophets. Where this argument breaks down

[45] E.g. the statement of Jesus in Matt. 22. 21 'Render to Caesar the things that are Caesar's', of Paul in Rom. 13. 1-7 or of Peter in 1 Peter 2. 13-17.

is that no society is changed by the most lofty moral generalisations. It was, for example, not the prophets but the Pharisees and their predecessors who eliminated idolatry within the Jewish people. A society is changed when it changes its objectives, when it reforms, modifies or alters the quality of its administration and the details of its legislation; when its citizens increase their sensitivity to moral principles in the actualities of daily life and its concrete problems. Man as person can be appealed to for a total change, for a single act of repentance, and a new truth can be suddenly appreciated and alter the whole direction of personal life. Society as such is not moved by such means. Mass repentance has again and again in history shown that it produces only mass hysteria, for the psychology of 'the herd' is different from that of the individual. Judaism is not wrong when, from the standpoint of a total society, it sees the prophets as commentators on the Law and not as its replacement.

In the issue before us we can, as we have said, see the attitude of Jesus to the Sinaitic revelation from at least two pronouncements whose authenticity is guaranteed by the fact that they are in sharp contrast with the attitude of the early Church at the time they were recorded. He asserted that not one jot or tittle of the Law should pass away, and he said that the scribes 'sat in Moses' seat,' and that their instructions should be followed.[46] On the other hand, he demanded of his followers, and so of the Church which continued his and their work, that they should go beyond what society was entitled to demand. He asked for a standard of forgiveness, of purity, and of love which no law could enforce. It is by setting these two statements side by side that we can see the nature of that new society which it was a function of the Incarnation to bring into being.

The Church is not the 'remnant' described in the Old Testament; it is a *new* form of society resting on the full understanding of the meaning of man as person, which had been prepared by the developments of Jewish thought during the previous centuries, and by the emergence of distinct communities within Judaism, such as the Pharisaic *Haberim* or the Essenes. It is for that reason that the recent discovery of the 'Dead Sea Scrolls' has an important place in the study of Christian origins, and not because we shall discover therein, as is sometimes suggested, the true source of Christian beliefs or practices. That which distinguishes the teaching of Jesus and the thought of the Church is the constant feeling of a basic tension—even conflict—with 'the world'. Pharisaism was a 'reformist' movement; the Essenes constituted a movement withdrawn from the world. Thus both evaded this tension. But Jesus again and again told his

[46] Matt. 5. 18 and 23. 2.

followers that there would be conflict between them and 'the world', and he never told them to withdraw from that conflict. The distinction from these previous communities within Judaism becomes even clearer when we consider what was to be the strength that sustained the Christians in the expected conflict; it was to be drawn from their Risen Lord, from Jesus himself. An entirely new note was struck when Jesus told his disciples that 'in the world you have tribulation; *but be of good cheer, I have overcome the world*,'[47] and it is even clearer in the closing verse of the first Gospel: '*Lo, I am with you always*, to the close of the age.'[48] It is his constant sense of unity with or 'in' the Risen Lord which makes the permanent contribution of Paul to Christian thinking, but it is a note which was already struck by Jesus himself, and is evidence, were evidence needed, that the attempt to distinguish the teaching of Paul from that of Jesus, and to argue that Paul 'founded the Church' by making of Jesus something he did not himself intend, is entirely untrue.

The same new note is struck in many sayings of Jesus which have shocked by their severity. None is more striking than that recorded by Luke: 'If any one comes to me and does not hate his own father and mother and wife and children and brothers and sisters, yes, and even his own life, he cannot be my disciple.'[49] Even if we make allowance for a deliberate hyperbole, this emphasis on the conflict between the loyalties demanded by natural relationships and those demanded by Christian discipleship is entirely new; at the same time it needs to be set in close connection with the equally novel hyperbole which some have detected in the sayings of Jesus summed up in 'love your enemies'. In both there is 'an emphasis on the unattainable', the absolute, which has distinguished Christian thinking, more perhaps than Christian practice, from the beginning. If Sinai brought into existence a society struggling to achieve the ultimately attainable (and that is the true function of a society[50]) Jesus penetrated into the heart of man as person by setting before him the goal of the unattainable, the perfection to which he would always be striving, the perfection which has made the greatest of Christian saints conscious that they were the most worthless of Christian sinners.

Such a goal is inevitably of universal significance to mankind;

[47] John 16. 33.

[48] Matt. 28. 20. Many will regret the change from the familiar 'even unto the end of the world' in this verse.

[49] Luke 14. 26.

[50] Compare the emphasis on the attainable in the great discourses of Deut. chs. 4-11, and especially the summary of Deuteronomic teaching in the passage beginning 'This commandment which I command you this day is not too hard for you, neither is it far off. . . .' (30. 11).

it cannot be limited to one nation, culture or tradition. That the early Church should have been quickly brought up against the problem of the admission of Gentiles was inevitable. But two cautions are necessary if we are to put their decision in the right perspective. We have to understand the full meaning of the Jewish origin of Jesus; and we have to consider the theological and historical identification of the Sinaitic society with the single Jewish people.

In relation to the first, what is of interest is not merely that Jesus was born a Jew but that he voluntarily confined his mission to the Jewish people, and apparently instructed his disciples, when he first sent them out to preach, that they were to do likewise.[51] It does not seem exaggerated to claim that this deliberate policy rested on the fact that the new revelation which he initiated was meant to stand in the context of the old for its full significance to be understood. In fact there have been many interpretations in the Christian tradition resting on this juxtaposition. Paul, wrestling with the problem in his letter to the Romans, suggests that Jews seeking to 'establish their own' righteousness 'did not submit to God's righteousness',[52] but it would be difficult to establish this distinction from a study of the history of the two religions. Both would equally produce examples of either alternative. Modern theologians have coined the phrase that 'the good is enemy to the best', but the same comment would apply and as a generalisation it is at best a half-truth. It would seem more natural to see in the action of Jesus a positive purpose—to put before men the tension which actually exists in life, the tension between society and the persons who compose it, and this he could not have achieved by basing his mission or the first essays of his followers on contacts with a pagan society to which they would have been totally opposed. Throughout his life Jesus acted and left to others the interpretation. So in this case he left to his followers the entire responsibility for the mission to the Gentiles, and he thereby left to them likewise the decision as to the relations of the new revelation to its predecessor. We shall, however, come to a wrong conclusion about this relationship if we ignore the second caution, and assume that a Gentile mission *automatically* implied a breach with Jewish tradition, an assumption frequently made by Christian

[51] It is Matthew who reports Jesus as saying 'Go nowhere among the Gentiles and enter no town of the Samaritans.' Neither Mark nor Luke has this verse. The harsh reply of Jesus to the Syrophoenician woman (unless, as W. R. Maltby has suggested, it was said with a smile which took all the sting out of it) is common to Mark and Matthew (Mark 7. 24-30 and Matt. 15. 21-28).

[52] Rom. 10. 3.

theologians even when they do not refer 'the rejection of Israel' directly to the teaching of Jesus himself.

There is no better *theological* reason for confining the activity which flows from Sinai exclusively to the Jewish people, because it was originally given to their ancestors, than there is for confining the Christian revelation to that people because it was originally communicated and lived by a Jew. When the claim is made, as it is in the present chapter, that the essence of the Sinaitic revelation is its disclosure of the divine activity to man in society, it is implicit that it is equally applicable to *all* societies. It began with Israel, but was not intended to end there. That it has so far done so is a product of history, not of theology, and the change in Jewish attitude is a consequence of historical pressures.[53] At this period the Jewish attitude to the Gentile seems to have been much more fluid and open, as was seen in the discussion of the position of Jewish communities in the Diaspora. [54] We must not assume that the decision to preach to, and accept Gentiles, would be automatically taken by supporter and opponent alike as equivalent to a statement that an 'old' Israel was rejected and a 'new' Israel had taken its place. That such came to be the belief of the Gentile Church, we owe to the language used by Paul in his letters and the Gentile interpretation of it.

It might appear that the logical consequence of the argument that neither Jesus nor the earliest Jewish or Gentile Christians saw in the foundation of the Church the complete replacement of one exclusive divine agent by another, equally exclusive, would be either that there was no reason for conflict between the Synagogue and the Church, or, alternatively, that the Church should have been content to remain a 'sect' within Jewry, timing its expansion to the needs or outlook of the major community. As to the first, we may and should be profoundly regretful that the conflict grew to the proportions which it did, but we reduce the Incarnation to very superficial dimensions if we assume that it would be easily digestible by any already constituted religious community or institution. As to the second, it would be to concede that man as person must be subordinate to the society of which he is born, or has become, a member, or, in modern terms of the argument, to admit that the state could override the rights and consciences of its citizens, an argument which Judaism and Christianity are at one in denying.

[53] So far as a direct missionary activity of the Synagogue is concerned we have to remember that both Christianity and Islam made such activity impossible, and that from the appearance of Hasidism in the eighteenth century the pastoral idea of the rabbinate has grown considerably.

[54] See above, pp. 109 f.

The true conclusion, then, appears to be that the Church sprang rightly and inevitably from the Incarnation, and that it was bound to be an independent and separate body even within the national community of Jewry. But the relations between Sinai and Calvary are basically those of creative tension arising out of the dual inheritance of humanity. Instead of this there has been substituted, by the tragic failure of both sides, stark opposition and a false 'either—or' from which neither has benefited.

Chapter Four

THE EMERGENCE OF THE CHURCH

1. THE DISCIPLES TAKE CONTROL

THE 'event' had happened. Now it was the time for men to seek and to proclaim its 'interpretation'. For the first years of the life of the Church we are dependent on a single source, the Acts of the Apostles, and much will depend on the attitude we take to the reliability of its evidence. It is generally agreed that the book was written at least forty years after the events which its opening chapters record; but this need not make it completely unreliable if we accept as authentic the claim which the author himself makes in the third gospel that he was recounting what was 'delivered to us by those who from the beginning were eye-witnesses and ministers of the word' and that he had himself 'followed all things closely for some time past'.[1] The author was undoubtedly writing with a purpose in both works; he was not just an 'academic historian'; but it is unfair to assume that the purpose involved automatically the distortion or suppression of the evidence which came to him in the preparation of his manuscript.

Acts falls into two parts: the growth of the pre-Pauline Church and the travels and activities of Paul. The best argument for the author's essential reliability lies in two facts. In the former half he describes a situation which, as we shall see, cannot reflect the time at which he was writing, or have been invented out of the picture which the Church presented at that time; in the latter he gives us a picture of Paul's successive defences after his arrest in Jerusalem which is at such variance with the apparent evidence of the letters, and so embarrassing to the attitude which the Church was coming to take at the time of writing, that it seems impossible to explain the author's action except on the basis of his recording what had actually happened.

[1] Luke 1. 2 f. It has always seemed to me a pity that those who legitimately deny the theory of verbal inspiration should not more readily recognise that divine-human co-operation is a reasonable belief, and that sincerity and humility may open the way to those intuitions which distinguish a good historian from a bad one.

The first speeches of Peter[2] almost apologise for the Crucifixion; they certainly contain no proclamation of the Cross as the messianic throne, but expect Jesus to make a second appearance to vindicate his messianic claims. But even more striking is the lengthy speech of the proto-martyr of the Christian faith. The composition of edifying addresses to be delivered by victims of religious persecution before their deaths was already a known *genre* of literature, as 2 and 4 Maccabees witness;[3] and it appears impossible to find any reason, other than that the author had irrefutable evidence that it actually happened, for what he has recorded of Stephen. He has given us a verbose, impertinent (for Stephen was addressing judges who were as familiar with the history of Israel as he was himself) and inconclusive discourse followed by an undignified loss of temper, instead of a splendid proclamation of the messiahship of Jesus or of the new life in his name.[4] From the standpoint of literary invention it would have been much more effective to have confined his narrative to the nobility with which Stephen accepted death. Moreover, the author describes that death as a lynching; for, as he himself makes clear, the trial had not been completed, Stephen had not been found guilty, and no sentence had been pronounced. Had the narrative been an invention we should surely have had an official condemnation by the Synagogue of the proto-martyr of the Church. At the least, Stephen would have said something for which a death sentence could have been judicially pronounced. With the same frankness the author has recorded an attitude of conformity on the part of Paul towards Judaism in his successive defences which no Christian writer, exercising his imagination at that period, would have thought of inventing.

[2] Acts 2. 14 ff. and 3. 12 ff. See C. S. C. Williams, *A Commentary on the Acts*, A. & C. Black, 1957, pp. 65 ff.

[3] E.g., the speech of the aged priest Eleazar in 2 Macc. 6. 23 ff. and 4 Macc. 5. 16 ff.

[4] For a discussion of the authenticity of the speech see Lake and Foakes Jackson, *The Beginnings of Christianity* both in the commentary *ad loc.* and in additional note 32 by Henry J. Cadbury. But the latter does not approach the problem that this particular speech seems to be the last that an author would wish to invent, an argument which does not apply to the speeches of Peter and Paul. It is true that Stephen, had he not lost his temper, might eventually have come to the point of comparing the rejection of Moses with that of Jesus, though the point is rather feeble; but his argument about the Temple, while it may represent an opinion current in the Diaspora that the Temple was not really necessary, did not represent a current opinion in the Church of the first days. As to the Almighty not dwelling in temples made with hands, this, oddly enough, occurred to Solomon himself in his prayer of dedication (1 Kings 8. 27).

We can, then, accept the account given in Acts as sufficiently reliable to give us a picture of the earliest days of the Church. Largely through the work of Professor Dodd, we can identify the message or 'good news' (*kerygma*) with which the apostles sought to convince the people of Israel of the authenticity of their experience. 'It re-recounted in brief the life and work of Jesus Christ, his conflicts, sufferings, and death, and his Resurrection from the dead; and it went on to declare that in these events the divinely guided history of Israel through long centuries had reached its climax. God himself had acted decisively in this way to inaugurate his kingdom upon earth'.[5] Side by side with the good news there appears to have been from very early times a brief code of ethical and moral conduct, since we find passages identical in style and content in all the New Testament letter-writers.[6] This was a true *interims-ethik*, for the earliest expectation of the apostles was that there would be but a short period before Jesus returned in the mantle of expected messianic dignity to carry into effect the ending of the present age.

This crystallisation of their proclamation together with a simple code of ethics was the easier part of the task of the leaders of the Nazarenes (as it is appropriate to call them at this time). Much more difficult was the development of an apologetic to explain why the career of Jesus of Nazareth had been so different from what might have been expected, and why it had fallen to them, an obscure group of peasants, to convey the truth to Israel. If we envisage realistically the situation in which they found themselves we shall see that the line along which they developed their apologetic was not merely natural but inevitable. That line, which has left its permanent mark on Christian history, was to enfold their new experience within the pattern of Israel's existing religious history as set forth in Torah and illuminated by the prophets. It comprised the great drama of creation, of the call of Israel, of the ritual of atonement and forgiveness accomplished in the national sanctuary, and culminated in the day of the Lord proclaimed by the prophets and the apocalyptists. Only by so doing were they speaking a common language with those whom they sought to convince.

The gospel parable of the vineyard, and the statement that the Christian leaders should 'sit on twelve thrones judging the tribes of

[5] The *kerygma* is discussed in detail in *The Apostolic Preaching and its development*, Hodder & Stoughton, 1936. The quotation is from the same author's *Gospel and Law*, Cambridge, 1951, p. 9.

[6] Dodd, *op. cit.*, p. 18.

Israel'[7] certainly indicate that they foresaw a new leadership in Israel and saw themselves supplanting the priests and politicians of the Temple. But they do not imply any 'new' Israel in the sense of a *different* Israel. The vineyard was not abandoned in the parable, only its cultivators rejected; it was still the chosen people the new judges would judge. But this was the extent of the change which was to take place. In both there is no hint that they, as apostles of Jesus, were to create a new and distinct Israel.

The enfolding of the new experience within the existing pattern is most dramatically expressed, among New Testament writers, by the author of the Epistle to the Hebrews. He is convinced that the Mosaic interpretation of the pattern has failed, but that the whole pattern, as fulfilled by Jesus, is there already in the Scriptures. The failure itself he regards (as does Paul in writing to the Romans) as a divine intention rather than a sole product of human wickedness. Indeed he emphasises that those who failed were 'well attested by their faith'.[8] By the argument that Jesus was a 'priest for ever after the order of Melchisedek'[9] he makes the action of Jesus retrospective, covering the whole period during which the Mosaic dispensation was an earthly shadow of the heavenly pattern existing simultaneously with it but revealed only in the Incarnation.

The contemporary school of 'Biblical theology' has worked out in detail the use by New Testament writers of the conception most fully expressed in Hebrews, showing the extent to which the whole pattern of history and revelation was adapted to the new situation.[10] It is not surprising that it is the events surrounding the Exodus which attracted most attention, for the Christian saw in Christ a new deliverance implementing that which his ancestors—physical or spiritual—had experienced from Egypt. As we shall see in treating of the teaching of Paul, it is an implementation which is in question and not a repetition, a point which is not always clear with the theologians of this school. It is because of the concentration on this

[7] The parable of the rejection of the cultivators of the vineyard is found in all three synoptists (Mark 12. 1 ff., Luke 20. 9 ff., and Matt. 21. 33 ff.). The promise that the apostles would judge Israel is not found in Mark, but is in Luke 22. 30 and Matt. 19. 28.

[8] Compare Heb. 11. 39: 'And all these, though well attested by their faith, did not receive what was promised' with Rom. 11. 30-32: 'Just as you were once disobedient to God but now have received mercy because of their disobedience, so they have now been disobedient in order that by the mercy shown to you they also may receive mercy. For God has consigned all men to disobedience, that he may have mercy upon all.'

[9] Heb. 6. 20 and 7. 15-17.

[10] Compare *The Way of At-one-ment* by W. J. Phythian-Adams. See especially chapters 1 and 2.

period of the history of Israel that we get the familiar symbol of Jesus as the paschal lamb; for in itself the symbol is not appropriate. Many Christian liturgies have the words 'O lamb of God that takest away the sins of the world', but the paschal lamb was not a sin offering. The sin offering *par excellence* was the scape-goat, and, though the author of the Epistle to the Hebrews uses the ritual of the Day of Atonement as the basis of his picture of the redeeming work of Christ, he compares the latter to the high priest, not to the offering itself. Nevertheless, in the various books of the New Testament there are constant verbal reminders of the events of Israel's sacred history and of the actual ritual and worship of the tabernacle in the wilderness. Paul has summed up this attitude in the opening verses of his letter to the Romans when he speaks of himself as 'set apart for the gospel of God which he promised beforehand through his prophets in the holy scriptures'.[11]

While such an apologetic could explain the stumbling block of the Crucifixion, and bring the suffering servant of Deutero-Isaiah into the centre of the picture of messianic activity, it still left unexplained the nature of the actual life which Jesus had lived, and was no answer to the expectation that the coming of the Messiah should be the end of history as they knew it. Jesus had spent his time in preaching and healing; and his death had been accompanied by no visible and fundamental alteration in the state of the world around them. It was from this dilemma that was evolved the theory that the actual life which had ended on the Cross was *not* the messianic appearance of Jesus as the Christ, but a preliminary, designed to give the world an opportunity for repentance. This was to be almost immediately followed by the culmination foretold in the Scriptures as the end of the great drama of creation, the 'day of the Lord'. The situation is made clear in Peter's second speech, that which followed the healing of the lame man: 'Repent therefore and turn again that your sins may be blotted out, that times of refreshing may come from the presence of the Lord, and *that he may send the Christ appointed for you, Jesus*, whom heaven must receive until the time for establishing all that God spoke by the mouth of his holy prophets from of old.'[12]

This curious theology is explicable as a first essay in interpretation and apologetic, for the material from which the earliest believers could draw their arguments was inevitably the Scriptures which both they and those with whom they discussed these things held to be

[11] Rom. 1. 2.

[12] Acts 3. 19-21. Compare 18. 5 where Paul at Corinth testified to the Jews 'that the Christ was Jesus'.

sacred. What it leaves entirely out of account is any appreciation of the independent originality of the Incarnation, or any apologetic based on actual experience of the present powers of the risen Christ. The Jesus which it expounds is a Jesus whose every action was already foretold and already embodied (even if in shadowy form) in the past revelation of the divine purpose in creation, and in the fast and festival of the ritual year of Judaism, especially as expressed in the Temple at Jerusalem.

The first evidence that the life of Jesus and the power of the risen Christ could not be so easily and conveniently fitted into this tidy scheme came as a consequence of the first persecution of the Nazarenes. So far as the persecution itself is concerned we must regard it as political, as a continuation of that caution which feared the effect of Jesus on the crowds in Jerusalem, and not as a religious condemnation of a new theology. When Peter was first brought before the high priest and the council, the charge was that he was accusing the authorities of the nation of having committed a judicial murder.[13] He was bringing them into contempt by telling the crowds that one whom they had handed over to the Romans for execution was, in fact, the Messiah.

It was at this session that Luke reports that Gamaliel intervened on behalf of the accused with the words: 'keep away from these men and let them alone; for if this plan or this undertaking is of men, it will fail; but if it is of God you will not be able to overthrow them. You might even be found opposing God!'[14] If we accept the account given by Luke of the first days of the Church as substantially accurate there is no reason why we should make an exception for the speech of Gamaliel, the leader of the 'Pharisaic' or 'Tannaitic' party. It does not imply acceptance of the teaching of Peter but, rather, disapproval of the Sadducaic policy of repression, and of seeing a political danger in every manifestation of religious effervescence. At the moment it apparently achieved a limited success but it did not save the apostles from a scourging.

The movement spread in Jerusalem, and brought in the hellenistic communities which abounded in the holy city. From them a new crisis arose, provoked by Stephen who, so far as our evidence goes, was a provocative rather than an effective apologist. We have only a few verses to describe, by vague allusions from his enemies, what the line of his apologetic was. He was said to have spoken 'blasphemous words against Moses and God'; and to have spoken against 'this holy place and the law', alleging that 'this Jesus of Nazareth will

[13] Acts. 5. 27 f.
[14] Acts 5. 38 f.

destroy this place and will change the customs which Moses delivered to us'.[15] The one point which would seem to be clear is that Stephen was feeling his way towards what would have been a commonplace of Christian thinking later, that the life and words of Jesus could not be as easily fitted into the primitive pattern as had been assumed. But more than that we cannot say. In any case the persecution which followed brought new problems of interpretation.

It is curious that New Testament scholars seem largely to have overlooked the significance of the first spread of the teaching about Jesus outside the Jerusalem area. It was among the Samaritans and, so far as all the subsequent evidence goes, it permanently healed the breach between Jews and Samaritans so far as the Nazarenes were concerned. Caesarea, which was to be the main bishopric of Palestine, was in Samaritan territory, and we hear of no protest that Jerusalem was subject to it until the importance of the latter as a centre of pilgrimage caused it to be made an independent patriarchate in the fifth century.[16]

The successful preaching among the Samaritans was followed almost immediately by a further advance: the acceptance of a few Gentile converts into the Nazarene fellowship. This was not in itself a revolutionary step, nor did it, of itself, involve a breach with Judaism. As we now know, there was a widespread missionary activity in the diaspora synagogues of the time,[17] and in this case prophetic expectation enabled the Nazarenes easily to fit the admission of Gentiles into the framework of their theological scheme. That a turning of the Gentiles to the God of Israel would be one of the manifestations of the 'last days' had been foretold on a number of occasions, and the Nazarenes believed that they were living, at least by anticipation, in the Age of the Messiah. That this is so is shown, better than by any argument, by the almost casual words in which Luke reports the innovation. After Peter had reported his experience with Cornelius, the centurion of Caesarea, 'the apostles and brethren who were in Judea' 'glorified God, saying, "then to the Gentiles also God has granted repentance unto life".'[18]

This phase of Nazarene theology does not end abruptly with the entry of Paul into the centre of the stage, although from now onwards it will be easier to use the word 'Christian' in place of 'Naza-

[15] Acts 6. 11-15.

[16] This is still a remarkable fact, even though the Jerusalem bishops were of Gentile origin from 135 onwards. There were still plenty of Christians of Jewish origin in the Church after that.

[17] See above pp. 109 f. and below, pp. 317 ff.

[18] Acts 11. 18. The narrative of the conversion of Cornelius begins with 10. 1.

rene'.[19] The eschatology of the letters to the Thessalonians is based entirely on the almost immediate return of Jesus as the Christ, and the idea of a speedy end to the Age never wholly disappears from Pauline thought, even though it passes into the background. Nevertheless with Paul a new period *is* reached, for with him we become acquainted with a new appraisal of the meaning of the life of Jesus and of the power of the risen Christ. It becomes less and less a question of fitting an account of the Incarnation into this or that previous experience of Israel, or this or that declaration of the prophets, and increasingly a challenge to 'know the truth in Christ' by the experience of membership of his body.

2. THE TEACHING OF PAUL AS IT AFFECTS THE JEWISH-CHRISTIAN RELATIONSHIP

THE statement that 'with Paul a new period is reached' needs the qualification: 'so far as our records inform us'. As a statement of fact it is almost certainly untrue. The power of the living Christ was not being manifested only in the most brilliant of his followers; and it must have been the general if unrecorded experience of the whole body that many things were happening to them *directly* and not just because it had been spoken by the prophets. That which built up the Church was the life of its members; that which brought in new converts was the enthusiasm and piety of those members and the evidence which they offered that they possessed a secret for which others longed. As the years passed, an increasing number of those members were of Gentile origin, and of them Kirsopp Lake acutely observes that 'they had accepted much of Jewish theology, and especially the doctrine of the Messiah, but the community which they desired to enter was the Messianic kingdom, not the Jewish Church, and to their mind it was plain that membership in this kingdom was the privilege of those who accepted the Messiah, and was independent of the Law which was an exclusively Jewish possession'.[20] Lake has oversimplified the situation by attributing to first century Gentiles only that attitude which is identical with that of the modern mind. We must not go to the other extreme and deny that it was one of the attitudes adopted, but we can detect at least two others.

There is plenty of evidence from the ancient world of the attraction

[19] Acts 11. 26. 'In Antioch the disciples were for the first time called Christians.'

[20] Kirsopp Lake, *The Earlier Epistles of Saint Paul*, Rivingtons, 1919, p. 27.

of the most complicated and exacting ritualism, and that customs such as circumcision could attract as well as repel. The presence of both in Judaism did not always have the effect which Lake predicates. Writing to his Galatian converts Paul reproaches them with becoming slaves to 'days and months and seasons and years'[21] and while Paul himself might regard such things as slavery to 'weak and beggarly elemental spirits' it is evident that Gentile Galatians ranked them much more highly, and regarded the spirits thus approached as divine. Moreover the language which Paul, speaking Greek, was obliged to use of Jesus as the Christ could be tied up with the language of the mystery religions,[22] and the combination of a saviour with a complicated ritual and a bodily mutilation exercised a fascination the modern mind is only beginning to understand from the studies of the anthropologists.

There was yet a third attitude to Judaism and the Scriptures which prevailed in the Diaspora, among both Jews and Gentile God-fearers. The history and law of the Scriptures was regarded as having a secret allegorical meaning which made them a clue at once to universal history and to universal morality. While our fullest expression of this view is in Philo, he opposed those Jews who saw *only* such meanings in the story of Israel.[23] The very fact of his opposition testifies to the existence of the view which he opposed, which the New Testament confirms; for such allegorical methods are used by Paul himself in addressing audiences which were both Jewish and Gentile. He entirely allegorizes circumcision and offers a complicated allegorical interpretation of the story of Hagar and Ishmael.[24]

Any one of these attitudes might be found equally well among Jews or God-fearing Gentiles, among those who accepted and those who rejected the identification of the Messiah with Jesus. We must guard against drawing a picture of clear-cut divisions where there was a wide diversity of opinions shading into one another, or of clear-cut alignments where men holding these diverse opinions, and of Jewish or Gentile origin, might be found for or against that identification.

The problem set by the group described by Lake was dealt with before Paul entered on the scene, when the Jerusalem Church accepted almost casually the earliest Samaritan and Gentile converts without any prescriptions as to how or in what measure they

[21] Gal. 4. 10. Compare the 'teachers of the Law' in 1 Tim. 1. 3-7.

[22] The mystery redeemer was *Kurios*, 'Lord', the phrase often used by Greek Christians as a synonym for the Hebraicism *Christos* or 'Anointed'.

[23] Philo, *On the Migration of Abraham*, 16.

[24] Rom. 2. 28 and Gal. 4. 24 ff.

were to conform to Jewish law and practice. Formal confirmation of this attitude came in the subsequent decisions at Jerusalem[25] after the conflict between Peter and Paul at Antioch. They were 'liberal'. There was nothing un-Jewish in this. There was a general agreement among Jews that the Messianic Age involved new relations with the Gentiles but there was no halakic decision as to what those relations should be. In the atmosphere of the time the decisions of the council at Jerusalem were perfectly reasonable, and the fact that they were put forward by James, whose Jewish orthodoxy was never under suspicion, was a guarantee that they would have the support of the bulk of the Jewish Christians. And indeed, though the Judeo-Christian community came under grave suspicion in the second century, and was excommunicated by both sides before the middle of that century, we never hear of any official demand that Gentile Christians should obey the whole of the law even from those circles whose own obedience enabled them to remain within the Jewish community into the third and fourth century.[26]

In fact there gradually grew up in rabbinic Judaism the conception of 'Noachic Commandments' which were obligatory on all mankind and which were very similar to the instructions to the Gentiles in Acts,[27] though it was never accepted that simple observance of these ethical standards entitled a man to admission to the Chosen People. But then rabbinic Jews did not believe that they were living, even by anticipation, in the messianic Age.

With the third group, the allegorizers, Paul had no quarrel. But in the second he saw the deadliest enemies to his gospel. It is too often assumed that this group was wholly Jewish. Indeed Christian scholars have gone further and considered it to be the only attitude possible, not merely for Jews but even for Jewish Christians. It is important to recognise that such a view has no support from the author of Acts. The Jerusalem council was precipitated by '*some men* who came down from Judea' to Antioch and told the Gentile Christians there that they needed to be circumcised.[28] A little later[29] he is more specific but still makes it clear that this was not an official action. The 'some men' of Judea become 'some believers who

[25] Gal. 2. 11-14, and Acts ch. 15.

[26] See below, p. 222.

[27] 15. 20. On Noachian Laws, see *The Jewish Encyclopaedia*, Laws, Noachian. That portion of the Pentateuch in which they are embodied has been extracted and published with notes as *The Universal Bible, being the Pentateuchal Texts at first addressed to all Nations*, by Solomon Schonfeld, Sidgwick and Jackson, 1955.

[28] Acts 15. 1.

[29] *Ibid.* 5.

belonged to the party of the Pharisees'. As Paul related in Galatians they swung Peter and even Barnabas over to their view—but only for a time.[30] Throughout they were only a minority within the Church—and it may well be that part of Paul's infuriated attack on them arose from the fact that he recognised in them just the kind of Pharisee which he had once been himself.[31] But there is no reason to suppose that this outlook was confined to Jews. It is a phenomenon of all religions that a convert can be 'plus catholique que le Pape'.

The problems created by the various attitudes to Judaism among Gentile believers were rendered more complicated by two other issues which were forcing themselves on the attention of the nascent Church. One issue particularly affected its Jewish members. We know that there were many opinions about the messiah in the Jewish world of that time, and it is possible that the Dead Sea scrolls will enrich our knowledge with evidence of messianic beliefs more akin to those held by the early Christians than we had hitherto encountered. But it must still have been a matter of extreme perplexity and acute distress to Jewish Christians that there was no Jewish mass movement to their side. It was a situation for which no prophet or apocalyptist had prepared them—that the messiah should have announced himself, and that the bulk of the people should not have believed him.

This perplexity was rendered still more poignant by the lack of any signs that their confident expectation of the immediate return of Jesus would be fulfilled. Almost a generation had gone by, many Christians were already dead. In the Holy Land itself the tension between Jews and Romans was increasing, political extremism was more and more adopting the evil methods of terrorism, and yet the Messiah delayed to return.

These three factors—uncertainty about the relation between Judaism and the Church, distress caused by the non-acceptance of their messianic proclamation by the majority of the Jewish people, and perplexity as to why the messiah delayed his return—form together the background to the immense, complex, and sometimes contradictory structure raised by Paul in his letters and his speeches in Acts.

In the factual situation which Paul had to meet there were *two* Israels. There was the Jewish people who, in the mass, remained faithful to the Mosaic Torah, and there was a new body, composed of Jews and Gentiles, who were coming to regard themselves messiani-

[30] It is Paul who says in Gal. 2. 12 that they came from James, but he has said already in v. 9 that James joined with Peter and John to approve the actions of Paul and Barnabas.

[31] Gal. 1. 14.

cally as a new and true 'Israel of God'. Paul did not accept this duality. He did not accept a rejection of the 'old' Israel and the substitution of a 'new' one. Like the rabbis he did not accept automatic membership of the Kingdom as a consequence of physical birth—there were Jews who by their own sin shut themselves out of the life to come—but he looked forward to the time when 'all Israel will be saved'.[32] That 'Israel' would be one with the Gentile believers without distinction in the messianic kingdom.[33] This was a position amply supported by reference to the prophets and there was no reason for Paul to feel 'un-Jewish' in putting it forward. There is also no evidence that he ever wavered in his convictions that this is how history would develop.

Paul is also clear and consistent on the secondary issue of the reasons for the delay in the return of Jesus as Messiah. The Church was living in an interim period, designed in the mercy of God to give the Gentile time to learn of the kingdom and so to catch up with the Jew and provoke him to emulation of his faith.[34] When this time had elapsed, all Israel would be found within the messianic kingdom and the end could come.

Thus far Paul's thought is clear and straightforward. The complications begin with the consequences of his conviction that entry into the messianic kingdom could only be by faith, and with the fact that when he uses the word 'nomos' or 'law' he uses it with three quite different meanings. In the seventh chapter of Romans and in some other places it means any external regulation of conduct, and is as applicable to his own ethical teaching as to any other. In some places it means Torah, that is Judaism as practised by Jews. In Galatians particularly it means primarily the ritual and ceremonial laws of Judaism as they concern Gentile converts.

It is in this last sense that the stark opposition between faith and works first emerges: 'O foolish Galatians! Who has bewitched you, before whose eyes Jesus Christ was publicly portrayed as crucified? Let me ask you only this: Did you receive the Spirit by works of the law, or by hearing with faith? Are you so foolish? Having begun with the Spirit, are you now ending with the flesh? Did you experience so many things in vain?—if it really is in vain. Does he who supplies the Spirit to you and works miracles among you do so by works of the law, or by hearing with faith?'[35]

[32] Rom. 11. 26.
[33] Gal. 3. 27-29, Rom. 10. 12, Eph. 2. 11-15, Col. 3. 9-11. Compare also Rom. 3. 20-22, 27-31.
[34] Rom. 11. 11 f. and 25-27.
[35] Gal. 3. 1-5.

The situation in Galatia was *not* that there was any move against the ethical living which Judaism inculcated in the God-fearers, but that the party within the Church which had caused trouble at Antioch wanted the Gentile adherents to the kingdom to be circumcised and to observe the whole ritual law.[36] In absolutely rejecting such a proposition Paul was fighting for the fundamental truth that with the Incarnation a *new* relationship between God and man was born, and that the entry into that relationship could only be by the faith of the entrant. The whole history of Christianity would support him in his contention. The words of A. M. Toplady in the hymn 'Rock of Ages' express the common conviction of all the Christian Churches through the ages:

'Nothing in my hand I bring,
Simply to thy Cross I cling'.

From the most clerical and ceremonial Church to the simplest Christian body this remains the common conviction. Christ asks for the surrender of man's whole personality to himself, and in return makes of him, as Paul well knew, 'a new creation'.

It is important to realise that this fundamental truth expressed a relationship with which Judaism had not dealt, or needed to deal. This was not because Judaism was a religion believing that spiritual benefit came from the mechanical performance of 'works'. In its own terms Judaism dealt with the problem of human merit with the same spiritual insight as Paul. The religion of a community is properly a religion of works, and the rabbis were perpetually pre-occupied in insisting on the importance of *the spirit* in which the works were performed. Already in the transitional period which followed 'the men of the Great Synagogue' Antigonus of Soko had made the statement: 'Be not as slaves that minister to the Lord with a view to recompense; but be as slaves that minister to the Lord without a view to receive recompense; and let the fear of Heaven be upon you'.[37] Later rabbis developed the doctrine of *kawwanah* or 'intention', emphasising that no work performed without the intention of serving God and fulfilling his will had any validity.[38] There was, in consequence, no opposition in Judaism between 'faith' and 'works' such as Paul posits. One could again say that Paul's thought is 'clear and straightforward' so long as the 'works' with which he is

[36] Gal. 5: 2 and 6. 12.

[37] Ab. 1. 3, p. 3.

[38] Compare the excellent section on *Kawwanah* in Ch. 10 of the *Rabbinic Anthology*, and the exposition of Hasidic *Kawwanah* in *The Legend of The Baal Shem* by Martin Buber, East and West Library, 1956, pp. 33 ff.

dealing are formal and not ethical. But, even in Galatians, he goes straight on from the practical issue of circumcision and Jewish ritual obligations to Torah itself.

He is led to this development by his conviction that it is not only the entry into the Christian life which rests upon faith and faith alone, but that man's eternal status is that of 'justification by faith' in the atonement made by his crucified Redeemer. And here he becomes involved in his deeper condemnation of Judaism. For he is convinced that by 'the works of the Law'—and this must mean more than just ritual—no man is justified before God.[39] His whole conception of 'justification' is linked to the purpose of the Incarnation and the belief in a future life. But the Law, in its full sense of Torah, never set out to provide such justification, and the idea itself has no natural place in its unfolding. We must remember that the people of Israel came late in their development to a conception of life after death. It has no place in the written Scriptures and, though it was a universal Pharisaic belief by the time of Jesus, there was still no definition of its nature or of the conditions on which it was obtained. Rabbis could with perfect freedom accept that 'the righteous of all nations have a share in the world to come' or, on the other hand, define in terms of the particular subject which they happened to be discussing that this or that class of Israelite would have no share in the life to come. Certainly there was never a definition, such as the strictures of Paul might imply, that the reward of eternal life was secured by the performance of particular 'works'. Moreover, Judaism never lacked the humility of consciousness of man's failure to fulfil God's purposes.[40]

We must recognise that, if Paul's adversaries could not make the new faith neat and logical by imposing on its adherents the formal duties of the old, neither could Paul make the old faith logically coherent with the new—and therefore liable to his condemnation—by judging it by standards to which, in the divine purpose, it was never meant to conform.

For Paul the issue of a future life was of capital importance. 'If Christ has not been raised, then our preaching is in vain and your faith is in vain . . . you are still in your sins . . . those who have fallen asleep in Christ have perished . . . we are of all men most to be pitied.'[41] Therefore, the conditions under which a future life was assured were of equal importance, and it was here that, however

[39] Compare Acts 13. 39; Gal. 2. 21, 3. 11; Rom. 3. 20, 9. 32.

[40] Compare the almost Pauline language of Ps. 143. 2 'in thy sight shall no man living be justified' (Prayer Book version).

[41] From 1 Cor. 15. 13-19.

much he owed his basic ideas to his rabbinic training, he saw a deep gulf fixed between his teaching and that of Judaism.[42]

In view of the enormous influence on subsequent Christian thinking which Paul has had, it is remarkable that at this point he entirely diverges from the attitude of Jesus himself. Jesus made no wholesale onslaught on the Law and distinguished that which seemed to him wrong and unworthy from the main stream of Torah which, he said, would not pass away. Paul, on the other hand, condemns Torah itself in a number of passages. It is one of the mysteries of history that it is Paul and not Jesus who has been the determinant in the Christian attitude to Judaism, and that this is so in spite of the additional fact that in the New Testament itself there is condemnation of his unrestricted opposition of faith and works. For it is impossible not to regard the second chapter of the letter of James as containing a direct answer to the interpretation which some of his adherents made of some of the arguments of Paul. For Paul on a number of occasions had derived his teaching about the role of Judaism from his view that the justification of Abraham rested exclusively on his faith[43] and James, after pointedly saying that faith without works soon became hypocrisy, referred explicitly to Abraham and pointed out that he also had 'works' to commend him.

The traditional acceptance of the strictures of the Pauline letters is all the more extraordinary, in that Paul himself affirms again and again in his speeches as reported in the closing chapters of Acts that 'neither against the law of the Jews, nor against the temple, nor

[42] W. D. Davies, who in *Paul and Rabbinic Judaism* has provided a most exhaustive study of the sources of the ideas of Paul, and found evidence of them in rabbinic literature, attempts to minimise the differences on this issue by arguing that Paul regarded the doctrine of justification by faith 'not as the essential pivot of his thought but as a convenient polemic' (p. 222). This seems to me an impossible position to maintain. So long as only a selected portion of humanity is believed to be assured of a future life, so long will the conditions of that assurance be of capital importance to the Christian theologian. The arguments of Augustine, Luther or Barth can be rejected only by the belief in the ultimate salvation of creation as an indissoluble unity. Justification by faith, though the excesses added to the doctrine by the theologians named may be otiose, is the only possible belief of a Christian who accepts that salvation is partial. It is therefore central to Pauline thought and cannot possibly be dismissed as a 'convenient polemic' weapon.

[43] Compare Gal. 3. 6 f., and Rom. 4, 3 and 9 with James 2. 14-24. In the succeeding verses he might be considered to be correcting the emphasis of the letter to the Hebrews equally, For the latter in his famous chapter on the heroes of faith not merely refers to Abraham in Pauline terms, but includes Rahab also as a heroine of faith (11. 8-10 and 31). James points out that the merits of Rahab derived from her 'works'.

against Caesar have I offended at all'.[44] The whole of these chapters merits much more careful study for their emphasis on the extent of Paul's conformity. The Church at Jerusalem 'glorified God' when they heard Paul's account of his mission, and asked him to disprove the precise charge that rumour circulated 'that you teach all the Jews who are among the Gentiles to forsake Moses, telling them not to circumcise their children or observe the customs'.[45] And Paul readily agreed to do so. When Paul was before the sanhedrin he prevented a decision against him by proclaiming that it was because of the Pharisaic doctrine of the resurrection that he was in trouble.[46] But the Pharisees would certainly not have been interested in this defence if they had definite evidence that he had said the things about Torah which we have in his letters (it is difficult for us to realise that at this period the letters were not 'Holy Scripture' and were probably buried in the archives of local Churches where the few we possess survived, almost by accident, until a later generation rediscovered them).

The Church fathers and modern scholars alike have been puzzled by the inconsistency these speeches reveal. The former adopted the view that Paul lied to save his life; the latter, aware of the psychological difficulties of so bald and brutal a statement, say the same thing in more moderate language.[47] It seems fairer to Paul to acknowledge that he believed his statement to be true. So far as the actual language of the letters is concerned we can reasonably accept the idea that Paul would not remember precise phrases of lengthy letters written a good many years previously. But the issue is more important than the language in which Paul expressed it.

To get the right perspective we must remember that Paul saw the historic people of Israel and the Gentiles as a unity, with equal status in Christ. When he says to the Galatians that he was entrusted with the mission to 'the uncircumcision'[48] we must not assume that it involves not preaching to Jews, and it is wrong to link this statement up with the two-fold utterance in Acts: 'since you thrust [the word of God] from you, and judge yourselves unworthy of eternal life, behold, we turn to the Gentiles'.[49] For in each case the author

[44] Acts 25. 8. Compare 22. 3 and 12 (the emphasis on the Jewish orthodoxy of Ananias who baptized him) and 23. 14.

[45] Acts 21. 20.

[46] Acts 23. 6-9.

[47] E.g., Professor Menzies in Peake's Commentary, p. 800 or Professor Rackham, in his commentary on Acts, p. 430.

[48] Gal. 2. 7.

[49] Acts 13. 46 and 18. 6.

relates that, at his next stop, Paul went as usual to the synagogue.[50] It is always on the basis of a unity in Christ that we must approach his references to Judaism and the history of Israel. For that unity is a matter of experience and not of theory, however grounded.

If the contention of the previous chapter be true, that Sinai and Calvary exist in creative tension by which neither can absorb the other, then we have here the basic reason for the contradictions in Pauline thought and the variety of means by which he sought to relate his experience to his theory.

In the period during which he entered the Nazarene community, the preachers of Jesus as Messiah sought, as shown in the previous section, to fit the Incarnation within the picture of what had been foretold by the Scriptures. This line of argument is apparent also in Paul. To understand it we need to remember, as Professor Davies reminds us convincingly in *Paul and Rabbinic Judaism*, that Paul's thought was essentially Jewish. He shared the outlook by which the suffering servant was at once an individual and a community within the nation, or, indeed, the nation itself redeemed, the outlook by which the psalmists moved without difficulty from singular to plural and from past to future, the outlook, in fact, by which a modern orthodox Jew insists in the Seder service that his generation was with that of his ancestors in the deliverance from Egyptian bondage. When, therefore, Professor Davies seeks to show that Paul thought of a *new* exodus or a *new* Torah,[51] he is transferring Paul's thought from its native background to one essentially alien to him. That which was fulfilled in Jesus was the history and revelation which was given in the Scriptures, and it had only one, not two, fulfilments. Paul's clearest expression of this idea, so strange to us with our hellenic background, is the statement that the children of Israel in the desert 'drank from the supernatural Rock which followed them, and the Rock was Christ'.[52] As there was only one rock, so there was only *one* exodus, only *one* sacred history.

Moreover, if we accepted the idea that Paul saw a *new* exodus, a *new* giving of a *new* Torah which involved a *new* covenant, there

[50] Acts 14. 1 and 18. 19.

[51] *Op. cit.*, p. 225.

[52] 1 Cor. 10. 4. The idea that the well of water followed the Israelites in all their wanderings is to be found in a number of rabbinic Midrashim. See L. Ginzberg, *The Legends of the Jews*, Vol. 3, pp. 50 ff. and Vol. 6, p. 21, notes 123 ff. It is worth comparing this idea in Paul with Rev. 13. 8; 'the Lamb that hath been slain from the foundation of the world', which certainly does not imply two Crucifixions. The text is that of the English Revised Version. The American Revised Standard Version translates differently. The Greek allows both and here the English seems preferable.

would be no reason for him to go beyond this thought. He could rest content with the statement that 'the Law was our custodian [schoolmaster] to bring us to Christ',[53] and with the splendid précis of Jewish history contained in the words 'to them belong the sonship, the glory, the covenants, the giving of the law, the worship, and the promises, to them belong the patriarchs, and of their race, according to the flesh, is the Christ'.[54] All this was glorious; there was no reason to attack it; but, on the other hand, Paul would have had to proclaim quite unequivocally that it had been only a preliminary, and had now been superseded by something which was essentially new.

That somehow this logical sequence did not cover Paul's thought is shown, not only by his violent attacks on the law as a 'ministration of death', as bringing a curse, as increasing sin and so on[55] but by the curious breakdown of his argument in the beginning of his letter to the Romans. After discussing the situation of the Gentiles Paul asks 'Then what advantage has the Jew? Or what is the value of circumcision?' and answers 'Much in every way'.[56] But after a beginning that the Jews were 'entrusted with the oracles of God', he cannot think of any argument that the Jewish situation was better than that of the Gentiles, and says explicitly nine verses later 'Are we Jews any better off? No, not at all'. Then, at the end of this particular argument he suddenly exclaims: 'Do we then overthrow the law by this faith? By no means! On the contrary, we uphold the law.'[57] No amount of ingenious commenting will produce evidence which an objective and fair-minded Jewish scholar could accept that the argument in this chapter was really upholding Torah. But if we acknowledge one side of Paul's thought to be that of his contemporaries, that the whole drama of the Incarnation and Redemption was already enfolded within the relations between Jahweh and Israel, then we can see that by rooting his insistence on faith in the original call of Abraham he did feel that he was bringing the whole covenant relationship of Torah within one scheme of salvation, however much Israel had fallen short of divine expectation. In fact he was doing so even on his own premise, for, as Martin Buber has

[53] Gal. 3. 24.

[54] Rom. 9. 4 f. Dr. Barth in his commentary on Romans *ad loc.* considers that the final phrase 'God who is over all be blessed for ever' should be amended to bring it within the series, since the knowledge of the true God also came from Israel.

[55] See for example, Rom. 2. 25; 3. 20; 8. 2; 1 Cor. 15. 56; Gal. 3. 10-14.

[56] Rom. 3. 1.

[57] Rom. 3. 31.

shown, there is an important, if subtle, difference between the Jewish and the Christian use of the word 'faith'.[58]

It is foolish to seek ingenious reconciliations of these passages or arguments by which an appearance of coherence is given to them, because they are true reflections of the real situation. It was impossible to give adequate expression to Paul's fundamental conviction that the centre of his gospel was suffering and triumphant love, love manifested when we were yet sinners,[59] and fit it into the history of Israel as revealed in the Scriptures, while at the same time maintaining, as Paul maintained, that the history of Israel was God's design covering the whole purpose of creation. Paul knew that without Israel there would have been no Christ. His experience told him that in Christ he was 'a new creation', not covered by the history of Israel. There was no alchemy by which these two facts could be fitted, by the subordination of one or the other, into a neat and logical whole. His thought and its contradictions reflect his dilemma. His subsequent interpreters have only increased it by their refusal to see that the dilemma cannot be resolved. And the result has been the tragedy of the Jewish people at the hands of the Christian Church through the centuries.

3. LEGAL IMPLICATIONS OF THE PAULINE MISSION

THE absolute unity and equality of Jew and Gentile 'in Christ' was basic to Paul's whole conception of the gospel. Unfortunately, it lacked any positive legal basis in the laws of the Roman empire, and especially in the Greek cities which were the scene of much of his work. It was not difficult for Paul to accept that the churches which he founded were considered by other Jews to constitute one of the many sects into which the Jewish people were in that period divided. As he says himself in his speech before Felix, Roman governor of Judaea: 'This I admit to you, that according to the Way, which they call a sect, I worship the God of our fathers, believing everything laid down by the law or written in the prophets.'[60] He would not have been involved in any legal difficulties had he confined himself to persuading other Jews to accept his 'Way'. Nor would there have been trouble if he sought to increase the number of God-fearers among the Gentiles. But, once he included in one body men and

[58] See *Two Types of Faith*, Routledge and Kegan Paul, 1951, *passim.*
[59] Rom. 5. 8.
[60] Acts 24. 14.

women of Jewish and Gentile origin, and insisted on considering them all equal, then a new legal situation arose. For Paul was then implicitly claiming for such Gentiles the privileges which successive Roman rulers had accorded to the Jewish people.

Basically such privileges were confined to those who were Jews both by birth and by religion.[61] It is true that Roman law did not make any general regulation forbidding a citizen or subject to adopt the religion of his choice, and such a law would have been alien to the whole spirit of Roman tolerance in matters of religion. But in the case of the adoption of Judaism special considerations existed. Jews had a position not of equality but of privilege, for they alone were allowed to refuse participation in the public worship of the empire or of its different cities; and no state can be indifferent to the indefinite multiplication of the beneficiaries of a privilege originally extended to a restricted group. In accordance with the general spirit of toleration in Roman law, the adoption of Judaism—either in whole or in part—was not defined as a crime but, *because of the special nature of that religion*, the law could not explicitly extend to such converts the privilege intended for those who were Jews by birth and faith. They therefore would have no defence if they were charged with the crime of atheism.

Atheism in Roman law was not a particular theological belief but the non-accomplishment of an act, viz: the worship of the gods, whether imperial, civic or domestic.[62] Of course, if a convert was at the same time prepared to continue his public or domestic religious obligations no issue arose; but such compliance was unlikely in any case, whether the man in question were a convert to Pharisaic or to any sectarian Judaism. A convert was more likely to be aggressive in his refusal to commit an act which was a basic disobedience to his new faith and condemned in the decalogue itself. Not every convert would, however, be called upon for a public confession of his faith. If he or she were an obscure person then only domestic worship would be affected and, since the husband was master of his household and could worship as he liked, only wives with pagan husbands would in practice be subject to severe penalties.[63] But public worship would be involved for any man who exercised any public function, or who belonged to the imperial entourage. If such

[61] J. Juster, *op. cit.*, I, p. 232.

[62] Juster, *ibid.*, p. 255 f.

[63] Juster, *ibid.*, p. 256, n. 3, quotes two prominent women who suffered in this way. Paul seems to be unaware of the distinction of the sexes in this matter, since he gives the same advice to husbands and wives with a pagan partner in 1 Cor. 7. 12-16.

a person refused to participate in public worship he had become positively guilty of the crime of atheism.

During the lifetime of Paul this guilt might be overlooked, or bring no legal charge with it. For it was not until the reign of the emperor Domitian at the end of the first century that Rome encouraged private informers to denounce the guilty, and this practice was in general opposed to Roman conduct in such matters, for Rome applied readily the precept *de minimis non curat lex*. So long as no public harm resulted, or the law was not conspicuously flouted, a certain amount of Jewish missionary activity was overlooked.[64] But what Paul set out to do could not easily be accepted as covered by this attitude, for wherever he went he preached publicly and sought to win Jewish and Gentile men and women to that unity in Christ which entering the Church involved.

There are three occasions in *Acts* where Paul was involved in the consequences of his anomalous position. In the sixteenth chapter is related at length the visit of Paul to the Roman colony of Philippi. There a slave girl 'who had a spirit of divination' brought a good deal of publicity to his activities. He exorcised the spirit to the loss of her owners who thereupon brought him before the magistrates on the charge that 'these men are Jews and they are disturbing our city. They advocate customs which it is not lawful for us Romans to accept or practise.' The accusation may have arisen maliciously but the charge was correct. Paul was preaching 'atheism' to Roman citizens, and doing it to a public particularly proud of its status as a Roman colony devoted to the worship, not of some provincial deity, but of the gods of Rome itself. In the end the magistrates were content with expelling Paul from the city.

The troubles which Paul encountered shortly afterwards in Thessalonica can be brought under the same category. The leaders of the riot against him on this occasion were Jews who stirred up some unspecified 'wicked fellows of the rabble', and their accusation is worded differently: 'these men who have turned the world upside down have come here also . . . and they are all acting against the decrees of Caesar, saying there is another king, Jesus.'[65] On various occasions during Paul's first journey Jews had stirred up similar trouble, but they had not previously brought a legal charge against

[64] That there were in practice limits to this complaisance we learn from Acts itself (18. 2) for it is believed that Claudius had expelled the Jews from Rome because of their missionary activity. See *The Beginnings of Christianity*, Vol. IV, *ad loc.* and Vol. V, p. 292.

[65] Acts 17. 6-7.

the apostle before the civic authorities.[66] The charge now brought falls into three parts. Firstly, the apostle was provoking a public disturbance wherever he went; secondly he was preaching 'atheism' to Gentiles; thirdly he was preaching disloyalty to the emperor to Jews. In making the third charge, which was false, the Jews were evidently desirous of dissociating themselves from any responsibility for the conduct of this Jewish Roman citizen, for the two other charges were true. But again the magistrates were content with 'taking security', presumably against a repetition of Paul's preaching, and sending the apostle and his companions away.[67] Doubtless they felt confident that the world was not really in danger of being turned upside down by a Jewish fanatic.

More interesting is a repetition of a similar sequence of events in Corinth.[68] Here, however, the preliminaries were different. Paul had earlier quarrelled with the leaders of the synagogue and had conducted for eighteen months a successful missionary campaign among the purely pagan population of the city. From the evidence offered by his letters to the Corinthians one can assume that some at least of his converts came from the slums of that sea port, and did not associate their salvation with any obligation to live moral lives. They were arrogant, quarrelsome and litigious; they allowed each other to practise incest, fornication, drunkenness and robbery, and openly derided the apostle's authority and mocked his rebukes.[69] To understand the subsequent action of the Jews, one must realise that these pagan converts had become, in their own eyes and in those of Paul, 'Jews', enjoying the protection of the privileged position of that people. With this background we can appreciate that, when the Jews in unison brought Paul before Gallio, the proconsul, there is a different implication in their accusation that 'this man is persuading men to worship God contrary to the law'.

This was not a charge of 'atheism', which would have come strangely from the lips of a purely Jewish assemblage, anxious to vindicate their own correctness *vis-à-vis* the Roman authorities. As the reply of Gallio makes clear, 'the law' in this case is Torah.[70] Paul was bringing a motley rabble within the protection of the

[66] Acts 13. 50; 14. 5, 19. That there had been occasions when Paul was brought before the synagogal authorities is shewn by 2 Cor. 11. 24: 'Five times I have received at the hands of the Jews the forty lashes less one.'

[67] Acts 17. 9 f.

[68] Acts 18. 12-17.

[69] 1 Cor. *passim.* See especially 1. 10; 4. 8; 5. 1, 9; 6. 6; and 16. See 2 Cor. on the subject of the Corinthian Christians' attitude to the apostle's rebuke of their evil ways, especially 10. 10.

[70] Acts 18. 15.

Jewish community while, at the same time, he was denouncing that Torah whose ethical influence secured that the Jewish community was composed of good citizens. They wanted to make it clear that they refused to accept any responsibility for Paul's converts and did not consider them to be Jews.[71]

The proceedings at Corinth are the last recorded until Paul arrived on his final visit to Jerusalem. There, as at Corinth, it was with Jews that he encountered opposition; and, after he had appealed to the emperor, the Roman authorities were still puzzled to know what it was all about. Festus confessed to King Agrippa that he had no idea of what Paul was supposed to be guilty, and that he felt embarrassed at sending him to Rome without being able to indicate the charges against him.[72] On the other hand, both the Christian Jews of Jerusalem and those who rejected the Christian claim appeared to know Paul well by reputation, and it was Jews of Asia who originally started the riot which led to his arrest.

When the author of Acts finally brings Paul to Rome he provides his story with the most unexpected denouement. The Jews of Rome admitted that they had heard of the sect of the Christians, and had heard nothing but evil of it. But what of Paul himself? What of the man who had suffered corporal punishment five times from the Jews and thrice from the Romans, who was accused by the Jews of Thessalonica of having set the whole world upside down, who was regarded in Jerusalem as such a deadly foe to his people and their religion that forty of them, with the full agreement of the high priest, banded themselves together neither to eat nor drink until they had killed him?[73]

With sublime indifference to dramatic effect, Luke informs us that Paul invited to a discussion the Jewish authorities of that city to which he had written the letter which has troubled the Church for nearly two thousand years by its profundity, its violence and its paradox. And what did they reply? That they would have nothing to do with that troubler of Jewry? No. They replied politely that 'we have received no letters from Judea about you, and none of the brethren coming here has reported or spoken any evil about you!'[74] If the writer be really the composer of an imaginary history, writing a century after the events he records, then he must rank not merely

[71] I have discussed the incident fully in my *Conflict of Church and Synagogue*, pp. 65 ff.

[72] Acts 25. 24-27. For a discussion of the whole position see *The Beginnings of Christianity*, Vol. V. Note xxvi.

[73] Acts 23. 12-15.

[74] Acts 28. 21.

with the most imaginative writers of any age, but also with the wittiest and most sardonic. Voltaire could not have done better; and Anatole France's superb story of the elderly Pilate who could not remember the name of Jesus of Nazareth is banal before such an utterly unexpected ending as that which Luke provides. The Jewish leaders of the capital city of the Roman empire had never heard of Paul![75]

The remark of the same leaders that 'with regard to this sect we know that everywhere it is spoken against'[76] is a reminder that the common view which attributes to Paul himself the expansion of Christianity into the Gentile world is wide of the mark. Not only did he not begin the mission to Gentiles but he was never the only one working in the field. That the infant Church could not have had many leaders of his intellectual and spiritual stature we can readily admit; but he owes his unique prominence in Christian history to his excellent biographer and the accident which has preserved some of his letters. Even in later hagiological literature we have not merely nothing comparable to Acts, but we lack even any reliable account of the doings of the twelve themselves. We do, however, have a common tradition describing intense hostility between Jews and Christians during this century, and to this Acts itself and Paul's letter to the Corinthians bear witness in their accounts of Paul's treatment at Jewish hands.[77]

But to what extent is Acts a genuine historical record? There is no book in the New Testament about which there is such dispute,

[75] In *The Beginnings of Christianity*, Vol. IV, *ad loc.* it is suggested that the Jewish leaders were anxious not to get involved in Paul's trial, and feigned an ignorance they did not possess because of the severe Roman laws against frivolous prosecution. But the Jews were not officially Paul's prosecutors, nor had Paul an official complaint against his nation. The appeal of Paul to Caesar is largely inexplicable because of our ignorance of the minutiae of Roman law. Paul's action secured for him the opportunity to preach his gospel before the emperor in Rome itself. What its precise legal significance was we do not know. Whether Luke really intended these verses to be the end of his MS. we shall never know. Scholars have long puzzled over the absence of any account of the death of Paul, but no one explanation has satisfied them. It might be objected to my account that Acts does not say the elders had not heard of Paul, but only that they knew nothing *against* him. This could lend itself to fascinating speculation as to who were the Jews that gave the Roman elders the *good* reports of him. For the case against the authenticity of this ending, see Jackson and Lake, *Beginnings of Christianity*, Vol. II, pp. 334 ff., in *The Case against the Tradition* by H. Windisch.

[76] Acts 28. 22.

[77] See my *Conflict of Church and Synagogue*, Appendix Five, p. 402. See also 2 Cor. 11. 23-29.

not merely as to its date, but as to the purpose for which it was written. Into much of the controversy it is unnecessary here to enter, and reasons have already been given for the view that it is substantially an accurate record of the early decades of the life of the Church.[78] But we are inevitably concerned with its purpose. It is generally agreed that Luke shows the Romans in a favourable light and that, in the Gospel, he is anxious to bring forward evidence that the message of Jesus was designed for a wider circle than the Jewish people, and to lay the blame for the condemnation of Jesus on the priestly faction rather than on Pilate. But to assume that the narrative is by that very fact tendentious or even imaginary implies that we know from other sources that the Romans played a quite different role, both in the trial of Jesus and in their first encounters with the Christian body. We have no such other sources, nor is the role attributed to them by Luke inherently improbable. None of the gospels suggest that the Romans took any initiative whatever in bringing Jesus to judgement; nor is the role of different Roman authorities in Acts so artificial that it is impossible to consider it historical.

Dr. B. S. Easton has, indeed, gone so far as to claim that Luke wrote to Theophilus with the intention of making them even more favourable by presenting the Church as the true Judaism, and by emphasising that every act of Paul was controlled by and reported to Jewish Christian authorities in Jerusalem. Gentile Christians were, therefore, entitled to the privileges originally given to Jews. According to Dr. Easton, 'if a Gentile wished to embrace Judaism, in whole or in part, Roman law gave him an unquestioned right to do so'.[79] As has already been shown this is technically correct, but Dr. Easton omits to say that it also retained an unquestioned right to condemn him for atheism, did he do so.

The picture which Luke gives seems much nearer to probability. The Christian Church at that time was a very small minority of a minority within a vast empire. It must have seemed of exiguous importance to a Roman official. To say that Luke persistently presents the Romans as acquitting Paul is exaggerated. While they apologised for scourging him uncondemned at Philippi, they also

[78] A Jewish scholar, Samuel Sandmel, in a recent book, *A Jewish Understanding of the New Testament*, Cincinnati, 1956, gives a sober argument for a date as late as A.D. 115. He considers the book a work of art not a history, designed primarily to show that Christianity was the true successor of Judaism. While I disagree with this estimate, I think Professor Sandmel is right in saying that Luke ignores or plays down the differences between groups within the Church.

[79] *Early Christianity*, S.P.C.K., 1955, p. 45.

expelled him from the city. At Thessalonica, they took surety from Paul's host, Jason, persumably to ensure that Paul did not continue his preaching, as his followers immediately sent him away. In the final act of the drama they were frankly puzzled. They consistently refused to be hustled into violent action by Paul's Jewish opponents. At the same time they took what seemed to them adequate measures to preserve public order in an affair of minor importance. It is difficult to see why this picture, which is what Luke gives us, should not be the truth.

Such a situation could not have been of indefinite duration; for it was a fact that the charge of atheism lay just below the surface did the Romans once wish to bring it. When the Church became publicly recognised as a separate body the charge was brought again and again during the two following centuries. That the Christians should have tried as long as possible to enjoy the protection of Judaism was natural. That they did so enjoy it for considerably more than half a century is remarkable, as we can see in tracing the steps by which the separation was effected.

4. THE FIRST CHRISTOLOGIES

TODAY, using too freely the rich inheritance in prayer and hymn of all the Churches, we frequently express in our public worship a devotion to Jesus Christ and a conviction of his uniqueness which correspond but little to our real experience or even to our inmost desires. The situation in the days of the first Christians was the opposite. They had a superabundant, an overflowing, experience of Christ for which they were constantly unable to find any adequate expression. The phrases which meant so much to them were obscure when they attempted to use them to outsiders. The words which recur in the New Testament writers, and which obviously expressed the common experience of the Christian communities, that they were 'in Christ', were not easy to make clear to a Jewish enquirer for there was nothing in Judaism corresponding to the idea which they expressed. As for the pagan, he might assume that they just implied the 'enthusiasm' which bound the worshippers in one of the mystery religions into union with their god, but the belief that the experience was familiar would only make it more difficult for the pagan to understand its meaning on Christian lips.

On the other hand, if we add the two words with which those already quoted are commonly associated in all ages of Christian history—'new life in Christ'—then the earliest Church seems to have had an experience more easily recognised, and therefore more easily appreciated or condemned, than the devotion of the more established and 'conventional' congregations of today. We could, indeed, more rightly compare the early communities of Christians to the Salvation Army, Moral Rearmament, or the Christian Healing Movement, if we wanted to get the full flavour of 'new life in Christ'. And the parallel has this value, that it is easier for critics to reject the explanations, than deny the facts, given by exponents of 'new life' experienced in these movements.

In all the books of the New Testament there is, to varying extents, the attempt to explain this new life in terms of old concepts. But there is a difference between the first three gospels and the rest. In the synoptic gospels we can reasonably assume that we have the reflexion of the earliest corporate interpretation of the life of Jesus of Nazareth. Even if the stories and narratives were drawn together by the second generation, they were given their original form in terms which seemed appropriate to the first years. The terms adopted might be called a 'modified apocalyptic' in the sense that they accepted an eschatological interpretation of the Incarnation; but by the happy belief that the coming of Jesus of Nazareth as Messiah was postponed to a subsequent appearance, they were able to describe in relatively non-eschatological terms the day to day life of which they already knew.

While the synoptists are thus based on the corporate mind of the earliest Christians in the very first years after the Incarnation, the fourth gospel and the rest of the New Testament contain individual explanations and interpretations of that 'real'[80] Christ in whom the Church possessed its new life. What effect that 'real' Christ could have on the most established conventions of messianic expectation we can most easily see from the book of Revelation. Its author has reproduced the belief of the first years on the full scale of the pre-Christian apocalypses. There are the same confused visions, the same mystifying symbolism, the same pseudo-scarifying events. But at the centre of it all there is no apocalyptic messiah, but 'between the throne and the four living creatures and among the elders . . . a lamb standing as though it had been slain'.[81]

There is no greater contrast in the New Testament than that which lies between the two works ascribed to a 'John'. The author of the fourth gospel is soaked in the ideas of Philo and draws from the

[80] By 'real' is meant 'in the purpose of God and in the mind of Jesus himself'. It is independent of human explanation or the 'mythology' of the period as described, for example, by Bultmann.

[81] Rev. 5. 6.

Alexandrian philosopher his interpretation of the Incarnation. It is worth noting that he draws nothing from Philo's views of the messianic age,[82] and that he explicitly rejects an apocalyptic significance in the life of Jesus by putting in his mouth the words 'I did not come to judge the world but to save the world.'[83] His interpretation of Jesus is drawn from the whole range of Philonic thought about the logos. Like the logos, Jesus is at the beginning united with God; like the logos he comes from God, carrying the fullness of the divine nature into creation; like the logos he dwells not only in God but also in those who accept him, and so unites the creation into God. Yet, when he comes to the heart of things, Philo fails him as completely as did the apocalyptists fail the other John. Philo would have made nothing of 'and the logos became flesh', and would have been still more estranged from the thought that, being flesh, the logos became a person—an individual—who could be born, be rejected, and be crucified. In Philo's thought it was no task of the logos to redeem creation by his suffering, or to proclaim that 'I, when I am lifted up from the earth, will draw all men to myself.'[84]

Between John and John stretches the whole range of the thought and experience of Paul; but it rests on the same foundation, the experience of the Cross. Undoubtedly the early Church was puzzled as to who Jesus was; undoubtedly it should officially be described as the Church of the *Resurrection*, not of the Crucifixion; and many and great books have been written, and will be written, on the developing Christology of the first century. But it was no thought-out religious philosophy which caused the spread of the Church. It was the acceptance of the fact that 'the Son of God' had suffered *for them*, that his blood had been poured out *for them*. The experience which they had undergone was an emotional and not an intellectual one; the language appropriate to describing it was emotional, even sentimental. It emphasised 'the blood of the Lamb' so vividly that within a century pagans came to believe that hideous rites accompanied the religious devotions of the Christians. It is only as we understand this that we can appreciate the profound bewilderment which the Christian message caused in Jewish circles, and even among Jewish adherents of the new faith.

In language more pictorial than metaphysical Judaism could accept that God shared in the sufferings of his people. When Jerusalem was in the hands of enemies Jews could speak of 'the exile

[82] There is no reference in Philo to a personal Messiah. See Wolfson, *Philo* II, pp. 413 f.

[83] John 12. 47.

[84] John 12. 32. Note the whole argument from v. 23 onwards.

of the Shekinah'. But this language of suffering and 'exile' prepared the Jewish founders of the Church but inadequately for the physical fact and extent of the sufferings of Jesus, or for the extraordinary effect which 'acceptance' of those sufferings produced. The most earnest rabbi would scarcely expect a Jew to be turned from sin to righteousness by the thought of sharing in the exile of the shekinah, but the book of Revelation spoke explicitly of the righteous Christians as owing their righteousness to their being 'washed in the blood of the Lamb'.[85] The early Christians had entered into a new dimension of religious experience, and they were at a loss to discover phrases from their traditional language in which that new experience could be expressed.

There is no more interesting or illuminating illustration of the Christian dilemma and its novelty than the situation which confronted Paul in Corinth at the time of his first letter. Different messages had been delivered and different spiritual experiences exhibited. There were parties claiming allegiance to Apollos, to Peter and to Paul—and, of course, there were those who claimed that *they* owed allegiance to Christ.[86] We can see that Paul longed to show his rivals up by exhibiting gifts at least the equal of theirs.[87] But he resisted the temptation and 'decided to know nothing among you except Jesus Christ and him crucified',[88] for it was at this point that 'the new dimension of religious experience' had to prove itself or fail. In so far as Paul acted on this choice it would mean that the gospel would not rest on his eloquence or on his intellectual skill, but would be solidly based on a 'demonstration of the Spirit and power'.[89] Exactly the same answer would be given by any of the pioneers or leaders of Divine Healing in the Churches of today. To preach the Cross is to release a 'demonstration of the Spirit and power'. At the same time Paul was under no illusion as to the difficulties of his decision. He had realised, as he said himself a few verses earlier, that to preach the Cross was to preach what is 'a stumbling block to Jews and folly to Gentiles'[90] and the words are carefully chosen.

Paul's preaching of the Cross was a stumbling-block to Jews for many reasons, but specifically because of the statement in Torah

[85] Rev. 7. 14.
[86] 1 Cor. 1. 12.
[87] *Ibid.*, 2. 1.
[88] *Ibid.*, 2. 2.
[89] *Ibid.*, 1. 17. 'not to preach . . . with eloquent wisdom, lest the cross of Christ be emptied of its power'.
[90] *Ibid.*, 1. 23.

that 'a hanged man is accursed by God'[91] or 'an affront to God'. On the contrary, declared Paul. The crucified Jesus is himself divine, and the Cross witnesses to the power of God by its redeeming action upon men. Likewise Paul's claim that Jesus suffered as other men suffered, with 'real' suffering followed by 'real' death, was foolishness to Greeks. Paul retorted that, so far from being foolishness, it showed the wisdom of God. The Greeks were quite familiar with the idea of a suffering demi-god; and they had no difficulty in accepting that Christ was divine—the use by Paul of the title 'Lord' would identify Christ in many Greek minds with the demi-gods of mythology and the mystery religions. But they did not take those sufferings personally or expect them to have any effect upon their lives or conduct. The agony of Prometheus or the sorrow of Demeter they regarded as exquisite poetical conceptions. But men did not go out as missionaries to preach that lives were changed by them. That would be 'foolishness' indeed. But Paul claimed precisely that the sufferings of Jesus did change lives because, though he was divine, his sufferings were real and 'human'. Paul's problem with the Greeks was thus the humanity revealed by the Cross.

With the Jews it was the other side that counted, and Paul was much more concerned to remove the stumbling block of the Jews than correct the folly of the Greeks if the emphasis of his message be any evidence. For Paul was little concerned with the need to prove that Christ was really human; he was much concerned to show that the Jewish idea of atonement was fulfilled in him, just because he was divine. Judaism had a deeply spiritual doctrine of the need and meaning of repentance. The Day of Atonement was already becoming the most sacred day in the calendar of Jewry, and it has retained that position into modern times. Paul did not need to explain to Jews that man needed repentance. He did not even have to show that he needed help in 'making atonement' for his sins. That was precisely what the national Day of Atonement with its profound and all-embracing ritual was designed to provide. What he had to argue was that God, as well as man, was factually concerned in the suffering and death of Jesus, and that by them God and man, separated by man's sin, were brought together again.

This was in any case to go beyond Jewish thought, but it was also to provide a further 'stumbling block' for Jews as it was presented by Paul. The author of the Epistle to the Hebrews had indeed associated the Crucifixion with the Day of Atonement, but he had attributed

[91] Deut. 21: 23. Rashi explains this verse by saying that the mutilation of a human body is an affront to God who made it. Compare San. 46a, p. 304.

to Christ the role of high priest who can 'sympathize with our weaknesses' and 'in every respect has been tempted as we are, yet without sinning'.[92] But Paul with great audacity identified the crucified Christ with the slain scapegoat, as he had identified him with the sacrificed paschal lamb.[93] But in the case of the scapegoat there was the additional stumbling block that much of the argumentation of Paul on the atonement could be—and was—so easily warped into a repulsive conception of a God who had to revenge himself upon his innocent son for the sins of guilty humanity. Once a 'price' was introduced into the teaching about the cost of man's sin—and it was Paul who introduced it—[94] then the question was inevitably asked as to who had been the recipient of the price paid. Whether the answer were God or the Devil it was equally disastrous from the standpoint of the simple Jewish conception of the character of God.[95]

Paul's difficulty was that a purely Jewish conception of the manner whereby God overcame men's sins was not easily understood by the kind of ignorant and humble Gentiles to whom his mission took him. He had to explain it in their language—and every explanation was a fresh stumbling block to his Jewish hearers. For in the analogies which he chose, while his emphasis was always on the freedom which was secured, he likened the work of Christ to release from debt or release from slavery, releases which were only effected by a payment of that which was owed to him whose authority was thereby cancelled. These releases were works neither of love nor of power, and the course of Christian theology would have flowed more smoothly had Paul not had recourse to them as analogies. But it must be said again that Paul's emphasis is not on the payment made but on the freedom secured, and this is how his Gentile hearers would probably

[92] Heb. 4. 15.

[93] Compare 1 Cor. 5. 7, with Rom. 5. 6, 11.

[94] E.g., 1 Cor., 6. 20 and 7. 23.

[95] Almost any Jewish work of polemic or apologetic would provide an example of the spiritual authenticity of this stumbling block. More because I happen to have come upon it recently than for any other reason, I would quote from *Why I am not a Christian; a reply to the Conversionists* by a Jewish layman, N. S. Joseph, published by the Jewish Religious Union in 1908. Note that this body is 'reformist'. Mr. Joseph thus speaks of the doctrine: 'Mingled with the Trinitarian doctrine, as still officially expounded, is the doctrine of vicarious Atonement—that unworthy, irrational and hateful doctrine that the All-merciful and All-just God made an atonement to Himself for sins committed against Himself by sacrificing to Himself a perfect being, an innocent and godly man, richly endowed with the divine spirit. . . .' (pp. 7-8).

have taken his words. For that is what they themselves would have been concerned with in their ordinary lives.

It is, however, not merely in his understanding of the atonement wrought by the Cross that Paul could puzzle and cause offence to religious Jews. Whether as an extension of his teaching of the atonement or from some other source, Paul expressed a belief in the unity of all worshippers in the body of Christ which was entirely novel. Dr. W. D. Davies in *Paul and Rabbinic Judaism*[96] claims that Paul was merely extending the Jewish concept of the solidarity of all Israel by which, for example, at the Passover each generation identified itself with that which undertook the Exodus. But, if this be so, Paul carried the concept to lengths which no Jew would easily have accepted. For Paul not merely identified Christ with the divine, but said outright to the members of the Corinthian church that they were 'the body of Christ'.[97] He thus 'makes at one' humanity and divinity in a way which the Church has even yet not understood or accepted, and which it has certainly not embodied in its teaching or dogma.[98]

This is not said in order to introduce a theological discussion. Whether the Church has followed or not, Paul genuinely saw the little Christian communities as scattered parts of the body of Christ in a way which allowed him to use language beyond that of any known Jewish experience[99] in identifying himself and them with his Lord. But such language is evidence of how soon it proved impossible to fit Christ into any previously known categories. Paul used, in addition, of course, the conventional 'mythological' language of his time. He drew from apocalyptic, from the Wisdom literature and elsewhere, titles and dignities which he ascribed to his Master. But they are not important. It is the struggle to find *new* language to describe a *new* experience which matters.

His double experience of the atonement compelled him to think of Jesus Christ as more than human. But into what category was he then to place him? For as a Jew he recognised only one being to whom the category divine was fully applicable, and that was God himself. Paul was not a trinitarian; he had not the resources which were to be made available by several centuries of hammering on the anvil

[96] pp. 101 ff. and elsewhere. See index, *Christ*.

[97] 1 Cor. 12. 27.

[98] In saying this it is assumed that such a doctrine is ultimately consistent only with a belief in the unity of all creation in the Creator, which has no place for a Last Judgment or a division into sheep and goats. For if I, as a Christian, be a member of the body of Christ, as a man I am certainly a member of humanity, and have no point at which I can genuinely dissociate myself from other men.

[99] E.g., Rom. 6. 3, 1 Cor. 10. 2.

of both experience and philosophic thought. For him Jesus was never the equal of God; whatever of divinity was to be ascribed to him was to be so ascribed because God had willed and planned it thus. The Cross was a manifestation of the wisdom and a demonstration of the power of God. To Paul, as to the author of the Epistle to the Hebrews, the Christ Jesus reconciling God and man was part of the very structure of creation. It was not something imposed from without at a moment in history; it was part of the very web of history. But no New Testament author worked out the implications of this revolutionary conception. There was no orthodoxy or heresy in the matter. Though it led to the fourth century doctrine of Nicea, nothing like the Nicene formula was in the minds of first century Christians. In any case the leadership at this time was Jewish, and to the Jewish mind there could be the greatest variety in intellectual formulation and outlook, provided there was conformity in conduct.

The two titles with which we are left after reading the New Testament are 'Lord' and 'Saviour'. Both imply something on the divine rather than the human side. But neither is sufficiently definite to compel any single interpretation or to exclude an alternative one. Moreover the characteristics which are applied to the pre-existent Christ in the New Testament in no way add to the Old Testament's doctrine of God. Qualities are transferred, tasks are committed, to the Son; but they are qualities already possessed, tasks already undertaken, by the Deity. But with the Incarnation, something new happens and provides the centre of the New Testament picture. It is the Atonement. But here also we must be careful in our language. The Atonement does not bring Christ into the centre of New Testament theology. That is always 'God', and distinguished from whatever title is ascribed to Christ. But it is by the Atonement that 'we have access to the Father'.[1] This is something entirely fresh to the Jewish thought of the apostles; and though the New Testament writers nowhere explicitly recognise it, it is the clearest evidence of the new centre to which Christian thought shifted, from the chosen people to the chosen person, from man in community to man in himself. For there could be no significance in the Atonement except as each man accepted it for himself by faith.

There could be three ways in which this new understanding of the divine-human relationship could be related to that already possessed in Judaism. They could be thought of as in opposition to each other; they could be so absorbed into each other that the clear edges of each were smoothed over to give an appearance of unity; or they could be held in creative tension. The first was adopted by the

[1] Rom. 5. 2; Eph. 2. 18; 3. 12.

Christian Church, largely through the influence of Paul; the third has not been tried; the second was attempted by those who came to be called 'the Judeo-Christians'.

Their existence was an inevitable consequence of the first century situation. For they were not the followers of some opinion produced by Christological controversy, and then condemned by the Church as heretical. They were basically those who desired to continue into subsequent generations the original beliefs of the apostles. 'Attending the temple together and breaking bread in their homes'[2] was once a fair description of the Jerusalem Church. The Judeo-Christians were those who wished both Jews and Gentile Christians to recognise that the continuation of this practice was what was demanded of those who accepted Jesus as the coming Messiah. That they thought themselves 'a bridge' it would be foolish to claim; for it would imply that they recognised the bulk of Jews and of Christians to be standing on opposite sides of a gulf.

Politically they offended the majority of Jerusalem Jewry when they would not take part in the defence of Jerusalem against the Romans; religiously Judaism took no notice of them until the last decades of the first century. Their fellow Christians among the Gentiles reacted sooner. When Paul, and those who thought like him, began to develop a Christology which emphasized the divine aspects of the career of Jesus of Nazareth, the Judeo-Christians regarded the development as heretical. When they accompanied this with ever increasing abuse of Judaism and proclaimed the impossibility of combining loyalty to Jesus of Nazareth with the acceptance of any Jewish practice, a rift became inevitable, and Paul came to be regarded as the arch-enemy.

There was no central Judeo-Christian authority, nor was there simply one Judeo-Christian doctrine.[3] But the many varieties of these doctrines have in common their rejection of aspects of orthodox (Gentile) Christology which would bring their teaching into flat opposition to Judaism. They preferred an adoptionist Christology, for in excluding both pre-existence and the virgin birth they ran no risk of impugning the uniqueness of God. They emphasized the

[2] Acts 2. 46.

[3] The fullest and best documented account of Judeo-Christianity is *Theologie und Geschichte des Judenchristentums* Tübingen, 1949, by H. J. Schoeps. An admirable shorter account is in Marcel Simon *Verus Israel*, Paris, 1948, Ch. 9 p. 277 f. The work of Schoeps rests on a theory as to the nature of Judeo-Christianity which has not won universal acceptance. See 'The Qumran Scrolls, the Ebionites and their Literature' by J. A. Fitzmyer, S. J., in *The Scrolls and the New Testament*, Ed. K. Stendhal, S.C.M. Press, 1958, especially the notes.

Resurrection, ignoring the Atonement, since the latter doctrine emphasised the divinity of Christ. In their adoptionism some could go so far as to make the basis of the adoption the faultless obedience of Jesus to the Law; and in their unwillingness to forfeit anything of their Judaism some could go so far as to reduce their concern with Jesus of Nazareth to belief that such would be the name of the Messiah when at last he came.[4] But these last, the *posh'e Israel* or 'sinners in Israel' could be paralleled among the Gentiles by those Christians who joined to an unimpeachable orthodoxy a constant lapse into 'judaising' by keeping Easter on the Jewish date, by getting rabbis to bless their fields and so on. They are familiar to us in the denunciations of the preachers and in the canons of early councils;[5] and they were 'sinners in Christendom' rather than separate sects. But the Judeo-Christians as such were different. It was not some trifle, but a whole position, which separated them from others and caused them to be organised in a group of sects identifiable to both Jews and Christians. It is a strange and tragic fact that, at the end of the first and at the beginning of the second century, when to the whole Church Christology was still fluid, the Gentile Christians excommunicated them not for an inadequate Christology but because they still observed 'the law'. Justin Martyr makes this clear in his *Dialogue with Trypho*, admitting that most Gentile Christians would have nothing to do with any Judeo-Christian, and emphasizing his own toleration by saying that he would only refuse fellowship to those who tried to propagate their views among Gentile Christians.[6] Such an attitude to Judaism is the disastrous consequence of setting the extravagance of Paul before the measured and sober attitude of Jesus himself, a consequence from which the Church is still suffering.

5. THE SEPARATION

In considering the manner of the separation between Christianity and Judaism we have to recognise the complete change which took place after the Jewish defeat and the destruction of the Temple in A.D. 70. For the view that the separation was inevitable, automatic, and operated either on the death of Jesus or immediately Paul denounced

[4] If A. Marmorstein is right in his identification of the Posh'e Israel. See his *Religionsgeschichtliche Studien I*, 1910, pp. 26 ff and *Studies in Jewish Theology*, Oxford, 1950, pp. 179 ff.

[5] See my *Conflict of Church and Synagogue*, pp. 164 and 174 ff.

[6] *Op. cit.*, ch. 47.

the Law, has no historic justification. It was a long process and included many incidents of which the adherents of neither religion can be proud, incidents where to a hostile Roman authority Jews denounced Christians and Christians denounced Jews.[7]

Such events took place after A.D. 70. Before that time it is extremely doubtful whether it would have occurred to either side that a separation was desirable, let alone inevitable. That the sect of the Nazarenes was attracting a number of Gentile converts was well known to the Jewish authorities; but so were the synagogues in the Diaspora. That some at least of these Gentile converts were undesirable did not alter the situation. In having a private Messiah they were doing no more than the Qumran sect. For the basic fact was that the Temple and the Synagogue possessed considerable disciplinary powers, that Jewish officials were prepared to use those powers; and there is no reason for assuming that they did not believe that they had adequate means for keeping within bounds this new sect which had appeared on the many-coloured tapestry of Jewish beliefs and practices.[8]

We are the more justified in believing this of the period before A.D. 70 in that the centre of Judaism was at that time the Temple, not Torah, and that neither Jesus himself, nor his followers, made the Temple the centre of continuous and consistent attack. Stephen may have been going to claim that the Temple was unnecessary; but in that he was merely voicing opinions held by some diaspora Jews and there was nothing specifically Christian in that outlook. Some Nazarenes may not have participated in Temple sacrifices, but neither did the Essenes who were certainly Jews in spite of that. At most they merited the title of being 'sinners in Israel', and such it was not the custom of the Jewry of that time to excommunicate. Such a situation may seem curious to us, to whom the whole idea of the Temple perpetually reeking with the stench of animal sacrifices is exceedingly unattractive. But it remains a fact that we have no evidence that it appeared to contemporaries to be inconsistent with a spiritual religion. Moreover, by its emphasis on the death of Jesus as a bloody sacrifice ending all sacrifices, the Church could appear to accept the bloodshed of sacrifices as basically part of religion. Their

[7] Cases of the former happened during the transition period when Christians were first emerging from the protection of being a Jewish sect, cases of the latter when, after the defeat of 135, Jews were forbidden to practise their Judaism. See my *Conflict of Church and Synagogue*, chs. 3 and 4, and compare Justin, *op. cit.*, ch. 110.

[8] We learn from Acts 8. 3 and 9. 1 f. that the authority of the high priest could make itself felt at Damascus, and from 2 Cor. 11. 23-25 that Paul had been severely punished by the synagogal authorities of various places.

condemnation of other sacrifices was not because they were cruel but because they were ineffective.

If the Temple authorities had no reason for completely severing relations with those who accepted Jesus as Messiah, the same was not true in the political field as the shadows of the revolt darkened in the sixties. But the Zealots and nationalists were concerned only with such Jews as lived in Jerusalem or at least in Palestine. The Jerusalem Church came under their condemnation because its members would take no part in the war; but the nationalists had no interest in their beliefs or in their communities in the Diaspora.

As to the Tannaitic rabbis, the Pharisees of the New Testament, they were still only a minority of the nation, but of them it must be likewise said that at that period they would not have considered that the Nazarenes had severed all connection with Israel. They had no quarrel with their idea of God, so long as Christology was in an undeveloped state. That of Paul was certainly unacceptable, but Paul was not the whole Church nor were his views considered the norm of Christian orthodoxy. Paul's ethics, a subject in which they were more interested, were entirely Pharisaic. It is often forgotten that the later chapters in his letters, when the theological issues have been dealt with and the apostle is telling his communities how to live, contain little with which a scrupulous rabbi would quarrel and much that he would commend. Of the letters it might well be said by such, as is said by Jewish critics of the New Testament as a whole, that it is what is new that is not good, and that what is good is not new.

So long as such a situation existed on the Jewish side there is no reason whatever for thinking that the Christians would take the initiative in seeking a separation. We have already seen that such an initiative would have resulted in their lacking protection did they, or any one of them, attract the unfavourable attention of a Roman official. Once they were known as a separate body they did not become an 'illegal' body, but an unlicensed one and, as such, with no permission to commit 'atheism'.

After A.D. 70 the situation changed completely. Although it would be exaggerated to claim that there existed no Sadducees or Essenes after the immense slaughter which accompanied the Jewish defeat, yet it is true that all parties save the rabbinic, the nationalistic and the Christian entirely ceased to have any visible influence on the destiny of the people. The nationalists aroused the nation once again and in A.D. 135 procured a still more disastrous defeat with its accompanying slaughter. The Judeo-Christians lived in increasing isolation. The real future lay only with the rabbis. One of their inevitable tasks was so to develop their teaching that they made a hedge about the dispirited and defeated people as effective as their ancestors had made around the Torah.

To do this they set out to procure a new uniformity in religion as the necessary basis for a new unity. Not only was the idea a new one among Jews, but the very thought of consciously creating and securing national unity by means of religious uniformity was without precedent in human history. A very grave enemy to this uniformity was the Judeo-Christian community. Moreover, behind them lay the growing and aggressive Gentile community, still attached to Jewish privilege, but increasingly hostile to Judaism even when it was represented by their own fellow-Christians of Jewish origin. This added politics to religion as a cause of separation. We are not sufficiently sure of the dating of events to say whether the rabbinical attack was simultaneous on both wings of the Christian Church, or whether they proceeded from the former to the latter. But in both cases their action was effective, indeed decisive.

So far as the Judeo-Christians were concerned, they introduced into the synagogal service a formula which Judeo-Christians could not pronounce.[9] This was an additional clause, the *Birkath ha-Minim*, in a series of benedictions and maledictions of which the number ultimately became eighteen, so that it is still known by that name in the synagogal prayers. The clause stated 'and for the Nazarenes may there be no hope'. That such was its original form has recently been discovered from an Egyptian papyrus, for the present form, rendered discreet by centuries of Christian censorship and scrutiny, conceals the word *Nozrim* behind the more neutral *minim* or *meshummadim*, words which could, or could not, include the Judeo-Christians according to the intention of the man who pronounced them.[10] In the original form it could detect a Judeo-Christian in two ways; he could be asked to lead the congregation at this point in the service, or if it was a service of Judeo-Christians alone, then a spy could observe whether it was included or not, for synagogal services were open to all. The clause is said to have been included in the 'Eighteen' by a rabbi, Samuel the Small, who lived before the end of the first

[9] Justin, *op. cit.*, ch. 96.

[10] On *Minim* and the *Birkath ha-Minim* see A. Marmorstein, *Studies in Jewish Theology*, index; also Travers Herford, *Christianity in Talmud and Midrash*, and H. Strack, *Jesus, die Häretiker u. die Christen nach den altesten judischen Angaben*. On the formula of the Benediction see M. Simon, *op. cit.*, p. 235, and I. Elbogen, *Der Judische Gottesdienst*, pp. 36 and 51. That it was originally aimed at the Christians is clear from patristic literature, e.g. Justin, *op. cit.*, para. 16.

century. The date would thus fit with the reforms introduced after the destruction of the Temple.

The other action taken by the synagogal authorities was to send out 'apostles' carrying a letter to all Jewish congregations in the Diaspora. The existence of this letter is known to us only from the constant references to it in Christian literature, and it is from that hostile source that we have to try to reconstruct its contents. Even apart from its contents or occasion it is, however, of particular interest as almost the sole example of communications passing officially by 'apostles' and in writing from the central Jewish authorities in the Land of Israel to the diaspora Jewries. If we are to take the text of Justin,[11] then the rabbis sent out

> chosen and ordained men throughout all the world to proclaim that 'a godless and lawless heresy had sprung from one Jesus, a Galilean deceiver, whom we crucified, but his disciples stole him by night from the tomb where he was laid when unfastened from the cross, and now deceive men by asserting that he has risen from the dead and ascended to heaven.' Moreover, you accuse him of having taught those godless, lawless, and unholy doctrines which you mention to the condemnation of those who confess him to be Christ and a Teacher from and Son of God.

What those 'godless, lawless and unholy doctrines' were we are left to speculate. Later fathers elaborated their denunciations of the letter to accuse the Jewish authorities of including all those accusations of promiscuous immorality which we find in Celsus or in the *Sepher Toldoth Jeshu*.[12] That they were to be found in such an official text is very unlikely. For Christians were not yet separated from Jews in the diaspora synagogues; and their manner of life was sufficiently well known for such libels to have discredited the entire letter. Nor is it necessary to believe them to explain the letter, for the official Christian attitude to 'the Law' was in itself sufficient to justify the excommunication, once the Synagogue had set out to bring within its fold all who were to be counted Jews.

It is difficult for the modern Christian to understand how it came to be acceptable to his Christian ancestors to speak with such vulgar and unbridled abuse of Judaism and the Jewish people. The doctrine that *autres temps, autres moeurs* explains everything has to be stretched to quite unconvincing limits to excuse the violence of

[11] *Ibid.*, ch. 108. The translation is from the edition of *The Ante-Nicene Fathers*, p. 235. Cf. Ch. 17.

[12] See Origen, *Contra Celsum*, VI. 27; Eusebius, *On Isaiah* 18. 1; Jerome, *On Isaiah* 18. 2.

their language and the indifference to veracity of their accusations. Later writers certainly went even further than those with whom we are concerned of the first and second centuries. But it is also true that the latter were addressing the Jewish people at an exceptionally tragic moment of their history, a moment which should have attracted sympathy rather than reprobation. They had seen their Temple utterly destroyed and their holy city in ruins, they had lost their high priest and their political autonomy, and yet there is only one reference in the considerable Christian literature which has survived which views these tragedies with pity. That is in a curious work entitled *The Teaching of the Apostles*, and calls on Christians to fast and mourn over the fallen city that they may rejoice in the world to come.[13] But the more typical reaction can be seen in Justin's attitude when he taunts Trypho with the Jewish rite of circumcision, alleging that God gave it deliberately to the Jewish people so that they could be easily distinguished from others and punished for their sins.[14] When we reflect that Justin is generally considered to have been exceptionally moderate in his approach, we can imagine the kind of thing that was said when Jews and Christians got into an argument in the inn or market place.[15] The letter to the synagogues was but the reaction to a situation already created by the Christians.

It is impossible to say whether by their abuse they wished deliberately to sever the *legal* link with Judaism which protected them against Roman judicial procedure. The date at which the Romans became cognisant of a separate body of Christians is much disputed, but it seems unlikely that this took place until roughly the same time as the *Birkath ha-Minim* and the letter to the synagogues, that is to say, in the last decades of the first century. From that time onwards the Gentile, and particularly the western, Church became more and more ignorant of what Judaism was. Few scholars knew Hebrew or could read Jewish rabbinical writings. Few Jews were converted to the Church. Moreover, the effective centre of Jewish thought was moving eastwards from Galilee to Mesopotamia where Jews were in contact only with 'heretical' or schismatic eastern Churches. It is not until the Middle Ages, when Jewish communities were well established in western Europe, that a physical contact was restored between the two religions in that vital area. Even then another half

[13] *Didascalia Apostolorum*, 2, 21. One may note that even in this case the Christian attitude is not quite disinterested.

[14] *Op. cit.*, ch. 16 and 92.

[15] See A. Marmorstein, *Studies in Jewish Theology*, pp. 69 ff. and my *Conflict of Church and Synagogue*, pp. 95 ff.

a millenium was to pass before Christian scholars, with but few exceptions, sought to understand Judaism with any motive save that of condemnation.

The story of the development of Christology has not been carried further because many books exist already dealing with its fascinating growth from the New Testament to Nicea.

Book Three

THE EMERGENCE OF RABBINIC JUDAISM

Chapter Five

THE VICTORY OF TORAH

1. INDEPENDENCE, TEMPLE AND TORAH

DURING the centuries preceding the destruction of Jerusalem by the Romans, the national consciousness and spiritual life of the Jewish people has been dispersed between the three concepts: *independence*, which was focused first on the Hasmonean then—albeit reluctantly—on the Herodian royal houses; *the Temple*, which exhibited in Jerusalem the national pride of the whole dispersed people of the Jews in being the people of Jahweh; and *Torah* which was the divinely appointed way in which that people, by their conformity and obedience, expressed their loyalty and their willingness to live according to the divine will.

Doubtless it would have been ideal to honour each of these three expressions of national life in such a way that it did not impair the honour done to the other two. But so devoted an attitude was beyond most ordinary people. There arose a secular nationalism, which was prepared to indulge in all the terrorism which such a nationalism can excite, and to make use of religion to inflame popular resentments, but which had little genuine interest either in Temple or in Torah. In the second place Pharisees and Essenes alike were more concerned with Torah than with Temple, and could exist without the Temple worship. But, thirdly, there were the Sadducees, concentrating on worship at the national shrine, a shrine which was venerated and respected throughout the eastern Mediterranean world, and they were prepared to sacrifice national independence and strict attention to Torah, provided the shrine were preserved. Hence they were prepared to accept a working agreement with Rome.

It was the gradual spread of Roman hegemony over the countries east of the Mediterranean which made the attitudes of Jews, as they considered their independence, their Temple and their Torah, decisive for their future. Both the survival and the dispersion of Judaism and the Jewish people were decided by the clash of Rome and Jewry, by the conflict of Roman paganism and laxity with Jewish ethics and morality. The grandeur and the tragedy alike of Jewish history were foreshadowed in that conflict which left the physical existence of both Jewry and Jerusalem in ruins.

2. ROME AND JUDEA

It was early in the Maccabean period that Jewish leaders became aware of the steady approach of a world power which stemmed from the central Mediterranean and neither from Egypt nor from Mesopotamia, seats of the empires whose contraction and expansion had hitherto largely determined their history. In their conflict with their next-door neighbour and overlord, Syria, it was natural for them to seek the alliance of a power which menaced Syria rather than themselves, for the Roman approach was from the north. At that period, that is the second century B.C., such an alliance fitted in with Roman policy, for, so long as Syria was independent, it suited Rome to have as allies states which would, in their own interests, resist any Syrian aggrandisement. Judea was such a state though, in fact, Rome never honoured her alliance by giving the Maccabees the slightest aid in their struggle with Syria.[1]

Once Rome had conquered Syria and added her territory to the Roman empire, no further advantage remained in the independence of Judea. Such was the situation when Pompey, having conquered the former country, entered the latter. He had no intention of leaving Judea independent. But to the Jews he was an ally, and in that capacity he was asked to judge between the claims of Aristobulus and Hyrcanus, the last two brothers of the Hasmonean dynasty. The fact that the former did not accept his adjudication gave him a pretext for the capture of Jerusalem and the despoiling of the Temple.[2] For some time the brutal fact of annexation was thinly disguised by the ascription to Hyrcanus of the rank of ethnarch. But Pompey made his mastery clear by refusing him permission to use the ancestral title of king, by deciding that the territory of Judea should be considerably reduced, and, worst of all, by imposing on the inhabitants of the country the payment of a tribute to Rome. Those Jews to whom the independence of their people was an almost axiomatic implication of their religion could not be deceived by the fact that Hyrcanus, in addition to being high priest, was ethnarch. They knew that they had

[1] For a full survey of this earlier period, see M. S. Ginsburg, *Rome et la Judée*, Paris, Povolzky, 1928, Chs. I—V.
[2] *Ibid.*, pp. 79 ff.

a master who was a pagan and who ruled a pagan empire, and they were not willing to accept it.[3]

Julius Caesar, once he had become master of the empire by the defeat of Pompey, was prepared to extend the narrow liberties which the latter had left to the Jews. His great design was to unify the Roman empire; and he considered that the Jewish people, widely dispersed through its territories, could be a useful adjunct and assistant to that unity provided that they were happy and contented under Roman rule. He recognised that Jews everywhere throughout the empire formed one people. Hence he made Hyrcanus ethnarch of the Jews, not ethnarch of Judea, and allowed him to collect the Temple tax from all communities. But his intention of making the high-priesthood and ethnarchy hereditary in the Hasmonean family was frustrated by Herod the Great. Finally, he allowed all Jews throughout the empire freedom to practise their religion, a privilege which, in the event, was more important than anything else.[4]

While Hyrcanus was thus authorised to exercise his religious authority outside the country, and did so exercise it, political authority was nowhere his. For Antipater, father of Herod the Great, was designated as 'Overseer' of Judea. Political power was, henceforth, entirely in the hands of Rome, who might designate a client king or a Roman procurator as it seemed good. Herod the Great pleased Augustus and was allowed great freedom from 37 till 4 B.C. But his son, Archelaus, was only allowed to exercise over a smaller area and with a lower rank such authority as Augustus designated. When even that proved beyond his competence, he was simply set aside for a Roman procurator.[5] From the beginning of the rule of Archelaus there had been disturbances, and at one period the whole country was involved in what was almost a civil war, such was the Jewish resentment against political subjection. During this time also two imposters, one a Herodian, one a Maccabee, appeared and won considerable popular support, for they held out the hope of freedom; but of more importance is the fact that conditions under Rome

[3] See Stewart Perowne, *The Later Herods*, Hodder and Stoughton, 1958, Ch. V.

[4] Ginsburg, *op. cit.*, pp. 89 and 96 f.

[5] The events of the following decades are described in too many books for detailed references to be necessary. But special attention can be drawn to Schurer, Division I, which contains references to all the original sources, and to *The Later Herods* which is of particular value because of Mr. Perowne's intimate knowledge of the country. The fullest account of this period is to be found in F. M. Abel, *L'Histoire de la Palestine depuis la Conquête d'Alexandre Jusqu'à l'Invasion Arabe*, Paris, 1952, but this work of 900 pages contains no index.

brought into permanent existence a group, later called Zealots, who were brigands, terrorists, messianists—whatever the situation at any one moment made possible. They reappear under different leaders with tragic persistency until the disastrous clash with Rome in A.D. 66.

For thirty-five years Judea was ruled by a Roman procurator dependent on the governor of Syria. For Judea was not sufficiently important from the Roman point of view to warrant raising it above the lowest provincial status. This meant that it was not men of first class character and ability who were appointed to rule it, and to deal with the difficult and delicate problems which any pagan government of Jews involved. In A.D. 41 the province reverted to Herod Agrippa I, grandson of Herod the Great. Agrippa was a friend of the emperors Caligula and Claudius, and was a man with all the diplomatic skill of his grandfather. His career with its ups and downs was singularly romantic, and produced a man whose pliancy was more conspicuous than his probity. But, as king of Judea, he was determined to seek the respect and support of the religious leaders of the nation, and this he succeeded in doing to a remarkable extent. In fact he so pacified the country as to make it seem possible that the link between Rome and Judea could be a peaceable one.

Agrippa died suddenly after only three years of kingship, and the country passed again to a Roman procurator. From then until the outbreak of open war the situation steadily deteriorated, each procurator appearing more venal and brutal than his predecessor. A fatal step was taken in 48 when the procurator, V. Cumanus, raised his garrison troops locally from the Greek population of Caesarea and the neighbouring Greek cities. Relations between the Jews and Greeks of Caesarea had, for some time, been bad and the troops, when they were sent to Jerusalem to act as guardians of the peace during Passover, acted instead as provokers of violence. The indecent gesture of a soldier from the battlements of the great castle of the Antonia above the Temple courts provoked the rage of the crowds attending the festival, and Cumanus so arranged matters that it led to a massacre in which thousands died. Jewish anger at this deliberate exploitation of a quarrel in which they were the aggrieved party was felt even as far away as Rome. For the Jews of that city were so stirred that their protests and unrest led the emperor to decree their expulsion from the city.

In 52 a freedman (that is a slave who had purchased his freedom) became procurator. He was Felix, brother of Pallas who was the favourite of the emperor Nero. Of Felix Tacitus coined one of his famous epigrams, saying that 'enjoying cruelty and lust in all their forms he exercised the powers of a king with the outlook of a slave'.[6] Under him rebellion, which had for some time been spasmodic, became endemic. He began, indeed, by strong action against the bands of open terrorists, whether they were operating under the guise of religion or not, but he succeeded only in driving opposition underground, not in either suppressing or conciliating it. It was during his eight years of office that the previous gangs became *sicarii*, that is, they armed themselves with the short curved dagger which was deadly at close quarters. As a political weapon the knife could achieve nothing, as a weapon of terrorism it was supreme—until the bomb was invented. For, his hideous deed performed, the murderer could sink into the background, and become part of the crowd, angry or terrified like the rest.

Felix not only did not try to extirpate the sicarii—and how difficult a task that would have been the British learned in twentieth century Cyprus—but he made secret use of them to murder his own enemies. In such a situation a reign of terror over the whole land developed, for any man of substance or of moderation, or just the personal enemy of someone, might be struck down at any time or place. But murder was not the only activity of the outlaws; properties were pillaged, houses burnt down, and acts of violence committed in all parts of the country. Governors more competent and more honest than Felix have found such a situation impossible to control. His successor, Porcius Festus, was apparently such a man, but he died less than two years after his appointment having achieved nothing, and his successors imitated the worst vices of Felix. L. Albinus, the first of these, was so open to bribes that it was said that only those remained in prison who could not pay enough to get out. His successor, Gessius Florus, the last procurator before open war began, was of such a character, says Josephus, that Albinus appeared an angel beside him.

That the Roman government of Judea was harsh, brutal, and insensitive to the values to which Jews attached the greatest importance, could not be denied. But there is no reason to suppose that it was essentially different from the government of other provinces, which were not in a state of perpetual ferment. We are, perhaps, better equipped than our immediately preceding generations, to understand that it may well have been neither the corruption nor the brutality which stirred the Jews, but the insensitivity. For that same region of the world, which we now call the Middle East, shows us repeated examples both of ferocious brutality for a supposedly

[6] *History* 5, 9. 'per omniam saevitiam ac libidinem jus regium servili ingenio exercuit'.

morally acceptable objective, and irrepressible unrest for a non-material gain. Cyprus has shown examples of both, and so have most of the Arab countries. It may well be that the treatment, not of the Jews, but of Judaism, was the real issue on which Rome and Judea came to open warfare.

3. ROME AND JUDAISM

In *The Later Herods* Stewart Perowne writes:

> 'Again and again Rome would try to establish an understanding with the Jews, and on each occasion there would not be lacking Jews, men of principle and integrity, to reciprocate Gentile goodwill. But in the end the breach widened until it became an abyss which engulfed the whole of Jewry. What was the reason for this tragic decline? Why could not Jews be the same as others? Must they, even in their relations with Rome, be different?
>
> The answer is that they must.[7]

With a deep insight Perowne contrasts the ethical and moral standards of Judaism with those which prevailed in the nations around it. Jews were obviously as exposed to temptations to lust and violence as other men. But they recognised lust and violence as moral wrongs which they ought to avoid. In that 'ought' lay the difference. They were called by Law and by prophets to a very different life from that which they saw in their Roman masters. Antiochus had attempted to pollute their religion, and they had replied with arms in their hands and won their independence. The assault of their Roman masters was no less serious. The very tax they paid them was to be used in the interests of paganism and wrong. Men, who could not appreciate what it meant, decided whether they might or might not practise this or that commandment of their religion. Men whose utter laxity in matters of sex and family life was an open scandal to the Jews, were set over them to rule their country—or rather God's country, for Israel was the land which he had chosen.

There was thus created an underlying *malaise* independent of any special act of any particular emperor or procurator, a *malaise* felt also by those who sought both to be loyal to their religion and to conciliate their masters. There were, however, many of those 'special acts' to inflame the situation, some perhaps unconscious, but far more deliberately intended to insult the religion and outrage the feelings of the Jews. It began with the entry of Pompey into the Holy of Holies in the Temple; for his act conveyed the assumption of the Romans

[7] *Op. cit.*, p. 31.

that, so far as they were concerned, there were no rights or prohibitions of others which could limit their own freedom to do what they willed. Pompey could do with Jewish things what no Jew could do, *because he was a Roman.* No Jew could handle indiscriminately the sacred robes of the high priest. But the Roman guard in Jerusalem could demand their committal to Roman care. Even though they were surrendered with great solemnity, and sealed in a room whence the high priest fetched them for the special occasions on which they were worn, it was Romans, not Jews, who controlled the entry to the room.[8] Another instance of the Roman exercise of arbitrary power was exhibited by Crassus in 53 B.C., when he shared with Pompey and Caesar the mastery of the empire. Though he was not at war with the Jews, he entered the Temple and robbed it of all the gold he found, whether in its treasury or among its sacred vessels. Three-quarters of a century later, Pilate assumed the same power to make use of the Temple treasury. In this case his object was a laudable one, indeed it was an object for which it was expressly stipulated that the funds might be used.[9] For he desired to improve the water supply of Jerusalem. But in Jewish eyes it was not for a Roman to decide the use of these funds which resulted from the freewill offerings of the whole Jewish people. So they showed their anger by noisy protest, and Pilate silenced it by a massacre in the streets of Jerusalem. It was another robbery of the treasury which precipitated the war.

Yet a third field of offence beside the entry into the Temple and the use of its treasures, lay in the Roman and Jewish attitudes to the representation of the human (or indeed any living) figure. A war was narrowly averted when the mad and degenerate emperor, Caligula, decreed that a golden statue of himself should be erected in the Temple. Mad though he was, it is unlikely that Caligula did not know the meaning of the insult he was offering to Judaism. Even the Roman governor of Syria, Petronius, sought to stay the emperor's hand at the risk of his own life,[10] but it was Agrippa who dissuaded him from his purpose. A few years later the attempt of Pilate to introduce Roman standards with human and animal images on them led to a bloody riot.[11] Though in both cases the proposed insult was withdrawn, Rome continued to possess the right to offer such insults, did she wish.

[8] On the complex subject of these vestments, see Josephus, *Antiquities*, 15, 11, 4 and especially 18, 4, 3.

[9] Shek. 4, 2, p. 13.

[10] The murder of Caligula enabled him not to put into execution that emperor's order that he commit suicide. The whole incident is described by Philo in his *Legatio at Caium* (*Caligulam*) 31 f.

[11] Perowne, *op. cit.*, has an illustration of such eagles facing p. 32.

A pietist might have claimed that all such things were but insults to the externals of religion, and did not touch any spiritual reality, for things of the spirit could not be touched by such actions. It was doubtless the fact that the period was filled with conflicts of this sort which encouraged the Essene withdrawal from society. But Judaism is not a religion which divides life into sacred and secular, and such actions of the Romans did vitally affect religious Jews. Nor was the Roman presence confined to such things. A reference has already been made to Roman sexual morality. The abyss surrounding the Jews is illustrated by the pathetic and disastrous story of the family of the emperor Augustus himself—who spoke so much of restoring the primitive purity of Roman family life.[12] Divorce, incest, secret murder, seemed to a Jew the basis of Roman habits—and it must be remembered that there were plenty of Italian Jews who, on pilgrimage to Jerusalem, would have related the life of the imperial family. Even the Romanised Jews were infected by it, and the lives of most of the Herods could not be approved by any standards of Torah. It could be said, succintly but truthfully, that the presence of *Rome* meant the dishonouring of Torah.

The presence of Romans too must have meant continual tension. For much of Judaism is orthopraxis and, while one can conceal orthodoxy, one cannot conceal orthopraxis. A very good example is provided by the observance of the sabbath. A Jew cannot conceal the fact of his observance if he lives in any close proximity to Gentiles. This is evident from the number of sneers at the practice found in the Roman satirists.[13] And soldiers are no less likely than the poets to have made the sabbath the subject of rude jests. The Jewish veneration for the actual scrolls of Torah is another matter which proximity might well reveal; and it is unlikely that the Roman soldier who tore a scroll into pieces with ribald sneers and insults, was unaware of the offence which he was committing. The occasion affords a good example of the confusion of political and religious incidents. The soldier was one of a body carrying out a punitive raid at the orders of the procurator Cumanus on a number of villages near the place on the main highway between Jerusalem and Caesarea where a Roman official had been robbed. It was a purely political, indeed criminal, affair. The public action of the soldier at once wiped out of Jewish minds the government's duty to punish a highway robbery, and made the Jews who lived in the villages into the innocent victims of an insult to their religion. The unfortunate soldier was also

[12] *Ibid.*, p. 3.

[13] See Th. Reinach, *Textes d'Auteurs Grecs et Latins relatifs au Judaisme*, Paris, Leroux, 1895, *Sabbat* in index.

made aware of the complications of life in Judea, for he was beheaded at the demand of a Jewish mob in Caesarea.[14]

Josephus says that the Jews cried 'that they could not bear to live any longer if the laws of their forefathers must be affronted after this manner', and that is, in fact, how many respectable and pious Jews came to regard Roman rule. Some doubtless adopted the Essene solution, retiring as far as possible from the ways of men; some joined the Zealots or other bands of outlaws, some tried up to the last to prevent matters from coming to a head. In this last category were the priesthood, especially those of higher rank. It had long ceased to be true that the high priests were in any sense leaders of the nation, or occupied an elevated position in the popular mind. But on the other hand it would be unfair to regard them all simply as time-servers, who led a profitable existence by keeping up the ceremonial of the Temple, and thereby collecting for themselves the considerable perquisites which accompanied its ritual and organisation. The office was obtained by some external appointment, either of a Herodian king or ethnarch or of a Roman governor, and it lay with such an outsider whether it was held for a long period or whether it was changed frequently, whether it was held by a scoundrel or by a man worthy of respect. The Caiaphas of the New Testament held it for eighteen years, but most of the appointments lasted a shorter time.

If we cannot speak of a leadership from the Temple, neither can we claim it from the synagogue. The Pharisees of the earlier period, the Tannaim of the later, were conscientious, spiritually minded, and devoted to Torah. But they were not able to hold the nation back from its destruction at Roman hands, whether in successive riots or in the ultimates of war. It would, perhaps, be fair to say that that which tipped the balance against the forces of religious responsibility was the prevailing messianic ferment.

The true crime of the apocalyptists was that they made violence seem part of the purpose of God, and sanctioned bloodshed in his name. This might not be a serious matter when Judea was either independent or under a ruler who was popular or, at least, tolerated by the people. It was disastrous in such a situation as existed in the first century. The rulers were inherently inacceptable to the Jews because they were pagans, and actually detested by them because they were both brutal and insensitive. They were just the kind of people apocalyptic denounced and threatened with a bloody end. In such a situation the ideas that God would even up the disparity of numbers and power, and that religion would cover murder, were likely to produce just what they did in fact produce—a situation in which

[14] Josephus, *Ant.*, 20, 5, 4.

counsels of moderation and patience would fall on unheeding ears. The anonymous authors of apocalyptic bear a large responsibility in the disasters which befell the people under Roman rule.

We know of continual messianic ferment, but we do not know how many of the leaders of the Zealot bands claimed to be either the messiah or to be assisting his coming. Theudas, in the time of the procurator C. Fadus, seems to have believed himself messiah,[15] and 'the Egyptian' for whom Paul was mistaken by the Temple guard, was probably another.[16] Josephus refers to them in general terms in speaking of the disorders under Felix, and there is no doubt that by his time (52-60) the political and religious motives for disorder were completely confused in the common mind. But it is interesting that the rabbis of that period seem to have kept silent on the messianic issue.[17] That they believed in the coming of a messiah, and that they foresaw him fulfilling both a political and a religious role, we may safely assume. But their silence in times of such general distress is most naturally interpreted as unwillingness either to seem to support the more spiritual conception of a messiah which was being put forward by the Judeo-Christians, or to give encouragement to the wild popular folly which sought divine sanction for every attack upon Roman authority.

When war actually came we know that the religious leaders, both Pharisaic and Sadducaic, counselled moderation, but it was too late for their pleas to be heard.

4. THE WAR WITH ROME

THERE is no need to attempt any detailed account of the war. It is to be found in any Jewish history, and its terrible details are irrelevant for our present purpose,[18] except in so far as they determined the

[15] Josephus, *op. cit.*, 20, 5, 1. The relevant material is discussed in Schurer, *op. cit.*, Vol., 1, II, p. 168, n. 6.

[16] Josephus, *op. cit.*, 20, 8, 6, and Acts 21, 38. There is a long discussion on the identity of the Egyptian in *The Beginnings of Christianity*, IV, pp. 276 f.

[17] Joseph Klausner, *The Messianic Idea in Israel*, Allen and Unwin, 1956, pp. 392 f.

[18] As all accounts are based on Josephus, the question of his reliability is important. There is, however, no consensus of opinion about it among scholars. But there is general agreement that in the main he gives a fair account. Most people place little reliance on his figures. Beyond that it is not safe to go. An interesting discussion of his character and career to be found in Perowne, *The Later Herods*, ch. 13. One of the best critical assessments of the war is in the relevant chapters of *The Fall of Jerusalem and the Christian Church*, by S. G. F. Brandon, S.P.C.K., 1951.

conditions under which the Jewish people remade its existence after the tragedy.

The 'step from which there is no return' was taken by Florus in 66 when he robbed the Temple treasury of seventeen talents. The Jews replied by mockery at his 'poverty'. Florus retaliated with massacre, but seeing that he had gone too far, withdrew his small forces from Jerusalem lest they should be completely annihilated. The Jewish mob retorted by stopping the daily sacrifice for the emperor. King Agrippa II, the high priestly leaders and the leaders of the Tannaim[19] all tried to turn the mob from its course. But the only result was civil war in Jerusalem in which a high priest was murdered with many of his followers, and the mob took complete control. It is possible that Simeon b. Gamaliel was murdered at the same time, for we hear nothing of him again, and it is his son, another Gamaliel, who is head of the house of Hillel after the war. During this bloody civil war between the different Jewish parties, Cestius Gallus, legate of Syria, arrived with a substantial army. Having half conquered Jerusalem, he suddenly withdrew, and his forces were badly mauled on their retreat northwards.

Josephus gives no clue as to the real reason for the withdrawal of Gallus.[20] But its effect on the Jewish rebels was electric. They saw in it a repetition of the miracle which had saved the city in the days of Sennacherib,[21] and were convinced that God was on their side, and would protect his city and Temple from the heathen enemy. From then onwards power lay more and more with the extremists. In both Galilee and Judea the moderates were ousted; but the extremists were divided among themselves. Only at moments of extreme danger would they unite, and their murderous dissensions contributed considerably to the Jewish defeat, while their constant massacres of moderate and responsible elements made it more difficult for the people to rise again when the terrors of war were withdrawn.

One of the points on which, it appears, we shall never get much information is the part played in the war by Jews outside the country. Josephus in his account of its beginnings tells of violent riots and massacres between Jews and Gentiles in the mixed cities which surrounded Judea, cities like Caesarea or the Greek cities of the Decapolis. We know that these riots spread as far as Damascus and

[19] L. Finkelstein in *Akiba, Scholar, Saint and Martyr*, pp. 46 ff claims that Simeon b. Gamaliel and his entourage were all Shammaites, and strongly nationalistic. The Talmud has little good to say of Simeon.

[20] The mystery is discussed and a list of authorities quoted by Brandon *op. cit.*, pp. 159 f.

[21] 2 Kings 19. 32-35.

Alexandria. But there were many powerful Jewish communities further afield, and there were the Jews of Babylon. On both he is silent; and as it would be contrary to his purpose to render Jewish inhabitants of the empire unpopular, or to encourage the Jews outside the empire to think of violence, his silence is suspect. Dio Cassius, a distinguished lawyer and administrator, in a history of the Romans written in about A.D. 200, says that they did take part. But he is separated by more than a hundred years from the Jewish war. Furthermore the part dealing with events of that period exists, not in Dio's own work but in a medieval Byzantine synopsis. It is therefore impossible to know how much reliance to place on the remark attributed to him that Jews 'not only in the Roman empire but from beyond the Euphrates' came to the aid of the Jews of Judea.[22]

We could place more reliance on Dio—for, after all, his statement is reasonable—if this support was referred to, even indirectly, in the literature of the time, Christian, Jewish, or pagan. But no such references are forthcoming, and there are no traces in what we know of contemporary Jewish-Christian and Jewish-Gentile relations of such a situation as would have been created by a widespread Jewish rising at this time. Until further evidence is discovered, judgement must be suspended, though the balance is perhaps inclined in favour of Dio's statement. For later revolts prove that diaspora Jewry was not completely satisfied with its status under the charter of Caesar, and after the war Jewish solidarity appears unimpaired.

Whether they took an active part in it or not, the whole of Jewry was affected by the conditions consequent on the Jewish defeat in the mother country. For nearly two thousand years there will be no such thing as Jewish political authority over any defined geographical area, though there will be various limited forms of personal authority over 'the Jews', or 'the Jews of. . . .'. Moreover the devastation wrought in Judea itself, that is in the southern part of Palestine, aided by the casualties of the second Jewish war, will make Galilee, rather than the south, the centre of Jewish population in the Holy Land until the nineteenth century. As to Jerusalem itself, it is not until the same century that it will regain its importance as the largest Jewish centre in the country.

A second result, to be confirmed by rabbinic action in the next generation, is the definite break with the Palestinian Judeo-Christian Church. The total break between the two religions was not complete until the beginning of the second century, but the refusal of the Christians to take part in the defence of Jerusalem, and the Gentile

[22] The quotation is from Bk. 66. 4. quoted in Reinach, *op. cit.*, p. 190.

Christian mockery of the Jews for their defeat, made a definite breach in the Holy Land.

There is a connection between these two consequences of the defeat. The disappearance of any political autonomy and any ultimate authority over a precise piece of territory, compelled the post-war Jewish leaders to seek some basis for the identification of 'a Jew' other than that he lived in Jewish territory, or was recognised as a Jew by the political authority of that territory. To be a Jew it was necessary to share in a corporate experience and accept the common interpretation of that experience. By rejecting the common interpretation, the Judeo-Christians were, by this new definition, rejecting membership of the Jewish community. Judaism remained primarily orthopraxis, but developed the power to decide what faith and works it would accept as being Jewish. Because there was no other way in which any continuity of Jewish history could be maintained, there was a new urgency in the search for unity, and for a common expression of the destiny of the chosen people.

5. RABBAN JOHANAN B. ZAKKAI AND HIS COLLEAGUES

AT the beginning, and through the early months of the siege, it seems that quite a number of the Tannaitic leaders were still in Jerusalem. But when their leader, Johanan b. Zakkai, became convinced that there was no further hope for the city, he decided to leave it. There is a picturesque account that he was carried out in a coffin, and asked of the Romans permission only to settle in the small town in the maritime plain, Jabneh, there to build up an academy of learning.[23] It was this academy which became the central college and court of Judaism, and made of the teaching of Torah the basis of survival. The very fact that the court was brought from the mountains of Jerusalem down to the plain (and subsequently still lower, to Tiberias) seemed to his contemporaries a sign of their humiliation but was proof to Johanan that it should be the means of redeeming Israel. To a rabbi who said that the court was truly brought down to the ground, he replied that 'from there they are destined to be redeemed, as it says, "shake thyself from the dust, arise!" '[24]

Johanan took with, or gathered round, him a distinguished group of both older and younger scholars, including the son of Simeon b. Gamaliel who was soon made the President of the Assembly.

[23] Gitt, 56a, b, p. 257.
[24] R. H. 31 a, b, p. 149. The quotation is from Is. 52. 2.

Gamaliel II was still a very young man when this honour fell to him and he did not always use his power wisely. There was also his brother-in-law, Eliezer b. Hyrcanus, who possessed a marvellous memory for the decisions of rabbis previous to the destruction of the Temple, but would accept the authority of no innovations, and would himself propound no decision if he could not say that he had heard it from his teachers.[25] There was another Eliezer, Eliezer b. Jacob, who was particularly acquainted with the Temple, as was Hananiah, who had been deputy high priest. These two provided constant information when the Temple was under discussion; for it must be remembered that the rabbis of Jabneh expected its rebuilding in due course. It had been destroyed before and rebuilt, and there was no reason why that should not happen again. One of the older men was Zadok, who had fasted forty years, because he foresaw the destruction of the Temple in punishment for the wickedness of the nation. But the most distinguished colleague of Johanan was Joshua b. Hananiah, who lived into the reign of Hadrian.[26]

The gathering represented many streams in the life of the people. Gamaliel and his brother-in-law Eliezer belonged to the class of wealthy landowners, and were still men of substance after the war. Several of them, as already mentioned, had been in the service of the Temple and were intimate with every detail of its life. But Joshua b. Hananiah was throughout his life a poor man, earning his living as a maker of needles. It is claimed that Johanan was a disciple of Hillel,[27] though he must have been very young when Hillel died, and many scholars doubt if the two men came into personal contact. But he was, at least, a disciple of the School of Hillel, and his familiarity with its traditions increased his value to the 'Vineyard', as the scholars called their academy at Jabneh. On various occasions it is quoted that the opinion of Johanan came from 'the teacher of his teacher'[28]—in other words it had a valuable antiquity, bringing it nearer 'the Men of the Great Synagogue'.[29] He was already a distinguished teacher in Jerusalem before the war.[30]

[25] Yoma 66b, p. 311. For a detailed study of R. Eliezer, see B. Z. Bokser, *Pharisaic Judaism in Transition*, New York, 1935.

[26] Brief biographies of these men, together with references to their sayings, will be found in *Die Lehrer der Mischnah*, by M. Braunschweiger, Frankfurt, 1890. See also *The Last Pharisee, The Life and Times of R. Joshua b. Hananyah, a first century Idealist*, J Podro, Vallentine, Mitchell, 1959.

[27] B.B., 134a, p. 563.

[28] E.g. Ed. 8. 7., p. 50.

[29] See above pp. 61 f.

[30] There is an excellent biographical sketch of Johanan in Finkelstein, *Akiba* pp. 60 ff. and *passim.*

The characters of the three leaders, Johanan, Gamaliel, and Joshua, were very different. Johanan is praised for the depth and comprehensiveness of his knowledge. 'He did not neglect Scripture or Mishnah, Gemara, Halakah, Aggada, or Supplements (aggadic midrash), the subtleties of Scripture, or the subtleties of the Scribes, or any of the Sages' rules of interpretation'.[31] Like Hillel he was both firm and liberal. He was a man of great strength of character, and his determination to leave Jerusalem and begin work at Jabneh shows both his courage and his initiative. But he had time to be courteous. It was said of him that no one was ever the first to greet him; even if it was a pagan, Johanan would salute him first.[32] Strong and gentle, Johanan was also humble, and his humility is shown in the account of his death bed, when he refused to trust in his own merits, but professed himself unworthy to meet an all-righteous Judge.[33] He showed his humility also by his willingness to receive advice from others, to subject his opinion to the criticism of others, and to accept the decision of the majority. While this is shown in various Talmudic arguments, one of the most delightful examples of his willingness to hear others is the story of how, when his son died, all the other scholars were unable to comfort him until R. Eleazar b. Arak arrived. When Johanan saw Eleazar come he knew that he would overcome his grief, because of the wisdom with which Eleazar would console him.[34]

That a man who was to have so decisive an influence on Jewish development should possess the characteristics of Johanan was of the greatest value to his and succeeding generations. The inevitable temptation, to which not a few rabbis succumbed, was to adopt a hostile attitude to the outside world, and Jewish history made it easy for Jews to regard Gentiles with contempt or dislike. It is, then, worth ending the account of Johanan with his verdict in a discussion of the interpretation of a verse of the Bible dealing with the sins of the Gentiles. To the hostile opinions of his colleagues, which he recognised to be superior to his own, he gave the final answer that 'charity makes atonement for the heathen'.[35]

Gamaliel was a very different character. He was intolerant and impulsive, and attempted to force unity on the Vineyard by bearing down opposition. As we shall see, the question of the unity and authority of Torah greatly exercised the Vineyard, and it was not in

[31] Ab. d. R.N. Ch. 14.
[32] Ber. 17a, p. 102.
[33] *Ibid.*, 28b, p. 173.
[34] Ab. d. R.N. Ch. 14.
[35] B.B. 10b, p. 51.

pursuit of personal power that Gamaliel showed his intolerance. But he considered that as President it was his right to give rulings, and that it was wrong of any scholar to challenge those rulings, and so introduce confusion into simple minds. Incidentally he considered that 'simple minds' should not be allowed to attend the lectures and discussions of the scholars, and stationed a keeper at the door to keep out all except those who had the President's permission to attend.[36]

The Talmud graphically expresses the confusion which Gamaliel thus introduced by pin-pointing his conflicts with a man of opposite temperament, but much older than himself, Joshua b. Hananiah. One issue arose from the date of the Day of Atonement. Gamaliel calculated wrongly the astronomical evidence, and Joshua told him so, giving him the correct interpretation. Gamaliel refused to make any change and ordered Joshua to appear before him in his working clothes and carrying his scrip on the day he, Joshua, thought to be the Day of Atonement. Joshua, to the surprise of the scholars, did so; and Gamaliel showed his essential generosity by exclaiming 'welcome my teacher and pupil, my teacher in wisdom, my pupil in obeying my decision'.[37] But conflicts between the two men continued, and rose to fresh heights of antagonism over the issue of the evening prayer. Joshua held that it was voluntary, wishing perhaps to excuse the tired labourer from repeating its long and complex clauses, but Gamaliel insisted that it was compulsory. Gamaliel in this case had the weight of the Vineyard behind him, but his vindictive treatment of the much older Joshua so angered them that they deposed him on the spot, and appointed a still younger man, Eleazar b. Azariah, as president.

Gamaliel again showed his good qualities. He recognised the rightness of his deposition, and took his place without rancour among the rank and file of the Vineyard. To Joshua he apologised humbly and, going to visit him in his home, realised for the first time in what poverty the majority of scholars dwelt.[38] For he found Joshua working at his forge in a smoke-grimed cottage. That Joshua was not elevated in place of Gamaliel was due, it seems, to his poverty and lowly origin. For the scholars recognised that their leader would need on occasion to meet and negotiate with the Roman governors. For this Gamaliel and Eleazar were fitted by their aristocratic descent.

[36] On the character of Gamaliel see Finkelstein, *op. cit.*, pp. 112 ff.

[37] R.H. 25a, pp. 108 f. The discussion turns largely on the importance of getting an agreed authority—even if it be a wrong one! Compare Bek. 36a, p. 230 for another argument.

[38] Hor. 10a fin., p. 71.

The scholars of the Vineyard were not other-worldly, and recognised the duty of seeking good relations with their governors, no easy task after the long and bitter war. But the task had to be attempted, and the best men chosen for it. For, as R. Haninia, who had been deputy high priest, said: 'We should pray for the government for, were it not for the fear thereof, one man would swallow up his fellow-men.'[39]

Joshua continued for long to be a member of the Vineyard, and what is recorded of his opinions is always gentle and liberal. He would even accept a proselyte who had been baptised but not circumcised and though he were of Moabite or Ammonite origin.[40] It was he who converted Aquila, and ordained Akiba. In spite of the feeling that they needed a rich aristocrat as negotiator, it was Joshua who went to Hadrian, and persuaded him to withdraw a harsh governor, and to allow the Temple to be rebuilt. But, as to the latter, difficulties arose and the permission led to nothing, until the second war nullified it. Even at the age of ninety, he visited Hadrian in Alexandria on behalf of his people, and died soon after his return, a scholar *sans peur et sans reproche*.

Of such a type were the leaders who assembled in Jabneh, while the siege of Jerusalem was still continuing. When the city fell, and it was possible to think of the future, there were two tasks which demanded their immediate attention. The first was the consolation of the survivors, and the second was a decision as to how they, as teachers of Torah and as judges, could bring the nation back to its obedience to the God of Israel. Neither task was an easy one, and neither could be accomplished in a single generation.

There is no sadder or more touching verdict on the destruction of the Temple than the words of a third century rabbi that, since the destruction of the Temple, the gates of prayer are locked (Lam. 3. 8) but the gates of tears are always open (Ps. 39. 13). But tears would not rebuild the nation, and the immediate task was not to aid the people to grieve, but to prevent exaggerated mourning. When Johanan was weeping over the ruins of the Temple with his disciples, he turned to them and said: 'be not grieved, we have another atonement as effective as this . . . acts of loving kindness'.[41] And in the same spirit, Joshua, learning that there were some who would eat neither meat nor wine, because such foods could no longer be sanctified by the Temple sacrifices, reminded the ascetics that, logically, they should

[39] Ab. 3. 2, p. 27.
[40] Yeb. 46a, p. 303.
[41] Ab. d. R.N. Ch. 4. The idea that money spent on charity equates money spent on sacrifices is to be found throughout the period. Cf. B.B. 9a, p. 41 ff. Study also equals sacrifice, cf. Men. 110a, pp. 679 f.

abstain also from bread and fruit, since both of these were offered at the Temple. But by doing so they would impose, in his opinion, an impossible burden on their fellow-countrymen. For, said Joshua, 'not to mourn at all is impossible, because the blow has fallen. To mourn over-much is also impossible, because we do not impose on the community a hardship which the majority cannot endure.'[42] This principle, that an impossible burden must never be placed on the people, became fundamental in the development of rabbinic Judaism. It is typical of Joshua that both its tenderness and its realism should have come from him.

The consolation of Israel, however, did not consist simply in moral exhortation. There were a number of practical religious duties which had been fulfilled by the Temple and its officers, and for which a substitute had to be found until the Temple could be rebuilt. Johanan was an admirable leader for such a purpose. His vast knowledge enabled him to judge the meaning of past acts, his generous and realistic temperament enabled him to find a dignified and practical substitute. The various prescriptions which he issued did not make Jabneh itself an equivalent for Jerusalem. But he laid on 'every place where there was a Beth Din' the responsibility for the carrying out of the correct ceremonial,[43] and thus began that extraordinary decentralisation which enabled Judaism to survive.

In view of the fact that the destiny of Israel depended now on the success of the scholars, it is interesting to find, not as the statement of one rabbi but as the opinion of the Vineyard, that a scholar must not esteem himself above a workman. For, they said: 'I am God's creature and my fellow is God's creature. My work is in the town and his work is in the country. I rise early for my work, and he rises early for his work. Just as he does not presume to do my work, so I do not presume to do his work. Will you say, I do much and he does little. We have learnt: one may do much or one may do little; it is all one provided that he directs his heart to heaven'.[44] A little earlier there had been a tendency among some Pharisees to separate themselves from the ordinary people, and to consider themselves superior, an attitude reflected in Gamaliel II's stationing of a porter at the door to regulate entry.[45] But this passage reflects the realisation of the scholars that, with the Temple destroyed and their political autonomy in ruins, they could only succeed in preserving the chosen people if

[42] B.B. 60b, p. 245. L. Finkelstein in *Akiba*, p. 348 n. 33 considers that this event did not occur then, but about A.D. 120.

[43] These regulations are found in Mishnah, R.H., Ch. 4. 1-3, pp. 137 ff.

[44] Ber. 17a, p. 101.

[45] Cf. John 7. 49.

they united themselves with the people and persisted in their task until their work had come to be accepted by all who called themselves Jews. We so easily overlook the unprecedented and extraordinary task to which they and succeeding generations of scholars were devoting themselves, that we overlook also that it took many generations before they had won that acceptance.

The oral law had grown in bulk from the days of the men of the Great Synagogue onwards. Hillel had made the first attempt, so far as we know, to get some order into the method by which the oral laws were deduced from the written Torah. He expounded seven rules: '*a fortiori*, analogy, deduction from one verse, deduction from two verses, inference from general and particular, from particular and general, similarity elsewhere, deduction from context'.[46] But in his day there were two Pharisaic schools of interpretation as well as that of the Sadducees. The Vineyard realised that, with such varied rules of interpretation, 'Torah would be forgotten in Israel' because no one could remember all the interpretations.[47] The first issue was, therefore, the choice of one school of interpretation and the rejection of the idea that they should pick and choose between different schools over each point, preferring now the view of Hillel, now that of Shammai, now of someone else. The debate was a vigorous one, and threatened to be interminable. But a *Bath Kol* intervened with the solution that 'the teaching of both schools are the words of the living God, but in practice the halakah of the School of Hillel is to be followed'.[48]

The decision that the school of Hillel gave the authoritative decisions was wholly in accord with the temperaments of Johanan and Joshua, both of whom sought always a liberal interpretation of a

[46] Ab. d. R.N. Ch. 37.

[47] Shab. 138b, pp. 699 f. There is an excellent discussion of the halakoth, of Shammai and of Hillel in L. Ginzberg, *On Jewish Law and Lore*, J.P.S. of America, 1955, pp. 88 ff.

[48] Er. 13b, pp. 85 f. The *Bath Kol* is an intervention, which cannot be properly described as 'the voice of God' or even literally as 'the echo of the voice of God', since rabbis felt themselves entitled to contradict it and deplore its intervention. It was, however, a formula for achieving a decision, which it is difficult for us to define closely. Cf. *The Rabbinic Mind*, Max Kadushin, Jewish Theological Seminary, New York 1952, pp. 261 ff. For arguments about the *Bath Kol* and similar miraculous interventions in discussions see Er. 6b—7a, pp. 34 f. and B.M. 59b. p. 353. On one occasion Eliezer b. Jacob invited a wall to fall in proof of his statement, when R. Joshua rebuked the wall, asking to know what it thought it was doing interfering in a debate between scholars! Attitude to the *Bath Kol* was at times similar. This decision in favour of the school of Hillel did not prevent the inclusion of some decisions of Shammai.

disputed question, and with the belief of the Vineyard that they must make those who were not scholars realise that they and the scholars alike were parts of Israel. The time when there could be many schools of interpretation had passed. Joshua, by his absolute obedience to Gamaliel II, testified to the importance of unity. Since a large part of the work of the Vineyard was the collection of past traditions, this decision made their work that much easier, though on a number of points they still recorded, as part of the debate on an issue, decisions that had been taken by the school of Shammai. Just as they had to choose between rival interpretations, so also they had to take a final decision as to the Scriptures with whose interpretation they were concerned. So far as the main bulk of the writing was concerned, they had nothing to do. The books of the Law, the prophets, including the historical books, and certain other works had long been canonised. But it was still unclear whether Ecclesiastes, Esther and The Song of Songs should be included. The decisive debate was delayed till the end of the century, and then all were included.[49]

While we may be astonished at the amount of time which they devoted to the ritual and appurtenances of the Temple, we must remember that it was not until after the second war that hope was given up that the Temple would be rebuilt. Even after that any incident in their favour could rouse again their expectations. When Julian became emperor in the fourth century, and dethroned Christianity from its position as a state religion, they hoped for a rebuilding; and in later messianic expectation the rebuilding of the Temple was thought of as part of the messianic age.[50]

Their main effort was directed at the securing of unity, because the nation as a whole was not yet accustomed to the idea that there was to be only one Judaism and one leadership, religious and social (political was not yet in question). The scholars of the Vineyard and their immediate successors had to cope with a nationalism which was still vigorous in spite of defeat and massacre, as well as with alternative forms of Judaism, including that of the Jewish Christians.

6. AKIBA B. JOSEPH

THE period of Johanan b. Zakkai was one in which conservation and innovation had to proceed together. To gather up the traditions of the past, before they were forgotten, was of prime importance for a

[49] Meg. 6b—7a, pp. 32 ff.

[50] The Temple also was one of the creatures which pre-existed the creation of heaven and earth. See Ginzberg, *Legends of the Jews,* VII Index p. 467, second column.

religion like Judaism where action was so important, and where a people already widely scattered had to be kept in some sort of unity. But, conservation having taken place, the next important task was that of the systematizing and ordering of the religious practices thus conserved. In this area the supreme authority was Akiba b. Joseph.

Akiba was born about A.D. 40 into the poorest class of the rural community and was for long too poor to study. It was only by the determination of his wife to go out to work separately that he could put together enough money for the poorest scholar's life, and the stories of his poverty are numerous. Akiba came into the field when it was still doubtful what form would emerge from the codification and systematization of the many ordinances deduced from the Scriptures. Though the *Bath Kol* had declared for Hillel, and though both Johanan and Joshua were keen Hillelites, there were important priestly, aristocratic and Shammaite influences in the Vineyard, especially the president, Gamaliel II and his brother-in-law, Eliezer b. Hyrcanus. Their attitude was repeated in the next generation by men such as Ishmael b. Elisha.[51] These leaders thought of the Jewish people as primarily a people of priests, landowners and farmers, with a certain amount of labour employed by them; and indeed that was a fair description of the Jewish people as it then lived in Palestine. But, had their development of halakah proceeded exclusively along the lines suited to such a people, it would have very soon become ill-adjusted to the life of Jews elsewhere and in coming centuries. For halakah was already so intimate and so detailed that, to be accepted, it needed to be firmly based on the actualities of existence, and even on the prosperity or adversity of the people who would express it in their daily lives at home and abroad. Akiba, thinking of a much more proletarian existence than his wealthy and land-owning colleagues, was a much better guide.

He spent a long period in study before he was equipped for any kind of leadership. The whole body of Scripture was largely new to him, and at first he saw only the literal acceptance or fulfilment of the written words. His theology was anthropomorphic, and his attitude to the halakah was one of unrelieved and literalistic severity. But even in his early days he had a deep intuition of the meaning of

[51] Finkelstein, *op. cit.*, completely systematizes the whole series of issues into a conflict between the patricians and the plebeians, the former priestly land-owning or farming, the latter largely urban and commercial. The same distinction is found in his work *The Pharisees*. While Finkelstein may carry his schematization too far, his basic theory is inescapable, and its importance for the future of Judaism is obvious. See especially L. Ginsberg, *On Jewish Law and Lore*, pp. 159 ff.

Scripture which enabled him to outgrow the simple, almost mechanical, outlook of his first essays in rabbinic scholarship. It is interesting, in view of his later development, that his first teacher was the aristocratic Tarpho, but the greatest influence of his early days was the more eccentric Nahum of Gimso. For Nahum foreshadowed the main contribution of Akiba to rabbinic studies by proclaiming that every letter and tittle of Torah was of direct significance, and that a meaning must be deduced from it.

This carried the question of deciding halakah beyond the idea that the duty of the rabbis was to understand what the sentences and words meant and to render their decisions on that basis. For, by emphasising 'jots and tittles', any interpretation could in actual fact be produced. This was recognised by the rabbis themselves, as is shown, for example, by the story that 'when Moses ascended on high he found the Holy One (blessed be He) engaged in affixing coronets to the letters. Said Moses, 'Lord of the Universe, who stays thy hand?' (i.e. who is it that stayed your hand from doing all that was necessary before you gave the Torah to me, that you have to do this now?) He answered, 'there will arise a man, at the end of many generations, Akiba b. Joseph by name, who will expound upon each tittle heaps and heaps of laws.' Moses asked that he might listen to him, but he found that he did not understand what Akiba was talking about.[52] Dr. Finkelstein, in writing of Akiba's system, says frankly that 'it is obvious that he considered the interpretation of the written law merely the form which had to be followed in the derivation of desirable rules from the scriptural text.'[53]

This method of Akiba's was of capital importance for the future, and represented the completion of a revolution which was implicit, though not explicit, in the work of the teachers of Torah from the beginning. The Mishnah, the work of the end of the second Christian century, sees no reason to quote a biblical verse or passage as authority for its decisions. It quotes them as self-justificatory, sometimes, but by no means always, giving the name of the rabbi who first enunciated them. The fact that a halakah is included in the Mishnah is its own authority. An example was given earlier of the form of the earlier halakic midrash, where each phrase was linked to a Biblical verse which authorised its purpose.[54] Except where we have a record

[52] Men. 29b, p. 190.

[53] *Akiba, Scholar, Saint and Martyr*, p. 171. This book is of the utmost value, especially for the reader unaccustomed to rabbinical activities. By putting Akiba into the normal framework of a biography Dr. Finkelstein helps greatly to the understanding of the period, and of the way in which a rabbinical decision was reached.

[54] See above Ch. 2. 4., p. 66.

of the discussion in the Gemara, we do not necessarily know from what Biblical verse, and by what methods, the present halakoth of the Mishnah derived.

The concept of the 'oral law' thus received an enormously increased significance, and the action of Akiba emphasised anew the responsibility of scholars. But it also made Judaism—potentially—entirely fluid, since the absence of a subject from the written Scriptures could no longer prevent a development that seemed desirable to the scholars of any generation. Rabbinic Judaism became a religion in its own right stemming organically (as did Christianity) from, but not identical with, the religion of Israel, that is, the religion of the Old Testament. Its nature and content will be discussed in the following chapter; but in the work of Akiba we can see already the crystallization of developments which had been maturing for centuries.

The task of the teachers of Torah was, from the beginning, unprecedented. With the destruction (even temporarily) of the Temple it was enormously extended, for it had to cover the whole life of the people at a period of constant change, and of new problems perpetually arising. In the past various interpretations of the duty of man could exist side by side, for it was not on them that national unity and survival depended. Obedience to God could be expressed in the fulfilment of a simple or of a complex system of duties. That those duties were always performed in the same way did not appear important. It was this position that was changed by the new need to build out of obedience to Torah a basis of that national unity which would alone secure survival.

The rabbis of the Vineyard carried out this task by transferring to daily life the conception of the performance of an exact ritual and ceremonial which had hitherto been associated only with the Temple. We must not think of them as doing this consciously or deliberately, or of choosing to exercise their leadership in this manner, after having considered and rejected alternative ways in which their responsibilities could be exercised. It is impossible to understand the developments of rabbinic Judaism until it is seen that *this was the natural thing to do.*

We have already seen that they transferred to ordinary life the discipline of purification which had formerly been associated only with the service of the Temple, and that in some quarters they had done this by the time of Jesus of Nazareth.[55] Now they did the same thing with regard to the whole of life as they passed it in review.

Scrupulous attention to detail, and scrupulous performance of a

[55] Mark 7. 3 f. See above, p. 169.

ritual, are not only natural to primitive people, but can be understood and remembered by ordinary people everywhere. The Jews had pelted a high priest in Maccabean times because he was performing a ritual incorrectly;[56] a Roman Catholic priest in celebrating the mass uses a great number of very precise gestures which express spiritual truths and which the congregation accepts as such; campanology—or the proper ringing of church bells—was practised by English villagers long before the days of education, and they correctly performed sequences which might take hours to be completed with the most intricate and ever changing patterns. Ritual neither depends on education nor is hostile to the spirit. No doubt there were minds which attuned themselves with difficulty to such precision of living,[57] and no doubt the extreme nationalists saw quite other methods for preserving the life of the nation. But it is a mistake to assume that the Vineyard and its successors were forcing Judaism into unnatural channels or making the spiritual life of the people 'legalistic' 'external' or 'formal', by turning them into paths to which they were not wholly unaccustomed, and in which they would have no difficulty in seeing as much spiritual vitality as each mind could compass. For the rabbis themselves, then as always, the centre of religion was that men should 'direct their hearts to heaven'. The detailed fulfilment of Torah was designed to help rather than hinder this.

The essential thing was to see that the halakoth which they issued were related to the actual life of the people, and directed their development towards a pattern which seemed to the rabbis morally and spiritually good. If we consider the methods and objectives of Akiba we can see that there was always an actual situation before his mind, and that it was for truly spiritual purposes that he extended so enormously the realm of the oral law.[58]

Dr. Finkelstein has summarised his 'juristic philosophy' by naming eight ideals which Akiba set before himself:

1. So to interpret the ceremonial laws that the poor were not excluded from participation in worship, or subjected to intolerable ritual burdens:

2. to ensure that civil law should be used, wherever possible, to rectify social inequalities;

3. to limit the prerogatives of the priests, especially towards the Levites;

[56] See above, p. 65.

[57] Compare Peter's attitude expressed in Acts 15. 10.

[58] Finkelstein, *op. cit.*, p. 95—106 illustrates this by giving a number of examples of the clash between Akiba and the patrician element, represented by Eliezer b. Hyrcanus.

4. to protect family life against disruption by the severest penalties against faithlessness;
5. to protect the rights and status of free labour, while bettering the conditions of the slave;
6. to defend observant merchants from the handicaps of their observances;
7. to eradicate superstitious practices;
8. to proclaim peace and human equality as fundamental principles of religion.[59]

In due course Akiba established his own academy, siting it under a fig tree at Bene Berak (near the present Tel Aviv), and gathering round him an eager band of teachers and disciples. This was probably the happiest time of his life; and as it was a time of peace for the nation, he was able to continue his work uninterruptedly for a dozen years. During this time it is believed that he fixed the order of the arrangement of the halakoth, which became the present Mishnah, dividing them into six main subjects, and into many of the subordinate tractates. It is perhaps during this period also that he experimented with mystical or gnostic metaphysics in company with three of his colleagues. From the results, it would appear that they were making some psychic experiment, and made contact with a power which resulted in some terrifying experience. For Akiba was the only one of the four who came out of the experiment with his faith and reason unimpaired.[60]

By the time that unrest was passing once again into war with Rome, Akiba was about ninety years old. That at some point he recognised Bar Cochba as messiah is undoubted,[61] but it is impossible to say what part he played in the revolt as a whole.[62] Dr. Finkelstein,[63] relates how the teaching of the aged scholar had become uncertain and hesitant and how he fumbled in his decisions. That he was carried away by the first facile victories of the rebels would argue a mind which had lost much of its discernment, and it is at least consonant with his whole

[59] *Ibid.* Summarised from pp. 177 f.

[60] Hag. 14b, pp. 89 f.

[61] Midrash Rabba Lam. 2. 2. Ed. Son. VII., p. 157.

[62] Dr. Finkelstein, *op. cit.*, p. 269, admits that he on one occasion 'went so far as to call him messiah outright,' but clearly ascribes this to the weakening faculties of extreme old age, and dissociates Akiba from any responsibility for the revolt. Graetz and Dubnow recount that he travelled widely throughout the east stirring up rebellion; Sacher and Margolis and Marx call him 'the soul of the revolt'; Roth and Grayzel say that he was the most prominent figure in the revolt; only Baron is much more circumspect, just recording his recognition on one occasion of Bar Cochba as messiah.

[63] pp. 265 ff.

life to acquit him of more than a senile error. He did not carry all of his colleagues with him in acceptance of the revolt, but we know much less of its details than we do of the earlier war, and we cannot allot a role to each of the rabbis of the period.

In the sad period which followed, Akiba rediscovered his authority and his clear vision. In despite of Roman prohibitions, he openly taught Torah to his disciples, and courted the arrest which followed.[64] After three years in prison he was martyred, proclaiming the *Shema* with his dying breath in words whose nobility still rings from the pages of the Talmud:[65]

> All my days I have been troubled by this verse 'with all thy soul' (which I interpret) 'even if he takes my soul'. I said: When shall I have the opportunity of fulfilling this? Now that I have the opportunity, shall I not fulfil it? He prolonged the word *ehad* [one] until he expired while saying it.

7. THE REBIRTH OF NATIONALISM

THE first war with Rome ushers in seventy years of very puzzling Jewish history. If we are to take our few and scattered authorities at their face value we appear to be dealing with:

1. A war in Palestine from 66 to 70 in which Josephus tells us of no co-operation from the Diaspora. (Dio Cassius, however, writes a hundred and fifty years later that the Diaspora did join in.)
2. Three curiously futile and scattered outbreaks in the Roman Diaspora and one in Babylon between 115 and 117, with which Palestine was apparently not concerned. (But Spartianus, writing at the end of the third century, refers to trouble in Palestine *at some time* in Hadrian's reign.)
3. A second war in Palestine, from 132 to 135, which may have had some support in the Diaspora. (Dio Cassius, at any rate, says so.)

It would be easier, though we cannot prove that it would be truer, if we could reassess the picture as follows:

There were three wars between Rome and the Jews.

For the first, the centre was in Palestine, where Jews felt the full effect of a harsh Roman government. Support from the Diaspora was slight and sporadic, because the diaspora communities were fairly happy under Roman rule.

The second was an opportunist attempt to exploit the absence in Mesopotamia of the Emperor Trajan. It was begun by the Babylonian

[64] Ber. 61b, pp. 385 f.
[65] *Ibid.*, p. 386.

Jews who, seeing for the first time a Roman army within their reach, determined to avenge the loss of Jerusalem and the Temple. As Trajan passed eastwards they rose behind him. They made every effort to persuade communities further west to rise also. The Palestinian Jews attempted to join their fellows and did, or did not, succeed. This is a logical reappraisement of a quite chaotic story, but it means that we must revise some of the dating, which at present implies that western Jews rose first.

In any case this second war was utterly futile and misdirected. Jewish historians are completely divided as to its causes,[66] and all that ancient historians really tell us is that it was very bloody and very violent. The Jews of Cyrene had a leader called Lucuas, but there seems no reason to think that they believed him to be a messiah, and there are no messianic implications in the other accounts.[67] It is impossible to decide whether there actually was trouble in Palestine or not. What is quite certain is that all the revolts were a complete failure, though they took some trouble to suppress. They seem to have left little trace on diaspora history; though they probably accounted for the fact that Jews seem to have lost their importance and influence in the following half-century. There is, for example, considerable evidence that they harried the Christians considerably during the period of the separation of the two religions, but there is little evidence of their playing a hostile part in the great persecutions which followed in the second century onwards.[68] But, while they may have lost influence, the period of their active repression was short.

The third war was much the most important and decisive for the Jewish future, but again we are in considerable doubt as to how or why rebellion seemed to the Jews a desperate necessity. It seems that at some short period after the series of troubles in the years 115-117, the Jews of Palestine were promised the rebuilding of Jerusalem and,

[66] Graetz starts the revolt in Mesopotamia, and has considerable respect for its planning. He calls the plan 'wohlberechtnete' and thinks there was a single powerful leader; Dubnow places the responsibility on refugees from Judea; Sachar agrees with Graetz; Roth ascribes it all to a vague messianism, but detects a 'master' mind; Margolis and Marx describe it as a plot of the Jews of Cyrene, Cyprus and Egypt with the Armenians and Parthians, but they put the Babylonian revolt later; Grayzel mentions no general planning, and calls it racial riots; Baron thinks that the Jews were settling old scores, but that there was a messianic background. The exact passages are not given as they are easily found in the respective histories.

[67] All the sources will be found in Schurer, *op. cit.*, I, 2, pp. 281 ff., but he seems unduly prepared to accept the veracity of the atrocities.

[68] See my *Conflict*, Ch. 4. and especially the list of saints and martyrs in App. 5, pp. 402 ff.

possibly, of the Temple.[69] The details are extremely vague, but, for some reason, the expectation that the Temple would be rebuilt was disappointed. Perhaps it was falsified by the event, when it was learned by the Jews that Hadrian contemplated a temple in his own honour not in that of the God of Israel, or perhaps it was withdrawn because of Samaritan or other opposition, and the plan of Hadrian was a later detail. In any case there was *some* expectation, and *some* failure to see it realised. This failure included seeing a pagan and impure temple on the spot, whose presence effectively prevented any restoration of the true Temple. A second subject for Jewish anger concerned the legislation of Hadrian concerning circumcision. He assimilated it to castration, and forbad it.[70] He may have been intending to make the practice of Judaism impossible; or he may have been ignorant of, and indifferent to, its effect on the Jews. But this edict seems to have been the basis on which the Jews of Palestine attempted again a suicidal resistance to Rome.

The rabbinic leaders were not at one on the question. They were divided first on the issue as to what concessions in observance should be made to Roman *force majeure*, and then on the question of resistance, if the concession was insufficient to save life. We are told that the rabbis met in an upper room of the 'house of Nithza at Lydda', and that a majority vote was given for a new regulation that 'if a man is commanded: "transgress and suffer not death", he may transgress and not suffer death, excepting if he be ordered to commit idolatry, incest (which includes adultery) and murder.'[71] In the same passage R. Dimi of Babylon, a much later rabbi, adds that this concession was made 'only if there is no royal decree; but if there is a royal decree, one must incur martyrdom rather than transgress even a minor precept.' That this reflects the opinion of some at Lydda is suggested by the fact that R. Ishmael seems to have definitely stirred up rebellion, proclaiming that 'when the people of Israel obey their judges, God gives them the victory over their enemies.'[72] Eliezer b. Hyrcanus and Joshua begged Ishmael to restrain his followers, but without success, and the deaths at this time of both Eliezer and Gamaliel II weakened the peace party. There were, in fact, three

[69] Finkelstein, *op. cit.*, pp. 313 ff. ascribes this to Trajan, but does not date it. Baron, *op. cit.*, ascribes it to Hadrian. Though the former adduces a great deal of evidence for his theory, it still remains difficult to see when Trajan could have done it. If he did it before the series of outbreaks, they are still more incomprehensible; and he died almost before peace was restored. Hadrian seems the more likely of the two.

[70] See Juster, *op. cit.*, 1. p. 265 and notes.

[71] San. 74a, p. 502.

[72] Finkelstein, *op. cit.*, p. 201, quoting *Midrash Tannaim*, 16. 18. p. 97.

distinguishable groups in the years before 132, the war party, who counselled concealment by appearing to accept any Roman prohibition (Ishmael at Lydda seems to have counselled this, but not to have convinced his colleagues), the apocalyptic party, who were willing to accept martyrdom (as reflected by the information conveyed by R. Dimi), and the peace party, who wished to obey Rome as far as was conscientiously possible. How power came into the hands of the first we do not know, but the next thing we hear is that Bar Cochba had been accepted as a national leader, and had embarked on a policy of violent resistance. That he began, as did his predecessors, with some successes, is not surprising. What is surprising is that these successes seem to have convinced the ninety year old Akiba that Bar Cochba was the messiah, and that God would give him the victory. They were followed by a strenuous resistance in a few fortified places, and it was three years before the final resistance of the rebels was overcome.

The people then had to pay the full price of their folly. All expressions of Judaism were forbidden. Many, scholars included,[73] crossed the frontiers into the Parthian empire, but many faced life in Palestine, resisting the determined attempt of the angry Hadrian to suppress all manifestations of Judaism. It is well for his reputation that it was his refusal to abandon the teaching of Torah, and not his foolish recognition of Bar Cochba as messiah, that led to the martyrdom of the aged Akiba. Many others gave their lives at the same time,[74] and were recognised permanently in Jewish hagiology for their courage. A contemporary, Nathan the Babylonian, says: ' "Of them that love Me and keep My commandments," refers to those who dwell in the land of Israel and risk their lives for the sake of the commandments. "Why are you being led out to be decapitated?" "Because I circumcised my son to be an Israelite." "Why are you being led out to be burned?" "Because I read the Torah." "Why are you being led out to be crucified?" "Because I ate the unleavened bread." "Why are you getting a hundred lashes?" "Because I performed the ceremony of the Lulab." And it says: "Those with which I was wounded in the house of my friends" (Zech. 13. 6). These wounds caused me to be beloved of My father in heaven.'[75]

[73] For ordination was prohibited. A.Z. 8b, p. 41.

[74] *Mekilta, Bahodesh*, Ed. Lauterbach, 2. p. 247.

[75] E.g. the trial and martyrdom of R. Hanina b. Teradion recounted in A.Z. 17a, b, 18a, pp. 88 ff. It ends: 'Why hast thou occupied thyself with the Torah?' He replied: 'Thus the Lord my God commanded me! At once they sentenced him to be burnt, his wife to be slain, and his daughter to be consigned to a brothel.'

8. IN PERIL OF DESPAIR

JEWISH history had been turbulent, distressing, and full of foreboding ever since the conflict with triumphant paganism had first developed in the time of Antiochus Epiphanes. The victories of the Maccabees had been fragile triumphs, which had turned too soon to disillusion and eventually despair. The 'glorious' reign of Herod the Great, filled with impressive external signs of magnificence, had not been a time of spiritual rest or refreshment. All this had produced the strange phenomenon of a series of writers proclaiming pseudonymously that they had seen visions of a divine retribution coming upon the world, and especially upon the oppressors of Israel, in the near future.

Then came catastrophe; the people were crushed after their first rebellion against Rome; but Rome grew steadily in power. Jerusalem was destroyed; but a Roman legion was camped upon its ruins. Worst of all, the Temple was no more; but the gifts to it of the whole people had been turned into a tribute paid to Jupiter Capitolinus. A generation of unrest, with bloody risings in the diaspora communities in both Parthian and Roman territories, had all ended in disastrous defeat and bloody massacre. Then had come a second struggle with Rome in the Holy Land itself, and thereafter the silence of death reigned over Judea and Jerusalem until Rome rebuilt the Holy City as a pagan centre with pagan temples. But no eschatological deliverance came. There was no sign that the might of Rome was lessened.

It is not surprising if, during and after this long martyrdom, the minds of writers turned to the older cosmic visions, and sought to reproduce them, fitted to the new situation. But there is a change. There is much less of the pretended prophesying, much less of the elaborate vision of talking animals and what not, and much more of serious, often pessimistic, analysis of the actual situation. There is also much less reference to a messiah. It is noteworthy in the unhappy incident of Akiba's acceptance of Bar Cochba that it reveals that he did not expect a messiah to be either a supernatural being, assisted with legions of angels, or a model exponent of Torah. The Christian proclamation of Jesus had undoubtedly made Jews chary of ascribing more than mortal attributes to a messiah or his messianic kingdom, and had at the same time made their religious leaders more wary of teaching the people to expect their deliverance from a messiah.

This change is most strikingly expressed in two of the most important eschatological works of the period, II Baruch and IV Ezra. Both are, in their present form, composite, so that contradictions may occur. In one stream of the material blended into II Baruch the messiah and his kingdom are part of this world of corruption. When the end comes, the messiah returns to heaven. In another stream there is no expectation of a messiah at all.[76] In the main part of IV Ezra there is neither messiah nor messianic kingdom; though one of its redactors has added to the original description of the judgement a messianic kingdom, of short duration and terminating with the death of the messiah and his companions.[77] It is thus evident that the expectation of the kind of supernatural deliverance for which men had earlier waited, and which had caused so much unrest in Herodian times, had ceased to comfort the people or strengthen their faith.

The two notes which are dominant in the literature of the period between the two destructions of Jerusalem are contradictory ones. On one side is an optimistic insistence on God's love for his chosen people, Israel, and on the other is a pessimistic note of utter bewilderment at the destiny which Israel has encountered, and the misery through which she is passing.

The first may be illustrated by two works. The author of the *Biblical Antiquities of Philo* (which has nothing to do with Philo) is described by its editor, M. R. James, as 'being neither of lofty mind nor of great literary talent'.[78] But to emphasise the divine choice of Israel he composed a haggadic midrash of the Old Testament. The part which survives tells the story from Adam to Saul. The work has somewhat the character, but none of the incisiveness, of the *Book of Jubilees*. Though it was written at the end of the first century, when the air was full either of lamentations for the lost Temple or of the subtleties of Akiba's expositions, the author shows no interest in either! But he refers again and again to the glories of Israel and the certainty of the promises made to her.[79] This was, indeed, a note which is struck on many occasions by the Tannaitic teachers, for it was one of the methods by which they attempted to cheer and encourage their contemporaries. They insisted that, whatever befell them, they were the people chosen of God.

The other 'optimistic' work is a very charming *Testament of Abraham*.[80] It recounts how, before his death, Abraham was taken

[76] *Apocrypha and Pseudepigrapha of the Old Testament*, Vol. 2. *Pseudepigrapha*, II Baruch, ed. R. H. Charles, p. 478.

[77] *Ibid.* IV Ezra, ed. G. H. Box, pp. 558 f.

[78] S.P.C.K., 1917, p. 65. For a discussion of the teaching about the election of Israel current among the rabbis of the period, see B. W. Helfgott, *The Doctrine of Election in Tannaitic Literature*, Columbia University, New York, 1954.

[79] *Ibid.*, p. 37.

[80] Ed. G. H. Box, S.P.C.K., 1927.

for a ride through the world on a fiery chariot, so that he might see the lives of all his children. He was horrified by the prevalence of sin, and, seeing some conspicuous sinners, asked that they might be struck dead. This was at once done, and Abraham repeated the prescription on subsequent occasions with gratifying success. But there came suddenly a voice from heaven: 'turn away Abraham that he may not see all the world. If he sees all that are living in sin, he will destroy every living thing. For, behold, Abraham has not sinned neither pities he sinners; but *I* made the world, and will not to destroy any creatures among them, but I delay the death of a sinner, until he repent and live.'[81] There is a still deeper note in the *Testament*, similar to that which distinguishes the best of the *Testament of the Twelve Patriarchs* from parallel passages in the Old Testament.[82] Abraham learned his lesson from the action of God. For, later, seeing that the good and bad deeds of a particular soul, when weighed by the angel, were exactly balanced, he asked whether he might not intercede, together with his conducting angel, for that soul. He was told that he might do so, and the instant effect was that the good deeds outweighed the bad, and the soul was saved.[83]

II Baruch and IV Ezra have component parts of very differing value; for both have had redactors of lesser spiritual strength who, like Elihu in the book of Job, sought to infuse a conventional and optimistic note into the pessimistic works which they were editing. Though they differ in many ways, they have in common the striking trait that they reflect the pre-exilic prophets in almost exclusively concerning themselves with the responsibility of Israel for its own destiny. They seek no *alibi* by denouncing other nations, as did the post-exilic prophets and the earlier apocalyptists. In II Baruch we find the oft repeated story of the final moments in the Temple:[84]

> Moreover ye priests, take ye the keys of the sanctuary
> And cast them up into the height of heaven
> And give them to the Lord, and say:
> 'Guard thy house thyself,
> For lo! we are found false stewards.'

The lesson is still further emphasised by the question:[85]

> Have ye not seen what has befallen Zion?
> Or do ye perchance think that the place had sinned

[81] *Op. cit.*, pp. 16 f.

[82] See above, pp. 58 ff.

[83] *Ibid.* pp. 23 f.

[84] II Baruch 10. 18, *op cit.*, p. 486. The same story is told of the First Temple. See Ta'an, 29a, p. 155.

[85] *Ibid.*, 77. 8-10, p. 520.

And that on this account it was overthrown?

* * * * * *

Know ye not that on account of you who did sin
That which sinned not was overthrown?

Though there are the typical messianic interludes in our present text, yet it is on Torah, not on the messiah, that Israel is told to rely. The lesson is repeated again and again: 'For lo! the days come when everything that existeth will become the prey of corruption, and be as though it had not been. But, as for you, if you prepare your hearts so as to sow in them the fruit of Torah, it shall protect you in that time in which the Mighty One is to shake the whole creation.[86]

That it is Torah and not a messiah who will deliver Israel is taught explicitly. When the people complain that they are left in darkness, Baruch replies:

Shepherds and lamps and fountains come from the Law:
And though ye depart, yet the Law abideth.
If therefore ye have respect to the Law
And are intent upon Wisdom,
A lamp will not be wanting
And a shepherd will not fail
And a fountain will not dry up.[87]

There are other points of interest in II Baruch, points which may reflect Jewish reaction to Pauline ideas, with which the leaders in Jerusalem must have been familiar. The most important is the denial of the Pauline doctrine of a universal fall in Adam and salvation in Christ.[88] The author of Baruch says explicitly:

Though Adam first sinned
And brought untimely death upon all,
Yet of those who were born from him
Each one of them hath prepared for his own soul torment to come
And again each one of them hath chosen for himself glories to come.

* * * * * *

Adam is therefore not the cause, save only of his own soul,
But each one of us hath been the Adam of his own soul.[89]

[86] *Ibid.*, 31. 5—32. 1. Compare 44. 3 ff. and 46. 5 pp. 498 and 503 f.

[87] *Ibid.*, 77. 15-16, p. 521.

[88] Rom. 5. 12. and I Cor. 15. 22.

[89] 2 Baruch 54. 15. Compare 56. 6, pp. 511 and 513. The deeper pessimism of IV Ezra accepts the universal responsibility of Adam: 'O thou Adam, what hast thou done? For though it was thou that sinned, the fall was not thine alone, but ours also who are thy descendants'. (7. 119, p. 591).

The author of II Baruch was an unhappy and puzzled man. But he is exceeded in sorrowful bewilderment by the much greater artist who wrote the *Vision of Salathiel*, which is the central part of IV Ezra.[90] There is no ancient Jewish work, canonical or uncanonical, of such a sad and pessimistic tone. It recalls, more than any other Jewish writing, Paul's despairing outbreak in his letter to the Romans, (ch. 7), but the author, like his great predecessor who wrote the book of Job, had no answer to the paradox that Torah is divine and man is sinful. He can only put into the mouth of the angel who reports the intentions of the Almighty to Salathiel: 'Thou comest far short of being able to love my creation more than I.'[91]

Like Paul, the author is crushed by the contrast of the holiness of the Law and his own inability to keep it.[92] But he is also utterly bewildered by the problem, to him insoluble, that Israel is being apparently heavily punished for her sins, while the nations, in whose hands her punishment has lain and who are prospering greatly, are no better than she is. In fact they are still more sinful.[93] But that is not all. Man himself seems made to master the animal kingdom, but he suffers far more than the animals.[94] To the author, the basic tragedy is that, when the Law was given, the evil inclination in man was not removed from him. In consequence he has fallen deeper and deeper into sin. In fact the author apparently accepts it as a fact that very few will be saved, and he tries to make this teaching acceptable by comparing the human situation with the rarity of precious stones and the prevalence of ordinary pebbles—truly a counsel of despair.[95]

The whole range of eschatological apocalyptic is preserved for us, either in Greek or in various oriental languages, by the eastern Churches. At what date they passed from Jewish to Christian pos-

[90] The allocation of the text is made in *op. cit.*, p. 550. There is no 'apocalyptic' in the genuine Vision, but in its present form it is set in the stock rubbish of the hack-writer eschatologist. Box considers that it must be written before 135 because it was known to, and preserved by, the Church. But this does not seem necessary. It sufficed for one individual convert to bring it over; and that may have happened after as well as before the final breach. And the despairing sadness of the book suggests the period following Bar Cochba's failure.

[91] 8. 47, p. 597.

[92] 3. 18 ff., pp. 562 f.

[93] 3. 28, and 5. 29, pp. 563 and 571. Compare the complaint of II Baruch, ch. 11 ff. The prosperity of Babylon (Rome) is contrasted with the misery of Israel. To the explanation of God (in part lost) the author pertinently asks: 'But how does that make it any better for us? The world, which was made for us, abides and we perish' (14. 19, p. 491).

[94] 7. 62-74, p. 586.

[95] 3. 36 and 7. 50-52, pp. 564 and 585.

session we have no means of knowing. The Hebrew original we can assume to be Jewish; the Greek translations may have been made for diaspora communities; but the rest are early Christian. In any case they left relatively little trace in the development of rabbinic midrash, and it was some centuries after the disaster of 135 before a messianic fervour broke out again.

A more permanent tribute to the distress of the second century is the emphasis and interpretations put upon the *Akedah*, the sacrifice of Isaac. Origen, in the third century, reported that Jews told him that 'as they had no altar, no temple, no priest, and therefore no offerings of sacrifices, they felt that their sins remained with them and that they had no means of obtaining pardon.[96] What was reported to Origen was a problem familiar to the rabbis of the first and second centuries. There were different experiences which were said to bring forgiveness of sins; but in the main it was on the efficacy of suffering that the rabbis relied.[97] For them the pre-eminent instance of suffering voluntarily undergone was the sacrifice of Isaac, and Isaac's willingness to be offered up makes him also the first martyr—the Stephen of the Synagogue. In fact many references to Isaac refer to his blood making atonement, and seem to forget that in reality he did not give up his life. The *Akedah* is referred to in the prayers of the New Year, and the reference seems to be as early as the first century,[98] and some other references also belong to the first and second century. It is natural to think that it was during this period, when they were facing together the disaster to their own hopes and the steady advance of their rival, Christianity, that the rabbis found an alternative to the death of Jesus in that of Isaac. It offered some balm to a despairing people.

9. IN PERIL OF APOSTASY

IN view of the mood which is reflected by much of the material just considered, the leaders of the dispirited people needed constantly to take precautions against apostasy. For they were surrounded by a double temptation to apostatize, on the one hand to the growing congregations of Christians, and on the other to the diverse mystery religions and philosophies of the heathen majority surrounding all the Jewish communities. The new leadership had a task of supreme

[96] *Homily on Numbers*, 10. 2., P.G. 12, c. 638.
[97] Ber. 5a, pp. 19 f.
[98] See the articles by I. Levi in R.E.J. 64, p. 161 and Marmorstein A. *ibid.*, 71. p. 190.

difficulty in finding a basis on which to make it attractive for Jews to remain Jews.

In such a situation mere abuse would have helped little, and we do not find in the discussions and pronouncements of the Tannaim either vulgar abuse of Christianity, or that contempt for idols which was possible to a Deutero-Isaiah. We have already noted that 'the letter to the synagogues' was in all probability a relatively dignified pronouncement, and did not contain the vulgar abuse which Christian writers attribute to it.[99] This is confirmed by the paucity of references to Jesus in the Jewish literature of the first century after the separation.[1] There is no reference to him or to the early Church in the Mishnah, that is before A.D. 200, nor is there any reference in the midrash of the Tannaim. Dr. Morris Goldstein accepts five references to Jesus and his disciples during this period, and says of them: 'what is likely to be recorded would be what is startling, dramatic, not customary. Thus the impression remained that here is one who performed unusual acts—regarded by some as miracles, by others as sorcery. A brilliant turning of a phrase of Scripture would be recalled by a rabbi. Confirmation of the non-abrogation of the Jewish law would be cited. It was remembered that Jesus was executed,[2] but this was interpreted in the light of Judaism. He left his disciples to carry on his work; certainly this is of importance, otherwise there would be no Christianity. Healing was performed in his name. This is always noteworthy and unforgettable.'[3] Dr. Klausner speaks in

[99] See above, p. 222.

[1] This literature is considered by a number of Christian and Jewish writers. H. Laible, *Jesus Christus im Thalmud*, Institutum Judaicum, No. 10, Berlin, 1891, is thoroughly biased. H. L. Strack, *Jesus, Die Haeretiker und Die Christen*, Institutum Judaicum, No. 37, Leipzig, 1910, is valuable for its Hebrew texts. R. Travers Herford, *Christianity in Talmud and Midrash*, Williams and Norgate, 1903, is much the fullest account of the material. On the Jewish side there is a full discussion of passages referring to Jesus in J. Klausner, *Jesus of Nazareth*, Macmillan, 1929. A very imporant work is Morris Goldstein *Jesus in the Jewish Tradition*, Macmillan, New York, 1950. Its value lies in two fields. For the first time it dates the references, distinguishing earlier and later mentions. Secondly, it shows that many of the references used by earlier writers, including those quoted above, cannot really be said to refer to Jesus or the Christian community; for Jesus was, after all, a common name among Greek-speaking Jews, and there were many other schismatics than the Judeo-Christians whom the rabbis might refer to.

[2] A Baraita in Sanh. 43a, p. 281, dealing with the trial and death of Jesus. The passage is a very puzzling one, and is discussed in all the books cited in the note above. See especially that of Herford, pp. 83 ff, and Goldstein, pp. 22 ff.

[3] Goldstein, *op. cit.*, p. 102.

very much the same tone: 'The Tannaim were at the end of the first Christian century far from regarding Jesus as more than 'a transgressor in Israel', and were still accustomed to come into close religious contact with Christians.'[4] The second Christian century, with the growing power of the Church on one side and the humiliation of the Synagogue on the other, saw a great increase in the bitterness with which Christianity was regarded. From the evidence of Origen, quoting the scandalous stories of Celsus[5], the vulgar abuse which was to issue in the *Sepher Toldoth Jeshu* began to accumulate in the second century, and grew in volume steadily thenceforward. But its beginning is not as early as is sometimes assumed by Christian writers.

The main effect on rabbinic teaching of the existence of the missionary activities of the Christian Church was to be seen in the clarity and frequency with which they repeated and emphasised the cardinal teachings of Judaism. A very obvious example is to be found in the emphasis on the unity of God, and the consequent denial of Christian beliefs in the divinity of Jesus. 'Why', they asked, 'was man created last? That the Minim[6] might not say: there was a partner with Him in the work.'[7] In the same way it was emphasised that the messiah had not yet come, and that, when he did, he would reign for only a short period, and in this world. He had no kingdom in the world to come. In view of the emphasis often put on miracles in popular Christian writing, the rabbis invented an amusing method of contradicting the idea that miracles could attest theological truth. The best known example of this method is the refusal of Joshua b. Hananiah and his colleagues to accept the argument of Eliezer b. Hyrcanus which he sought to strengthen by invoking miracles. 'On that day R. Eliezer brought forward every imaginable argument, but they did not accept them. Said he to them: "If the *halachah* agrees with me, let this carob tree prove it!" Thereupon the carob tree was torn a hundred cubits out of its place—others affirm, four hundred cubits. "No proof can be brought from a carob tree" they retorted.'[8] Eliezer tried in succession a stream running backward, a wall falling down, and finally a *Bath Kol.* But Joshua and his colleagues refused to be moved by anything except argument, and that Eliezer could not produce.

[4] Klausner, *op. cit.*, p. 37.

[5] Origen, *Contra Celsum*, 1. 32, 38 and 52. P.G., 11.

[6] *Minim* here obviously refers to the Christians. But it does not do so always, for there were other sectaries. See Goldstein, *op. cit.*, pp. 45 ff.

[7] Tosephta, Sanh. 8. 17., quoted by Goldstein, p. 84. On the whole range of these indirect references to Christian teaching, see also Herford, *op. cit.*, Table of Contents, pp. xii and xiii.

[8] B.M. 59b, pp. 352 ff.

The force of Christian arguments could be reduced, one by one, by such methods, but it was also necessary to drive continuously into the minds of the Jewish communities that they were a people chosen by God for a special service and that God did not change his mind. The constant claim of the Christians that the election had passed to them and left the original Israel derelict was something which almost every Tannaitic leader was called upon at some time to deny.[9] For the economic distress of the common people, as well as the collapse of the national autonomy, made it an argument which the ordinary Jew might well find difficult to answer, and therefore an argument which Christians were always ready to use. Thus 'Joshua b. Hananiah was once at the court of Caesar [Hadrian]. A certain unbeliever showed him by gestures: A people whose Lord had turned his face from them. He showed him in reply: His hand is stretched over us.'[10] The unbeliever in the story came to a bad end, and the compilers of the Talmud doubtless wished that it might always be so.

But, generation by generation, the challenge was continued. R. Meir, of the generation following Akiba, offered this comfort: 'Even though the Israelites are full of blemishes, they are still called "his sons" (Deut. 32. 5). Isaiah calls them "sons who act corruptly" (1. 4). If they are called "sons" when corrupt, how much more would they be his sons did they not act corruptly! Jeremiah calls them "sons wise to do evil" (4. 22). If they did good, how much more would they be his sons! Beloved are Israel, for whether they do God's will or no they are called his sons'.[11] This generous doctrine did not pass without criticism from his colleagues, for it could imply that Israel had no duty to keep the Torah. R. Judah b. Ilai, therefore, taught that 'when you behave as sons, then you are designated sons; if you do not behave as sons, you are not designated sons.'[12] Yet, whether sternly or mildly, the rabbis of the Tannaitic period left Israel in no doubt that the choice had not been repealed.

Jews being but human, it may be suspected that there must have been also some down-to-earth and commonplace reasons for remaining loyal to Judaism, reasons that did not depend on argument, however convincing. In the first place, it is, after all, natural to any human society to continue in the tradition of its forefathers. It is only in modern times that a cosmopolitan and changing life has

[9] Helfgott, *op. cit.*, contains a most careful study of this subject up to the time of Judah the Prince. Quotations are given from each of the outstanding Tannaim, showing in what manifold form the question could arise.

[10] Hag. 5b, p. 21.

[11] *The Rabbinic Anthology*, p. 103.

[12] Kid., 36a, p. 177.

become almost the norm, and then it is only for a small section of humanity. Even now, the majority of the human species lives by following, with moderate amendment, the lives and customs of its predecessors. *Vis inertiae* is a potent and universal factor. Moreover we must not contrast the strait and burdensome life of the Palestinian town and village with some alternative elysium. Everywhere in the Roman world men lived under the burden of harsh taxation, and the poor had to accept a basic insecurity in the face of wealth or military power. The lot of Jews was not so intolerably worse than that of others. But this is not enough. There *was* a positive reason for remaining within the Jewish fold for the ordinary decent man and woman. That reason was Jewish family life, with its warmth of affection, its strict morals, and its permanence. It was one of the most powerful props on which the leaders could rely, that so much of the essential Jewishness of their faith was expressed within the home. With reason it was said that the sabbath was the centre of Judaism; but the festivals also made their annual presence felt at the domestic hearth.

It is curious that Christianity has made less of the home and more of the church, but so it is; it may be that the Christian emphasis on asceticism militated against the centring of religion in family life. But these two contrasting emphases must have militated somewhat against the conversion of Jews, quite apart from theology.

The arguments in favour of Jewish living must have been much stronger when the alternative to be considered was paganism. And yet it is not from Jewish authors that we learn of the atmosphere of pagan society in the first and second centuries. It is the Greek and Latin literature of the time which reveal its hopelessness, its cruelty, its vulgarity. Judaism and its daughter Christianity were much more attractive to the pagan than was paganism normally to the Jew.

The Mishnah tractate of *Abodah Zarah* (strange worship) deals with the issues facing a Jew by his contact with idolatry. It is interesting that the rabbis of the generation of Johanan b. Zakkai are scarcely cited at all in its discussions and decisions. It is evident that apostasy to paganism was not a vital problem after the first Roman war. But it was very different for the generation involved in the last one. The discussions which fill the pages of *Abodah Zarah* are largely between R. Meir, R. Judah b. Ilai and R. Simeon b. Gamaliel II, all of whom flourished between A.D. 130 and 160. It is evident that in the despair of that generation apostasy to paganism was a real problem. It is particularly interesting that there is a consistent pattern governing the relationship between their attitude and that of earlier generations, represented in the tractate under the general appellation of 'the Sages'. The rabbis of the second century have tightened up regulations condemning the attraction of pagan worship, but they have been a little more generous in regulating commercial relations. It would appear that they feared idolatry more, but the seductive influence of a pagan merchant or neighbour less, than their predecessors. Such an attitude is found in the epigram of R. Joshua b. Levi at the end of the second century: 'Which is the commandment that is as weighty as all other commandments? Surely it is that concerning idolatry.'[13]

There is another point of interest in the contents of *Abodah Zarah*. It is a tractate in which one would expect some recognition of the position of the diaspora communities, surrounded as they were by a wide variety of 'strange worships'. But apart from a trifling reference to selling or renting houses and land in Syria, there is no reference whatever to the problems of a typical diaspora community. On the other hand, almost every section bears evidence of the fact that in the Holy Land itself Jews lived in continual contact with pagans, and that a wide variety of common activities flowed from this association. Different discussions and decisions imply that a Jew was now the employer, now the employed, of a Gentile, that he was now the tenant now the landlord of a Gentile, that he was now the borrower, now the lender of house, land, or animals to and from a Gentile. In such a situation abuse would have served no purpose; but it would also have served no purpose just to forbid such associations. They were inevitable, and the only sensible course was to accept them, and to ensure, as far as possible, that they were innocuous.

10. IN PERIL OF THE AMME-HA'ARETZ

THE Talmud and other rabbinical literature contain an enormous number of references to 'the people of the land', the *amme-ha'aretz*. Many of these references are hostile, many contemptuous and some imply an appalling bitterness between them and the scholars. It has frequently been assumed by Christian writers that these people are identical with the poor, the *anavim* of the psalmist and the prophet, and the outcasts and sinners of the New Testament.[14] In consequence

[13] Hor. 8a, p. 55; Hul. 5a, p. 19.

[14] On this identification see, for example, A. Büchler, *Die Galiläische Am-Ha'Arec des Zweiten Jahrhunderts*, Wien, 1906, and *The Political and Social Leaders of the Jewish Community of Sepphoris in the Second and Third Centuries*, Jews College Publications, No. 1., n.d., or C. G. Montefiore, *Synoptic Gospels*, Vol. 1., p. cviii. and Vol. 2, a special article by I. A. Abrahams, pp. 647 ff.

it is assumed that there was a continuing gulf between the scholars, as learned men, and the ordinary rank and file Jews of town and country, and that this gulf the scholars disdained to cross.

This is a misunderstanding of the evidence. There was indeed a class of 'sinners' who rejected all moral teaching, whether of the rabbis or of anyone else, and we may assume that Jesus and his followers were more gentle in their positive tenderness towards this class than were the rabbis. But these outcasts of society were, in any case, a small minority, and they are not referred to in the Talmud under the term am-ha'Aretz, but in the more abusive word, Bôr. In so far as an am-ha'Aretz was an ordinary Jew, he was the man at whom rabbinical teaching was directed, not the man whom the rabbis wished to avoid; and so far from the rabbis wishing to dissociate themselves from the rank and file of the community, they were themselves in many cases working men, and it was by the working men that they were particularly respected. It was by their support that rabbinic Judaism ultimately became the norm for the whole nation.

All abusive generalizations must, therefore, be balanced by other remarks which indicate a tenderness towards the ordinary man. We have already quoted a favourite statement of the Vineyard on the subject—their work and that of the scholar were of equal merit, provided the heart of each was directed to heaven.[15] In a second century discussion, R. Johanan said in the name of R. Simeon b. Yohai: 'Even though a man reads but the Shema morning and evening, he has fulfilled the precept: "This book of the Law shall not depart out of thy mouth". It is forbidden, however, to say this in the presence of an am-ha'Aretz. But Raba said, "It is a meritorious thing to say it in the presence of an am-ha'Aretz".[16] Of the same tenor, and reflecting the actuality of the problem, are stories of different rabbis who were caught out in their attempt to demand a superior status for themselves.[17] Of these one of the most telling relates how a scholar mistook a very well-conducted stranger for a scholar like himself, and invited him home. There he found him to be completely ignorant even of the correct grace to say before meals. When the scholar attempted to turn out his unwelcome guest, the latter seized him and accused him of robbing him of his inheritance. How so, said the

[15] Above, p. 248. The saying is from Ber. 17a, p. 101.

[16] Men. 99b, p. 609. The contradiction is not based on disagreement about the principle. Simeon said: 'Don't tell him this is the minimum, for he will take it as a maximum.' Raba replied: 'He will be led on from this minimum to fuller obedience to Torah, so tell him to start here.'

[17] E.g. B.B. 8a, p. 33, where the Patriarch Judah is caught out in trying to feed scholars only during a famine, or Ta'an. 20ab, p. 100.

scholar. The guest replied that he had heard the school children repeating the verse 'Moses commanded us a law as a possession for the assembly.'[18] It was no private inheritance of the scholar's and he had withheld it from him improperly.[19] From such stories we can legitimately deduce that scholars *did* make supercilious remarks about ordinary Jews, and that they were sorry for these remarks afterwards, since they told these stories against themselves in their own literature.

In the main, the distinction between their own order, the *Haberim*, and the common folk was quite factual, and indicated clearly what it was, in terms of orthopraxy, that they wished the common folk to accept. The distinction was not one which implied that the amme-ha'Aretz were outside the fold of Judaism. This is shown in discussion of fundamentals, in which the amme-ha'Aretz could be trusted, and need not be suspected of infringements.[20] It may be compared to Peter's asseveration in Joppa that he had never eaten anything unclean in his life, though, from the rabbinic standpoint, he was certainly an am-ha'Aretz.[21] There are various places where the particular observances are specified which distinguish them. They are those who do not eat non-sacred food in a state of ritual cleanness; who do not tithe their produce properly; who do not recite the Shema morning and evening; who do not put on *tefillin*; who have no fringes to their garments; who have no *mezuzah* on their doors; who do not bring up their sons to study Torah.[22] There is in these statements the usual rabbinic mixture of matters which the ordinary Christian would consider fundamental with what he would consider secondary; but Judaism makes this distinction much more rarely. The important thing is that all the matters specified lie in the realm in which an ordinary religious teacher would expect to instruct his ordinary pupils, young or adult. They imply no hostility on the one side or especial turpitude on the other.[23]

Finally, there was no permanent barrier between the scholar and this kind of am-ha'Aretz. A scholar could, by failing in his observances, fall back into the common pool of ordinary men whence he had

[18] Deut. 33. 4.

[19] Midrash Rabbah. Lev. 9. 3. Ed. Son., p. 109.

[20] E.g. Hag. 24b, p. 155.

[21] Acts. 10. 14.

[22] Ber. 47b, pp. 286 ff. and Sot. 22a, p. 110. These are only given as examples. Questions of tithing and of ritual cleanness are constantly discussed elsewhere. See, for example, the Tractate *Demai* on tithing.

[23] An excellent account of these amme-ha'Aretz is to be found in the article by I. A. Abrahams, quoted above. Abrahams points out that G. F. Moore in his treatment (e.g. in *The Beginnings of Christianity*, 1. App. E., p. 439. Cf. his *Judaism*, II, pp. 159 ff.) does not make sufficient allowance for differences of date of different pronouncements.

risen; and an ordinary man could be accepted into the ranks of the scholars, and become a *haber*, if he was punctilious in his behaviour and had educated himself by attendance at the academies. The rabbis, not unnaturally, differed as to whether the path should be made easy or difficult for him, but all agreed that the path was there.[24] Yet this clearly does not exhaust the meaning of amme-ha'Aretz in rabbinic literature. It does not explain why, no doubt in a mood of exasperated exaggeration, a sober rabbi could say that it was a meritorious act to kill an am-ha'Aretz on the Day of Atonement when it fell on a sabbath![25] It was certainly not by such an attitude towards ordinary Jews that the rabbis ultimately won their places as the unquestioned leaders of the nation.

That such was their aim is, in fact, the clue to the identification of the amme-ha'Aretz and the reason why they are liable to be treated with such venom in rabbinic literature. They were the rivals to the rabbis for the leadership of the people. From some descriptions in both Jewish and Christian writers, one might assume that the rabbis, almost spontaneously and with universal acceptance, assumed the leadership of the dispirited and ruined nation, and led them straight into the paths—viewed with approval or disapproval by these writers—of rabbinic precision and orthopraxy. The truth is very different. There was no universal obedience given to the rabbis or their discipline, and there was no immediate acceptance of the court at Jabne and its successors as being the natural inheritors of the powers of the pre-70 sanhedrin. There was a long and bitter struggle, and one waged under excessively difficult conditions, before it would be possible to speak of rabbinic Judaism as the norm of Jewish ethical and religious behaviour.

Dr. Adolf Büchler, in works already quoted, was one of the first to draw attention to the fact that the amme-ha'Aretz were rivals of the rabbis, not rebellious members of their flocks. In particular it is possible to specify three groups of Jews, who might well overlap in individual cases, who rejected rabbinic demands upon them. They are to be more easily identified in second century Galilee than in first century Judea, where the situation following the two wars must have been wholly abnormal. The three groups are composed of *priests*, who were still enjoying the offerings due to them, though they now gave nothing in return, of *landowners* who had no intention of paying the tithes the rabbis demanded or of supporting the whole class of poor scholars, and of *judges*, who were appointed by the

[24] Bek. 30b, pp. 191 ff.

[25] Pes. 49b, p. 236. The passages contain many other abusive references to the class, their wives and daughters as well as themselves.

Romans, or by non-rabbinic Jewish leaders of the community, who did not judge according to the rabbinic interpretation of the Law.[26]

We must realise that the whole battle was fought out by leaders who were no longer free, or represented a free people. The Roman hand lay heavy on the land. It was Rome who had the last word in administration, in the dispensation of justice and in taxation. The issue was fought out in Galilee, after the arrival of the rabbinic academies from Judea in the first half of the second century.[27] It may well be that, as Galilee had been less directly involved in the wars than Judea, the rich and leading men of Galilee had reached a relatively comfortable *modus vivendi* with the occupying forces and the Roman authorities, which they feared that the rabbis would upset. No doubt the *modus vivendi* was fairly costly, and Roman taxes were rarely light. One can well imagine the resistance which would be offered to the rabbinical demand for still more payment of tithes, and for greater, and therefore more difficult, discrimination in matters of ritual cleanness. But there was another side to it; in many ways the rabbis were demanding more generous and kindly treatment of the poor, and were the representatives of a people downtrodden and oppressed, not by the Romans, but by their own priests, landowners and judges.[28]

The question of the amme-ha'Aretz judges is particularly interesting, for we have already seen in many places that the function of judge had been inherent in that of rabbi. In purely religious issues their decisions may well have been acceptable, but Judaism in those days was not a religion where it was easy to define the jurisdiction of a purely ecclesiastical court, and there is no doubt that the rabbis, on their coming from Judea at the end of the Hadrianic war, found Roman law, custom, and Sadducaic law being administered by Jewish judges.[29] Their opinion of the consequences is expressed in the remark: 'Your hands are defiled with blood' refers to judges—'your fingers with iniquity' to judges' clerks—'your lips have spoken lies'

[26] For these last, see especially H-P. Chajes, *Les Juges en Palestine de l'An* 70 *a l'An* 500, in R.E.J., 39, pp. 39 ff.

[27] They had some difficulty in establishing themselves. R.H. 31ab, p. 149, says that they went from Jabne to Usha, then back to Jabne, back again to Usha, and thence to Shefar Am and Beth Shearim before they settled in Sepphoris where they stayed for fifty years. Their pleading for support at Usha is related at length in Midrash R. Song of Songs II, 5. 3 ff. Ed. Son., pp. 106 ff.

[28] Büchler, *Jews of Sepphoris*, pp. 6, 37 and *passim*.

[29] Büchler, *op. cit.*, p. 21 deals with the appointment of judges by the Romans. On p. 32 is a reference to Sadducaic law (based on T. J., Sanh. I, 1. 18a, 37 and T.B., B.M. 30b, p. 189). See also Chajes, *op. cit.*

to lawyers—'your tongue muttereth wickedness to the litigants'.[30] It would appear that a change came only gradually when from time to time individual rabbis were appointed judges, either by the Roman or by the Jewish authorities. It was from their individual merits, not from the cession of authority to their courts corporately, that the inhabitants of Galilee slowly came to acknowledge the superiority of the rabbinic sense of justice.

Such a situation, protracted over several generations, would explain the bitterness of rabbinic language. But even so, Dr. Büchler takes it too literally in his masterly surveys. It cannot be used as evidence of insuperable hostility and division within Jewry. *Odium theologicum* never trips off the tongue in chaste and measured phraseology. We should be wrong in thinking that some community of professional prostitutes was referred to by a seventeenth or eighteenth century Anglican divine who grew warm about the followers of the Scarlet Woman, and we can equally assume that the non-rabbinic priests, landowners and judges of Galilee were not constantly guilty of the revolting and inhuman bestialities which the rabbis in their exasperation attributed to them.

11. THE UPHILL ROAD TO VICTORY

We cannot tell exactly how or when the claim of the rabbis to be the true leaders of the chosen people could be considered to be accepted by the majority of their fellow-countrymen. If this is true for Palestine itself, where we can consult the immense mass of rabbinic literature, it is still truer for the communities of the western Diaspora, about whose religious life we are extraordinarily ill-informed. In Babylon it may well be that the problem was easier; for Babylonian Jewry had never been an independent state, and its leadership had always been a social and religious one.

In their battle with custom, with indifference and with the positive alternatives offered by priests and landowners, the rabbis had four points in their favour. In the first place they were themselves representatives of all classes in the community, and their society was itself classless. Some of them were patricians, and they had the great and growing advantage that the patriarchal house, which won increasing recognition from Rome from the middle of the second century, was itself of rabbinic origin. At times this was counterbalanced by an ignorant or indifferent patriarch, for the honour was hereditary; but nevertheless it was a great asset. If some of the rabbis were patricians,

[30] Shab. 139a, p. 701.

some were from the poorest urban or agricultural classes; and in their classless society this was no disadvantage. They went as far as to say, with their habitual capacity for exaggeration, that 'if a bastard were a scholar, and the high priest an ignoramus, the learned bastard takes precedence over the ignorant high priest.'[31]

Their second advantage may well have lain in the contrast between the tenderness and scruple of a rabbinic judge, and the harshness of other courts. There are scattered references to rabbis winning respect as judges, but there is not enough to build up a positive case. The negative case that justice was ill administered in other courts, is unquestionable and has been given in the previous section.

The third and fourth advantages may be considered together. It was the rabbis and their disciples who occupied themselves with the local synagogues and schools. In fact the two were often held in the same building, and under the same direction. We have little information as to the attendance of the amme-ha'Aretz at the daily or weekly services. It was, no doubt, less than the rabbis desired, but that does not mean that it was without importance, or that their synagogal leadership was without significance. The best evidence lies in the enormous body of midrash which has survived, and which indicates that there must have been ample opportunity for using that particular medley of parable, homily, story and exhortation which makes up the midrashic literature.[32] It was essentially popular, not scholarly. In this period we can assume that schools existed in most Jewish communities but attendance doubtless varied. It was one of the signs of an am-ha 'Aretz that he did not send his sons to school, implying that he could have done so. Schools must, therefore, have been available throughout the community; and, in fact, in this period we have the beginnings of discussions of conditions and curricula.

The rabbis needed all these advantages in their struggle for control. What they had to offer could appear cold comfort to a highly emotional, passionate and courageous people smarting with anger under the bitterness of repeated defeat and renewed oppression, and facing in grinding poverty the destruction of their homes and the ruin of their cities. They were offering a way of life which was either accepted as bringing those who observed it into the presence of God, or was meaningless, meticulous pedantry. No wonder that they laid such enormous stress on the immense responsibilities of the scholar. For if he could not make the rabbinic way of life attractive by his

[31] Hor. 13a, p. 99.

[32] Midrash Rabba has been published *in toto* by the Soncino Press. A wide variety of midrashic material is to be found in Louis Ginzberg, *The Legends of the Jews.*

example, he could do nothing by his precept. No priest was ever more continuously warned and groomed for the priestly office than was the scholar for his task. In addition, the scholar, unlike the priest, was told that scholarship would never be enough. He had to work side by side with the congregation, if he was to influence them by his scholarship.

There is in the tractate Aboth a description of the perfect scholar, and it sets an ideal high enough to be a challenge to the leadership of any religion:

> The possessor of Torah is one who recognises his place, who rejoices in his portion, who makes a fence to his words, who claims no credit for himself, is loved, loves the All Present, loves his fellow creatures, loves righteous ways, welcomes reproofs of himself, loves uprightness, keeps himself far from honours, lets not his heart become swelled on account of his learning, delights not in giving legal decisions, shares in the bearing of a burden with his colleagues,[33] uses his weight with him on the scale of merit, places him upon a groundwork of truth, places him upon a groundwork of peace, composes himself at his study, asks and answers, listens to others, and himself adds to his knowledge, learns in order to teach, learns in order to practise, makes his teacher wiser, notes with precision that which he has heard, and says a thing in the name of him who said it.[34]

Admonition and warning about the close relationship between the study and practice of religion, and between study and work in the life of the scholar, are to be found all through rabbinic literature. It may be that sometimes the constant repetition of a theme in the literature of any religion implies that the subject in question was constantly neglected by its faithful, so that they needed constant reminders; but it may also mean that the subject was constantly and universally held to be of the highest importance. The latter is certainly the case here. The very centre of the rabbinic outlook was the complete integration of understanding and practising the will of God for human life, and the complete integration of the scholar into the community which he was to lead, both by the classlessness of the rabbinic society and by the injunction that a man must earn his living, and not expect his scholarship to support him.[35]

[33] This and the three following clauses deal with conduct in court. He inclines his fellow-judges to leniency, and is careful to see that all the facts are placed before them.

[34] Ab. 6. 6, pp. 85 f.

[35] Rather than illustrate this paragraph by individual quotations, I refer the reader to the *Rabbinic Anthology*, Ch. VI, 'Study, Practice and Goodness' where these points are admirably illustrated and commented.

Finally the rabbis kept constantly in the forefront of their teaching the claim that it was because Israel was a people specially chosen of God, and with a special responsibility towards him, that they had a duty of obedience to his revealed will. In return, they offered a singularly intimate and attractive picture of the concern of God for Israel, a picture which lacked all the philosophical metaphysic of the Christian theology which was emerging simultaneously, but which was, as we shall see in subsequent pages, extremely well adapted to their purpose. And their purpose was to give spiritual depth and significance to the whole life of their people, and to make that life a thing so characteristic and distinctive that it provided a basis for survival which could prove independent of any other support. It had to take the place not merely of Temple, throne, and geographical contiguity, but of the sport, culture and intellectual diversions of the peoples who surrounded the Jewish communities.

Chapter Six

THE RELIGION OF SURVIVAL

1. THE NATURE OF RABBINIC LITERATURE

THOSE who have sought to give the Christian reader a sympathetic and positive interpretation of rabbinic Judaism, whether they be orthodox Jews or Christian theologians such as R. Travers Herford or George Foot Moore, have been at pains to work out a systematic exposition of its theological and moral concepts. They have shown that the rabbis had in no wise lost the spiritual values of the religion of Israel as revealed in the written Torah, but had maintained, refined, and developed them. In particular there are four fields in which their ideas mark considerable progress over those expressed in earlier centuries. They are more conscious of the importance of individuals. Even though their central effort throughout had to be the preservation of the nation, the problems of Jeremiah and Ezekiel and, above all, of the author of the Book of Job, had not been forgotten. There is also a much more developed doctrine of repentance, and a consciousness that all men are sinners. Coupled with this, there is an insistence on the importance of prayer in the spiritual life of the individual. Finally much is revealed in the change in the meaning of the word *Zedakah*. In the Scriptures it means 'justice', but in rabbinical literature it means 'love'.[1] Those who have drawn attention to this continuation and deepening of spiritual vitality have been able to do this with sincerity and without tendentious evasions. For the material is there, though in its natural state it is widely dispersed and in no way consistently arranged.

But those, on the other hand, who have attacked rabbinic Judaism, whether they be atheistic or liberal Jews, or antisemites or, indeed, the average Christian theologian, have had no difficulty in by-passing any serious examination of the theology and morals which can be distilled from rabbinic texts, by exposing the exceedingly curious character of the texts themselves, from which they quote without difficulty sentiments and opinions which are trivial, ridiculous, barbarous, irrelevant to any uplifting or religious purpose whatever,

[1] On these four points see Max Kadushin, *Organic Thinking*, Jewish Theological Seminary, New York, 1938, pp. 219 ff.

and even indelicate. They also are able to do this without misquoting or distorting the text, for in the vast and incoherent mass of rabbinic literature all this is to be found.[2]

So far as I know, none of the scholars of the former group have ever attempted to meet those of the latter point of view on their own ground, admitting the existence of material of this kind, as well as a great deal which is repetitive, tedious and mediocre, and explaining how this situation came into being. For there is no self-evident transition from the majestic words of Scripture to the conversational gambits of the rabbis,[3] and it is at first difficult to see how a people, passionate (as they have shown in their politics), poetic (as they have shown in their worship) and with a high standard of morality (as Gentiles have shown by the respect with which they were regarded by the Romans), came to compose, accept and delight in such a literature, and be content with nothing else for more than half a millenium. There are more than seven hundred years between the writing of IV Ezra (c. A.D. 150) and the philosophic and religious works of Saadiah (892-942). During that long period we know of no independent historical, poetical, religious, prophetic, or other

[2] An example of frivolous irrelevancy, chosen at random, may be quoted from Gitt. 31b, p. 129 f. 'R. Huna and R. Hisda were once sitting together when Geniba passed by them. Said one of them: Let us rise before him, for he is a learned man. Said the other: Shall we rise before a quarrelsome man? When he came up to them he asked them what they were discussing. They replied: We were talking about the winds. He said to them: Thus said R. Hanan b. Raba in the name of Rab: Four winds blow every day and the north wind blows with all of them, for were it not so the world would not be able to exist for a moment. The south wind is the most violent of all, and were it not that the Son of the Hawk [this is the name of an angel] keeps it back, it would devastate the whole world; for so it says, Doth the hawk soar by thy wisdom, and stretch her wings towards the south? (Job 39: 26).'

Raba and R. Nahman b. Isaac were once sitting together, when R. Nahman b. Jacob passed by in a gilt carriage and wearing a purple cloak. Raba went to meet him, but R. Nahman b. Isaac did not stir, for he said: 'Perhaps it is one of the court of the Exilarch, and Raba needs them, but I do not. When he saw R. Nahman b. Jacob approaching, he bared his arm and said: 'The south wind is blowing'. Raba said: Thus said Rab: A woman bears prematurely when this wind blows. Samuel said: Even pearls in the sea rot away . . .' and further illustrations come under the category of indelicate!

[3] How disastrous an honest explanation can be may be seen in the otherwise admirable book of Dr. E. R. Trattner, *Understanding the Talmud*, Nelson, New York, 1955, in which it is explained that the Mishnah is the new testament of Judaism. (pp. 20. f). In fact there is no equivalent to the New Testament in Judaism, and no equivalent to the Mishnah in Christianity. If there were, the subsequent history of the two religions would have been different.

work from an individual Jewish hand, except a few synagogal poems, written in Palestine after the Arab conquest. All that we have are halakic and haggadic compositions, and innumerable tales making up the rich folk-lore of the midrash. Such a literature is an extraordinary, indeed a unique, incident in the long history of a people with a high cultural level and an established literary tradition.

If there be one strange problem in the disappearance of individual contributions to the literature of the people, yet another is to be found in the curiously unequal value of what they did create and preserve. There are many gems to be found in rabbinic writings—a collection such as the *Rabbinic Anthology* already quoted will reveal them—and a religion which is orthopractical needs as many discussions of its orthopraxy as does a religion which is orthodox demand copious theological treatises. But even after allowance has been made for full discussion of orthopraxy there remains in the vast confusion of Talmud and Midrash much that is so utterly trivial that the mind gropes with difficulty for a reason why it was considered worth preserving. It makes little difference whether we accept the traditional belief that only the Scriptures themselves were written down, while all the oral law and the discussion therefrom were preserved in the memory, or adopt the view of many modern scholars that the material of Mishnah, Gemara and Midrash must have been committed to writing much earlier than we know. For it is equally difficult to imagine why the memory was burdened with such matters as to explain why costly writing material was expended upon it.

There are, of course, innumerable cases in which the sublime rises unexpectedly from the ridiculous. No Christian theologian would have deduced that a man must give his life 'for the Sanctification of the Name' from the behaviour of the frogs which afflicted the Egyptians during the ten plagues. But a certain 'Thaddeus, the man of Rome' did so, and earned immortality thereby.[4] In the same way a seemingly irrelevant narrative or some chance remark may hide a much more vital principle than would appear on the surface. The famous egg laid on the Sabbath is a case in point.[5] The question was whether, if preparations for its use existed, it might be used. Yes, said the school of Shammai; for the existence is a *fact*. No, said that of Hillel, for when the preparations were made, there could have been no *intention* to use an egg which did not yet exist, and

[4] The steps in the surprising argument are told in Pes. 53b., p. 261.

[5] See the discussion on this and similar issues in L. Ginzberg, *On Jewish Law and Lore*, pp. 118 ff. T. R. Glover once made the egg a symbol of Paul's Judaism, and found thereby that it was a poor alternative to Christianity.

what distinguishes men from beasts is that they should act on properly motivated intention. Where the intention does not exist, the mere fact itself is without significance. I am indebted for this explanation to the work by Professor Ginzberg quoted in the note. The explanation accepted, one can readily admit that the issue of intention is an important one and worthy to be discussed; but it still remains a mystery that the vehicle for the discussion should be so obscurely hidden in an egg!

It became the delight of later ages, when Jews were confined to ghettoes and lacked all contact with the outside world, for rabbinic students to elaborate fanciful arguments by which the most disparate facts were brought into an apparently logical sequence. Such activity was called *pilpul*; and there is no doubt that the pages of the Talmud and other writings provide ample opportunity for the diversion. But the fact that these passages were so used centuries later scarcely explains why they were originally collected and preserved.

To some extent it may always be a mystery why so much of rabbinic literature possesses this triviality, even when every allowance has been made for the ignorance and misunderstanding of the modern reader who, whether Jew or Gentile, is not brought up within the rabbinic tradition or even the common *Weltanschauung* of those days. We must recognise that their minds and outlook were very different from our own. To take an evident example from a different source: when Paul spoke of 'principalities', 'powers', 'the world rulers of this present darkness' and 'the spiritual hosts of wickedness in the heavenly places'[6] he provides the modern reader with fine phrases to roll off his tongue; but to himself and his readers, the reference was to something well known, concrete and real, with which their daily life and ultimate salvation were alike concerned.

We can, however, go a stage further. The Talmud and other rabbinic writings are not 'the religious literature' of the Jews of the period; they are *the whole literature*, and it was the definite intention of the rabbis that this should be so. One might reverse the preceding paragraphs and argue that it was no more surprising that such trivia should be found in religious books than that such profound spiritual insight should be shown in such commonplace and routine discussions of matters of minor importance. In the same way it may be argued that the Midrash is just Jewish folk-lore, and not of great literary quality; but, if so, it is folk-lore with an amazingly consistent and spiritual outlook.

[6] Eph. 6. 12.

It was intended that the Jewish community, wherever it might be, should be hedged in from every pagan and competing influence. The rabbis of Palestine and Babylon were not even prepared to accept the writings of Philo, because they were in Greek; and other communities, though Greek must have been their language of every-day use, followed suit, so that the memory of the Alexandrian sage perished among his own people. And yet they contained nothing that the rabbis would have categorically rejected. Their philosophic language was different from his, but their ethics and monotheism were identical. But his writings, with their references to Greek philosophies, were a doorway to the world outside, and so the rabbis shut them out.

Rabbinic literature has been compared by Christian writers with the output of the Church fathers, to the disadvantage of the former. But the comparison is not a fair one. We should compare the contents, written or retained in memory, of a Jewish academy with the contents of a monastic or episcopal library; and we should then find that the latter were not confined to the writings of the Church fathers. Lurking, perhaps, in the corner were the philosophers, dramatists, historians and humourists of the Greek and Latin world, so that we must compare a Talmudic student sniggering over the indelicacies of Akiba or some other rabbi with a monk giggling at the coarseness of Aristophanes or the vulgarity of Plautus. For it is only by the Christian Church that these authors have been preserved for us. By such comparisons rabbinic literature compares favourably with the reading matter available to those of other faiths at the same period. What is unique about it is the disordered combination of all human interests and recreations within its pages. Nothing could more dramatically illustrate the thesis that Judaism has no water-tight compartments, and knows no distinctions between what is sacred and what is secular.

The result is undeniably disconcerting to the reader who has taken his definition of a 'religious' book from other sources; and almost any comparison which may be made therefrom will almost certainly be much to the disadvantage of the rabbis. But those who make such comparisons will probably be attempting to compare things which are really not susceptible to comparison. The position of the Jewish rabbis was not parallel to that of either the Christian theologians or the Greek philosophers, and they were not seeking to produce a religious literature which would compare favourably with theirs. For what was the dominant problem with the former was not even an issue which the others had to take into account. It was a whole people down to its most stupid and recalcitrant members that the rabbis were concerned with, and neither theologian nor philosopher thought in terms of more than a selected community from within nations; and it was a whole every-day life that they were concerned with, not with that portion of life which might be subsumed under the heading of 'religion'.

In consequence, the measure of their success cannot be gauged by the collection of their noblest sentiments in an Anthology, important though it is to make such collection. The evidence for the success of their method lies, not in a comparison between its noblest sentiments and other sentiments, but in the fact that, while they were the leaders and moulders of national life, the Jewish people *did* survive. This does not mean that their method was ideal. Because we have to rely on their compositions for what we know of the history and sociology of the Jews, we may well wish that they had had more sense of history, had been more accurate in many of their statements, more comprehensive in others and so on. But these are side-issues. They set out to secure survival and they succeeded. Later chapters of Jewish history show that they had dulled neither the intellectual nor the spiritual wits of their people in the process. In Saadiah, in Maimonides, and in the whole galaxy of the writers in the western caliphate, Jewry showed that after more than half a millenium of rabbinic leadership Jews could still take full and immediate advantage of any doors into the intellectual and spiritual life of the gentile world which were opened to them.

2. LIVING BY THE MIZWOTH:

a. THE ORDERING OF HALAKAH

A *mizwah* is a divine call to action in relation to a particular and concrete situation. But the word is frequently used for 'the good deed' which results from the divine call, and it is in that sense that it is used in this chapter. The rabbis firmly believed that the main purpose of God in giving the Torah to Israel, whether in the written Scriptures or the oral law, was to give to men a complete set of halakoth, that is, if we may so call it, a blue print of a human society so acting in the whole of its life as to do honour to its Creator and to enjoy to the fullest possible extent the good gifts, material, spiritual and intellectual which he had given them. The halakoth were definite commandments by which the rabbis believed that the community might be constantly guided to that end. There would never be a time in this world when halakoth were not needed, and when their constant re-examination in the light of existing situations would become unnecessary. For, as the author of IV Ezra remarked sadly, God in giving Torah had not destroyed the evil impulse in man.

To obey joyfully one of these commandments was to perform a *mizwah*. Judaism is the religion of teaching and performing these duties. We can see the beginning of this development in the teachers of Torah from the days of Ezra onwards; but it was when there was no other sign by which a Jew could be identified, or identify himself, that the rabbis came to lay such exclusive emphasis on Torah as the conveyance of halakoth which men answered by performing mizwoth.

Judaism is not a religion of salvation, and much misunderstanding comes from the Christian assumption that it must necessarily be such. In fact the future life was one of the subjects on which the rabbis were prepared to be light-hearted. A Palestinian rabbi of the third century gave it as his opinion that the day when rain fell was more important than the day of the resurrection of the dead, since the latter benefited only the righteous whereas the former benefited sinners as well.[7] In the same spirit their allotment or denial of a place in the world to come might be determined, not by a fixed eschatological theology, but by a competition to find the most appropriate text allotting either salvation or its denial.[8] Reference has already been made[9] to the method by which the rabbis countered Christian doctrines, and it may well be that in such apparent frivolity they were making fun of the Christian preoccupation with the next world.

Because Judaism is not a religion of salvation, it is important not to describe their concern with action rather than belief as a doctrine of 'justification by works' in opposition to the Christian doctrine of 'justification by faith'. The fact is that they did not believe in justification itself as a theological doctrine. They emphasised, according to the subject of their discussion, man's complete responsibility for his actions, and his right to reward or punishment according to his merits, or else they reminded him of his complete dependence on

[7] Ta'an, 7a, p. 24. One can never tell where the dialectic of argument will lead the rabbis. The rest of the discussion is worth reading, so long as it is not taken seriously. The rabbis did not really think a day's rain more important than the giving of Torah.

[8] Mishnah, Sanh. Ch. 11 in Ed. Son. (but Ch. 10 in Ed. Danby) is full of such discussions, and the prize goes to the best quotation, not to the merits of the deceased. See, for example, Ed. Son. pp. 738 and 759.

[9] See above, p. 267.

God's grace.[10] But they had not worked out anything as subtle as the Pauline doctrine of justification, and would probably have had difficulty in understanding it. They certainly would not have accepted it, substituting 'works' for 'faith' in the Pauline interpretation of either. In spite of much that is said about Judaism, they were probably less concerned with rewards than were Christians, because they were less concerned with the future life.

The doctrine of justification depends on the acceptance of the idea that a man is ultimately judged by merits other than his own. For the Christian, these merits are naturally those given him by Jesus Christ. Christians have tried to see the same doctrine, palely reflected in Judaism, in the Akedah, the sacrifice of Isaac to which reference has already been made,[11] and in 'the merits of the fathers', or 'the patriarchs'. It is indeed probable that the rabbis occasionally took refuge in extolling the merits of the patriarchs in countering Christian propaganda, but that is very different from making a Jewish dogma out of these references.[12] Their real feeling is probably better expressed in the categoric opinion, 'a man must not trust in the work of his ancestors. . . . No man will eat in the time to come of his fathers' works, but only of his own.'[13]

We do right to disclaim the idea that any doctrine of 'justification by works' was in their minds. But we must not go to the other extreme, as do too many Christian writers, and assume that there was nothing in their minds except a legalistic and narrow delight in making ordinary life as full of meaningless rules as possible—to the great detriment, of course, of all religious and spiritual values. We have spoken already of the exalted nature of their conception of

[10] A striking example of the extremes of contradiction possible is to be found by comparing the two following passages: R. Judah ha-Nasi said: 'Be thou careful with a light precept as with a grave one, for thou knowest not the grant of reward for the fulfilment of precepts. . . . Apply thy mind to three things, and thou wilt not come into the power of sin: know what there is above thee: an eye that sees, an ear that hears, and all thy deeds written in a book. (Ab. 2. 1, p. 11 f.). R. Judah said in the name of Rab, in the passage about Akiba quoted above (p. 252, note 52). 'Moses said, Lord of the Universe, thou hast shown me his Torah, show me his reward. 'Turn thee round', said He; and Moses turned and saw them weighing out his flesh in the market stalls. 'Lord of the Universe', cried Moses, 'such Torah and such a reward!' He replied, 'Be silent, for such is My decree.' Men. 29b, p. 190.

[11] See above, p. 265.

[12] There is a discussion of the Jewish Doctrine of Merit in *The Rabbinic Anthology*, pp. xxxvi (by Montefiore) and c, ci and 689 (by Loewe). See also A. Marmorstein, *The Doctrine of Merits in Old Rabbinic Literature*, Jews College, 1920, especially pp. 31 ff.

[13] A midrash on Ps. 146. 3. quoted in *The Rabbinic Anthology*, p. 221.

Torah, and we must not forget that by the third Christian century, when we can first speak of their being in control of the people, they had behind them the gradually growing experience of seven or eight hundred years of the teaching of Torah, and the gradually growing conviction that in its observance lay the most effective way to knit together, and to preserve the identity of, a people which was ever growing more and more dispersed.

It is a mistake to seek in any way to water down the basic rabbinic teaching that God gave the Torah with all its many commandments that man might take full responsibility for every action of his life, and that he might so live as to fulfil the will of God and please him. The rabbis would never have tolerated the suggestion that God did not mean man to understand his will, and it is in this sphere of *understanding* that we find the emphasis on study, the statement that to reject the interpretation of Torah is worse than to reject Torah itself, and the insistence that study and action cannot and must not be separated.[14]

The basis of the distillation from the written Torah of the precise commandments that God wished to be obeyed is contained in the Mishnah. As G. F. Moore has said, the Mishnah is not itself primarily a legal code 'but an instrument for the study of the law, an apparatus of instruction'.[15] It was meant to open, not to close, the door to further interpretations, and it is in this context that the occasional remarks are made, contradictory on the surface, on the relative importance of the written and the oral Torah.

The Mishnah states categorically: 'There is greater stringency in respect to the teachings of the scribes than in respect to the Torah',[16] but the quotation occurs in a passage dealing with the responsibility of the scribe or rabbi, and the severity with which false teaching must be repressed. The reason why a greater stringency is needed in his case is that the false words of a rabbi cannot be easily detected by an ordinary man, whereas he can check a misquotation of the written Scriptures. Another reference to the same subject (also somewhat illusive since it comes at a point where R. Judah wishes to cause a diversion in an argument on cheese!) was brought by the indefatigable R. Dimi[17] from Palestine in the fourth century. He reported that 'the congregation of Israel declared to the Holy One,

[14] On the study of Torah and resulting action see M. Kadushin, *Organic Thinking*, pp. 59, 71 ff. and 78.

[15] *Judaism*, Vol. I., p. 96.

[16] Sanh. 88b, p. 587.

[17] R. Dimi apparently acted as an interpreter between the academies of Babylon and Palestine. His contributions to the Talmud are nearly always based on knowledge of what was being discussed in the other country.

blessed be He: Master of the Universe, the words of thy beloved ones are more pleasant to me than the wine of the Torah.'[18] These two quotations justify us in believing that the rabbis saw that, just as it was impossible in Christian theology to have grades of God-head, so in the matter of Torah it was impossible to refuse the same recognition of a divine imperative to all the halakoth alike, whether they stemmed directly from the written Torah or from a rabbinic interpretation. They held that the sincere and devoted student of Torah, living a kindly and upright life, was inspired by the spirit of God, and that his words had the authority of that inspiration.[19] On the other hand the written Torah was complete, whereas they not merely did not claim finality for the oral Torah, but recognised that this made a difference 'since what is written in Torah cannot be annulled, but that which is a Rabbinical ordinance can be annulled'.[20] But even so, they were not prepared to say so too categorically, since their whole work would be ruined if the Jewish communities did not accept willingly their decisions, but wanted to know on every occasion on what precise authority they were made.

It was possible for succeeding generations of rabbis to maintain their hold upon the people only by the most realistic approach to their task. If they had once allowed the community to be burdened with a number of regulations which were outmoded and which they were unable to support, then the whole fabric of their system would have broken down. We have seen already that in the days of Johanan b. Zakkai his colleague Joshua forbad the people to mourn over-much, on the ground that excessive mourning would be insupportable. In the time of the patriarch Simeon III, in the middle of the second century, it became a basic principle that 'we make no decree upon the community unless the majority are able to abide it.'[21] His contemporary, R. Ishmael b. Elisha, went even further. Reflecting that the only correct and logical reply to Hadrian's prohibition of basic Jewish practices would be to cease from begetting children, he said nothing of this to the people, for 'it is better that

[18] A.Z. 35a, p. 169.

[19] Cf. Max. Kadushin, *op. cit.*, pp. 27 ff.

[20] A.Z. 52b, p. 265. Another mention of the subject is in Hor. 11a, p. 80, where the situation is repeated. The disregard of Torah is the worse, but the disputants do not want to be categoric about it. There is also this interesting point. Where a halakah occurs in the written Torah, the interpretation must adhere strictly to its plain sense, but a halakah of the rabbis may be interpreted leniently. A.Z. 7a, p. 31.

[21] A.Z. 36a, fin. p. 175. Compare Ber. 12b, p. 71. A concise statement of the authority of the rabbis will be found in G. Horowitz, *The Spirit of Jewish Law*, New York, 1953, Ch. X., pp. 90 ff.

they should err in ignorance than presumptuously.'[22] To a third rabbi of the period, Nathan, was attributed the merit of having discovered a scriptural basis for granting such freedom to the rabbinic leaders. He interpreted Ps. 119. 126 as 'It is time to work for the Lord; they have made void Thy law.' In a 'time to work for the Lord' it was permitted to add, repeal or alter the Torah. A later rabbi added the comment that 'it is better that one letter of the Torah should be uprooted than that the whole Torah should be forgotten.'[23] Finally there was the verse, 'Ye shall therefore keep My statutes and My judgments; which if a man do he shall live in them.' *Live* in them, not *die* in them, said the rabbis, authorising the ordinary Israelite to violate all Torah save the prohibitions of murder, unchastity and idolatry, under external compulsion.[24] A Beth Din was allowed astonishing liberty when this same external compulsion threatened the community. Without any Pentateuchal authority it might order flogging, or even death 'not for the purpose of transgressing the words of Torah, but in order to make a fence about the Torah'. R. Eliezer b. Jacob, another contemporary of Akiba, quotes a case which occurred three hundred years earlier, showing how soon life according to Torah involved the modification of the words of Torah. A man was executed for riding a horse on the sabbath, 'not because he deserved the penalty, but because of the exigencies of the hour'.[25]

The rabbis, then, had no excuse if they neglected to watch over the real interests of the community. They had every authority for seeing that the observance of the mizwoth was not made intolerable, and rabbinic literature gives ample evidence that they took full advantage of this authority. In a number of cases they simply abolished laws of Torah which had fallen into complete disuse, in others they made modifications suited to the needs of the days in which they lived. In view of the controversy of Jesus with the Pharisees of his day over a healing on the sabbath, it is interesting to note that the laws governing the sabbath were ever more and more relaxed, first when there was danger to life, then when there was *the possibility* of danger to life. Exceptions made for the benefit of the sick were continually modified and enlarged, but there is a special charm in finding that the sabbath rule might be broken lest a child, who had fallen into a

[22] B.B. 60b, p. 246.
[23] Ber. 54a, p. 329 and Tem. 14b, p. 99.
[24] Sanh. 74a, p. 502.
[25] Yeb. 90b, p. 615. For another early case, recounted with some humour, see Gen. Rabbah. Ch. 91. 3. Ed. Son., p. 836.

pit or locked himself into a room, should be frightened, though he was in no danger of death.[26]

Their modifications are found in various questions of marriage and divorce, in matters where primitive laws of the Pentateuch offended the more sensitive consciences of later generations,[27] and in cases in which the strict adherence to the Biblical law would have made for undue hardship in commercial or financial matters.[28] They could certainly claim that no human affairs lay outside their interest, and we cannot make any grave charge against their methods or their decisions. The life which they directed was disciplined and, to some extent, austere; but it was not ascetic, it made every allowance for recreation, and history shows that it served its purpose.

3. LIVING BY THE MIZWOTH:

b. THE JOYFUL BURDEN

THE society which we are now describing was not living in some utopian Elysium sundered from the cares of time, but in the troubled ages which saw the breakdown of the western Roman empire, the rise of Parthia and the coming of Islam. Jews were living dispersed through all the regions affected by these events. Yet in relation to other societies contemporary with it and in its own intrinsic qualities, the Jewish community could not be called either unhappy or futile. The life of seeking and carrying out the mizwoth was one in which its burdens were cheerfully borne and its discipline was accepted with contentment. We have the most simple but incontrovertible evidence for this assertion. The religions and philosophies surrounding Israel were not all ignoble, the temptation to apostasy not necessarily synonymous with a craving for lust and vice. But Jews remained Jews, and this could be for one reason only. They preferred to.

Living by the mizwoth was necessarily living by a life which attached continuous importance to the performance of precise actions at a precise moment. It is, therefore, important to remember that there were two matters, which are the constant subject of rabbinic emphasis, but which are the subject of no halakah—the love of God and the love of neighbour. For these were immeasurable

[26] Yoma. 83a, p. 407 and 84b, p. 415 f.

[27] The most famous example is 'the eye for an eye'. See B.K. 83b, p. 474.

[28] For a full account of these matters see S. Zucrow, *Adjustment of Law to Life in Rabbinic Literature*, Stratford Co., Boston, 1928.

obligations, and their limits could not possibly be defined. But even in that which was defined, it is also important to distinguish the subtle balance in the mizwoth themselves. Whether consciously or unconsciously, the rabbis compounded a most delicate harmony of duties, wherein simple delight was as much a duty as onerous performance. There were three kinds of duty involved in the mizwoth. The duty of remembering that all life was a gift of its Creator, and the duty of obedience to his will stood on one side. On the other God offered an exceedingly full life, by the care with which he had foreseen men's domestic, economic, social and spiritual needs and provided for their fulfilment.

To a Christian, one of the most unexpected sections of a Jewish prayer book, or a summary of Jewish observances, is that dealing with the number of occasions on which should be said a special blessing in gratitude to God for his gifts.[29] There are many different forms of the blessing to be said over food and drink, and over the religious enjoyment of festivals. These might be expected. But there are also special blessings to be said on encountering a beautiful perfume, on seeing the wonders of nature, or the beauties of the animal or vegetable kingdom—even on seeing the first fruit tree in blossom. Nor is it forgotten that God made men, for there are special blessings to be said on meeting a sage or wise man, or a king and someone in authority. One final example illustrates once more the consistent view of Judaism that men should not seek to shift the blame on to others for their misfortune. There is a special blessing to be said on hearing evil tidings: Blessed art Thou, O Lord, King of the Universe, the true Judge.[30]

The essential quality and purpose of these blessings is that they bring continually before one who says them the presence of his Creator. They are constant reminders of God in his creation, and in so being they pass easily into the second set of mizwoth, those concerned with ritual matters. It is, of course, true that both sets of mizwoth can be observed in a meaningless and mechanical manner; but so

[29] Apart from Graces before and after meals, they occupy six pages of S. Singer's *Authorised Daily Prayer Book* (pp. 287 to 292), and thirty pages of Gerald Freidlander's *Laws and Customs of Israel*, Schapiro Vallentine, n.d. II. The discussion of precise blessings in *Berakoth* begins with Ch. 6. The basis is 'the fact that it is a reasonable supposition that it is forbidden to a man to enjoy anything of this world without saying a blessing.' (35a, p. 220).

[30] 'A man is bound to say one hundred blessings daily.' Men, 43b, pp. 263 f. Compare *The Blessings of the Jewish Prayer Book* by Mary R. Bede in *The Bridge, A Year Book of Judaeo-Christian Studies*, II. Pantheon Books, N.Y., 1956.

can all religious duties in all religions. But the essence of the many prescriptions affecting the preparation of daily food, the tithing of produce, and the preservation of the externals of the sabbath is that 'they inculcate the idea of the holy in daily life.'[31] Because the house-wife has to remember to prepare a meal in such and such a manner, because a man has to remember to set aside parts of his produce in such and such a way, because on the sabbath one must avoid such and such, the whole people have set before them constant reminders that God is concerned with the preparation of food, with the social obligations of property, with the general observance of the sabbath rest. They are made to feel his constant presence with them, which is the ultimate objective of mystical experience.

It is interesting to note that the rabbis were well aware that some of the halakoth calling forth such ritual mizwoth defied any human explanation. But in such especially they saw opportunities to remember their God. Some commandments dealt with such obvious moral necessities that they would have to be obeyed, even had the Lord never written them. Such are commandments dealing with murder, robbery, immorality and so on. The fact that these were forbidden might not of itself lead men to think of God. Any reasonable society would forbid them. But there were other commandments, beginning with circumcision, which were not self-evident. The sceptic or scoffer might well challenge them, and he could not be answered rationally. God gave such commandments in order that men might remember him, for he was the sole reason for their existence. *He* had given them.[32]

Such was one aspect of the mizwoth. They constantly emerged all through the business of daily living with the reminder of the goodness and existence of God. But a life based on such would be one-sided, if there were not the second group of mizwoth: those based on halakoth designed by God to enable the community of Israel to have the fullest possible enjoyment of the world which he had made. These are concerned with the domestic, social and economic affairs of the community and its members.

There is one subject whose justification or condemnation always provokes lively controversy—the attitude of the rabbis to women.

[31] Max Kadushin, *Organic Thinking*, p. 105. The same author in *The Rabbinic Mind* calls these observances 'normal mysticism', i.e. mysticism which is not related to some paranormal experience, but arises out of ordinary daily living. See pp. viii, 203 and 207. The whole study is well worth reading.

[32] Yoma, 67b, p. 316. There is a whole page of such quotations in *The Rabbinic Anthology*, p. 148. See also A. Buechler, *Studies in Sin and Atonement*, Oxford, 1928, p. 36.

On the surface, their conception of a community was ridiculously masculine, and they allotted women a very inferior place. But then, so did every society of their day; and it is fair to make comparisons only between contemporaries. But what makes the issue controversial is that, on the one hand, a large proportion of the references to women are silly and downright offensive, and that a good deal of the rabbinic preoccupation with sex is due to their prohibition of almost every occasion on which the sexes could meet each other on a normal and healthy footing; but that, on the other hand, their literature abounds with references to the joy of a happy married life, to the exaltation of the good woman; and that what we know of the Jewish communities of the time shows them to be a good deal healthier and happier than the non-Jewish communities of their environment.

This paradoxical attitude to women can be easily illustrated. There is, for example, only one reference to the greatest woman of the written Scriptures, the prophetess Deborah, which is concerned with the fact that she was a woman. R. Nahman remarked that 'haughtiness does not befit women. There were two haughty women, and their names are hateful, one being called a hornet (Deborah) and the other a weasel (Hulda). Of the hornet it is written, "she sent and called Barak", instead of going to him. Of the weasel it is written. "Say to the man" instead of "Say to the King".' The witticism was doubtless greeted with masculine guffaws, but one hopes that the wife of R. Nahman was sufficiently familiar with her Bible to remind her husband of Ecc. 7. 6. On the other hand we learn that 'he who has no wife dwells without good, without help, without joy, without blessing and without atonement.' He is also without peace, and is an incomplete man.[33]

The reason for the two contrary views is probably to be found in the fact that we are describing a society which at the same time elevated education to a height achieved by none of its contemporaries, and made no provision for the education of woman; a society which at the same time praised scholarship above all things, and yet placed the celebration of much of its feast and festival within the home, where the co-operation of the wife was essential to the maintenance of its spiritual quality. Had the rabbis used the appropriate verses of Scripture to authorise the introduction of some similar education for their daughters as for their sons, the paradox would have been resolved. As they did not, one can with equal sincerity laud or blame their attitude to women, while agreeing in regretting the number of

[33] Meg. 14b, p. 85, and Gen. Rabbah, 17. 2, p. 132.

silly and unworthy remarks which they allowed to be circulated.[34] Their minds were sufficiently acute for them to be held responsible for not seeing the obvious connection between the lack of education and the frivolity of mind of which they constantly held their womenfolk guilty. However, in a number of formal issues they did improve the status of women, for example in stipulating that, where there were both sons and daughters to inherit, it was more important to see that the daughters were not left destitute than the sons, so that, if the estate were small, the daughters might take all of it, leaving the sons to go begging.[35]

It is, perhaps, best to reckon the offensive remarks about women as being part of that comprehensiveness which sets rabbinic literature apart from other religious literature. For, outside their religious books, the contemporaries of the Jews said and did far worse things than the rabbis. We can, then, turn to other aspects of Jewish society, and we are bound to admit that it envisaged a more satisfying life than any society with which we can compare it. Indeed, in many respects, the world is still far from reaching the refinements of social and economic practice which the rabbis successfully inculcated among their followers.

It is obviously impossible to offer anything like a comprehensive survey of the whole subject, and it is more useful to illustrate a few particular points than to make a more comprehensive catalogue. Three subjects have been chosen, and each of them is illustrated by quotations which are to be found in Dr. A. Cohen's *Everyman's Talmud*. In this way the reader can turn to a single comprehensive introduction for further material, whereas if quotations were taken indiscriminately from rabbinic literature, as has been done reasonably elsewhere in this book, it would be little help to him. And the issue is important for the Christian reader in that the whole of this aspect of rabbinic Judaism is almost unknown and difficult to explore. Even the splendid *Rabbinic Anthology* collected by Dr. Montefiore omits altogether the social, economic and sanitary regulations of Judaism, while concentrating upon the 'religious and ethical'. An orthodox Jew, in Talmudic times or today, would not agree that the three subjects here chosen—relations between employer and

[34] For a representative group of opinions one can cite, on the favourable side, A. Cohen, *Everyman's Talmud*, Dent, 1932, Ch. V., pp. 168 ff., G. F. Moore *Judaism*, Vol. II, pp. 119 ff., and H. M. Loewe in *The Rabbinic Anthology*, pp. 656 ff. On the unfavourable side there is Montefiore in the same *Anthology*, pp. xviii and 507 ff., and S. Zucrow, *Women, Slaves and Ignorant*, Boston, 1932, Ch. IV, 'The Social Status of Women in Talmudic Times', pp. 74 ff.

[35] B.B. 139b, p. 594.

worker, slavery, and bodily health—were devoid of religious and ethical significance. They are essential to an understanding of the *Jewish* meaning of both 'religious' and 'ethical'.

The society envisaged by the rabbis was not socialistic. It accepted the existence of rich and poor, and had no condemnation for the possession of property. On the other hand there is no trace of hereditary privilege, nor the recognition of the existence of an 'upper class' above the law. There were responsibilities both on the employer of labour and on the labour employed. For example, an employer in a place where workmen are not accustomed to start early or to continue late, may not compel them to act otherwise. Where it is customary for the workmen to receive a meal, he must feed them. On the other hand, the workman may not work on his own plot all night and go out for wages at day, for he will be too tired to give his employer good service. He may not interrupt his work for his private devotions, for to do so is to rob his employer.[36]

In the ancient world slavery was universally practised, so that it is not surprising to find it accepted by the rabbis. But it is doubtful whether in any other community could have been coined the phrase that 'whoever acquires a Hebrew slave acquires a master for himself.'[37] A considerable distinction was made between the slave who was of Gentile origin and one who was of Jewish birth. The latter was to be regarded more as an 'indentured labourer' whereas the former was the servant for life of his master. But, while in many ways he was treated as an inferior, there were a number of methods by which he could gain his freedom and the Biblical law was enforced that severe physical ill treatment entitled him to go free.

Yet a third subject of special interest is physical health. There was unquestionably an element in Christian thinking which condoned neglect of healthy conditions, and approved dirt; and it was likewise true that such subjects as public hygiene became prominent only in modern times. The London of as late as the time of Charles Dickens must have been a city of abominable filth and appalling stench. In the nineteenth century such conditions may have applied only to the poorer districts. In the medieval city they would have been universal. In such an environment it is interesting to note that a Jew was advised not to live in any city where there was not some adequate sanitation, and that personal and domestic cleanliness ranked very high among the primary duties of a good Jewish family. The whole house had to be cleaned out once a year at the

[36] *Everyman's Talmud*, pp. 207 ff. On these three subjects the symposium *Die Lehre des Judenthums*, Leipzig, 1930. Vol. II can also be consulted.

[37] *Ibid.*, pp. 210 ff.

time of Passover, and its members were advised to wash face, hands and feet every day.[38] Though in many of their ideas they shared the common superstitions of their time, yet there is so much of common sense and experience in their rules of health that it is not surprising that Jews have been prominent in the medical profession from Talmudic times onward. The rabbis emphasised the need for regular habits, for moderation in eating and drinking, for securing enough sleep, but above all for cleanliness in living, so that it is not surprising if it was often true that the Jewish quarter escaped the epidemics which ravaged the cities of the ancient and medieval worlds.

To take seriously all such things, right relations between employer and employee, the right treatment of slaves, and the right observance of the laws of health was to fulfil the mizwoth as much as to say the right benedictions or to observe the ritual rules separating milk and meat in the kitchen. Jewish life was a unity, and it was in the fullest participation in the life of the community that it reached its fullest expression. The ascetic withdrawal from the community was never approved by the rabbis, certainly it was never regarded as giving greater opportunities for holiness and the service of God than was the every-day life of work and play within the family and the community. As the mizwoth pervaded every sphere of living, so they sanctified every sphere of living. Of course there were many who observed them in a slovenly or mechanical manner. But that is not the general picture. And there were doubtless some who found them burdensome. But that was not the common experience.

On the other side, it must be emphasised that so exacting and comprehensive an inclusion of all life within a rabbinically ordained and controlled framework is only successful where the rabbis are fully conscious of the *whole* of the environment and its possibilities. Once the rabbinically ordered life comes to be something separate from *the best* that can be obtained outside it, then difficulties arise. An obvious example of this danger lies in the complete contrast offered by the success of the rabbis in piloting their communities into the first 'emancipation' of early Islamic society between the tenth and the thirteenth centuries, and the failure of their successors to pilot Jewry undivided into the modern world with Jewish emancipation in eighteenth and nineteenth century Christian societies.

4. THE VALUES BEHIND THE MIZWOTH

It is very easy for the Christian reader to make a false estimate of

[38] For physical health, see *ibid*, pp. 253 ff.

the spiritual value of life as described in the two previous sections. For he is likely to attach unthinkingly the Jewish life based on the mizwoth to some Christian pattern of belief and conduct. Such an attachment is fatal. We cannot, for example, imagine an orthopraxy, which made a mizwah of reciting a special blessing over a fruit tree in bloom, attached to a Puritan theology which was quick to threaten Hell-fire for any slight disobedience. But it would be equally wrong to attach it to a conception of a priesthood-laity relationship which expected confession and penance for infringement. It is because they have, probably unconsciously, made such a Jewish-Christian hybrid, that so many Christian writers have denounced the practice of rabbinic Judaism as either an arid and unspiritual legalism or an intolerable burden. It would be both those things if it were attached to either a Puritan theology or a priest-laity relationship.

Historically however, rabbinic orthopraxy was lived with an entirely different background. Especially in the period of which we are writing the discussion and recording of halakoth and mizwoth was, as has already been said in a different context, continually interspersed with the enunciation of fundamental moral principles. It was, perhaps, a dubious service to Judaism when men like Maimonides or Joseph Caro made logical collections of the halakoth. For it made it possible for a Jew to read nothing but the precise commandments applying to his daily life, and this could easily create a false perspective. No tractate of the Mishnah or Talmud would produce this result; and, in consequence, the reader is constantly brought back to some central underlying principle.[39]

The duties which could be confined within no halakah were constantly before the eyes of the rabbis. A favourite saying of Raba was: 'The goal of wisdom is repentance and good deeds.'[40] In line with this G. F. Moore makes the remark that 'in no ancient religion is normal piety so pervaded by the consciousness of sin, the need for repentance, and the conviction that man's sole hope is in the for-

[39] Compare, for example, Dr. Abrahams' introduction to the tractate Hagigah, Ed. Son p. x. 'Despite the apparently chaotic heterogeneity of the subject matter, and complete lack of system in arrangement, the student who seeks to understand the tractate with heart as well as mind will sense beneath the surface of the variegated discussion a current of thought and feeling that binds the three chapters into a unity. Throughout Hagigah the answer to one question is being sought: How must the pilgrim approach the presence of his God? . . . The diverse topics, both *Halachic* and *Aggadic*, ritual as well as mystical, that form the contents of the tractate are only varied aspects of one great quest—the eternal quest of Israel for the *Shechinah*, the Presence Divine.'

[40] Ber 17a, p. 102.

giving grace of God'.[41] Such a remark emphasises the spiritual atmosphere behind the halakoth and reminds us that in speaking of rabbinic Judaism we are speaking of a religion *different* from Christianity, but not thereby either superior or inferior. For it is obvious that such a remark could be made with equal truth about Christianity, though from different premises. Parallel to the 'conviction of sin' could be placed the rabbinic emphasis on humility. Of two of the greatest heroes of Judaism, Moses and Hillel, their humility is a central characteristic to which attention is drawn.[42] Not only are such basic religious principles constantly enforced in discussion and exhortation, but a Jew was naturally liable to come upon them when seeking the halakah upon some minor matter of practice. The famous dictum of Hillel that the whole law is comprised in the statement that 'what is hateful to you, do not do to your neighbour' is to be found in the discussion of a passage in the Mishnah dealing with blowing out the lamp on the sabbath to allow an invalid to sleep![43]

One final example may be given of this quality of rabbinic literature. Starting from an extremely technical discussion of the water libation in the non-existent Temple, the rabbis came to the exquisite pronouncement that 'deeds of loving kindness are greater than charity. . . . Charity can be done only with one's money, but deeds of loving kindness can be done with one's person and one's money. Charity can be given only to the poor; deeds of loving kindness both to the rich and poor. Charity can be given to the living only; deeds of loving kindness can be done to the living and the dead. . . . He who executes charity and justice is regarded as though he had filled all the world with kindness.'[44]

Just as Judaism is not exclusively a religion of commandments, so also it is not a religion of salvation. Its qualities are not concentrated on the one purpose of assuring the salvation of its members. This freedom permitted, indeed compelled, a different development. Concentrated as Christian teaching was upon salvation, the Christian could not help remembering that salvation was the privilege of a selected minority. This gave enormous power and responsibility to the priesthood who could open and close the gates of heaven and

[41] *Judaism*, II, p. 214. Moore quotes especially the prayer which ends the services of the Day of Atonement. See also A. Buechler, *Studies in Sin and Atonement*, which has a detailed Table of Contents.

[42] E.g. Er. 13b, p. 86. The reference to Moses is in Num. 12 3. Compare also Kadushin, *Organic Thinking*, p. 149. God's greatness is often coupled with the divine humility. See Moore, *op. cit.*, I, p. 440.

[43] Shab. 31a, p. 140.

[44] Suk. 49b, p. 233.

hell. Jews, less interested in the future life and believing that all Israel would be saved, gave no similar power to the rabbi, and their religion was focused upon a different objective—doing the will of God here and now. The Jew believed that the fulfilment of that objective was a possible one, and in that fulfilment he saw the messianic age of the future. It was in guidance toward this end that lay the rabbi's responsibility. He could, therefore, legitimately stress action with the same single-minded enthusiasm as his Christian counterpart stressed faith. For in the two religions each played a similar part in giving to the choices of life significance and meaning.

A third quality of Judaism affords yet another interesting comparison with the parallel growth of Christianity. Both were, once they had developed, truly 'popular' religions. While in the local community or the parish the rabbi was distinguished by his learning and the priest by his ordination, in both religions local leader and people were of the same class, and shared the same general beliefs. But there is a striking difference, one which helps in the understanding of the different tasks and destinies of Judaism and Christianity.

The latter, ever reaching out towards the pagan world, absorbed people after people into its bosom; and each brought with it its age-old inheritance of folk-lore and of newly abandoned paganism. The early and the medieval Christian worlds were in consequence full of strange and terrifying beliefs, of gods but half subdued, of ancient and primitive forces still but half understood, and of whispered tales of strange beings who owed no allegiance to the Christian God. It is easy to overlook the amazing work done by our Christian forefathers in doing battle with, and in large measure overcoming, relics of the past in which both priest and congregation still half believed. It was inevitable that in the course of such a protracted battle religious authority should have been centralised, and theology should have mounted a pedestal where it defied the pagan assault.

The rabbi had to cope with no such problem. There were no such dark forces impending above him and threatening to overwhelm him and his congregation. A millenium had passed since the influences of Babylon had been absorbed and purified, still more since his forefathers had done battle with the evil forces of Canaanite religion. A bishop might well watch with anxiety while his parish priest decorated his church with holly at what was now Christ's mass: the rabbis of the great academies had no fear that in some local congregation the prohibition of milk with meat would stir ancient Canaanite superstitions from their forgotten graves. Judaism could, then, be a truly 'popular' religion in that rabbi and people could really share one another's confidence, whether in judging and accepting some detailed definition of halakah, or in weaving one of the innumerable tales which make up the Midrash. This is what the canon of Holy Scripture had done for Judaism. It had made even its folk-lore ethical and monotheistic.[45] In stories, however fantastical, there would be no suggestion that God regarded with envy the happiness of his children, or that there were dark forces which owed him no allegiance, and realms where the distinction of good and evil did not obtain.

It is this common origin of both halakah and haggadah in the same Bible, and often in the same passage, which blends Jewish life into a single whole and combines the apparent 'legalism' of the halakah with the warm, homely world of the haggadah. A single example will give the picture. The third commandment of the Decalogue is: 'Thou shalt not take the name of the Lord thy God in vain.' In a number of tractates of the Talmud the exact character and consequences of this prohibition are discussed, and the appropriate action is prescribed for its violation.[46] But the third commandment is also treated in the haggadah: 'Swearing falsely has terrible consequences, not only for one who does it but it endangers all the world. For when God created the world, He laid over the abyss a shard, on which is engraved the Ineffable Name, that the abyss may not burst forth and destroy the world. But as often as one swears falsely in God's name, the letters of the Ineffable Name fly away, and as there is then nothing to restrain the abyss, the waters burst forth from it to destroy the world. This would surely come to pass if God did not send the angel Ya'asriel, who has charge of the seventy pencils, to engrave anew the Ineffable Name on the shard.'[47] One can, then, take one's choice as to the reason why a Jew avoided swearing falsely by the name of God. The mizwoth were continuously entwined in the warmth of folk-lore.

It has been said above that you cannot fit life by the mizwoth into life governed by threats of eternal punishment for any infringement. It is equally difficult to see it as a means of combatting original sin.[48]

[45] 'Folklore, fairy tales, legends and all forms of story-telling akin to these are comprehended . . . under the inclusive description Haggadah, a name which can be explained by a circumlocution, but which cannot be translated. . . . The fancy of the Jewish people was engaged by the past, reflected in the Bible, and all its creations wear a Biblical hue for this reason,' L. Ginsberg, *The Legends of the Jews*, I, p. ix f. Compare also A. Rappoport, *Folklore of the Jews*, Soncino Press, 1937, pp. 5, 7, 264 and *passim.*

[46] See especially Sheb. 20b, 107 f., and 39a, p. 234.

[47] Ginzberg, *op. cit.*, III, p. 99.

[48] Buechler, *op. cit.*, see especially Ch. 4.

The rabbis did not have to because they had a most interesting substitute for the Christian doctrine of original sin. The latter can be understood by any who contemplate the struggle of the constantly expanding Church with the environing darkness of paganism. The Church had need of a clear separation between black and white such as the doctrine of original sin afforded. But the Jewish situation was different. Looking out into the world from the standpoint of a chosen people scattered among the nations, the rabbis wisely did not emphasise the universal wickedness of man, but stressed instead the basically ethical quality of that which distinguished *all* men from beasts. This was embodied in their teaching about *derek eretz*, a term applied to 'whatever is typical or characteristic of man'. A very broad concept, it joins together human interests at the farthest remove from one another.[49] It does not describe a specifically *Jewish* quality. 'It refers to what is universally human. . . . As such it is the perfect frame for the category of the ethical . . . because every human trait is *potentially* of ethical import.'[50] The phrase means literally 'the way of the world', and it is interesting that, from their standpoint within a closed and secure community (by comparison with the Christian, battling all the time with paganism), the rabbis could so contemplate the basis of human conduct. But, again, it had its importance in setting life by the mizwoth in its proper framework. That life was normal human life intensified, not a life in contrast to the human norm.

Into this life, based as we have seen on harmonies rather than contrasts, rabbinic Judaism could incorporate its thought of God without the necessity of constructing a formal metaphysic. It had, in fact no formal theology whatever. One might well say that, metaphysically, Judaism allowed either Christianity or Islam to create, by the struggles of their theologians, the monotheistic atmosphere in which the Jew was at home. Judaism *assumed* the existence and the unity of the Godhead, it troubled neither to argue nor to demonstrate it. In place of a metaphysic, the foundations of Judaism are four concepts, constantly interrelated to each other. These four concepts, organically linked, are: *the loving kindness of God* and *his justice*, and the expression of these qualities in *the Torah* and in *Israel*. These four concepts, in different combinations, constantly recur in rabbinic thinking and constantly determine rabbinic beliefs and ideas. Though they are not knit together in a formal theology, they play the same role in Judaism as credal definition does in Christianity. They are

[49] Kadushin, *Organic Thinking*, pp. 118.
[50] *Ibid.*, p. 119.

the test by which other ideas are accepted or rejected.[51] They are the basis on which life and its activities are given significance and meaning.

We are, then, presented with a very closely knit whole in the life of the Jewish community as moulded and developed by the rabbis. Its parts were interlocked and cannot, without distortion, be presented in isolation. In particular the mizwoth, which have afforded so much misunderstanding to Christian writers, cannot be considered apart from the whole set of values in which they are embedded, and from which, in this period of Judaism when logically ordered codes had not been isolated from the mass of rabbinic literature, they cannot be separated.

Finally, work is linked to worship, which we shall consider in the following section, by the fact that the Hebrew word *emunah* 'signifies alike faith—trust—in God, and faithfulness—honesty, integrity—in human relations. These two concepts of emunah do not conflict with each other, on the contrary, they complement and supplement one another. . . . Faith is a dynamic, a motive for faithfulness, and is of value only in so far as it is productive of faithful action: nor is there any faithful action that is not rooted in faith in God'.[52]

5. THE SABBATH, THE SYNAGOGUE, AND THE SCHOOL

THE observance of the Sabbath and the worship of the synagogue gathered together the whole of what has been separately described in the previous sections and moulded it into the life of the community of Israel. For the Sabbath was as central and distinctive a feature of Judaism as was life lived by the mizwoth; and the worship of the synagogue, already formed before the period which we are now considering, is so comprehensive that it has been accepted as the pattern of worship in the two other monotheistic religions which are daughters of Judaism.

By common agreement, even of those writers who are not friendly to Judaism, the Jewish Sabbath has always been a day of happiness and relaxation. There is evidence of this from all countries and from all periods, so that it needs no demonstration. 'The emperor [Hadrian] said to R. Joshua b. Hanania, "Why has the Sabbath dish such a fragrant odour?" "We have a certain seasoning," replied he,

[51] See Kadushin, *Organic Thinking*, p. 6, or *The Rabbinic Mind*, pp. 14 and 110.

[52] I. Epstein, in the *Introduction to Seder Zeraim*, Ed. Soncino, *Berakoth*, p. xv.

"called the Sabbath which we put into it, and that gives it a fragrant odour." "Give us some of it," asked he. "To him who keeps the Sabbath," retorted he, "it is efficacious; but to him who does not keep the Sabbath it is of no use."'[53] The rabbis regarded the Sabbath as central, for they equated its profanation with idolatry, considering both to be equally a total rejection of Torah.[54] And they emphasized its importance positively as well, asserting that if Israel kept even one Sabbath perfectly then the Messiah would come.[55]

It helps to place the multifarious mizwoth of Judaism in perspective to set this estimation of the Sabbath beside the fact that the Talmudic tractate on the subject is almost the longest of the whole Talmud and has much fewer digressions than usual, so that it is almost entirely occupied with the multiplication and sub-division of the prohibitions affecting that day. If the mizwoth on any subject could prove an intolerable burden it would surely be these, for their observance was demanded, not of a particular profession or in particular circumstances, but of the men, women and children of every household in the Jewish community in every land. Moreover, the rabbis recognised that their prohibitions were not Biblical, but their own additions to the single sentence of the Decalogue, and compared them to 'mountains hanging by a single thread'.[56] But the Talmud shows no feeling that these regulations, many of them sanctified common-sense, impeded the happiness or relaxation of the day.

The importance given to the Sabbath helps us also to correct the perspective of the rabbinic view of women to which reference has already been made. For, if the Sabbath was a queen, it was the housewife who was her chief minister. It was she who lit and blessed the Sabbath candles; saw to the cleaning of the house and prepared the special food with which the Sabbath was honoured. It was pre-eminently *her* day, and in the blessing granted her, the whole family moved to the centre of the stage and emphasized the importance Judaism attached to the home and its spiritual values.

The home always shares with the synagogue the chief place in the spiritual life of the people. As to the latter, the origin of congregational worship had, by this time, been completely forgotten. By Philo and Josephus it was already regarded as an institution of Moses,

[53] Shab., 119a, p. 587.
[54] Hull. 5a, p. 19.
[55] In Shab. 118b, p. 582 R. Simeon b. Yohai makes this statement of *two* Sabbaths. Other references are given in G. F. Moore, *op. cit.*, II, p. 26, n.1.
[56] Hag. 10a, p. 50.

and it was universally accepted throughout the whole Diaspora.[57] In fact there is somewhat quaint evidence during this period that the synagogue services had become so much the affair of the congregation that scholars frowned upon them.[58]

It may well be that this breach between the scholar and the synagogue officiants was due to the widening gap between the halakic and the haggadic or midrashic approach to the text of Scripture.[59] As the synagogal interpretation of the original Hebrew text of the Scriptures, spoken of already in the time of Ezra, came to permit of illustration and expansion of the Biblical narrative, a school of preachers grew up who more and more entertained the congregation by the liveliness and variety of their imagination. As we can see from collections of such preachings,[60] while some of the stories and parables have a deep moral significance, much of it was story telling 'pure and simple', and it is not surprising that the increasingly precise scholar, dealing with the minutiae of interpretation, found it distasteful. But the existence and volume of the synagogal midrash on the Scriptures reminds us that we must not speak of Judaism as being simply a religion for the scholar and the intellectual. The ordinary man, woman and child, had plenty on which to feed. Nor were Jews the only people to enjoy the stories of the midrash. They were widely known to Christians and are often found in patristic literature.'[61]

There is plenty of material to show that the leaders of Israel considered the assembling of the community in common worship to be a fundamental part of Judaism. In fact it was not only on the Sabbath and at festivals, but on ordinary weekdays, that they expected there to be always some who, going to or coming from their daily work, spent some time in private study and devotion in the synagogue.[62] Rabbi Nathan, a Tanna of the end of the first century,

[57] I. Elbogen, *Der Jüdische Gottesdienst*. 3rd Ed. Frankfurt, 1931, pp. 245 and 246.

[58] The evidence is found in Ber. 8a, p. 41 and Shab 10a, p. 34. Moore, *op. cit.*, II, p. 241, considers that this situation was both local and temporary.

[59] On the development of this distinction, see the introduction by Dr. I. Epstein to the Soncino Edition of Midrash Rabbah.

[60] For example, L. Ginzberg, *The Legends of the Jews*, in six volumes, or R. Asher Feldman, *The Parables and Similes of the Rabbis*, Cambridge, 1924.

[61] Ginzberg, *op. cit.*, 1, p. xiii, says 'In the rich literature of the Church Fathers many a Jewish legend lies embalmed which one would seek in vain in Jewish books'. See index under 'Christian'.

[62] Ber. 4b, p. 13. Note also the quaint saying in the same tractate (6b, p. 26) that when God enters the synagogue he would always expect to find a minyan present.

was expressing the general rabbinic view when he stated that God regarded study, deeds of charity and sharing in the worship of the community as the three principal duties of his children.[63]

As to the liturgical service itself, its main lines had already been fixed in the period when the Temple was still standing, a reason why communal worship was able to adjust itself to the destruction of the Temple with so little disturbance.[64] Until the attacks of the Christians caused the latter to be dropped, the central points of the service had been the Shema and the Decalogue, Israel's assertion of belief in God, and God's revealed will for Israel. Around the Shema grew preliminary and subsequent prayer and praise, and this was followed by a composite prayer, containing both praise and petition, which is known either as the Amidah (because it was said standing), the Tefillah (the prayer *par excellence*), or the Shemone Esreh (the eighteen benedictions), though their number was increased to nineteen in the time of the Vineyard, to include an exclusion of the Judeo-Christians from participating in synagogue worship.[65] The general form of these benedictions was settled at Jabne, where Gamaliel II is credited with a special interest in liturgical development, but the wording itself was left to the celebrant for some centuries to come. In fact the generation of Akiba was still preoccupied with the basic question whether more real devotion would be found in the extempore framing of the words or in the copying of an established formula—a dispute which has lasted in all religions with a fixed liturgy until this day.[66] It was not until the ninth century that a fixed and complete prayer book was collected by R. Amran, embodying the many phrases and decisions of Tannaim and Amoraim and their successors.[67]

The other main element in the service was the reading of the Scriptures. It is here that the rabbinic concentration on a religion of halakah and mizwah reveals a certain weakness. For, whereas the first five books are read consecutively and according to their meaning,

[63] Ber. 8a, p. 39.

[64] I. Elbogen, *op. cit.*, pp. 250 ff. considers that the Tannaim never regarded prayer as a substitute for sacrifice. See above, p. 247, for their discussions of what would replace the Temple cult. But see also A. Z. Idelsohn, *Jewish Liturgy and its Development*, New York, 1932, p. 26 for a contrary view, and for rabbinic texts in support of it.

[65] The birkath ha-Minim or ha-Nozrim was composed by Samuel the Lesser at the end of the first century. See Ber. 28b. fin., p. 175.

[66] Idelsohn, *op. cit.*, pp. 28 f.

[67] For material on the development of the synagogue liturgy see Elbogen and Idelsohn already quoted, or the introduction by I. Abrahams to the annotated edition of the *Authorised Daily Prayer Book* of Simeon Singer.

the other books receive much less attention. The great messages of the prophets are lost in the selection of a few verses to be read in a second lesson, not according to the sense of the prophetic message but because of some fancied association, possibly merely verbal or geographical, with the reading from the Pentateuch. So likewise only a selected number of the psalms were included in synagogue worship,[68] though it is as true of Judaism as it is of Christianity that the psalms were also a treasure house of private devotion.

That a religion possesses a beautiful and deeply spiritual liturgy is, unhappily, no evidence that many of those who say it or hear it will genuinely understand and mean the words with which they become perhaps too familiar. The problem is common to Judaism, Christianity and Islam, but it had a special urgency in Judaism because the synagogue was used for every kind of communal purpose[69] religious and secular, so that no specially 'religious' atmosphere or association assisted the congregation at its devotions. But there is yet another reason why proper attention to the prayers was a problem perpetually exercising the minds of the more spiritual rabbis: the tradition by which certain prayers were said both privately and then publicly came to mean that during the repetition those who had already said the prayer felt free to converse with their neighbours. Right into modern times Judaism has been more troubled by this destruction of the atmosphere of its worship than the Christian Churches, as is evidenced by the legend that 'R. Eleazar b. R. Jose once met Elijah driving four thousand camels heavily laden, and at his question concerning the nature of the load he received the following answer from the prophet: "These camels are laden with wrath and fury for those who talk during their prayers." '[70]

There is one use of the synagogue to which Elijah himself would not have taken exception. That was its use as a school. It is on a par with the generally ambivalent attitude of the rabbis towards women that Rab says simply: 'Whereby do women earn merit? By making their children go to synagogues to learn Scripture.'[71] But this saying also reflects the serious interest of the rabbis both in children and in education.[72] There are a number of statements, both charming and

[68] See Abrahams, *op. cit.*, pp. xxxiii ff.

[69] S. W. Baron, *Social and Religious History*, 2nd Ed., II, p. 284.

[70] Ginzberg, *Legends*, VI, p. 329.

[71] Ber. 17a, p. 102.

[72] On the general question of Jewish education during this period see Nathan Morris, *The Jewish School*, Eyre and Spottiswoode, 1937, and also Baron, *op. cit.*, II, pp. 274 ff., and Moore, *op. cit.*, I, pp. 316 ff.

profound, about children in rabbinic literature. A certain R. Zera enunciated the wise apothegm: 'One should not promise a child to give him something and then not give it him, because one will thereby teach him lying.' R. Judah remarked that to teach a child no craft by which he can earn his living is to teach him brigandage. For charm the palm must go to a saying in Abodah Zara that during the fourth quarter of the day God himself teaches Torah to those children who have died too young to learn it on earth.[73]

It is part of the expected discursiveness of the Talmud that the main practical discussion of education, with important historical information, is given during an argument as to who may or may not set up business in a common courtyard.[74] From this passage we learn that the beginnings of communal responsibility for primary education date back to the last decade in which the Temple was standing, and are due to the initiative of a high priest, Joshua b. Gamala. After trying unsuccessfully to keep older boys under discipline he fixed the age of entry at six or seven, and gradually extended the range of primary schools from Jerusalem throughout the country, and so into the diaspora communities. When a community found that there were twenty-five children among its families, it should engage a school-teacher, and Jews are warned not to settle in a town where there were too few families for such a teacher to be appointed.[75] When the children came to number forty, an assistant should be appointed. At fifty, a second 'qualified' teacher should be added. Teachers were the first people who were allowed to make a living out of their knowledge of Torah, but it seems that their pay was small, for they were not regarded as desirable sons-in-law![76]

It is not surprising that it took some centuries for so far-reaching an innovation as public primary education to win general acceptance, and there was never any question, during the period under discussion, of 'universal', or 'compulsory' education. But by the fourth century one can say that there were very few children who had not been taught, either by their father or by a communal teacher, the elements of their religion. That, at any rate, is implied in a story that three Palestinian Amoraim were sent to inspect the teaching in the towns

[73] Suk. 46b, p. 217; Kid 29a, pp 137 f; A.Z. 3b, p. 10. See also remarks about children, in Shab. 119b, pp. 590 ff. and Midrash Rabbah, Lamentations, 1. 5. 32. Ed. Son., p. 105. See also *The Rabbinic Anthology*, ch. xxiv, pp. 516 ff. The souls of unborn children heard the Laws being proclaimed at Sinai. Ginzberg, *Legend of the Jews*, III, p. 97.

[74] B.B., 20b—21ab, pp. 105 ff.

[75] San. 17b, p. 90.

[76] Pes. 49b, p. 236.

of Palestine and were horrified to find one town in which there were no teachers.[77] Even if this falls short of 'compulsory' education, yet it meant that the Jewish community possessed a degree of literacy far above that of its neighbours, a situation which has continued right into modern times.

The Sabbath, the synagogue, and the school between them emphasized the communal element in Judaism and the communal responsibility for the lives of members of the community. No man could perform his mizwoth for another, but no man could perform a synagogal service by himself. In the widely scattered Diaspora these institutions maintained the unity of Judaism and provided an element of uniformity within its multiplicity of circumstances. Besides, the sabbath and the synagogue provided a very practical basis for that unity in the hospitality which they encouraged, a hospitality all the more necessary for an isolated traveller. For the Sabbath table was not really filled without guests, and the synagogue provided a lodging place for strangers.

6. AUTHORITY AND JUSTICE

THE religion of the rabbis showed its ability to survive not only by the total pattern of life which it worked out to the smallest detail, but also by the unusual delegation of authority and the sensitive administration of justice which became characteristic of Jewish communities.

As the high priesthood in Jerusalem had decayed more and more in the last decades before the destruction of the Temple, so—though by no official or formal act—there grew up side by side with it the enduring authority which affection had vested first in the person of Hillel and then in his descendants. Apart from the brief interregnum of Johanan b. Zakkai, supreme authority was vested in the house of Hillel, and recognised by Rome, from the days of the Vineyard until the office, to which the Romans had granted the name and dignity of a patriarchate, dwindled and died at the hands of Christian emperors in the beginning of the fifth century.[78] It was symptomatic

[77] *The Rabbinic Anthology* No. 1460. Compare Morris, *op. cit.*, pp. 21 ff. and Sheb. 5a, p. 15 of which the meaning seems to be that by the fourth century only the most unusual circumstances would explain a child having no education.

[78] The patriarchate and its development in Roman law is treated in J. Juster, *Les Juifs dans l'Empire Romain*, I. pp. 391 ff. I am doubtful if they had as much actual authority as Justers infers from the law. See pp. 105 f. above.

of the insecurity in which Jewish life was henceforth to be lived that Arcadius, emperor of the eastern provinces, should issue an edict in 396 that 'the illustrious patriarch' was not to be insulted, and that three years later his western colleague, Honorius, should refer to him as 'that person' or as *depopulator Judaeorum*, and confiscate all his revenues.[79] It was little comfort that both titles and income were restored in 404[80] for they brought neither lustre nor safety. In 415 Theodosius II degraded the occupant of the office with insulting language and in 429 he abolished it and confiscated to himself all its revenues.[81]

Though the patriarch had been unquestionably one of the great officers of the eastern provinces, yet it is extremely difficult to assess the actual extent to which he was able to exercise his authority. He was entitled to receive revenue from all Jewish communities within the empire, and to send his officials to collect it. But it must have been to some extent at least voluntarily given. One may therefore presume that the communities received some benefit from his existence though it is impossible to define closely what it was. It would be easier to assess his importance if there were fewer obscurities surrounding the question of the exercise of his powers of ordaining rabbis. As with the Christian 'apostolic succession', so there was supposed to be a succession from Moses through Joshua, vested in the hands of the patriarch, and inalienable from whoever possessed the supreme authority *in Palestine itself*.[82] But there is no real evidence that the patriarch really 'appointed' the rabbis of the diaspora communities, and there is considerable evidence that the ceremony of ordination lapsed before the patriarchate was extinguished.[83]

The office of the patriarch was respected within the great Jewish community beyond the eastern frontiers of the empire, but the Jews of Babylon did not recognise his authority, save in fixing the calendar.

They had their own leader, likewise hereditary and likewise considered one of the great officers of the kingdom. An 'exilarch', tracing in some shadowy manner his descent from the house of David, was the supreme officer and judge of Babylonian Jewry. But the exilarchs shared their authority and the office of judge with the presidents of the great Babylonian academies, the geonim, and

[79] C.T., 16. 8. 11 and 14.
[80] *Ibid.*, 16. 8. 15 and 17.
[81] *Ibid.*, 16. 8. 22 and 29.
[82] On the extremely complex subject of ordination (Semikah) see J. Newman, *Semikah*, Manchester University Press, 1950.
[83] On the patriarchate see Baron, *The Jewish Community*, I., pp. 140 ff.

both offices gradually dwindled in importance as Babylonian Jewry itself declined when Mesopotamia became again a centre of continuous disorder and misrule.[84]

Both patriarch and exilarch may be considered necessary elements in the transition from the authority of the Maccabean and Herodian princes and high priests, as recognised by Rome, to the complete decentralisation which made each Jewish community throughout the world its own master. But they had no successors. Indeed, there is no vestige in either east or west of any attempt to create such. They had served their purpose and had become *functi officio*. What took their place was a Jewish adaptation of a legal device known already elsewhere. As codes developed in complexity in any administration covering a substantial area, it became necessary to have some method by which local judges or public bodies could secure, by correspondence, information from the centre as to the exact situation or decision covering some matter which had arisen in the locality. In the Roman administration of the early empire, this system was highly developed and standardised. Only those allowed by the emperor to give such rulings could do so. They were known as *juris consulti*, and their answers were called *responsa*. Later the Muslims were to evolve a somewhat similar system, by which the ecclesiastical authorities and the lay judges were able to keep in step.[85]

While they were still recognised as supreme religious authorities from their position as heads of the great rabbinical academies of Babylon, the geonim began to issue such *responsa* to communities which submitted questions to them. But, as they lost authority through the unsettled conditions of the country, the custom grew up by which a community needing to ask a question became also the judge deciding to whom the question should be put. They chose the most learned rabbi of whom they had heard, wherever he happened to be. The system could thus continue without any loss when there was no central authority left in Jewry; for these Jewish *responsa*, unlike those of the Romans, were of consultative, and not of executive, authority. Each local society was responsible for deciding whether and how a *responsum* given was to be put into effect.

Thus even in religious matters, and in connection with the ever increasing development of the oral law, rabbinic Judaism came to have no need of any central authority. And this was the more valuable

[84] On the authority of exilarchs and geonim see Baron, *op. cit.*, pp. 145 ff. and 173 ff.

[85] On the whole question of Responsa, see S. B. Freehof, *The Responsa Literature*, Jewish Publication Society of America, 1955. On Roman and Muslim parallels, see p. 22.

as the times were becoming such that any central authority would only have weakened Jewish life. For the barbarian invasions brought disorder to the western world in the fifth century, and Islamic power in the east fell into increasing decline as authority passed from the brilliant Abassid califate to ruder and less principled Turkish successors. Local self-reliance could mean local security because a local minority was obscure. There is yet another reason why reference to a central authority would have been a weakness and not a strength. The centuries of 'dark ages' in both east and west were centuries in which the geographical range of Jewish life was considerably extended, even though the main routes of communication were becoming impassible or more dangerous. We hear of more and more communities in 'barbarian' western Europe, whether on the Rhine or in France, Burgundy and Spain; and at the same time we have evidence of Jewish caravans penetrating further and further into the wilds of Asia and Africa and into what we would now designate as 'Russia'. Had communities so widely dispersed felt themselves incapable of managing their own affairs, the result must have been the collapse of Jewry and Judaism, for no central authorities could have found means of continuous contact and control. The early history of Christianity in Britain, with its struggles between a 'Celtic' and a 'Roman' form, illustrate what might have happened in Jewry. The survival of the Jewish community in China, for centuries after the stronger and more numerous Nestorian Church had vanished, is another example of the strength which lay in the complete decentralisation of Judaism.

This transference of power was not to the synagogal authorities. Judaism and the Jewish people did not become a series of 'autocephalous' churches. It was by the community, not by the congregation or its rabbi, that power was inherited, and the community was governed by laymen, who, in varying ways, were elected to their office. There does not appear to have been any single system, nor was any particular method of choice a matter of 'orthopraxis'. The evidence which has survived, scattered and fragmentary as it is, is enough to show that a wide variety existed.[86] But some form of election was essential, as a pleasant story confirms: 'R. Isaac said: We must not appoint a leader over a community without consulting it, as it says: "See the Lord hath called by name Bezalel the son of Uri." The Holy One, blessed be He, said to Moses: "Do you

[86] Baron, *Social and Religious History*, II., pp. 198 ff. and *Jewish Community*, I., pp. 96 ff.

consider Bezalel suitable?" He replied: "Sovereign of the Universe, if Thou thinkest him suitable, surely I must also." Said God to him: "All the same, go and consult them".'[87]

There was one condition which was essential, if this decentralisation was not to mean destruction. The community had to have judicial autonomy. This it could usually get, for the ancient world found a wide variety of local autonomies an acceptable form of local government. It relieved the central machinery, and it helped to secure tranquillity in empires which depended on conquest and not on any natural coherence for their frontiers. To grant this autonomy to Jewish communities, as it did also in certain cases to Christian communities, involved a risk. For Jews, like Christians, were scattered everywhere and might be more powerful and numerous in some enemy of the authority which granted autonomy.[88] Thus, when the Roman empire became Christian, Persian rulers were at first hesitant about giving too much power to Persian Christians—though in the event they were saved by the divisions on matters of orthodoxy between the Byzantine and Nestorian Churches. Here Judaism scored by its lack of any place where Jews formed the government, but Judaism also needed more than did a Christian congregation. There were no specifically *Christian* laws dealing, for example, with contracts or bailments, and there were no specifically 'Christian courts' in the Christian Roman empire for dealing with such issues. With Jews the situation was different. There is nothing in the wide range of patristic literature corresponding to the extensive Jewish material on legal matters. A whole section of the Talmud is entitled 'Seder Nezikin', 'The Order of Damages', and contains some of the longest and most complex tractates.[89] As Dr. Herzog says in his monumental but unfinished study of Jewish law, 'in Judaism what would generally be described as civil law is an integral part of the Jewish religion'.[90] There is yet another characteristic which distinguishes it. It is a commonplace of judicial systems that laws need constant reframing to meet with changing situations. In many such

[87] Ber. 55a, p. 336. We do not know enough to give an exact meaning to 'We . . . appoint'.

[88] Compare the situation in the time of Trajan above, p. 256.

[89] It is a pleasant example of the confusion which can attend those who seek to transfer by way of comparison matters appropriate to the one religion to the other, that the original title of this collection of books dealing wholly with legal matters was 'The Order of Salvation'. Any theological deductions from this fact would be sure to be wrong! Compare Newman, *op. cit.*, p. vii.

[90] I. Herzog, *The Main Institutions of Jewish Law*, Soncino Press, 1936. I. p. 381.

systems, for example the British, the result is a double code, of statute law and of equity. There are not two codes in Judaism, for the same judges were at once the framers and the continual interpreters of the code which they applied,[91] and both alike were based on the same written Torah.

Autonomy for a Jewish community meant therefore some measure of judicial independence, for the situation in a modern state, which grants full citizenship to its Jewish members and expects of them in return that they would conform to the laws of the majority, could not apply to the position anywhere in the ancient world. Here also rabbinic common-sense helped the communities to exercise their responsibility wisely. In the first place there were no privileged classes in Jewish society, and all Jews were under the authority of the same judicial code. There was, thus, no group which could automatically escape the jurisdiction of the humblest community by assuming some superior status.[92] In the second place, Jewish courts were not graded hierarchically, so that there was no automatic appeal from the ordinary court of a small community to some higher court at a distance. A right of appeal certainly existed in certain cases, and, within a fixed delay, it was possible to demand a retrial by the original court on the basis of fresh evidence. But the question is an obscure one, and the obscurity itself shows that appeals were not part of the routine of Jewish justice.[93] Each community had to be content with the justice which it could receive from its own officers.

Because of their position as scattered minorities, Jews were always conscious of the parallel existence of a code of laws other than their own, and this caused a number of special adjustments. For example, the rabbis assimilated into their *civil* code many issues which, in other codes, would have been matters of *criminal* jurisdiction. The reason is evident: they were much more likely to be allowed to judge their own civil cases than those which involved public crimes. Thus theft and burglary were dealt with as civil injuries to the man robbed, and not as offences against the standards of the whole society. By retaining such cases in their own hands, the rabbis were obeying a deep moral impulse. In all the environing societies of ancient Jewry torture, often of the most brutal kind, was a commonplace, and physical mutilation a normal sentence. There is no single passage in the whole mass of rabbinic literature which even discusses

[91] *Ibid.*, pp. 55 ff.
[92] Cf. *ibid.*, p. 41.
[93] See *ibid.*, pp. 14 f. and compare A.Z. 36a, p. 174.

the possibility of torture being applied in a Jewish court.[94]

While this may be an extreme case, there were many others in which the Jewish conscience exhibited a sensitivity which would have made Jews unwilling to go to other courts, and which gradually drew Gentiles, when involved in a suit involving a Jew, to prefer to be judged by Jewish law.[95] We may legitimately assume that this sensitivity in purely legal matters was, in part at any rate, a consequence of the quality of rabbinic literature already discussed—its ability to switch attention from one subject to another in the shortest possible time. There is in biblical law so much attention paid to the helpless, the needy and the dependent—the stranger, for example, and the widow—that it would be unnatural if the temper of mind thus cultivated changed suddenly when a different type of need came to be considered. When even an animal had rights and was entitled to consideration, it would have been unnatural had the claims of justice and charity between human beings been neglected.[96] The protection of the rights of women and slaves was among the subjects where the quality of Jewish law shows most characteristically.[97] In some cases provisions originally uniquely Jewish seem to have been taken over by the Gentiles among whom Jewish communities lived.[98]

While, then, it was natural for Jews to keep as many cases as possible within their own jurisdiction, the limits of that jurisdiction were inevitably determined by the government under which they lived and not by themselves. They had, therefore, constantly to decide upon an attitude to non-Jewish law which they would inculcate into their communities. An extreme example of the consequent situation can be quoted from a later period—it was not in force

[94] Compare C. G. Montefiore, *The Hibbert Lectures 1892*, Williams and Norgate 1892, p. 490.

[95] How such a situation was reached is a very human story. In the days of the Tannaim, it was crudely stated that a mixed case might be judged by the law which would be most unfavourable to the Gentile (B.K. 37b, p. 211 and 113a, p. 664). Jews learnt by experience that this was a foolish policy for a minority, always weaker than the majority which surrounded it. Later rabbis propounded the law that a Gentile must be treated just like a Jew, or even better 'for the sake of the Name'. (Horowitz, *op. cit.*, p. 237).

[96] Horowitz, *op. cit.*, pp. 105 ff., lists sixty out of the 613 commandments which deal directly with humane behaviour.

[97] On women see the introduction to *Seder Nashim* by J. H. Hertz in the Soncino Talmud, and on slaves cf. Herzog, *op. cit.*, p. 45 and Horowitz, *op. cit.*, pp. 244 ff.

[98] See J. J. Rabinowitz, *Jewish Law: Its Influence on the Development of Legal Institutions*, New York, 1956, Ch. V.

during the period under discussion. In no medieval non-Jewish legal code does the crime of *informing* exist. The medieval rabbis made it a capital offence for a Jew to inform against his brethren to an outside authority, and allowed an informer to be taken and killed wherever he was found.[99] In passing a measure of such extraordinary severity, the rabbis were only putting into practice the principle, already mentioned, that extreme measures might be taken when the very life of the community was in danger.[1]

Apart from such energetic reaction to needs which were special to the Jewish community, the rabbis adopted one of two attitudes to the Gentile laws affecting their lives. In many cases they just accepted them—having no alternative—but in their own discussions emphasized their disagreement from the current Gentile practice; but in other cases they themselves endorsed the action of Gentile courts.

Of the first kind the most interesting example concerns the capital sentence. The evidence is, on the whole, convincing that Jews lost the right to try cases involving capital punishment towards the end of the Herodian period, and the same seems to be true of cases involving severe corporal punishment.[2] Their many discussions were, therefore, academic, and revealed their general attitude to punishment rather than their executive experience. In fact, the patriarch Simeon b. Gamaliel II in the time of Akiba remarked that the rabbis had become so opposed to capital punishment or conviction for murder that the only consequence—had they the power to carry out their proposals—would have been 'to multiply shedders of blood in Israel'.[3] The question is academic, but there is this justification for the view of the patriarch: the rabbis never considered an alternative punishment, on the basis of which they would have been ready to admit a conviction. Instead they complicated the laws of evidence to such an extent that a conviction would never have been possible, and this was scarcely a practical manner of approaching the issue of serious crime.

In the day to day life of a complex society there were, however, inevitably many occasions when Jews were brought up against the consequences of their minority position on less grave matters than murder. Such matters were often not based on an ethical point but merely on differences of procedure; at other times they involved relations with non-Jews where it was impossible for a Jew to demand that his views prevail. Wherever they lived, Jews were bound to be

[99] Horowitz, *op. cit.*, pp. 228 ff. and 621 ff.
[1] See above, Section 2, n. 25 and Horowitz, *op. cit.*, p. 100.
[2] See Herzog, *op. cit.*, p. xxi.
[3] Mak. 7a, p. 35. See also Mishnah, *Sanhedrin*, *passim*.

brought into contact with Gentiles in buying and selling, in contracts and partnerships, and in a dozen other matters of commerce and business. With regard to such issues Mar Samuel, the great Babylonian jurist of the first half of the third century, made the epoch-making pronouncement that 'the law of the land is law', that is to say that its action is endorsed by Jewish law. Such a pronouncement had, obviously very definite limits. It could not, for example, license a Jewish wife to become a temple prostitute, just because such prostitution was 'the law of the land'. No matter of Jewish ritual or ethic could be affected by it. But that still left a considerable scope for its action in commercial matters, in the registration of documents and so on. But the limits were vague and the subject of continual debate.[4] In any case it was for the Jewish authorities and not for any individual Jew to decide in each case that 'the law of the land' was acceptable when it was at variance with Jewish law.

The principle did not, in fact, render some measure of judicial autonomy unnecessary. It only made possible an alternative solution in some doubtful issues. In every community, therefore, there had to be some source of judicial competence. The government of the community was in the hands of a layman; if the community was large and possessed a number of synagogues, each synagogue was also presided over by a layman, assisted by a hazan, who was competent to intone the liturgical portions of the service. In a small community this official might also be school-master and ritual slaughterer. He was, in fact, the first paid official of the community. But neither he nor the honorary officers were necessarily competent to act as judges, or to interpret the portion of the Torah read in the synagogue. It was here that the scholar and the rabbi found their place, the one with the spiritual leadership of the community, the other also with its judicial needs and responsibilities. The two functions could be, but were not necessarily, combined in one man.

All through rabbinic literature there is an insistence that a man does not study Torah for himself. The knowledge he acquires must be shared through action, and in return the community owes the scholar a measure of support so that he can continually perfect himself in his studies.[5] The highest honour that a scholar could receive was that he should become a judge. 'Every judge who judges

[4] There is a full discussion of the principle of *Dina de-Malkutha dina* in Herzog, *op. cit.*, pp. 24 ff. and in Horowitz, pp. 74 f. The main Talmudic references to the statement are Git. 10b, pp. 36 f., B.K. 113a, p. 663, B.B. 55a, p. 223.

[5] E.g., Yom, 72b, p. 346 and Shab. 114a, p. 558. See also *Rabbinic Anthology* No. 944, p. 353, with note by H. Loewe *ad loc.*

with complete fairness even for one hour, the Scripture gives him credit as though he had become a partner to the Holy One, blessed be He, in the creation'.[6] In another place it is said that 'a righteous judge causes the Shechinah to dwell in Israel'.[7] In some way that we cannot precisely define the grant of the title 'rabbi' was an authorisation to become a judge; and, in a religion like Judaism, this could well mean a position even more powerful than that of the elected layman who presided over community or synagogue, for the judge was both a civil and a religious authority. In any case the rabbi-judge in some measure represented the common element in Jewish life, while the lay officer emphasized the local independence. Safety and tranquillity within the community could, then, best be secured by a proper balance between these powers, and by preventing either from becoming so powerful that it could crush the other. Jewish life needed both the wealthy and skilful layman and the devoted and incorruptible judge. That Jewry survived in its dispersion shows that, in the main, these two elements were held in creative and not in destructive tension.[8] For if the one could preserve the Jews, the other could preserve their Judaism.

7. THE WORLD OUTSIDE

WHAT has been true of so many sections of the present chapter is true again with regard to the Jewish attitude to the world outside. It is not safe to pass judgment simply by analogy with the Christian situation. For the latter there has never been the slightest doubt that 'all the world is Christ's own field'. The missionary command laid upon the Church is central, original and unequivocal. Because in Judaism there are remarks hostile to the idea of Gentile converts, it is assumed that these imply the rejection of an obvious duty, as would such remarks were they found in the mouth of a Church father. But a mission to the outside world is not explicit in the Torah. There is no Sinaitic commandment requiring it, and it is only in the messianic age that there is an expectation—not universally expressed—that all nations would seek the truth in Jerusalem.

The result is that missionary activity, and the attitude to be adopted towards the convert, or proselyte, is the subject of lively discussion among the rabbis. Different opinions are expressed, depending some-

[6] Shab. 10a, p. 35.
[7] Sanh. 7a, p. 27.
[8] On the judges and their relation to the lay officers, compare Baron, *Community*, I., pp. 126 ff.

times on individual temperament, and sometimes on the situation in which the Jewish people found themselves at that particular moment of their history, in that particular place, or with regard to that particular stranger. The conservative Shammai, and the equally conservative Eliezer b. Hyrcanus, at times made remarks which were hostile to converts, and brought them into opposition to the liberal Hillel or Johanan b. Zakkai.[9] But at other times the opinions of all four coincided, as far as their temperaments allowed. For Eliezer constitutionally found it difficult to get on with his colleagues,[10] and Shammai found it difficult to control a hasty temper!

The attitude to the potential convert could also appear to depend on the circumstances. Thus there was one school of thought which insisted that in the time of the messiah converts would not be accepted for there would be no evidence that they were genuine, since they waited to come until Jews were prosperous and secure.[11] On the other hand, a would-be convert in the second century, when Judaism was under a heavy cloud, and who had been warned of this, was accepted as obviously genuine. It is laid down that he is to be addressed with the words: 'Do you not know that Israel at the present time are persecuted and oppressed, despised, harassed and overcome with afflictions?' If he replies, 'I know and yet am unworthy' he is received forthwith.[12]

Yet another determinant was the ever-present rival, the Christian Church. In a number of places it is insisted that a convert must at once scrupulously observe every jot and tittle of the law, though in the passage quoted above the more sensible method is laid down that he should be taught gradually, with a suitable mixture of light and serious commandments, until he has understood the whole. It is suggested that the insistence on every detail may be a Jewish reply to the continuous denunciations of Torah by the Church, and to the Pauline antinomian appeal to those who had, perhaps, not made up their minds whether to accept the monotheism and ethical standards of Judaism or those of Christianity.[13] The rabbis were de-

[9] Shab. 31a, p. 140 and Mid. Rabbah. Eccles. 1. 8. Ed. Son., pp. 28 ff. (But B. J. Bamberger, *Proselytism in the Talmudic Period*, H.U.C., Cincinnati, 1939, p. 235 interprets the passage differently.)

[10] A favourable attitude of Eliezer to proselytes is to be seen in Mekilta, Amalek, 3. Ed. Lauterbach, II., pp. 172 ff. On his temperament see B. Z. Bokser's biography of Eliezer, *Pharisaic Judaism in Transition*. Bloch, New York, 1935.

[11] On passages reflecting different views about the messianic period, see W. G. Braude, *Jewish Proselyting in the First Five Centuries of the Common Era*, Brown University, 1940, pp. 34 ff. and 45 ff.

[12] Yeb. 47a, pp. 310 f. The whole passage is well worth reading.

[13] See Braude, *op. cit.*, p. 98.

termined not to compromise, and so made themselves more rigid than they would normally be. But the most interesting example of Christian influence is, if a theory of Professor Braude be correct,[14] the reason for the most famous Talmudic statement on proselytes—at least according to Christian writers who love to quote it. R. Helbo, a Palestinian Amora of the end of the third and the beginning of the fourth century, made the Hebrew pun that a convert is as dangerous to Israel as the itch.[15] Dr. Braude connects the remark with the Constantinian legislation that attached the death penalty to the convert to Judaism.[16]

When we discount these various exceptions, the general picture confirmed by a much greater weight of evidence from every kind of rabbinical source, is of a religion which took very seriously its missionary privilege and responsibility. There is, however, no trace in Judaism of anything equivalent to the dedicated priest of Christianity, who gives his whole life to preaching and winning converts among the heathen, nor is there any trace of missions to 'foreign parts'. It was the synagogue service and the Jewish community in any locality which attracted individual men and women from the Gentile environment, and there is no doubt whatever that, as long as Jews were free to do so, these converts received a sincere welcome. Of course there were some who distrusted—Jews would not be human if that type did not exist among them—and suspected them of inadequacy or insincerity. But that was not the general opinion, as is revealed from the words of both halakists and haggadists; and a convert, once he was received, was in every way equal to a born Jew. It was a definite offence to remind him of his pagan past.[17]

We possess not only charming parables to illustrate God's love for converts,[18] but the summary of a sermon addressed to a congregation at the reception of such—at least that is what it appears to

[14] *Ibid.*, p. 42.

[15] It is quoted a number of times in T.B., e.g., Yeb., 47b, p. 312 and 109b, p. 762, etc. It is not a very good pun and might be rendered 'a conversion is as dangerous as a contusion.'

[16] C.T., 16. 8. 1. The Edict of Milan made the Christian Church a legal body in 313. It did not unhappily take long for the persecuted Church to turn persecutor. The death penalty by burning was attached to converts to Judaism in 315. It is an omen of things to come, that the language of the law is already vulgar and abusive. Judaism is a *feralis*, or a *nefaria* sect and the word for synagogue, *conciliabulum*, is slang for a brothel.

[17] 'You should not say to him: But yesterday you were worshipping Bel, Kores, Nebo and until now swine's flesh was sticking out from your teeth. . . . Mekilta, Nezikin, 18, Ed. Lauterbach, III., p. 137.

[18] Mid. Rabbah on Numbers 8. 2 (on Num. 5. 2 ff.) Ed. Son., p. 204, quoted above, p. 67.

be. For with the text 'beloved are the strangers' there is composed a midrash, supported by a vast array of quotations, on the verse 'you shall not wrong a stranger or oppress him, for you were strangers in the land of Egypt.'[19]

The belief that Judaism, by its very nature, does not seek converts is entirely erroneous.[20] What happened historically was that the increasing cruelty of the hostility of Christianity and Islam ensured the death of any Jew who sought to make a convert, and of any convert who was made. Even so, it was only gradually in Christian countries that Jews resigned themselves to this situation, as the constant legislation of Church councils and Christian emperors shows.[21] It may have been the same in the early days of Islam, but we have less information about it and, in any case, the situation was different. The Muslims represented an invading and conquering force and were less likely to be influenced by their new subjects. Jews thus came to compensate themselves by regarding converts first as unnecessary, and then as undesirable. Doubtless the words of R. Helbo came to be quoted by them as well as by Christians. Yet, even when this affected the majority of the Jewish people, missionary activity went on beyond the fringes of Christian and Islamic influences, witness the dramatic conversion of the ruling class of the Khazars in the eighth century.[22]

It was said at the beginning of this section that there was no Sinaitic authority for a general missionary programme. The best evidence of the sincerity of the rabbinic desire to spread Judaism is the determination with which they overcame the various exclusions of Ammonites, Moabites, and others in the written Torah. The two former are excluded 'for ever' and the Canaanites and others are not even to be allowed to live.[23] But these stern decrees had been cancelled so early by rabbinic authority that the surviving

[19] Mekilta, Nezikin, 18, Ed. Lauterbach, III., p. 138.

[20] On the whole issue of the missionary activity of Judaism, see the works of Braude and Bamberger, already quoted. Earlier works must be used with great caution, for it is a subject which has aroused much biassed writing. Schurer II., 2 pp. 291 ff. is both an example of this and an excellent source for bibliographic details of earlier Christian writing on the subject. Moore is valuable on the question of 'demi-proselytes'. For a discussion of the Matthean denunciation that the Pharisees 'compass heaven and earth to make one proselyte', see Bamberger, pp. 267 ff., and sources there quoted. It is greatly to be regretted that neither Bamberger nor Braude possess indices.

[21] See App. I. of my *Conflict of the Church and the Synagogue*.

[22] D. M. Dunlop, *The History of the Jewish Khazars*, Princeton, 1954, Chs. 5 and 6.

[23] Deut. 20. 17 and 23. 3.

sources simply assume that everyone knew this to be so. When the matter came up for discussion between R. Joshua b. Hananiah and Rabban Gamaliel, the former simply declared that Sennacherib had by his policy brought about a general confusion of races so that the old prohibitions no longer had a factual basis for enforcement.[24]

Finally we may quote the legend, twice repeated, that some of the greatest persecutors of Jews and Judaism were themselves converted, or became the ancestors of converts. 'A Tanna taught: Naaman was a resident alien; Nebuzaradan was a righteous proselyte;[25] descendants of Haman taught the Torah in Benai Brak; descendants of Sisera taught children in Jerusalem; descendants of Sennacherib gave public expositions of the Torah.'[26]

A revision of the conventional attitude to the missionary activity of the rabbinic period necessarily entails a re-examination also of the attitude adopted towards the Gentile world. It is too often assumed that the sneers and denunciations of Roman writers expressed the whole truth. But those who are filled with an *odium humani generis* do not attract others or desire to do so. In the period of the Hadrianic persecution, and in the decades following it, there is naturally a good deal more hostility than there is at other times, and it is expressed, as already shown, in the tractate Abodah Zara.[27] But, given the circumstances, the bitterness shown is not excessive and has often been exceeded by the hatred between one Christian sect and another Christian sect. It contains nothing of the spirit of 'kill all, God will know his own', but instead a number of rather mean and petty little unfriendlinesses, or silly bombast like the magnificent array of rabbis who endorse a death sentence which, in any case, Jews could not inflict: 'Rabina said to R. Ashi: Come and hear: R. Hiyya b. Abbah said in the name of R. Johanan: A son of Noah is put to death for stealing less than a prutah's worth of the property of an Israelite.'[28]

Much more in character are a number of statements commanding generous treatment of the Gentile 'for the sake of peace', 'to prevent profanation of the Name' or so that the Gentile may say 'Blessed be the God of the Jews'. A story in the Jerusalem Talmud

[24] Yad., 4. 4, pp. 563 f. The same argument is used by R. Jose in Yom. 54a, p. 254.

[25] Captain of the body-guard of Nebuchadnezzar, and responsible for the massacre of the population of Jerusalem subsequent to the capture of the city. 2 Kings 25. 8.

[26] Git. 57b, p. 265 or Sanh. 96b, p. 652.

[27] See above p. 269.

[28] A.Z. 71b, p. 343. A prutah is the smallest coin. It was revived by the State of Israel to express one thousandth of an Israeli £.

reflects both this attitude and the existence of a less worthy tradition. When Simon b. Shetah received a valuable pearl with an ass brought from an Arab, he insisted on it being returned. But his disciples protested that 'all the world agrees that if you find something belonging to a heathen, you may keep it.'[29] One may well call the attitude of Simon 'sanctified common-sense', in that Jews were entering on the long period when their prosperity, or even their lives, depended on the most varied collection of neighbours, civilised and barbarian, to the east, west, north and south of the original homeland.

In the enormous mass of literature, theological, legal and historical, which has survived from the early centuries of the Church we have ample material for a just assessment of the relations between Jews and their Christian neighbours.[30] So far as ordinary relations are concerned, they would lead us to expect that the teaching of the religious leaders must have been what, in fact, we find it to be. It is not a teaching of either hatred or contempt, but is well expressed in the words 'our rabbis have taught: we support the poor of the heathen along with the poor of Israel, and visit the sick of the heathen along with the sick of Israel, and bury the dead of the heathen along with the dead of Israel *in the interests of peace*'.[31] Such 'sanctified common-sense' might be inadequate and even dangerous if it had not some deeper spiritual motives behind it. But these were not lacking in rabbinic teaching. In many passages and in many contexts Jews were reminded that God was the father of all nations, and cared for them all equally. By the methods of rabbinic thinking already discussed,[32] we can accept that they held these views quite sincerely in the contexts appropriate to them, while also holding that Israel was viewed with a special love. It was, therefore, with complete sincerity that they could put into the mouth of God the words 'there is no favouritism before Me. Whether Gentile or Israelite, whether man or woman, whether male or female slave, he that has done a mizwah, the reward thereof is at hand.'[33] It was a commonplace that the

[29] *The Rabbinic Anthology*, p. 393. cf. No. 1084, p. 398.

[30] See my *Conflict of the Church and the Synagogue*, pp. 118 ff., 144 ff., 189 ff., 305 ff., 342 ff. These various passages deal with relations in the Roman empire, and in the Christian East and West up to A.D. 800. For Islamic material see Baron, *Social and Religious History*, III., Ch. 18, pp. 121 ff.

[31] Git. 61a, p. 287.

[32] See above pp. 301 f.

[33] From the Seder Eliahu, quoted by Kadushin in *Organic Thinking*, p. 99.

Torah was offered to all nations, and it was the general belief that all nations would ultimately be gathered under the Shekinah.[34] Indeed the belief that this would be so was expressed daily in the *Alenu* prayer in synagogue worship, where both the special love for Israel and the universal love for all men find expression.[35] The conversion of the Gentiles was the divine motive for the dispersion of the Jews[36] according to Eleazar, an early Tanna.

The religious history of the West would have been very different if there were nothing more to report of the relations between Jewry and the outside world. But an exception has unhappily to be made for relations with the Christian Church, first with its theologians, then, after our period, between ordinary Jews and Christians. There are various stages to be considered. At first there was the natural uncertainty of the Jewish authorities in facing a new and somewhat aggressive sect. Then the open expression of their views was prohibited and Saul of Tarsus was sent to Damascus to arrest members of the new sect.[37] But then came the far more bitter counter-attack of the now converted Paul, the leading, but not the only, missionary to the Gentile world. It is the Pauline abuse of Torah, and its repetition and accentuation by Gentiles who knew very little of what they were attacking, which has been the main and most impassible barrier between the two religions ever since.[38] The vulgarity of the abuse of Judaism which is to be found in the works of such men as John Chrysostom,[39] the entire falsification of biblical history which we meet in writers such as Eusebius of Caesarea,[40] inevitably produced a Jewish reaction. Contrary to the usual Christian assertion, the Roman persecutors of the first three centuries did not secure, after the period of definite separation, any consistent or violent Jewish co-operation.[41] But the period witnessed the beginning of a Jewish picture of the founder of Christianity comparable in its dis-

[34] Compare Ber. 57b, p. 358.

[35] Singer's *Daily Prayer Book*, pp. 76 f. Abrahams, Annotated Edition, pp. lxxxvi ff. On this dualism see also M. Guttman, *Das Judentum und Seine Umwelt*, Berlin 1927, Ch. 7.

[36] Pes. 87b, p. 463.

[37] Acts 9. 1 f.

[38] I have dealt with this at length in my *Conflict of the Church and the Synagogue*, which treats of the subject down to the time of Charlemagne. M. Simon, in *Verus Israel*, Paris, 1948, treats in fuller detail the first half of this period.

[39] *The Conflict*, pp. 163 ff.

[40] *Ibid.*, pp. 160 ff.

[41] *Ibid.*, Ch. 4, pp. 121 ff.

tortion to the Christian picture of Jewish history and religion.[42]

The Jewish life of Jesus the Nazarene, balancing the Christian picture of Torah and of Judaism, ultimately ensured that the adherents of each religion were almost wholly ignorant of the real tenets and character of the other. The Founder of Christianity was regarded as a sinner and seducer, the follower of Torah was regarded as a son of the devil, a liar, a cheat, with his hand against every man and seeking nothing better than the overthrow of the Gentile, especially Christian, world. And this picture is not wholly dispelled today. To the Christian tradition it has meant a distortion and a loss; to the Jews it has brought far more deadly results, culminating in the appalling massacres of our own days. It is inevitable that century after century of a life which was, at best insecure, at worst that of a hunted pariah, should affect the character of its victims as well as of those who inflicted such sufferings on fellow human beings. But, if the picture presented in the last four chapters be in any way true, then those distortions, deeply rooted as they are, are not of the true essence of either religion.

[42] There are many texts of the *Sepher Toldoth Jeshu*, giving many variant presentations of the story. Wagenseil gives the first translation into Latin. The best modern study is Dr. Morris Goldstein, *Jesus in the Jewish Tradition*, New York, 1950, as Dr. Goldstein is careful to date references whereever possible.

Epilogue

TWO RELIGIONS: TWO CHOSEN PEOPLE

It is the Christian claim that all that was spiritually valid in Judaism was taken over by the Church. Early father and modern writer speak with the same voice on at least this subject. Justin in the second century had written concisely 'your Scriptures or rather not yours but ours'[1] and had claimed with the Scripture all the spiritual gifts mentioned in their pages.[2] Almost identical words are used by the Very Rev. S. C. Carpenter, D.D. in a Pelican book published in 1953 entitled *Christianity*. For him, as for Justin, Judaism is just its predecessor. In a chapter entitled 'The Antecedents of Christianity' phrases abound such as these (the italics in all the quotations are mine): 'The Christian disciples of the first generation *inherited*, unhesitatingly and enthusiastically, *the great and splendid things for which Judaism had stood*' (p. 18). The *had* marks Judaism as already outmoded. Quoting the magnificent passage of Isaiah 40 which begins: 'To whom then will ye liken God?', he asserts that 'all this wealth of affirmation *became at once the property of the Christians*' (p. 20). On the same page we find: 'Old Testament religion was a historical religion . . . depending on *what God had done* for [Israel] as a nation. All this the Church took over'. On the following page we read: 'A third element of the Old Testament religion which *was taken over* by the Christian Church was belief in a Messiah.' The ordinary reader for whom a Penguin book is published would not gather from such passages that in no case had Judaism surrendered or abandoned any of these ideas, or repudiated them as part of her possession. The word 'sharing' is never used: indeed both Dr. Carpenter and Justin would find it inappropriate. For, like Justin, he finds that the divine purpose 'had never been understood, had in fact never been clearly disclosed, until it was realised in Christ' (p. 18).

Painful as such a conception of their history would be for loyal Jews, yet it would be inevitable for Christians to make such a claim, *had they in fact taken over the heritage of the Old Testament*. The astonishing thing about this iterated claim is that not only has the

[1] *Op. cit.*, Ch. 29.
[2] *Ibid.*, Ch. 82.

Church not done so but, without realising it, has constantly repudiated her intention of doing so. Every time she makes a distinction between 'secular' and 'religious' she repudiates the Old Testament. Every time she condemns 'religion mixing in politics' she emphasizes that she does not accept the values of Judaism. No one could imagine the religion described in the previous chapter to be the Christianity of the early Church. Whether it be right or wrong, the Christian conception of being a chosen people is completely different from the Jewish, and is a consequence only of the Incarnation, not of either the Law or the prophets. To both it would have been inappropriate and 'born out of due time'.

Both religions accept the belief that God has chosen from humanity certain men as vehicles of his universal purpose and design. Neither, at its best, considers the choice a privilege; both regard it as a responsibility. But,[3] since Christians are apt to think that the Jewish conception of being a chosen people sets Jews apart, and narrows their religion down to tribalism, it is perhaps well to emphasize that the original word for the Church, the Greek word *ecclesia*, means those who are called out from among others or chosen, and that the Latin word *electi*, the elect, a favourite title for a Christian community, means just the same thing. Christians as much as Jews believe themselves subjects of a divine choice.

Christianity, however, sees the divine choice enshrined in the biblical story narrowing down to the single figure of Jesus the Messiah, then, after his Incarnation, it sees this same choice widening out again to embrace mankind without distinction of Jew or Greek, bond or free, or, one may add, white or coloured. But within boundaries limited only by mankind, it still holds that only some are chosen, chosen as the elect from every nation, to receive the mystery of salvation, and to become, in the words beloved of Paul, 'new men in Christ', the new Israel, the new chosen people.

To Judaism it is the whole of one people which is chosen for a divine responsibility, chosen as it now is, in its present condition, with its imperfections and its good and bad members. This is not tribalism as opposed to universalism; for the choice is to responsibility not to privilege, and is related to the same assertion of the universal dominion of God, and of the ultimate responsibility of those he has chosen towards the whole of his creation.

Both religions, then, rest on the idea of choice. Both see that

[3] The text from here to the end of this chapter reproduces, with small alterations, pp. 6—11, of a lecture entitled *The Concept of a Chosen People in Judaism and Christianity* delivered at Chicago in 1954 and published by the Union of American Hebrew Congregations.

choice within a universal framework. But the result of these two different conceptions of the nature of the choice was to be naturally and logically to make the two religions differ in almost every conceivable emphasis and interest.

Both religions start with the acceptance of the divine authority of certain written Scriptures, but their differences began already in the two attitudes developed to these Scriptures. The Judaism which survived the destruction of Jerusalem, of the Temple and of the whole apparatus of sacrifice, drew its inspiration from the Pharisaic doctrine of interpretation—a doctrine most frequently misunderstood by New Testament scholars. The rabbis saw in the written Torah the focusing point through which the infinity of God's wisdom and design in creation reaches out to meet the infinity of men's needs as generation succeeds generation in a never static world. Each generation had the task of interpreting it anew, in terms of its own needs; and an interpretation once accepted by the scholars of a generation had the same divine authority as the original. In a sense it had more, for they regarded it as a greater sin to deny that God is continuously speaking to man, than to deny that he had once so spoken at Sinai.

Christianity made a sharp distinction between the Old and the New Testaments and interpreted the former only in terms of its 'fulfilment' in the latter. The main interest in the Old Testament of the Church fathers was as a quarry of proof texts that Jesus is the Christ foretold by the prophets. They had no conception of its unity comparable to the Jewish doctrine of Torah, and no doctrine of its interpretation. They used it in its literal sense, often with unhappy results especially on the development of law and the justification of wars.[4] From a doctrinal point of view the only sphere in which they regarded it as a focusing point between two infinities is in the development of Christological doctrine. And here we must come back to the two conceptions of a chosen people.

The development of Judaism was determined by the belief that a divine way of life was set before a whole people, here and now; and that its primary mission, and its primary contribution to mankind, was to explore, understand and express in every aspect of its daily life that divine plan for a whole community. In the literature of rabbinic Judaism there is to be found practically no interest in theological speculation and nothing which could be called a systematic theology. Having accepted the existence and the unity of God without hesitation, the rabbis concentrated all their interest on his activities in creation as they were to be embodied in the living

[4] See p. 81.

of the chosen people. A number of consequences flowed from this determination of interest.

In the first place it demanded a strong emphasis on education, for *understanding* occupies in Judaism the same key place as *faith* in Christianity. In the second place it put an end to the reasons for the existence of a clerical or priestly hierarchy. The priesthood disappeared with the Temple except for some trifling concessions to past prestige. The Judaism which grew in the second century was a religion of educated laymen. Moreover, it was a religion whose details were worked out by men following every occupation open to the community. The rabbis of the Talmudic period were not merely not priests; they were not even in the modern sense 'professionals'. If some gave almost the whole of their lives to study, they did it for love of Torah not because they were salaried or held official posts. Some were wealthy landowners, some were merchants, some were artisans taking only such time off from their studies as would ensure the most meagre and frugal existence.

Because they represented every aspect of the life of the community, they dealt freely with every aspect. Their discussions of education, of economics, of agriculture, of family life, of social relations, of communal responsibilities, in spite of the curious techniques which they employed, were infused with an astonishing realism just because they knew from experience what they were talking about. This realism reached its culmination in their conceptions of the functions of a law court, since it was an obligation of a scholar to be ready to judge in disputes. It is important to emphasize this point since Christian scholars are so apt to assume that 'Jewish' conceptions of justice are still based on the more primitive sections of the Pentateuch. I have again and again seen Christian and Jewish attitudes compared by contrasting 'the law of love of the Gospel' with 'the Jewish belief in an eye for an eye'. In fact, it is only in some parts of the Christian world, and in the nineteenth and twentieth centuries, that Christian justice has begun to approximate to the sensitivity and compassion of Jewish rabbinical courts fifteen hundred years earlier.

Finally the rabbis, in their perpetual concern with interpretation, were constantly conscious of the fact that it was a whole community, not a select body of saints, with which they were dealing. This concern is charmingly illustrated by a midrashic interpretation of the reason why, at the Feast of Tabernacles, Jews hold a sweet smelling citron, and wave the *lulav*, a nosegay with twigs of palm, myrtle and willow.[5]

[5] Lev. 23. 40 in *Midrash Rabba on Leviticus* 30. 12. Ed. Soncino, pp. 392 f.

> The fruit of the hadar tree symbolizes Israel: just as the citron has taste as well as fragrance, so Israel have among them men who possess learning and good deeds. Branches of palm tree, too, applies to Israel; as the palm tree has taste but not fragrance, so Israel have among them such as possess learning but not good deeds. And boughs of thick trees likewise applies to Israel; just as the myrtle has fragrance but no taste, so Israel have among them such as possess good deeds but not learning. And willows of the brook also applies to Israel: just as the willow has no taste and no fragrance, so Israel have among them such as possess neither learning nor good deeds. What then does the Holy One, blessed be He, do to them? To destroy them is impossible. But, says the Holy One, blessed be He, let them all be tied together in one band, and they will atone, one for another. If you have done so [says God] then at that instant I am exalted.

This tenderness for 'the willow in the lulav' runs all through their activities. They were concerned with the attainable. They certainly did not make Judaism a soft religion, but they were concerned that men should not fail and fall away through despair of ever attaining a loyal conformity to the will of God for their lives; and to this end they made 'a fence about the Torah' by which men could be aided in their daily loyalty. Sometimes the fence may seem to us too high, or the bricks of which it is composed too small; but its provision was in modern terms good psychology and wise therapeutics. For Christendom and Islam saw to it that a Jew should have every temptation to be disloyal and to desert his ancestral faith. The fence was not the core of Judaism, but it kept the core inviolate through nearly two thousand years of unparalleled external pressures.

The Christian conception of a chosen people was no less profound than the Jewish, no less universal in its implied responsibilities, but it rested on the idea that men were chosen individually and personally to receive salvation in Christ without regard to their race or status—without regard indeed even for their family ties. As the Church soon discovered, once the apostles had begun their preaching, this conception could easily be abused. Men could and did arise, falsely proclaiming that they held the key by which the longed for salvation could be assured. Men could and did so fashion redeemer Christs that they fitted into the pattern of every eastern mysticism and occult cult. The insistence on the finality and fullness of the divine choice could lead to even darker consequences; and men could proclaim a rigid predestinarianism, and even that, once saved, there was no indulgence of the flesh which need be avoided, since to wallow in sin only exalted the divine mercy and the wonder of the choice. In such a situation Christianity emphasized the unattainable as rightly as Judaism was emphasizing the attainable. To human duty to love God and to love men, neither religion set any limits. But a religion calling on men to be 'saved' had always to remind them that salvation was a beginning not an end, lest they should believe that no further spiritual growth was required, or that faith had no further experience to offer.

This totally different picture was reinforced by the fact that, while Judaism was coping with the appallingly difficult problem of finding a new centre for the survival of a people whose every natural insignia—government, land, public religious centre—had been destroyed, Christianity, proclaiming that the saved were from every people and nation, had to struggle to maintain its proclamation in competition with the religions, philosophies, temptations and peculiarities of every people and nation. And so it became an intensely theological religion. It created and strictly determined its official interpreters in a clerical hierarchy geographically covering every Christian community. Above all, it built around the person of the Redeemer and Saviour a fence of Christology as high, and with bricks as small, as that of the rabbis about the Jewish way of living; and with the same justification, and the same vindication by history.

It is only as we contemplate the task which was set to the Christian Church by its chosenness that we can understand sympathetically the bitter heresy hunts, the condemnation of men of the most upright lives and sincere beliefs for false views on what may seem to us academic trifles, and the long story of schism and excommunication which mars Christian history. For, just as the rabbis knew that it was vital to safeguard their way of life, so the theologians knew that it was vital to safeguard the historic Jesus of the gospels, the historic crucifixion and Resurrection, against interpretations which might deny the unity of God or the true humanity of Jesus, which might take Jesus out of actual history or God's activity out of the world he had created. Credal definition and credal conformity had as natural a place in Christianity as the sabbath and *kashruth* in Judaism. Christianity was as naturally a faith directed by educated clergy as Judaism a practice directed by educated laymen.

It is surely unnecessary to seek to substitute one conception for the other or to deny the validity, in the present world, of both. Christianity is not a substitute for Israel, nor is its mission made unnecessary by the survival of Judaism. But the reverse is true to a precisely equal degree. Judaism is not a substitute for Christianity, nor is its mission made unnecessary by the existence of the Christian Church.

Index One

BIBLE

Index Two

APOCRYPHA AND PSEUDEPIGRAPHA

Index Three

RABBINICA

BABYLONIAN TALMUD

General Index